ISSUES IN CONTEMPORARY RETIREMENT

ISSUES IN CONTEMPORARY RETIREMENT

Rita Ricardo-Campbell
Edward P. Lazear
Editors

HOOVER INSTITUTION PRESS

STANFORD UNIVERSITY STANFORD, CALIFORNIA

Hoover Press Publication 370

First printing, 1988

Manufactured in the United States of America

94 93 92 91 90 89 88   9 8 7 6 5 4 3 2 1

Library of Congress Cataloging in Publication Data

Issues in contemporary retirement

   Includes bibliographies and index
   1. Retirement—United States—Congresses.
2. Aged—Employment—United States—Congresses.
3. Social security—United States—Congresses.
I. Ricardo-Campbell, Rita.   II. Lazear, Edward P.
HQ1064.U5I88   1988   306'.38'0973   88-8081
ISBN 0-8179-8701-0

CONTENTS

PART III: POLICY IMPLICATIONS

CONTRIBUTORS

STEVEN G. ALLEN is Professor of Economics and Business at North Carolina State University and a Research Associate at the National Bureau of Economic Research. His most recent publications include "Post-Retirement Adjustments of Pension Benefits" (with Robert L. Clark and Daniel A. Sumner), *Journal of Human Resources* (1986); "Unions, Pension Wealth, and Age-Compensation Profiles" (with Robert L. Clark), *Industrial and Labor Relations Review* (1986); "Can Union Labor Ever Cost Less?" *Quarterly Journal of Economics* (1987); and "Declining Unionization in Construction: The Facts and the Reasons," *Industrial and Labor Relations Review* (1988). He is currently working on a study of how pension plans affect labor mobility.

JERE R. BEHRMAN is the William R. Kenan, Jr. Professor of Economics at the University of Pennsylvania. His recent publications include "Empirical Studies of Agricultural Supply" in J. Eatwell, M. Milgate, and P. Newman, eds., *The New Palgrave: A Dictionary of Economic Theory and Doctrine* (1987); "The Distribution of Public Services: An Exploration of Local Governmental Preferences" (with S. G. Craig), *American Economic Review* (1987); "Will Developing Country Nutrition Improve with Income? A Case Study for Rural South India" (with A. B. Deolalikar), *Journal of Political Economy* (1987); and "Schooling in Developing Countries: Which Countries Are the Under- and Overachievers and What Is the Schooling Impact?" *Economics of Education Review* (1987).

B. DOUGLAS BERNHEIM is Associate Professor of Economics at Stanford University and a Research Associate of the National Bureau of Economic Research. His recent publications include "Economic Growth with Intergenerational Altruism" (with Debraj Ray), *Review of Economic Studies* (1987); "Comparable Worth in a General Equilibrium Model of the U.S.

Economy" (with Perry Beider, John Shoven, and Victor Fuchs), *Research in Labor Economics* (forthcoming); and "Is Everything Neutral?" (with Kyle Bagwell), *Journal of Political Economy* (forthcoming).

MICHAEL J. BOSKIN is Burnet C. and Mildred Finley Wohlford Professor of Economics and Director of the Center for Economic Policy Research at Stanford University; Senior Fellow (by courtesy) at the Hoover Institution; and Research Associate at the National Bureau of Economic Research. Among his recent publications, several on Social Security include *Too Many Promises: The Uncertain Future of Social Security* (1986); "Social Security: A Financial Appraisal Across and Within Generations" (with J. Shoven, L. Kotlikoff, and D. Puffert), *National Tax Journal* (1987); and "Concepts and Measure of Earnings Replacement During Retirement," in Z. Bodie, J. Shoven, and D. Wise, eds., *Issues in Pension Economics* (1987).

RICHARD V. BURKHAUSER is Professor of Economics and Senior Research Associate of the Institute for Public Policy at Vanderbilt University. He has published widely on the behavioral and income distribution effects of government policy toward aged and disabled persons. He has co-authored *Disability and Work: The Economics of American Policy* (with Robert Haveman; 1982) and *Public Policy Toward Disabled Workers: Cross-National Analyses of Economic Impacts* (with Robert Haveman et al.; 1984).

EILEEN M. CRIMMINS is Associate Professor of Gerontology and Sociology at the Andrus Gerontology Center of the University of Southern California. She received her Ph.D. in demography from the University of Pennsylvania in 1974. Her recent publications include "Evidence on the Compression of Morbidity," *Gerontologica Biomedica Acta* (1987); "The Social Impact of Recent and Prospective Mortality Declines Among Older Americans," *Sociology and Social Research* (1986); "Life Expectancy and the Older Population," *Research on Aging* (1984); and "Implications of Recent Mortality Trends for the Size and Composition of the Population over 65," *Review of Public Data Use* (1983).

KINGSLEY DAVIS, sociologist and demographer, is a Senior Research Fellow at the Hoover Institution and Distinguished Professor of Sociology at the University of Southern California. He is known for his work on population growth, urbanization, and development in various parts of the world, and he has written on demographic factors affecting marriage and the family. His publications include editing *Contemporary Marriage* (1986) and, with Mikhail Bernstam and Rita Ricardo-Campbell, *Below-Replacement Fertility in Industrial Societies* (forthcoming).

ROBERT HUTCHENS is Associate Professor in the New York State School of Industrial and Labor Relations at Cornell University. He received his Ph.D. in Economics from the University of Wisconsin in 1976. His recent publications include "Layoffs and Labor Supply," *International Economic Review* (1983); "Delayed Payment Contracts and a Firm's Propensity to Hire Older Workers," *Journal of Labor Economics* (1986); "The Effects of the Omnibus Budget Reconciliation Act of 1981 on AFDC Recipients: A Review of Studies," *Research in Labor Economics* (1987); and "A Test of Lazear's Theory of Delayed Payment Contracts," *Journal of Labor Economics* (1987).

ALEX INKELES is Senior Fellow at the Hoover Institution and Professor of Sociology—and, by courtesy, of Education—at Stanford University. Formerly he served as Margaret Jacks Professor of Education at Stanford; at Harvard University he served as Professor of Sociology and as Director of Studies on Social and Cultural Aspects of Development in the Center for International Affairs. He received his Ph.D. from Columbia University in 1949. Dr. Inkeles is an authority on the social and cultural aspects of economic development in the developing nations, on the Soviet social system, and in the fields of personality and social structure. His recent books include *Becoming Modern: Individual Change in Six Developing Countries* (with Smith; 1974), which received the first Hadley Cantril Award, and *Exploring Individual Modernity* (1983).

RICHARD A. IPPOLITO is Chief Economist at the Pension Benefit Guaranty Corporation. He is the author of *Pensions, Economics and Public Policy* (1986).

LAURENCE J. KOTLIKOFF is Chairman of the Department of Economics at Boston University and a Research Associate of the National Bureau of Economic Research. He received his Ph.D. in Economics from Harvard University in 1977 and subsequently taught at the University of California, Los Angeles and at Yale University. Professor Kotlikoff has published extensively in professional journals, newspapers, and magazines; his book publications are *Determinants of Savings* (forthcoming); *Dynamic Fiscal Policy* (with Alan Auerbach; 1987); *Pensions in the American Economy* (with Daniel Smith; 1983); and *The Wage Carrot and the Pension Stick: Retirement Benefits and Labor Force Participation* (with David Wise; 1988).

EDWARD P. LAZEAR is Senior Fellow at the Hoover Institution and is Isidore Brown and Gladys J. Brown Professor of Urban and Labor Economics at the University of Chicago. He received his Ph.D. from Harvard University in

Economics in 1974 and his B.A. and M.A. from the University of California at Los Angeles in 1971. Dr. Lazear is Editor of the *Journal of Labor Economics* and Associate Editor of the *Journal of Economic Perspectives*. He has written numerous articles in a variety of areas, including "Why Is There Mandatory Retirement?" in the *Journal of Political Economy* (1979) as well as articles on retirement, pension policy, and general issues of worker compensation. Dr. Lazear is a frequent lecturer on the domestic and international circuit, most recently having presented lecture series in Paris and Vienna.

OLIVIA S. MITCHELL is Associate Professor of Labor Economics at Cornell University and Research Associate at the National Bureau of Economic Research. She also serves on the ERISA Advisory Board, appointed by the Secretary of Labor. She graduated magna cum laude in Economics from Harvard University and received her M.S. and Ph.D. from the University of Wisconsin at Madison. She co-authored *Retirement, Pensions, and Social Security* (with Gary S. Fields; 1985), and her publications forthcoming in 1988 include "Worker Knowledge of Pension Provisions," *Journal of Labor Economics;* "The Baby Boom's Legacy" (with P. Levine), *American Economic Review;* and "The Impact of Government Regulations on the Labor Market" (with A. Mikalauskas), in D. Salisbury, ed., *Mandating Benefits.*

MALCOLM H. MORRISON is Professorial Lecturer at the Graduate School of Arts and Sciences, George Washington University. He is a national expert on employment and retirement policies and has written and lectured widely both in the United States and abroad. From 1979 to 1982 he was the director of major national studies about the consequences of the Age Discrimination in Employment Act conducted by the U.S. Department of Labor. Dr. Morrison's recent publications include "National Survey of Retirement Policies and Practices," *Personnel Administrator* (1988); "Work and Retirement in an Aging Society," *Daedalus* (1986); and "Corporate Practices: Personnel Programs and Management Strategies for Older Workers," for Travelers Insurance Companies (1986). He also edited *Economics of Aging: The Future of Retirement* (1982).

MICHAEL D. PACKARD is an economist on the Program Analysis Staff of the Office of Research and Statistics, Social Security Administration. His interests comprise a wide range of topics relating to retirement and the economic status of the elderly. Recent publications in the *Social Security Bulletin* include "Income of New Disabled-Worker Beneficiaries and Their Families" (1987); "Health Status of New Retired-Worker Beneficiaries" (1985); "Slowing Down Pension Indexing: The Foreign Experience" (with Daniel

Wartonick; 1983); and "Retirement Options Under the Swedish National Pension System" (1982).

DONALD O. PARSONS is Professor of Economics at the Ohio State University. His recent publications include *Poverty and the Minimum Wage* (1980); "The Male Labor Force Participation Decision: Health, Reported Health and Economic Incentives," *Economica* (1982); "Demographic Effects on Public Charity to the Aged," *Journal of Human Resources* (1982); and "The Employment Relationship: Job Attachment, Work Effort, and the Nature of Contracts," in Orley Ashenfelter and Richard Layard, eds., *Handbook of Labor Economics* (1986).

MARIA T. PRAMAGGIORE is a pre-doctoral student in the Department of Economics at the University of Southern California. Her support is provided by a grant from the National Institute on Aging to USC entitled Multidisciplinary Research Training in Gerontology.

DOUGLAS J. PUFFERT is a doctoral student in the Department of Economics at Stanford University. His recent papers include "Social Security: A Financial Appraisal Across and Within Generations" (with M. Boskin, L. Kotlikoff, and J. Shoven), *National Tax Journal* (1987); "Social Security and the American Family" (with M. Boskin), in Lawrence Summers, ed., *Tax Policy and the Economy* (1987); and "Means and Implications of Social Security Finance in Developing Countries" (1987).

ROGER L. RANSOM is Professor of History and Economics at the University of California at Riverside and has held a Fellowship from the Guggenheim Foundation. With Richard Sutch, Dr. Ransom has been co-director of the University of California's History of Saving Project since 1984 and has co-authored a book, *One Kind of Freedom: The Economic Consequences of Emancipation* (1977), as well as over a dozen articles in economics and history journals. Their article "The Labor of Older Americans," *Journal of Economic History* (1986), was awarded the Cole prize by the Economic History Association.

VIRGINIA P. RENO is Director of the Program Analysis Staff in the Office of Research and Statistics of the Social Security Administration. Her research interests include social security and income maintenance issues, retirement and disability programs and behavior, and issues about the treatment of women and families in tax and benefit systems. Her recent publications include "Economic Security, 1935–85" (with S. Grad), *Social Security Bulletin* (1985); "Relationships Among Retirement, Disability and Unemployment:

The U.S. Experience" (with D. N. Price), *Social Security, Unemployment and Premature Retirement* (1985); "Distribution of Income Sources of Recent Retirees: Findings from the New Beneficiary Survey" (with L. D. Maxfield), *Social Security Bulletin* (1985); and "Women and Social Security," *Social Security Bulletin* (1985).

RITA RICARDO-CAMPBELL, PH.D., is Senior Fellow at the Hoover Institution. She is a member of the President's Economic Policy Advisory Board and the National Council on the Humanities; she also serves as a member on the Board of Directors of the Gillette Company and the Watkins-Johnson Company. Dr. Ricardo-Campbell has written several books, including *The Economics and Politics of Health* (2d ed., 1985); *Social Security: Promise and Reality* (1977); and *Drug Lag: Federal Government Decision Making* (1976). Her latest article, "U.S. Social Security Under Low Fertility," appears in *Below-Replacement Fertility in Industrial Societies* (forthcoming), which she co-edited with Kingsley Davis and Mikhail Bernstam.

SHERWIN ROSEN is Bergman Professor of Economics at the University of Chicago and Senior Research Fellow at the Hoover Institution. He is also Editor of the *Journal of Political Economy*. His recent publications include "Dynamic Animal Economics," *American Journal of Agricultural Economics* (1987); "Some Economics of Teaching," *Journal of Labor Economics* (1987); "Prizes and Incentives in Elimination Tournaments," *American Economic Review* (1986); and "Implicit Contracts: A Survey," *Journal of Economic Literature* (1985).

MARY ROSS is Director of the Legislative Reference Staff, Office of Legislative and Regulatory Policy, Social Security Administration. She has been with the SSA Office of Legislative and Regulatory Policy and its predecessor organizations, working primarily on legislative planning and evaluation in the Social Security retirement and survivors insurance area. In the late 1960s and early 1970s Miss Ross served as Chief of the Health Insurance (Medicare) Benefits Branch and in various capacities dealing with then-current welfare reform proposals. She also worked closely with major Advisory Councils on Social Security in 1965, 1968, 1971, 1975, and 1979. In 1968 and again in 1982 she received SSA's highest award, the Commissioners' Citation, for her legislative planning work.

GARY D. SANDEFUR is Associate Professor of Social Work and Sociology, and Associate Director of the Institute for Research on Poverty, at the University of Wisconsin at Madison. He has written widely on a variety of topics in social demography. His recent work includes forthcoming articles in *Demography* and in *Social Forces* on American Indian income and earnings, as well as an article (with Nancy Brandon Tuma) on methodological issues in the study of mobility forthcoming in *Social Science Research*. He is co-editor of *Minorities, Poverty, and Social Policy* (with Marta Tienda; forthcoming).

JOHN SHOVEN is Chairman of the Department of Economics at Stanford University. He is active in the Center for Economic Policy Research and the National Bureau of Economic Research, and he has been a long-term consultant with the U.S. Treasury Department. Dr. Shoven's recent publications include "General Equilibrium Computations of the Marginal Welfare Costs of Taxes in the United States" (with C. Ballard and J. Whalley), *American Economic Review* (1985); "The Effects of Interest Rates on Mortgage Prepayments" (with J. Green), *Journal of Money, Credit and Banking* (1986); and "Are There Lessons for the U.S. in the Japanese Tax System?" (with J. Makin), in P. Cogan, ed., *Contemporary Economic Problems* (forthcoming).

ROBIN SICKLES is Professor of Economics and Statistics at Rice University. His recent publications include "An Analysis of Youth Crime and Employment Patterns" (with D. Good and M. Priog-Good), *Journal of Quantitative Criminology* (1986); "An Analysis of the Health and Retirement Status of the Elderly" (with P. Taubman), *Econometric* (1986); "Allocative Distortions and the Regulatory Transition of the U.S. Airline Industry" (with D. Good and R. Johnson), *Journal of Econometrics* (1986); and "Union Wage, Hours and Earnings Differentials in the Construction Industry" (with J. Perloff), *Journal of Labor Economics* (1987).

GORDON F. STREIB is Graduate Research Professor at the University of Florida at Gainesville. He is also Joint Professor of Community Health and Family Medicine, College of Medicine, at the University of Florida and is Professor Emeritus of Cornell University, where he taught for 26 years. Dr. Streib received his Ph.D. from Columbia University and has been a Fulbright Professor to Denmark and Ireland. In 1984, he was the first recipient of the American Sociological Association's award as Distinguished Contributor to the Sociology of Aging. Dr. Streib's publications include *Programs for Older Americans: Evaluations by Academic Gerontologists* (1981) and *Old Homes—New Families: Shared Living for the Elderly* (1984).

RICHARD SUTCH is Professor of Economics and History at the University of California at Berkeley and has held a Fellowship from the Guggenheim Foundation. With Roger L. Ransom, Dr. Sutch has been co-director of the University of California's History of Saving Project since 1984 and has co-authored a book, *One Kind of Freedom: The Economic Consequences of Emancipation* (1977) as well as over a dozen articles in economics and history journals. Their article "The Labor of Older Americans," *Journal of Economic History* (1986), was awarded the Cole prize by the Economic History Association.

PAUL TAUBMAN is Professor of Economics at the University of Pennsylvania. His recent publications include "Birth Order, Schooling and Earnings" (with J. Behrman), *Journal of Labor Economics* (1986); "The Effect and Number of Position of Siblings on Child and Adult Outcomes" (with J. Behrman), *Social Biology* (1986); "A Multivariate Error Components Analysis and the Retirement Status of the Elderly" (with R. Sickles), *Econometrica* (1986); and "Kinship Studies" (with J. Behrman), in G. Psacharapoulos, ed., *Economics of Education Research and Studies* (1987).

NANCY BRANDON TUMA is Professor of Sociology at Stanford University and Senior Fellow by Courtesy of the Hoover Institution. She has written widely on a variety of topics related to labor mobility, child-bearing, and marital formation and dissolution; she is also known for development methods for studying change over time in social phenomena. Her recent work includes articles on child-bearing in the United States, Sri Lanka, and the Federal Republic of Germany as well as an article (with Gary D. Sandefur) on methodological issues in the study of mobility forthcoming in *Social Science Research*. She is coauthor of *Social Dynamics: Models and Methods* (with Michael T. Hannan; 1984).

PETER UHLENBERG is Associate Professor of Sociology at the University of North Carolina at Chapel Hill and a Fellow at the Carolina Population Center. His recent publications include a chapter, "Aging and the Societal Significance of Cohorts," in James E. Birren and Vern L. Bengtson, eds., *Theories of Aging: Psychological and Social Perspectives* (1987), and an article, "Does Population Aging Produce Increasing Gerontology?" *Sociological Forum* (forthcoming).

CHIKAKO USUI is Assistant Professor of Sociology at Tulane University. She received her Ph.D. from Stanford University in 1987. Her major areas of research are comparative social welfare and state policies and the sociology of aging. In 1983 her article, "Indicators of Contraceptive Policy for Nations at Three Levels of Development," was published in *Social Indicators Research*.

DAVID A. WISE is at the J.F.K. School of Government, Harvard University.

INTRODUCTION

The origin of the conference on "Issues in Contemporary Retirement" began with Dr. Richard Suzman of the National Institute on Aging, who walked into Dr. Rita Ricardo-Campbell's office at the Hoover Institution and proposed such a conference, with funding from the NIA.

The resulting interdisciplinary conference on contemporary retirement, held February 26–27, 1987, brought together economists, sociologists, historians, and demographers from across the country to explore some of the puzzling issues accompanying the increasing percentage of the aged in the population.[1] Foremost among these issues is that men are retiring earlier and earlier although national policy increasingly has been to encourage later retirement. Several of the papers in this volume discuss why the former is so; other papers discuss the changing age of old age, whether or not productivity declines as individuals age, retirement, and other relevant topics.

Trends

In their paper, Gary Sandefur and Nancy Tuma present a massive data analysis using census data from 1940, 1950, 1960, 1970, and 1980. Their goal is to document the general social and economic trends among the elderly population. Since the data set is enormous and the topic quite broad, it is difficult to summarize the findings in any simple way. Nevertheless, some points stand out: the aged population has grown more rapidly than the population as a whole over the 1940–1985 period; it has become less white and more female, especially among the very old; improvements in Social Security benefits led to a decline in labor force participation among the elderly; institutionalization is less common for the younger aged but more common for the older aged group than in the past; employment rates have declined for men and increased for women (this is also documented in the Ricardo-Campbell and the Ransom and Sutch papers); and the elderly are substantially better off now than they were in 1960. Sandefur and Tuma conclude that, if a primary social concern is to lengthen the worklife expectancy of men, it will have to be accomplished by changing Social Security entitlements.

Roger Ransom and Richard Sutch present evidence that retirement was common among American men as early as 1870. Further, they argue that, if anything, retirement was declining (labor force participation among older men was rising) until the late 1930s among men in manufacturing. They point out that the reversal of this trend coincides with the passage of the Social Security Act in 1935 and with the Revenue Act of 1942, which they suggest provided some incentive for earlier retirement. They go on to claim that an incentive story can be told to explain the changes in labor force participation. Upward-sloping age-earnings profiles can provide incentives to workers that raise lifetime productivity.[2] The higher productivity is consistent with postponed retirement. Although less than compelling, the theoretical suggestions provide an interesting interpretation of the numbers.

Rita Ricardo-Campbell focuses on retirement among women, using a new data set that she compiled from a nonprofit organization and from a profitmaking firm. The data base from a large company of 5,000 active women workers aged 40–50 and a data set of 900 recent women retirees of the same company provide detailed labor supply information. Because the data were new and the number of interview respondents from the larger data base was small, this is regarded as a pilot study. Nevertheless, there are a number of interesting findings.

Perhaps among the more important results of Ricardo-Campbell's analysis is that it is not unlikely that currently working women will retire at younger ages than have recently retired women. In addition, a comparison of active and retired women in the larger data set makes it clear that women workers will be better off at retirement in the future than are current female retirees, because the former will have earned more and because the greater number of years worked will entitle them to larger private pensions.

The main gender difference in labor force participation is that men have shortened their worklives while women have lengthened theirs. Ricardo-Campbell sees forces operating in both directions so that predictions on worklife lengths for the future are less certain. She concludes the analysis with a discussion of the financial status of widows.

Health and Retirement

Prior to the 1970s, many people believed that most early retirement—that is, before age 65—was due primarily to ill health. Recent economic studies have questioned this belief and pointed to the coincidental sharp drop in older male labor force participation with the availability of early retirement benefits at age 62 and monthly permanent disability payments, enacted in 1956. Disability benefits are converted at age 65 into a retired-worker benefit. Because a "disability freeze" is used in calculating the average monthly disability benefit starting in the year when the disability occurs, that benefit is higher than a Social Security retirement benefit would be. Moreover, the freeze on use of disability years "usually results in a higher subsequent Social Security benefit than would otherwise be payable, because it does not include in the calculation those years during the worker's prior period of disability when his or her earnings were likely to have been zero or insignificant" (Wilkin 1986, 3–4).

The economic incentive to apply for disability benefits in later years, but prior to age 62, and the Disability Amendments of 1980 were not discussed in the conference papers. However, three causal factors encouraging early withdrawal from the labor force were stressed by separate papers: health, economic resources, and cultural patterns.

Eileen Crimmins and Maria Pramaggiore use Health Interview Survey data for 1969–1981 to argue that the health of older men aged 55–61 and 62–64 may have been declining despite the increase in their life expectancy. They state that "the decline in the percentage of people disabled by heart disease is more than offset in most groups by the increase in the percentage suffering paralysis. In the case of those retired for reasons of health, there is an increase in both heart disease and paralysis categories."

Crimmins and Pramaggiore conclude that "the overall pattern of changes in the proportion of men working and in the health of those working and retired is consistent with some deterioration in health as well as an increasing tendency to withdraw from the labor force when a health condition is diagnosed." As economist Donald Parsons states in his comment on this paper, "the health deterioration . . . hypothesis is not mutually exclusive with the major competing hypothesis (the work disincentive model)." The paper recognizes that the individual perception of how well one feels in relationship to work has been changing. Individuals today may claim disability benefits whose level of impairment would not have induced them to retire many years ago.

It is of interest that the medical literature is beginning to document that there has been a steady decline in work disability due to cardiovascular and other diseases (Fries 1987). Incidence rates of heart attacks have declined 26 percent for men aged 45–54 and 22 percent for those aged 55–64 in at least one study, which gathered data on the employees of a large company for a period of more than twenty years (Pell and Fayerweather 1985). It is also becoming increasingly true that benefits from new drugs should enable many more persons suffering from chronic diseases to continue to work.

Jere Behrman, Robin Sickles, and Paul Taubman use the National Longi-tudinal Retirement History Survey and the Dorn sample to examine how age-specific death rates are related to socioeconomic and lifestyle variables. The basic statistical approach is to use a time-to-failure analysis. The key findings are as follows: regular tobacco users have a shorter life, as previ-ously documented; economic variables are independently important; pen-sion and Social Security eligibility are strongly correlated with life expec-tancy, though having a child at home or a working wife for men in their sixties is correlated with shorter life spans; and professionals and managers live longer.

Mid-Session Remarks

Kingsley Davis gave the dinner speech at the conference, where he exam-ined long-run changes in retirement behavior and focused on differences between men and women. He points out that women who work in the home never retire from their jobs. This makes the transition to old age less traumatic for women, but perhaps more difficult physically. He worries about the effects of changes in female labor force behavior on fertility rates, and he raises the point that women do not receive compensation or pension accrual for their time out of the labor force, even though that time is socially produc-tive. Davis outlines several possibilities for public policy. One alternative seeks greater equality in household and labor market responsibilities, whereas another seeks to reinforce the division of labor by sex. He concludes with what he believes to be the more likely scenario.

Early Retirement

Michael Packard and Virginia Reno examine the receipt of Social Secu-rity benefits and pensions in relationship to early retirement of men. They found that in 1980–81 only 25 percent of newly entitled male Social Secu-rity beneficiaries (not self-employed or receiving disability benefits) gave poor health as their reason for retiring, as compared to earlier surveys in which poor health was self-reported as the primary reason for retirement. Packard and Reno found that male beneficiaries who had stopped working well before age 62 were more likely to give poor health as their response. The authors stress that women were less likely than men to state in the 1980–81 survey that poor health was their reason for retirement. Earlier self-selection by women in poor health *not* to work for pay—at least among older cohorts—may account for the reported, sizable discrepancy by sex. The authors nowhere state that the rising percentage of replacement of income is the prime reason for increasingly earlier retirement, although their data imply this.

Sociologists Alex Inkeles and Chikako Usui explore the role of attitudes toward work, leisure, and acceptable values in their paper on cross-national perspectives in retirement decisions. Drawing on a 1982 Japanese study of retirement and labor force participation, Inkeles and Usui report that 57 percent of Japanese men continued work after age 60, as compared to 33 percent in the United States, 13 percent in the United Kingdom, and 8 percent in France. The authors explain that both the Japanese and Americans believe that a person should save while working and not have to rely on the state, one's family, or Social Security. The Japanese study states that 60 percent of Japanese and 64 percent of Americans are in general agreement on attitudes favoring self-reliance, whereas those percentages are much lower in the United Kingdom and France.

Inkeles and Usui argue that the reason the Japanese and Americans in the Japanese survey advise not to rely on public benefits cannot be because Social Security benefits in Japan and the United States are inadequate or unavailable. Rather, the reason is because of "preferences, basic values, and conceptions about what is good and proper." However, their limited data on private pensions indicate that 10 percent of men "over 60 in the labor force" in Japan and 29 percent in the United States receive pensions, as compared to 46 percent in the United Kingdom and 54 percent in France. An "almost universal private pension system" exists in France (Horlick 1987).

Lifetime Productivity

Laurence Kotlikoff offers a clever way to estimate the age-productivity relationship. His idea is that when a worker is hired, his lifetime expected productivity equals his lifetime expected wage. Thus, by comparing workers who start working in a firm at, say, age 50 with those who start at age 51, an estimate of productivity at age 50 can be obtained as being equal to the difference between the present values of the two wage streams. He estimates the model using data obtained from a large firm.

Kotlikoff's results suggest that age-earnings profiles are steeper than age-productivity profiles. This is consistent with Lazear's (1979) view that steep age-earnings profiles, coupled with mandatory retirement, are used to motivate workers over their lifetimes. Thus, the relation of productivity to compensation over the life cycle is at the center of labor economics today and is the key to understanding mandatory and other forms of induced retirement. As such, this paper provides a true contribution.

Retirement Age and Mandatory Retirement

Peter Uhlenberg challenges the idea that age 65 marks old age, and he cites—in contrast to the Crimmins and Pramaggiore paper—several researchers who question the continuing use of age 65. "With increasing life expectancy . . . the age of old age should be rising." Uhlenberg is concerned about the effect of increasing life expectancy on the U.S. Social Security system and other transfer payments to the aged, and he makes four proposals to lessen the tax burden on the working population. In essence, each of Uhlenberg's proposals would increase the chronological age of entitlement to old-age benefits. Uhlenberg recognizes the potential impact of this on disability benefit expenditures. In view of the differential in life expectancy between men and women, blacks and whites, some modifications of his proposals might be desirable.

Malcolm Morrison discusses the potential impact on the older male labor supply if the mandatory retirement age were eliminated. If this policy is followed without requiring employer pension accruals for people beyond age 65, a 10 percent increase in labor force participation by older men aged 60–70 is projected for the year 2000. The bulk of the increase would occur among those aged 65–67. If a mandatory age retirement of 70 is set, the increase would be about 5 percent. Generous private pension accrual for workers over age 65 would further increase older workers' labor force participation rate.

Financial Aspects of the U.S. Social Security System

Michael Boskin and Douglas Puffert examine by age cohorts the present value of future Social Security retirement benefits, and they discuss the long-run financial status of the Social Security system. Boskin and Puffert present various combinations of the Social Security Administration's four sets of assumptions, ranging from pessimistic to optimistic, for the beneficiaries. Several scenarios of the probable use of the developing large surplus in the Old Age, Survivor and Disability Insurance (OASDI) trust funds are given. These include future loans to the Hospital Insurance trust fund, which is expected to run out of money a few years hence, and raiding of the surplus to pay higher unfunded benefits. How different age cohorts would fare under different scenarios is projected.

B. Douglas Bernheim presents an interesting analysis of individuals' expectations and actual receipts of Social Security benefits. In order for individuals to do a thorough job of life-cycle planning, it is important that they estimate accurately the amount of payment they are going to receive upon retirement. He uses data from the Retirement History Survey and obtains the following results. First, responses are noisy in that they do not predict precisely the amount of benefits. But the estimates do not seem to be biased in that they pick out the expectation of the distribution reasonably well. Second, consumers do not use all the information available in forming their expectations, but they do tend to use the same information to form expectations on a number of different variables. Third, widows and single women make the most conservative and most accurate forecasts. There are two possible explanations: widows and single women may be better data processors, perhaps because the information is more important to them, or there may not be as much real variation in Social Security payments among women and widows, so that it is easier to predict. However, this question is not investigated in the paper.

At the conference, the presentation of each paper was followed by formal discussion, and these remarks are included in this volume after each paper.

Informal discussion from the floor was lively and informative. A few points made in that discussion were not raised by the papers or formal remarks. For example, the self-reported explanation of primarily financial incentives to retire has grown in importance because this explanation has become more acceptable. The potential impact of two-worker families on retirement age and the important nonpaid work by older volunteers were also discussed. It was pointed out that the potential labor shortage by the 1990s would increase the demand for labor of older persons and thus increase their wages, resulting in some individuals delaying their retirement.

Not discussed, however, was the increased opportunity cost or greater utility of foregone leisure. Higher income levels, greater choice of leisure activities—such as enjoyable travel, sports, computer games, craft hobbies, and adult education courses—and more widely disseminated information about their availability—may well in total be a major factor in early retirement.

The coeditors would especially like to thank Bette Childers, Muriel Karr, and Christina Peck of the Hoover Institution staff for their excellent help and patience in handling the myriad of details in running the conference.

Notes

1. The topic of involuntary retirement (that is, when plants close and jobs disappear) was intentionally omitted in the selection of papers.

2. Ransom and Sutch build on the analysis in Lazear (1979, 1981).

References

Fries, James F. 1987. "Reduction of the National Morbidity." *Gerontologica Perspecta* 1:54–65.

Horlick, Max. 1987. "The Relationships Between Public and Private Pension Schemes: An Introductory Overview." *Social Security Bulletin* 50:17.

Lazear, Edward P. 1979. "Why Is There Mandatory Retirement?" *Journal of Political Economy* 87:1261–64.

———.1981. "Agency, Earnings Profiles, Productivity, and Hours Restrictions." *American Economic Review* 71:606–20.

Pell, Sidney, and William E. Fayerweather. 1985. "Trends in the Incidence of Myocardial Infarction and in Associated Mortality and Morbidity in a Large Employed Population." *New England Journal of Medicine* 312:1008.

Wilkin, John C. 1986. "Present Value of OASDI and Medicare Benefits for Newly Entitled Disabled Workers." Actuarial Note no. 128. Washington, D.C.: U.S. Department of Health and Human Services, Social Security Administration.

ISSUES IN CONTEMPORARY RETIREMENT

PART I
LABOR FORCE ACTIVITY

I

THE DECLINE OF RETIREMENT IN THE YEARS BEFORE SOCIAL SECURITY: U.S. RETIREMENT PATTERNS, 1870–1940

Roger L. Ransom
and Richard Sutch

The history of retirement in the United States needs to be reassessed. A significant misunderstanding, which has influenced much recent work on contemporary retirement, is the view that retirement was uncommon before 1940. Actually, the expectation of retirement for a 30-year-old man in 1900 was over 35 percent. It is often assumed and sometimes explicitly stated that retirement became quantitatively significant about the time of World War II, after a gradual evolution driven by rising affluence and declining mortality produced a substantial substitution of retirement for labor by older men.

The data referred to in this paper will be archived at the Laboratory for Historical Research at the University of California at Riverside. Communications and requests for data should be addressed to the authors in care of the University of California History of Saving Project, Institute of Business and Economic Research, University of California, Berkeley, Calif., 94720. This paper has benefited from discussions with George Akerlof, Susan Carter, William Dickens, Claudia Goldin, Edward Lazear, and Robert Whaples. Participants of the Mellon Foundation Seminar on the Evolution of Labor Markets offered many helpful suggestions. Support from the National Science Foundation, the Guggenheim Foundation, the Institute for Business and Economic Research of the University of California at Berkeley, the Academic Senate of the University of California, the Inter-university Consortium for Political and Social Research, and the Laboratory for Historical Research of the University of California at Riverside is gratefully acknowledged.

Actually, national retirement rates for men were about the same in 1870 as they were in 1930.

There are several underlying misconceptions that need to be cleared up. First, there were no significant trends changing the life expectancy for adult men during this period. Second, retirement, as we shall see, was relatively common among American men as early as 1870. Third—and this point provides the title for this article—the incidence of retirement among nonagricultural workers was declining before the late 1930s. Therefore, the postwar increase in the propensity to retire—a trend that has received much journalistic and academic attention—cannot be viewed as the continuation of a prewar trend. Instead, there was a sharp reversal of direction in the trend at a time that falls between the passage of the Social Security Act in 1935 and the granting of tax incentives to corporate employers that established company pension plans with the Revenue Act of 1942.

The importance of these points for a contemporary study of retirement should be fairly obvious. Our view of why retirement exists, what role it plays in motivating private saving, the impact of Social Security, and a number of other issues in contemporary retirement may well be—and should be—influenced by our understanding of retirement's origins, its changing patterns, and its long-run trends. For example, the widespread misperception about the role of retirement before the 1940s has led to an exaggeration of the importance of intergenerational transfers in motivating wealth accumulation.[1] In this article, we also suggest a connection between the pre-1940 trends in retirement and the spreading practice of paying "incentive wages" and the associated establishment of internal labor markets by U.S. corporations prior to World War II.

Incentive wages are the consequence of wage contracts that pay young workers less than their marginal product and older workers more than their marginal product as a device to reduce turnover, reduce the cost of monitoring, and increase the productivity of the worker. In large firms, these wage policies are accompanied by work rules and bureaucratic personnel procedures that protect workers from arbitrary dismissal and increase job security with seniority. Historically, incentive wages have been generally associated with the establishment of internal labor markets. These are employment procedures designed to fill the firm's requirements for skilled workers by promotion from within rather than recruitment from outside the firm. Toward this end, jobs are ordered into a structured sequence through which workers advance as they gain seniority.[2] In this report we can only hint at the possible connection between the retirement patterns we observe and the adoption of these modern labor market institutions. Our primary task is to describe and explain the historical patterns. We hope that this will stimulate those engaged in direct confrontation of contemporary problems.

Mortality Trends

Mortality did not begin to fall in the United States until sometime after 1880. Before that, if there was any trend, it was upward. Mortality rates, at least in New England, were slowly increasing in the eighteenth and early nineteenth centuries.[3] In the late 1880s, public health measures, particularly water filtration and the installation of urban sewer systems, reversed these trends and brought the first measurable progress (Meeker 1972). Life expectancy at birth rose from about 43 years in 1880 to 63 years in 1940. What is often unrecognized is that most of this increase in life expectancy was the result of dramatic improvements in the infant mortality rate, which fell from approximately 160 per thousand births in 1880 to 43 per thousand in 1940. Nearly all of the remaining improvement in life expectancy was produced by a decline in the maternal mortality rate (U.S. Bureau of the Census 1975, I:series B107, B126, B142, B145, B148).

The life expectancy of men measured at age twenty, by contrast, actually fell between 1860 and 1900 before beginning to increase at a moderate rate between 1900 and 1940. The trend since 1880 is plotted in Figure 1.1.[4] In that figure we also illustrate the expectation of life for men at age 60. This measure hardly changed before World War II. Since retirement decisions are made by adults, it is difficult to argue that infant mortality would have had an important influence on those decisions. During this period, there simply were no changes in mortality significant enough to influence retirement patterns one way or another.

Retirement Patterns

Retirement patterns are usually analyzed using statistics on labor force participation. This presents a momentary problem for a review of prewar retirement trends, since the scientific concept of an aggregate "labor force" was first conceived in the 1930s and was not institutionalized in the United States until it was incorporated as part of the census-taking apparatus designed for the Sixteenth Census of 1940. There are no direct measurements of labor force participation that predate a 1937 experimental census designed to test the new labor force concepts.[5] However, earlier censuses dating back to 1870 did collect data on occupation and duration of unemployment. These can be used to construct estimates of employment, unemployment, and labor force participation for men that are reasonably consistent with modern definitions. Our work with these census records has led us to conclude that a reliable picture of retirement patterns for the period 1870–1940 can be reconstructed from the data.[6] To do so, we begin by establishing a benchmark estimate for the year 1900.

FIGURE 1.1
LIFE EXPECTANCY OF U.S. WHITE MEN

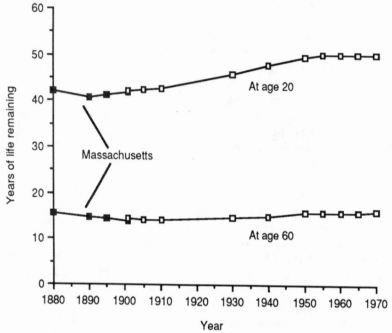

SOURCE: U.S. Bureau of the Census (1975, I: Series B118, B122, B128, B132).

NOTE: For 1900–1919, U.S. data refer to twenty states; for 1920–1929, they refer to 34 states; thereafter, for all states. These changes in the scope and coverage of the data probably exaggerate the improvements in mortality, but the bias is believed to be small.

Labor Force Participation Rates for Men in 1900

The published returns from the censuses of 1890 through 1930 cannot be used for our purposes, since the concept of occupational status then in place was quite different from the concepts of employment and unemployment that have been used since 1940 to define labor force participation. There is evidence that, in those early censuses, a considerable number of persons who were retired or permanently disabled were reported with a "gainful occupation" in the enumerations that constitute the published reports (Durand and Goldfield 1944, 11; Durand 1947, 81; Ransom and Sutch 1986a, 8–9). The individual-level returns from these censuses are preserved in the National Archives in the form of the original manuscripts returned by the enumerators, and these can be used to make inferences about the labor force status of individuals. To date, however, only the returns from the 1900 census have been converted to a machine-readable format.[7] For that year, a "public-use" sample of one in 760 has been collected from the entire national population recorded in the enumerators' manuscripts.[8]

Elsewhere we have described procedures we use to determine the labor force status of men included in this sample.[9] In the Appendix to this paper we present a tabulation of the resulting labor force statistics by single years of age. In Figure 1.2 we present the age profile of labor force participation rates for men. To smooth the profile we display the three-year moving cohort averages on the diagram. What is immediately striking about these data is that they indicate there was a significant propensity to retire at the turn of the century. Participation rates began to decline for men in their early fifties and the rate of decline became quite pronounced after age 55. These data, together with the age-specific mortality table for men in 1900, allow us to calculate that the expectation of retirement for a 30-year-old man would have been 36.1 percent.[10]

FIGURE 1.2 _____

LABOR FORCE PARTICIPATION RATE OF MEN, 1900

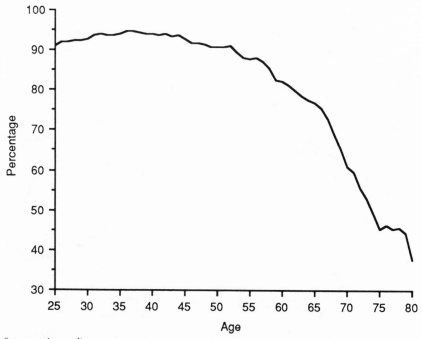

SOURCE: Appendix.

The length of the average retirement period at the turn of the century was substantial. In Figure 1.3 we present the expectation of life by age in 1900 for white men. A 55-year-old man could expect to live 17.4 additional years, a 65-year-old had a life expectancy remaining of 11.5 years, and a 75-year-old could anticipate another 6.8 years according to the life table. These figures may exaggerate somewhat the average length of retirement periods begun at each age, since retirees are likely to experience a higher mortality rate than people remaining at work. But, even after a plausible correction for differential mortality, the average retirement periods are of substantial duration.[11]

These findings have relevance for the debate over the importance of life-cycle motivations for saving. Darby (1979) and Kotlikoff and Summers (1981) have suggested that intergenerational transfers must have been a more important motivation than retirement for saving during the early twentieth century, because they believe, we think incorrectly, that retirement was

FIGURE 1.3 _____

LIFE EXPECTANCY OF WHITE MEN: YEARS OF LIFE REMAINING BY AGE

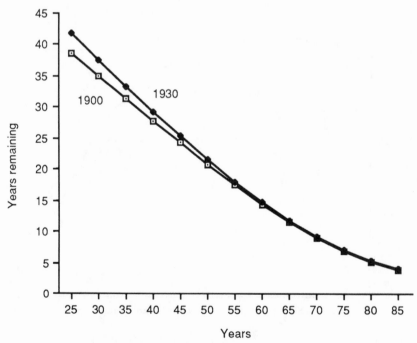

SOURCE: U.S. National Center for Health Statistics (1978, 5–13).

FIGURE 1.4

LABOR FORCE PARTICIPATION RATES OF MEN,
1900, 1930, 1950, AND 1980

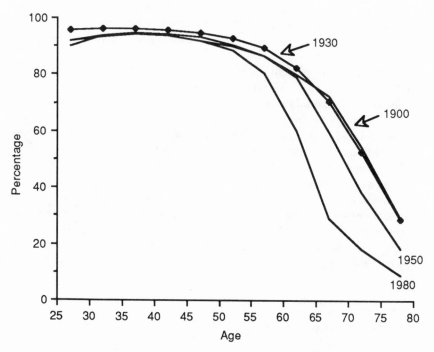

uncommon and retirement periods were brief (Ransom and Sutch 1986b). However, the labor force participation profile exhibited in Figure 1.2 predicts a sizable saving rate using the "stripped-down" Modigliani-Brumberg (1954) model of saving that smooths male consumption over the expected lifetimes. We estimate on this basis that an average saving rate of 16.2 percent of lifetime income would be required to completely smooth consumption.[12] If we had allowed for the fact that the age of death is uncertain and the possibility that annuity markets may not have been available, the rate of life-cycle saving predicted would have been even higher (Davies 1981; Abel 1985).

Retirement Trends Since 1900

In Figure 1.4 we superimpose the labor force participation profile we have estimated for 1900 on top of comparable profiles for 1930 (dashed line), 1950, and 1980. The 1900 and 1930 profiles are nearly identical. This suggests that retirement propensities were the same in 1900 and 1930 and that the increasing propensity to retire evident today did not appear until sometime after the onset of the Great Depression. Since the improvement in mortality for men over age 30 was negligible between 1900 and 1930 (see Figure 1.3), we can conclude that the expectation of retirement, the expected length of retirement, and the strength of the life-cycle motive were about the same in 1900 and 1930.

In Figure 1.5 we present the trends in labor force participation for older men from 1900 to 1980. The data for 1940 are not plotted on this diagram because of a substantial misreporting of age and employment status of older men associated with the introduction of Social Security (U.S. Bureau of the Census 1940, 31; Ransom and Sutch 1986a, 11–13). In Table 1.1 we present the results of the special census of labor force participation taken in 1937 together with estimates for 1930 that have been adjusted to put them on a more comparable basis. There is only a slight increase in the apparent retirement rates for those aged 55–74; the picture that emerges is one of relative constancy in the labor force participation rates of older men between 1900 and 1937.[13] Since 1950, however, retirement has become increasingly common (Tuma and Sandefur, Chapter 2 of this volume). This suggests that a significant break occurred about the time of World War II.

FIGURE 1.5

LABOR FORCE PARTICIPATION RATES OF OLDER MEN

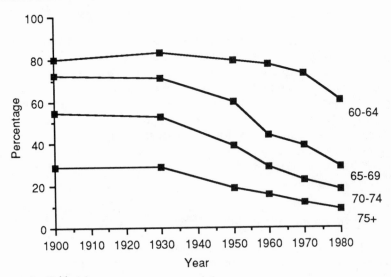

SOURCE: See Table 1.2.

TABLE 1.1

LABOR FORCE PARTICIPATION RATES OF OLDER MEN, 1930 AND 1937; ADJUSTED FOR COMPARABILITY (PERCENTAGES)

Age	April 1930	November 1937
55–59	89.5	90.9
60–64	82.6	83.7
65–74	63.1	57.7
55–74	78.1	77.0

SOURCES: Durand (1948, 97); the average for the consolidated group 55–74 was calculated using 1930 population weights (U.S. Bureau of the Census 1930, 115).

Retirement Trends Before 1900

The constancy of the propensity to retire may predate the 1900 census. If it were available, a national sample drawn from the censuses of 1870 or 1880 could be used directly to create a participation profile that might be compared to the ones shown in Figure 1.4.[14] The definition of "productive employment" in use at that time was close in concept to the modern definition of the labor force.[15] Only those people actively employed or temporarily unemployed were recorded with an occupation.[16] Although we cannot as yet present complete profiles for those early years, the published returns give figures for men aged 60 and over. Although it may be that these early census returns reflect an underenumeration of occupations for older men, the magnitude of the error is likely to be small.[17] In any case, the published figures are presented in Table 1.2 along with comparable labor force participation rates for 1900 through 1980. In Figure 1.6 we plot this data to illustrate the trend in retirement. It is remarkably flat for the entire period from 1870 to 1937.

The Decline in Retirement for Nonagricultural Workers

The figures we are examining refer to the entire male population of the United States. Retirement, however, was primarily an urban, nonagricultural phenomenon. Farm owners and tenants were less likely to retire, or at least less likely to report themselves as being without an occupation. This point has great significance for evaluating the trends in retirement in 1870–1940, since the fraction of the labor force engaged in agricultural occupations fell steadily throughout the entire period. It was over 50 percent at the

TABLE 1.2 _____

LABOR FORCE PARTICIPATION RATE OF MEN
AGED 60 AND OVER, 1870–1980

Year	Percentage rate	Source
1870	64.2	U.S. Census Office (1870, III:832)
1880	64.3	U.S. Census Office (1880, 714)
1900	66.1	Ransom and Sutch (1986a, 14)
1930	64.5	Durand (1948, 199)
1937	61.5	Enumerative Check Census[a]
1940	54.7[b]	U.S. Bureau of the Census (1940, pt. 2, p. 90)
1950	54.5	U.S. Bureau of the Census (1950, p. 247)
1960	45.4	U.S. Bureau of the Census (1960, p. 487)
1970	40.4	U.S. Bureau of the Census (1970, p. 679)
1980	32.2	U.S. Bureau of the Census (1980, table 272)

a. See Ransom and Sutch (1986a, 13n.33).

b. As noted in the text, the rate given for 1940 is inaccurate and the trend line displayed in Figure 1.6 does not pass through the point for 1940.

outset and less than 25 percent at the end of the period (U.S. Bureau of the Census 1975, I:series 0152–53). This trend alone would have operated to increase the overall proportion of the elderly population that was retired. Thus, it must have been the case that the retirement rates among the nonagricultural segment of the population were declining. As a rough indicator of the magnitude of this effect, we have adjusted the labor force participation rate trend to remove the effect of the proportional decline in agriculture.[18] The result is displayed in Figure 1.7.

The upward trend evident in the adjusted figures between 1870 and 1930 suggests that retirement was declining for nonagricultural workers before the Great Depression. This finding, though certainly surprising given the usual presumption of a positive income elasticity of demand for free time in old age, can nevertheless be buttressed with additional evidence on the age distributions of employees in specific industrial occupations.

About 1910 the U.S. Immigration Commission conducted an extensive investigation of employment conditions in several manufacturing industries. Part of its work included a report on the age distribution of wage earners by industry of employment.[19] In 1929 the Industrial Relations Counselors, a professional organization, conducted a companion survey based on responses from a "number of large corporations." According to the report of this survey, returns which are thought to be adequate samples have been received from three industries—iron and steel, oil refining, and slaughtering and meat packing. Data were secured also from several firms in the agricultural implements and bituminous coal mining industries which are indicative of the age distributions in those industries although they are not so complete as for the first three groups. (Latimer 1932, 2:815).

The data for all five industries are presented in Table 1.3 in a format designed to illustrate the increasing proportion of the employees in these industries that were aged 45 and over. Particularly marked are the increases in the relative proportions of workers aged 55–64. Although the evident shifts in the age distribution of workers toward those 45 and over may partially reflect a slowing down in the growth of these industries, we think it is likely that they also reflect a tendency toward later retirement. As we have noted, it is unlikely that there would be a noticeable shift produced by increasing life spans.

When we reported the possibility of a decline in retirement for nonagri-

FIGURE 1.6 _____

LABOR FORCE PARTICIPATION RATE OF MEN AGED 60 AND OVER

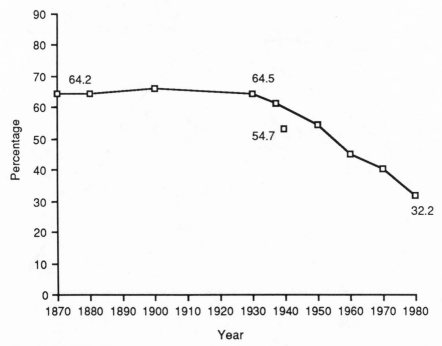

SOURCE: See Table 1.2.

cultural employees in another article, we suggested the possibility that the growth of the service sector of the economy might explain the declining trend in retirement (Ransom and Sutch 1986a, 18). Jobs in the service industries were generally less physically demanding than those in manufacturing, and the growth of employment opportunities for older men could have raised relative wages for that group and induced a lower rate of retirement (ibid., 19–27). An analysis of the data in Table 1.3, however, suggests that there was also a tendency to later retirement within the manufacturing industries.

Several explanations are possible. First, a decline of involuntary retirement brought on by illness or disability might have caused the overall downward trend in propensity to retire. Second, the introduction of seniority systems with rising age-earnings profiles might have increased the attractiveness of working to later retirement ages. Third, the implicit labor contracts that came with incentive wages, internal labor markets, and seniority systems may have protected older workers from dismissal.

FIGURE 1.7 _____

ACTUAL AND ADJUSTED LABOR FORCE PARTICIPATION RATES OF MEN
AGED 60 AND OVER

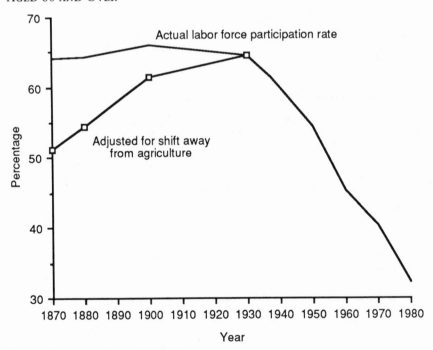

SOURCE: Ransom and Sutch (1986, 18).

TABLE 1.3

THE DECLINE OF RETIREMENT: AGE PROFILE OF
OLDER EMPLOYEES IN FIVE INDUSTRIES, 1910 AND 1929

Age	PROPORTION RELATIVE TO NUMBER OF EMPLOYEES UNDER AGE 45	
	1910	1929
Agricultural Implements Manufacturing		
Under 45	100.0	100.0
45–54	16.2	22.6
55–64	5.8	9.1
65 and over	1.4	2.1
Bituminous Coal Mining		
Under 45	100.0	100.0
45–54	12.4	17.8
55–64	4.1	6.1
65 and over	0.7	1.3
Iron and Steel Manufacturing		
Under 45	100.0	100.0
45–54	11.0	20.3
55–64	3.6	9.9
65 and over	0.8	2.3
Oil Refining		
Under 45	100.0	100.0
45–54	14.9	21.6
55–64	4.5	8.4
65 and over	1.0	0.9
Slaughtering and Meat Packing		
Under 45	100.0	100.0
45–54	13.3	14.5
55–64	4.8	5.4
65 and over	1.1	1.0

SOURCE: Latimer (1932, II:817).

The Possible Decline of Involuntary Retirement

In the presentation of data up to this point, the term "retirement" has been used as a synonym for "not in the labor force." Although this usage is standard when referring to older men, in this case it is also dictated by the nature of the pre-1940 census records. They provide few clues by which we might identify the circumstances of an individual's lack of remunerative employment. The only records of national scope on the ability to work come from the census of 1940 and are reproduced in Table 1.4. They suggest that the majority of the retired men in that year were physically unable to work.[20]

These 1940 census data do not, however, speak to the cause of the worker's retirement. Many of the respondents may have become incapacitated sometime after the date of retirement. A study of the reason for retirement was undertaken by the National Civic Federation in 1926. The basis of the federation's report was a survey of 6,703 men aged 65 and over residing in eleven eastern cities.[21] The National Civic Federation survey reported the cause of retirement for 2,418 of the 2,564 retired men included in their canvas (94 percent). The results are summarized in Table 1.5. According to the survey, 55.1 percent retired for ascertainable physical reasons (12.6 percent because of a disability and 42.6 percent because of ill health); the remainder presumably could have continued working. In Table 1.6 we pro-

TABLE 1.4

INABILITY TO WORK AND RETIREMENT: 1940 CENSUS

	PERCENTAGE OF THE MALE POPULATION			*Percentage of retired population unable to work*
		RETIRED AND		
Age	*In the labor force*	*Unable to work*	*Able to work*	
25–34	95.9	2.7	1.5	65.9
35–44	95.5	3.5	1.1	77.8
45–54	92.8	5.4	1.9	75.0
55–59	88.5	8.2	3.3	71.3
60–64	79.6	14.2	6.2	69.6
65–74	51.6	34.7	13.8	71.7
75 and over	18.3	65.6	16.1	88.3

SOURCE: Durand (1948, 33).

NOTE: The subtotals do not sum to 100 percent of the male population in every case because of independent rounding.

TABLE 1.5 _____

MEN AGED 65 AND OVER REPORTING WHY THEY RETIRED:
1926 SURVEY IN ELEVEN CITIES IN NEW YORK,
NEW JERSEY, PENNSYLVANIA, AND CONNECTICUT

| | | PERCENTAGE REPORTING EACH SPECIFIC CAUSE FOR RETIRING | | |
| | | All retired men 65 and over | MEN WHO RETIRED | |
Cause of retirement	Number		Before age 65	At age 65 or over
Disability	304	12.6	13.4	12.3
Accident	132	5.5	5.9	5.3
Blindness	127	5.3	6.5	4.8
Deafness	45	1.9	1.0	2.2
Ill Health	1,029	42.6	53.7	38.6
Chronic illness	439	18.2	20.8	17.2
Mental illness	29	1.2	1.1	1.2
Paralysis, shock, etc.	158	6.5	9.1	5.6
Rheumatism	291	12.0	15.3	10.9
Other sickness	112	4.6	7.5	3.6
Voluntary	1,085	44.9	32.9	49.1
Old age[a]	680	28.1	11.1	34.1
Not physical condition[b]	405	16.7	21.8	15.0
Total reporting	2,418	100.0	100.0	100.0

SOURCE: National Civic Federation (1928, 52).

NOTE: The percentages for the subtotals are not equal to the sum of the percentages reported in every case because of independent rounding.

a. No "exact physical cause" could be ascertained.

b. Persons who stated they had accumulated sufficient wealth or had children well able to support them.

vide details on the proportion of men retiring "voluntarily" by the age of retirement.

Interpretation of these tables is somewhat hampered by the fact that a substantial fraction gave the reason for retiring as "old age." Even so, the figures suggest that a substantial fraction of retirement was motivated for reasons of health or physical incapacity. This being so, it opens the possibility that the long-run declining trend of retirement was the consequence of improving health and declining rates of disability. Indeed, it is usually be-

TABLE 1.6

VOLUNTARY RETIREMENT OF RETIRED MEN AGED 65 AND OVER:
1926 SURVEY IN ELEVEN CITIES IN NEW YORK,
NEW JERSEY, PENNSYLVANIA, AND CONNECTICUT

Age at retirement	Proportion of retirement not caused by ascertainable disability or illness
Before 60	32.1
60–64	33.2
65–69	44.9
70–79	52.1
80 and over	57.1
60 and over	45.8

SOURCE: National Civic Federation (1928, 52).

lieved that the general state of health of the population had been improving prior to 1940. However, there is scant evidence of this. The only time trends on illness that come from this period are for men enlisted in the U.S. Army and Navy. These men would, of course, have been predominantly young, most of them under 30, and very few near retirement age. In any case, the data show a steady decline in the number of cases of illness reported from 1860 to 1940, but the rate of improvement is slower than the rate of decline in mortality for men of the same age group (Collins 1945, 157–59). Since the expectation of life of older men did not improve significantly in this period, we might suppose on this evidence that there was little improvement in the health of older men. It should be emphasized, however, that our knowledge is sketchy, and this inference is based on indirect and not very compelling evidence.

It should also be noted that, even when the date of retirement was dictated by illness or disability, it does not follow that the retirement was unexpected or that the individual was financially unprepared. If involuntary retirement is not uncommon, individuals ought to be able to anticipate its possibility. They could accumulate assets or purchase insurance as a precaution.[22] Of course, some individuals would nevertheless be caught prematurely or poorly prepared for forced retirement, and if their numbers were large this would appear as a serious social problem. In this regard, it is worth noting that the movement for social insurance that culminated in the Social Security Act was motivated by a concern about poverty and dependency among the elderly (see Squier 1912; Lubove 1968; Fischer 1978; Achenbaum 1978).

Unfortunately, our survey of the meager data available on the national trends in health and the causes of retirement do not permit a definite conclusion about the contribution of improving health to the decline of retirement. We are inclined to the proposition that whatever improvements occurred were of minor consequence, but clearly more work on this topic is needed.

The Impact of Rising Relative Wages for Older Men

Today, as is well known, the age-earnings profiles for workers generally rise with age. It is commonly supposed by labor economists that this fact reflects the workings of an "internal labor market" which, because of seniority systems, internal job hierarchies, and the use of "efficiency wages," pay older workers more than their current marginal product while paying younger workers less than their current marginal product (Lazear 1979). What is perhaps less well known, but nevertheless well documented, is that the internal labor market arose in the United States in the interwar period (Jacoby 1984).[23]

There is ample evidence drawn from samples of industrial workers collected around the turn of the century that typical age-earnings profiles for workers' families displayed a humped shape with peak earnings coming before age 40. There are two distinct reasons for this. First, the age-earnings profile for a cross section of workers in the same occupation shows a decline for older workers, presumably because productivity on the job declined as the worker aged. Second, in the late nineteenth century industrial workers frequently changed jobs late in life, moving to less demanding but also less remunerative employment. For example, a machine operator might take a job as a floor sweeper or doorman.

Evidence for the first of these phenomena can be found in surveys of working conditions collected in the late 1880s and early 1890s by government agencies. One of the most extensive was the family-budget study undertaken in 1890 by the U.S. Bureau of Labor. This survey covered 6,809 working-class families in 24 states and 9 industries (U.S. Commissioner of Labor 1890, 1891).[24] In Figure 1.8 we present the age-income profile for the husbands included in the survey. The curve for earnings of the head of household shows a pattern markedly different from that of post-World War II workers. Earnings rise sharply through the cohort of 20- to 33-year-old workers, peak, and then decline.[25] Because of the contribution from earnings of other family members (principally children) and the increased importance of "other income" (principally property income), the total earnings profile for the worker's family peaks at a later date. Nevertheless, total family income peaks at age 53 and falls sharply after age 58.

The downward occupational mobility is evident in the age distributions of workers by occupation. A special report based on the 1875 census of Massachusetts revealed substantial underrepresentation of the older population among industrial occupations and a corresponding overrepresentation in the unskilled and agricultural occupations.[26] The same pattern of under-representation of older workers among the skilled industrial trades is observed in U.S. census figures for 1870, 1880, and 1900.[27] This cannot be readily explained as the result of an unequal distribution of older workers between rural and urban areas. The same pattern of underrepresentation of older workers among skilled industrial jobs is evident in a canvass of wage workers undertaken in Detroit in 1883 and in a detailed survey of Michigan furniture workers in 1889.[28]

The significance of the humped-shape age-income profile for workers in 1890 is that it most likely represents spot wages paid to workers with little

FIGURE 1.8 _____

AGE-EARNINGS PROFILE, 1890

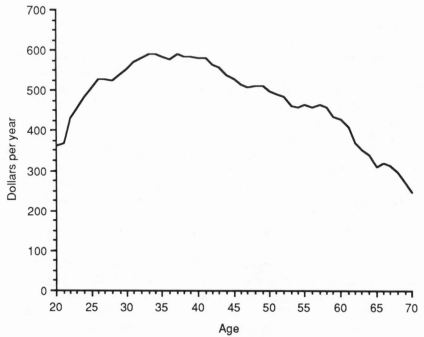

SOURCES: U.S. Commissioner of Labor (1890; 1891).

or no job security. If so, a gradual increase in the relative wage paid older workers brought about by the introduction of internal labor markets may have induced a longer attachment to the labor force. It might also be noted that the humped-shape earnings profile would have induced a considerable amount of life-cycle saving even without retirement.

Job Security

A third possibility is that retirement declined between 1900 and 1937 because job security for older workers increased. The usual theory of incentive wages implies that older workers would face less risk of layoff than would be the case in a system with spot wages before the introduction of internal job ladders (Akerlof and Yellen 1986, 1–21). Experienced older workers would be protected from dismissal as part of the implicit contract that establishes the incentive wage structure. Union contracts and seniority

FIGURE 1.9

UNEMPLOYMENT RATES BY AGE, 1900, 1940, AND 1970

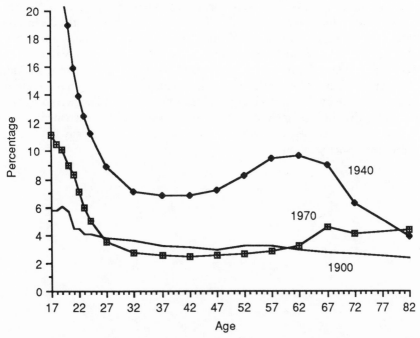

SOURCES: For 1900 data, see Appendix. For 1940, see U.S. Bureau of the Census (1940, table 24). For 1970, see U.S. Bureau of the Census (1970, 1-679).

preference rules might codify such an understanding. We would expect as a consequence that the unemployment rates in 1900 would be largely independent of age, whereas modern unemployment profiles are likely to decline with age.

If layoffs and terminations became less common for older workers as internal labor markets spread, then we might suppose that the inducement to retire would be reduced. This proposition, however, is not easy to assess, since we have no direct data on layoffs by age that span the period in question. However, the available data on unemployment by age does not support the hypothesis. In Figure 1.9 we present our estimates of the male unemployment rate by age for 1900 based on the sample from the 1900 census. Compared to the 1940 or 1970 age profile of unemployment rates for men, the 1900 profile is, as predicted, much flatter. Also as predicted, both the 1940 and the 1970 age profiles show higher unemployment rates among teenagers and young adults relative to the total than was true in 1900. However, both the 1940 and 1970 profiles show a puzzling increase in unemployment rates for older cohorts. By contrast, the 1900 profile remains flat out to the cohort of men aged 75 and over.

The rapid decline in reported unemployment for the cohorts aged 65 and over in 1940 is also somewhat surprising. We are tempted to argue that the increased relative job security for older men was a factor in the decline of retirement between 1900 and 1940 and that the increased relative incidence of unemployment of older men evident in the postwar profiles was a factor that helps explain the reversal of the retirement trend about 1940. Yet the 1940 data may have been affected by the events of the Great Depression in ways not related to the introduction of seniority systems. Furthermore, it is not clear why the age-unemployment profiles turn up for older men in the postwar period. Until more work on these issues is done, it may be best to withhold a conclusion on the matter.

LABOR FORCE PARTICIPATION: EMPLOYMENT AND UNEMPLOYMENT IN THE 1900 CENSUS SAMPLE

| | | IN LABOR FORCE | | | | NOT IN LABOR FORCE | | |
Age	Sample total	Total	Employed	Temporarily unemployed	Total	Permanently unemployed	No Occupation
10	1,166	125	114	11	1,041	16	1,025
11	1,008	145	134	11	863	22	841
12	1,130	200	184	16	930	30	900
13	966	213	196	17	753	15	738
14	1,017	344	321	23	673	44	629
15	1,018	460	430	29	558	45	513
16	1,041	586	545	41	455	47	408
17	948	665	626	38	283	47	236
18	968	704	664	41	264	50	214
19	892	717	674	44	175	40	135
20	983	807	761	46	176	40	136
21	940	801	766	35	139	36	103
22	958	821	785	36	137	37	100
23	920	793	760	32	127	36	91
24	957	858	823	35	99	30	69
25	935	860	827	33	75	31	44
26	906	825	796	29	81	33	48
27	831	774	740	34	57	19	38
28	866	794	765	29	72	30	42
29	708	652	628	24	56	27	29

APPENDIX (continued)

Age	Sample total	IN LABOR FORCE			NOT IN LABOR FORCE		
		Total	Employed	Temporarily unemployed	Total	Permanently unemployed	No Occupation
30	1,013	940	901	39	73	36	37
31	676	635	610	25	41	23	18
32	734	694	671	23	40	22	18
33	687	643	624	19	44	24	20
34	679	632	611	21	47	21	26
35	744	703	676	27	41	21	20
36	638	604	585	19	34	19	15
37	604	572	550	22	32	13	19
38	725	688	670	18	37	16	21
39	674	632	614	18	42	26	16
40	832	777	749	28	55	27	28
41	541	517	505	12	24	9	15
42	616	569	550	19	47	20	27
43	502	475	461	14	27	19	8
44	501	468	452	17	33	16	17
45	620	576	559	17	44	20	24
46	457	420	408	12	37	21	16
47	438	396	383	13	42	24	18
48	434	402	388	14	32	15	17
49	426	386	376	10	40	24	16

50	25	35	60	18	499	517	577
51	14	13	27	8	323	331	358
52	15	17	32	13	324	337	369
53	22	14	36	10	272	282	318
54	30	10	40	8	276	283	323
55	26	19	45	10	314	324	369
56	28	9	37	9	261	270	307
57	13	14	27	6	212	218	245
58	21	19	40	7	200	208	248
59	24	17	41	7	199	205	246
60	32	32	64	11	264	275	339
61	18	16	34	4	158	163	197
62	25	17	42	4	160	163	205
63	30	20	50	5	164	168	218
64	32	12	44	4	150	154	198
65	36	19	55	5	184	190	244
66	31	13	44	3	125	128	172
67	26	15	41	4	109	114	154
68	34	13	47	2	110	111	158
69	48	10	58	3	93	96	154
70	52	16	68	4	115	118	186
71	41	11	52	2	59	61	113
72	42	4	46	2	62	64	110
73	41	5	46	0	52	53	99
74	45	2	47	0	39	40	87

APPENDIX (*continued*)

Age	Sample total	IN LABOR FORCE			NOT IN LABOR FORCE		
		Total	Employed	Temporarily unemployed	Total	Permanently unemployed	No Occupation
75	106	51	50	1	55	4	51
76	71	29	27	2	42	7	35
77	44	22	22	0	22	0	22
78	55	26	26	0	29	2	27
79	37	14	14	0	23	1	22
80	55	25	24	1	30	2	28
81 and over	182	64	64	0	118	9	109
Total	38,243	28,971	27,829	1,142	9,272	1,492	7,780

SOURCES: 1900 census sample provided by the Inter-university Consortium for Political and Social Research; see Graham (1981). See also Ransom and Sutch (1986a, 1985) for more detail.

DEFINITIONS:

Labor force = sample total less those not in the labor force;

Employed = labor force less those temporarily unemployed;

Temporarily unemployed = total number of months of unemployment during the previous year reported by members of the labor force divided by twelve;

Not in the labor force = permanently unemployed plus those with no occupation;

Permanently unemployed = those reporting six months or more of unemployment in the preceding year;

No occupation = sum of those with no occupation reported (blank), those with nonoccupational titles such as "pensioner," "pauper," and "tourist" as well as underworld titles such as "gambler," and those who reported themselves as "retired," "landlords," "capitalists," and inmates of institutions.

DISCUSSION

Gordon F. Streib

Professors Roger Ransom and Richard Sutch have drawn our attention to the need to understand historical trends and patterns if we are to have a firmer grasp of contemporary issues about retirement. With considerable ingenuity they have amassed statistical information related to labor force participation and the changing industrial and occupational structures in the United States. They make an interesting observation that participation in the nonagricultural labor force at ages 60 and over actually increased from 1870 to 1930 when we adjust the rate for the declining percentage of agricultural workers.

Another important fact they highlight is the need to be clear about life expectancy for adult men. Using nineteenth-century data for Massachusetts, they show that although there was considerable change in life expectancy at birth, life expectancy at age twenty did not display such remarkable improvement. For example, expectation of life at birth in Massachusetts was 41.7 years and at age twenty was 67.2 years for white men. These expectancies had shifted by 1980 to 70.7 years at birth and 72.4 years at age twenty.

One of the interesting comparisons of the earlier period and today, presented in Table 1.5, is the reasons that men over age 65 stopped working. This 1926 survey of older men in eleven eastern cities indicated that 43 percent of the men reported they stopped work because of health reasons. Parnes and his associates (1985, 70–71) found in their longitudinal survey of a national probability sample of older men that 34 percent of the whites and 47 percent of the blacks gave poor health as their major reason for retirement. The 1926 study also had a category called "old age—no exact physical cause could be ascertained," and 28 percent of the retired men gave this as the reason for leaving the work force. Contemporary knowledge of the performance of older men on the job suggests that a considerable proportion of those men were probably in poor health.

Ransom and Sutch's interpretations of trends regarding work and retirement are somewhat problematical, because the statistical series are fragmentary and some artificial figures must be created based on estimates and incomplete data. Given the shortcomings of the available data, we can say there is room for doubt about some of their interpretations.

Nevertheless, we must acknowledge the difficulty that these investigators had in trying to reconstruct the labor force participation in the late nineteenth and early twentieth centuries and their ingenuity in attempting to present a coherent picture. Because there was no direct measurement of labor force participation before 1937, the authors used census materials on employment and unemployment. One of the difficulties with using old census data is highlighted by the authors' disagreement with Achenbaum (1978, 179–81, 217) about the interpretation of occupational data in the 1870–1880 census. Ransom and Sutch consider the reporting of an occupation as probably indicating employment. Other careful observers, such as Haber (1983, 166), found that almost all older men reported having an occupation and continued to see themselves as part of the labor market, whether or not they were employed. This makes it difficult to report with accuracy what proportion of older men were actually retired.

The authors speculate that the internal labor market may have operated to protect older workers and give them job security, but no evidence is presented for this suggestion. It is hard to reconcile this opinion with data from other sources, which report a high turnover of workers and indicate that few men stayed long enough with one firm to build up much seniority or receive any kind of a pension. For example, Alfred Dodge and Sons proposed a pension program in 1882. Over a period of twenty years, 2,046 employees were hired but only ten remained for fifteen years (ibid., 165).

It is regrettable that the authors are reluctant to draw any conclusions from their careful and detailed perusal of a variety of complicated statistical sources. We would hope that their study of 70 years of U.S. economic history yielded some results that would help contemporary analysts and policymakers to understand the current conditions. Part of the difficulty they faced is the lack of a sharp historical awareness that nonparticipation in the labor force is not the same as retirement. They state that "retirement was relatively common among American men as early as 1870." But we know nothing of why the older men were not working. Were they unemployed? Were they sick or disabled? Had they been laid off because their skills were obsolete in new industries, or they were unable to keep up with younger workers? Had they moved in with other family members and therefore could get along without a steady income? The authors are somewhat aware of this important issue but do not bring it to the reader's attention until more than halfway through the paper, when they note that they have used "retirement" as a synonym for "not in the labor force." And in Note 6, they point out the difficulty in differentiating between "temporary" and "permanent" forms of unemployment and hope that their arbitrary judgments "will preserve comparability with modern definitions and at the same time coincide with reasonable historical judgment about the individuals' experience."

A careful reading of a variety of historical sources indicates that retirement was a slowly emerging pattern in the period Ransom and Sutch studied and that 1940 was truly a watershed year, as it was the one in which Social Security payments were started as a universal right for those in the program. There is a lack of clear awareness in this paper of the changing nature of retirement and of the fact that receiving a pension, either public or private, is a central issue in late life when one does not work. The emergence of the position of retiree in society was accompanied by the knowledge that retirement has three aspects: it is an event, a process, and a social institution. Retirement as a multifaceted social and economic institution came to the United States gradually, and the concomitant pension system was integral to the institution.

The American Express Company is credited with having established the first private pension plan in 1875, but the first plan that was truly in place and operational was the one developed by the Baltimore and Ohio Railroad in 1884 (ibid., 113). The provision of economic support in old age was a major index of the emergence of retirement as a social institution. In 1887 President Grover Cleveland was willing to sign into law a bill granting pensions for veterans of the Mexican War, but not for older Civil War veterans. It was not until 1904 that President Theodore Roosevelt decreed a Civil War veterans pension scheme, and in 1907 the plan was enacted into law by Congress. These pension plans were created first for soldiers, then for government employees, and slowly for private-sector employees (ibid., 112–17; Graebner 1980). Railroads, certain paternalistic companies, and some unions organized plans that established the concept of retirement as a fixed status.

The discussion by Ransom and Sutch is helpful in laying out with broad strokes the fact that older persons in the nineteenth century continued to work when possible, but "retirement" in the period under review bears little relation to what we consider as retirement today. Their work does not have the conceptual apparatus to deal with the historical dynamics of what was happening from 1870 to 1940 at the societal level to affect the specific situations of older persons. This approach is defined by Donahue, Orbach, and Pollak (1960, 331): "Retirement is the creation of an economically nonproductive role in modern societies which are capable of supporting large numbers of persons whose labor is not essential to the functioning of the economic order"; they add that we need a perspective broad enough to deal with the range and variety of social patterns encompassed by retirement as a role, a status change, and an emerging form of social life.

Ransom and Sutch express the hope that their work will "stimulate those engaged in direct confrontation of contemporary problems." However, their work is not relevant to the principal contemporary problems such as the long-term funding of Social Security, the issues of intergenerational transfer, the solvency of private pension plans and the milking of pension assets, the enormous number of two-income families in which retirement is a joint decision, and the continued early retirement patterns (see, for example, the chapters by Ricardo-Campbell, Packard and Reno, and Bernheim in this volume).

Ransom and Sutch assert that the significant misunderstanding about the incidence of retirement before 1940 "has influenced much recent work on contemporary retirement." Readers will be puzzled as to how contemporary research has been affected one way or another by patterns of 50 to 100 years ago. Could they give us some examples? When current researchers note that retirement was uncommon before 1940, they refer to retirement as we know it now—that is, not working, a steady income supplied by Social Security and often by a private pension, a separate household (not being supported by one's children), and a new and accepted life style. Furthermore, contemporary researchers have not based their studies on the fallacies that Ransom and Sutch claim. A careful reading of the major research on retirement shows the precise way that retirement is now defined (Parnes et al. 1985; Palmore et al. 1985; Streib and Schneider 1971). It is much more sophisticated than simply not being in the labor force.

The study of retirement before Social Security was enacted is an interesting subject and might give a scholarly background for the study of contemporary issues. It is a formidable task that Professors Ransom and Sutch have set for themselves. Unfortunately, the available data they use are ambiguous and are not adequate to fit the model they utilize to explain their position that retirement was common before 1900 and then declined until the 1930s.

NOTES

1. Darby (1979) and Kotlikoff and Summers (1981) have incorporated their view that retirement was rare before World War II in their attempts to minimize the importance of life-cycle behavior. For a corrective, see Ransom and Sutch (1986b).

2. Incentive wages are an important part of an explanation of seniority systems and mandatory retirement in the internal labor market framework; see Lazear (1979, 1981). When incentive wages are set above the market-clearing wage they are called "efficiency wages." Efficiency wage models have been offered as an explanation of involuntary unemployment and sticky wages (Solow 1979). For a collection of essays on this issue, see Akerlof and Yellen (1986). The extensive theoretical literature is reviewed in Stiglitz (1987).

3. On early nineteenth-century trends in mortality see Potter (1965, 646, 663), Yasuba (1962, 86–96), Vinovskis (1972), and McClelland and Zeckhauser (1982, 54–68). The lack of any downward trend in death rates perhaps reflects two offsetting tendencies. On the one hand, there was probably some improvement in mortality, particularly infant mortality, in both rural and urban areas during this period. On the other hand, the shift in population from rural districts to cities, where mortality was significantly higher, more than offset any improvements in rural areas.

4. Vital statistics for the United States begin only in 1900. However, data for the Commonwealth of Massachusetts begins in 1880. Vinovskis (1972, 211) has calculated a life table for a large sample of Massachusetts towns in 1860.

5. The modern definitions of labor force participation, involuntary unemployment, and retirement were the product of the intensive study of unemployment by academic economists and government agencies during the 1930s. See Durand (1947) for a discussion. The trial census in which the labor force concept was first employed was the Enumerative Check Census conducted in 1937 by postal carriers.

6. The only area of real uncertainty is the difficult problem of distinguishing between "temporary" and "permanent" forms of unemployment using the early census records. We have made several arbitrary judgments that we hope will preserve comparability with modern definitions and at the same time coincide with reasonable historical judgment about the individuals' experience.

7. The returns from the 1890 census were destroyed in a fire. Work is underway to draw a sample from the returns of the 1910 census. The 1920 and 1930 returns remain closed to public examination.

8. The sample was collected and processed by the Center for Studies in Demography and Ecology of the University of Washington for the National Science Foundation under the direction of Samuel Preston. A data set including 99,034 individuals is now archived at the Inter-university Consortium for Political and Social Research (Graham 1981).

9. Our treatment of unemployment is subject to a degree of arbitrariness. We

excluded from the labor force those who reported six months or more of unemployment during the preceding twelve months (Ransom and Sutch 1986a, 10–11).

10. The expectation is calculated by estimating the experience of a hypothetical cohort of 1,000 men aged 30. The projections are based on the 1900 cross section of labor force participation rates and the 1900 life table reported by the U.S. National Center for Health Statistics (1978, 5–13). The life table is used to estimate the number surviving at each subsequent age. The number of survivors who were not in the labor force is then estimated from the age profile of participation rates. We assume that the probability of death was independent of the labor force status of the individual and calculate that, of the original 1,000 men in the synthetic cohort, 639 would die while in the labor force (employed or temporarily unemployed) and 361 would die after they had left the labor force. This method yields a conservative estimate of the probability of dying while retired, since in all likelihood retired men would have a higher age-specific mortality than men remaining at work. Retirement is often induced by illness or disability.

11. Darby (1979, 23) has calculated the expected length of the retirement period in 1900 at only 1.9 years. However, we find little merit in his estimation procedure. Darby's estimate is obtained by subtracting the estimated age of retirement from the life expectancy calculated at age twenty. Curiously, Darby's definition of the age of retirement excludes the possibility of retirement before age 65 (p. 22). Our own calculation suggests that the estimated age of retirement (measured at age 30) was 59 and the expected number of years of life remaining at age 59 was nearly 15.

12. The basic Modigliani-Brumberg model is discussed in Modigliani (1966; 1986, 300–301). The calculation assumes a stationary population, no economic growth, a known age of death, perfect annuity markets, and no bequests; it also assumes that the average consumption of retired men over age 30 and their dependents is equal to the average consumption of workers and their dependents. A growing population, positive growth, uncertain age of death, imperfect annuity markets, a net bequest motive, or higher expenditures in old age (say, because of expensive medical care) would all increase the saving rate predicted by the model.

13. A detailed study of employment of older men in Boston from 1890 to 1930 confirms this conclusion for that city; see Gratton (1986, 61–65).

14. A small (741) national sample of men aged 65 and over has been drawn from the 1880 census by Smith (1978). The sample, however, excluded institutionalized individuals and thus greatly underrepresented retirees among the aged population. It was also collected using a relatively complex stratified sampling procedure that unfortunately overrepresented men aged 65–70 and underrepresented those aged 75 and over; see Jensen et al. (1985).

15. The gainful occupation concept used from 1890 through 1930 replaced the "productive employment" concept used in 1870 and 1880 (Ransom and Sutch 1986a, 6–7).

16. There is some uncertainty about the treatment of unemployment in the census of 1870. An explicit enumeration of unemployment was not introduced until 1880. Even then the results were not published or tabulated. The definitions of employ-

ment and unemployment used in 1880 suggest to us that the number of men reported with "productive employment" included those actively employed at the time of the census, those not working because of illness or layoff, and those looking for new employment with a recent history of past employment.

17. Achenbaum (1978, 179–81) has suggested that the 1870 and 1880 censuses seriously underenumerate employment. However, the 1870 and 1880 data seem to be quite reliable for men in the prime working ages (16–59). If there were a tendency to underenumerate occupations in those censuses, it would have to have been a tendency confined to the elderly (Ransom and Sutch 1986a, 7). This possibility seems to be unlikely, since the sample collected from the 1880 census by Jensen et al. (1985) reported an "occupation" for 78 percent of the men aged 65 and over. Their data set is now archived at the Inter-university Consortium for Political and Social Research.

18. The adjustment was made by redistributing the male labor force in 1870, 1880, and 1900 to the agricultural and nonagricultural sectors using the distribution observed in 1930. The observed age distribution of agricultural and nonagricultural workers was used to calculate adjusted labor force participation rates (Ransom and Sutch 1986a, 18).

19. U.S. Immigration Commission (1911, II:1117, 1147, 1197). The exact date of the Immigration Commission figures is not reported, but they were collected sometime between 1907 when the commission was created and 1910 when its report was submitted.

20. It is possible that 1940 data exaggerate the extent of involuntary retirement relative to voluntary retirement for the earlier years, since retirement for industrial workers was near an all-time low that year. It may be supposed that the Great Depression and the associated collapse of many banks and financial institutions reduced the asset holdings of many workers, necessitating attachment to the labor force longer than originally intended. If so, the overall rate of labor force participation would have been raised.

21. The survey excluded military pensioners and those residing in public and private institutions (National Civic Federation 1928, 28–29, 53). Also, according to the report, "an especial effort was made to cover . . . workers in occupations other than manual" (p. 13). This would have underenumerated the extent of retirement, if our conjectures about the effect of service sector occupations on retirement are correct.

22. Disability insurance was not available in this era. There were, however, other types of insurance that might have imperfectly substituted for it (Ransom and Sutch 1987).

23. The highly successful introduction of the "five-dollar day" by Henry Ford in 1914 can be taken as the beginning of the trend toward incentive or efficiency wages in industrial employment (Raff and Summers 1987).

24. For a discussion of the survey see Haines (1979, 1985). This data file is archived at the Inter-university Consortium for Political and Social Research.

25. The decline is briefly interrupted at ages 53–58. In 1890 many men of this

age would have served in the Civil War armies. The slight rise in earnings may be attributable to the impact of the Civil War pension system that permitted veterans with "disabilities" to retire.

26. Massachusetts Bureau of Statistics of Labor (1878, pt. 6). The data are summarized in Ransom and Sutch (1986a, 21).

27. See U.S. Census Office 1870, 832–42; 1880, 744–51. A detailed breakdown of the percentage of male workers aged 60 and over by occupations for 1870, 1880, and 1900 is given in Ransom and Sutch (1986a, 22).

28. The Detroit canvass included 11,259 workers (Michigan Bureau of Labor and Industrial Statistics [MBLIS] 1884). In 1889 a survey was conducted of 5,419 workers in the furniture industry of that state (MBLIS 1890). For a summary of the evidence discussed in the text, see Ransom and Sutch (1986a, 23, 25).

References

Abel, Andrew B. 1985. "Precautionary Saving and Accidental Bequests." *American Economic Review* 75:777–91.

Achenbaum, W. Andrew. 1978. *Old Age in the New Land: The American Experience since 1790.* Baltimore, Md.: Johns Hopkins University Press.

Akerlof, George A., and Janet L. Yellen, eds. 1986. *Efficiency Wage Models of the Labor Market.* New York: Cambridge University Press.

Collins, Selwyn D. 1945. "Sickness and Health: Their Measurement, Distribution, and Changes." *The Annals of the American Academy of Political and Social Science* 237:152–63.

Darby, Michael R. 1979. *The Effects of Social Security on Income and the Capital Stock.* Washington, D.C.: American Enterprise Institute.

Davies, James B. 1981. "Uncertain Lifetime, Consumption, and Dissaving in Retirement." *Journal of Political Economy* 89:561–77.

Donahue, Wilma, Harold L. Orbach, and Otto Pollak. 1960. "Retirement: The Emerging Social Pattern." In Clark Tibbitts, ed., *Handbook of Social Gerontology.* Chicago: University of Chicago Press.

Durand, John D. 1947. "Development of the Labor Force Concept, 1930–40." *Social Science Research Council Bulletin* 56:80–90, appen. A.

———. 1948. *The Labor Force in the United States, 1890–1960.* Social Science Research Council.

Durand, John D., and Edwin Goldfield. 1944. U.S. Bureau of the Census, Sixteenth Census, 1940. *Population: Estimates of the Labor Force, Employment, and Unemployment in the United States, 1940 and 1930.* Washington, D.C.: GPO.

Fischer, David Hackett. 1977. *Growing Old in America: The Bland-Lee Lectures*

Delivered at Clark University. New York: Oxford University Press (expanded ed., 1978).

Graebner, William. 1980. *A History of Retirement: The Meaning and Function of an American Institution*. New Haven, Conn.: Yale University Press.

Graham, Stephen N. 1981. "The 1900 Public Use Sample Users Handbook." Draft version, no. 7825. Inter-university Consortium for Political and Social Research, Ann Arbor, Mich.

Gratton, Brian. 1986. *Urban Elders: Family, Work, and Welfare Among Boston's Aged, 1890–1950*. Philadelphia: Temple University Press.

Haber, Carole. 1983. *Beyond Sixty-Five: The Dilemma of Old Age in America's Past*. Cambridge: Cambridge University Press.

Haines, Michael R. 1979. "Industrial Work and the Family Life Cycle, 1889–1890." *Research in Economic History* 4:289–356.

———. 1985. "The Life Cycle, Savings, and Demographic Adaptation: Some Historical Evidence for the United States and Europe." In Alice S. Rossi, ed., *Gender and the Life Course*. Hawthorne, N.Y.: Aldine.

Jensen, Richard, et al. 1985. "Old Age in the United States, 1880." First edition, no. 8427. Inter-university Consortium for Political and Social Research, Ann Arbor, Mich.

Jacoby, Sanford M. 1984. "The Development of Internal Labor Markets in American Manufacturing Firms." In Paul Osterman, ed., *Internal Labor Markets*. Cambridge: MIT Press.

Kotlikoff, Laurence J., and Lawrence H. Summers. 1981. "The Role of Intergenerational Transfers in Aggregate Capital Accumulation." *Journal of Political Economy* 89: 706–32.

Latimer, Murray Webb. 1932. *Industrial Pension Systems in the United States and Canada*, 2 vols. New York: Industrial Relations Counselors.

Lazear, Edward P. 1979. "Why Is There Mandatory Retirement?" *Journal of Political Economy* 87:1261–84.

———. 1981. "Agency, Earnings Profiles, Productivity, and Hours Restrictions." *American Economic Review* 71:606–20.

Lubove, Roy. 1968. *The Struggle for Social Security, 1900–1935*. Cambridge: Harvard University Press.

Massachusetts Bureau of Statistics of Labor. 1878. *Ninth Annual Report of the Bureau of Statistics of Labor, February 1878*. Public Document 31. Boston: Rand, Abery.

McClelland, Peter D., and Richard J. Zeckhauser. 1982. *Demographic Dimensions of the New Republic: American Interregional Migration, Vital Statistics, and Manumissions, 1800–1860*. New York: Cambridge University Press.

Meeker, Edward. 1972. "The Improving Health of the United States, 1850–1915." *Explorations in Economic History* 9:353–73.

Michigan Bureau of Labor and Industrial Statistics. 1884. *First Annual Report of the Bureau of Labor and Industrial Statistics, February 1, 1884.* W. S. George.

———. 1890. *Sixth Annual Report of the Bureau of Labor and Industrial Statistics, 1890.* Robert Smith.

Modigliani, Franco. "The Life Cycle Hypothesis of Savings, the Demand for Wealth, and the Supply of Capital." *Social Research* 33:160–217.

———. 1986. "Life Cycle, Individual Thrift, and the Wealth of Nations." *American Economic Review* 76:297–313.

Modigliani, Franco, and Richard Brumberg. 1954. "Utility Analysis and the Consumption Function: An Interpretation of Cross-Section Data." In Kenneth K. Kurihara, ed., *Post Keynesian Economics.* New Brunswick, N.J.: Rutgers University Press.

National Civic Federation. 1928. *Extent of Old Age Dependency: Report by Industrial Welfare Department, The National Civic Federation, upon Economic and Physical Status of Persons 65 Years of Age and Over, New York, New Jersey, Pennsylvania and Connecticut, Includes Additional Data from Massachusetts.* Educational Movement to Secure Improvements in Working and Living Conditions of Employees by Employers.

Palmore, Erdman B., et al. 1985. *Retirement: Causes and Consequences.* New York: Springer.

Parnes, Herbert S., et al. 1985. *Retirement Among American Men.* Lexington, Mass.: D. C. Heath.

Potter, J. 1965. "The Growth of Population in America, 1700–1860." In D. V. Glass and D. E. C. Eversley, eds., *Population in History: Essays in Historical Demography.* Leeds, England: Edward Arnold.

Raff, Daniel, and Lawrence H. Summers. 1987. "Did Henry Ford Pay Efficiency Wages?" Paper presented to the Twenty-Seventh Annual Cliometrics Conference, Allerton Park, Illinois.

Ransom, Roger L., and Richard Sutch. 1985. "Retirement and Changes in Occupation with Advancing Age: American Men in the Late Nineteenth Century." *Working Paper on the History of Saving,* no. 4. University of California at Berkeley.

———. 1986a. "The Labor of Older Americans: Retirement of Men On and Off the Job, 1870–1937." *Journal of Economic History* 46:1–30.

———. 1986b. "Unequalled Thrift: An Inquiry into the Saving Behavior of Americans at the Turn of the Century." Paper presented to the American Economic Association, New Orleans, Louisiana.

———. 1987. "Tontine Insurance and the Armstrong Investigation: A Case of Stifled Innovation, 1868–1905." *Journal of Economic History* 47:379–90.

Smith, Daniel Scott. 1978. "A Community-Based Sample of the Older Population from the 1880 and 1900 United States Manuscript Census." *Historical Methods* 11:67–74.

Solow, Robert M. 1979. "Another Possible Cause of Wage Stickiness." *Journal of Macroeconomics* 1:79–82.

Squier, Lee Welling. 1912. *Old Age Dependency in the United States: A Complete Survey of the Pension Movement*. New York: Macmillan.

Stiglitz, Joseph E. 1987. "The Causes and Consequences of the Dependence of Quality on Price." *Journal of Economic Literature* 25:1–48.

Streib, Gordon F., and Clement J. Schneider. 1971. *Retirement in American Society: Impact and Process*. Ithaca, N.Y.: Cornell University Press.

U.S. Bureau of the Census, Fifteenth Census [1930]. *Population*. Vol. 5, "General Report on Occupations." Washington, D.C.: GPO.

———, Sixteenth Census [1940]. *Population*. Vol. 4, "Characteristics by Age: Marital Status, Relationship, Education, and Citizenship." Pt. 1. Washington, D.C.: GPO.

———, Seventeenth Census [1950]. *Census of the Population: 1950*. Vol. 2, "Characteristics of the Population: Number of Inhabitants, General and Detailed Characteristics of the Population." Pt. 1. Washington, D.C.: GPO.

———, Eighteenth Census [1960]. *Population*. Vol. 1, "Characteristics of the Population." Pt. 1. Washington, D.C.: GPO.

———, Nineteenth Census [1970] *1970 Census of Population*. Vol. 1, "Characteristics of the Population." Pt. 1. Washington, D.C.: GPO.

———. 1975. *Historical Statistics of the United States, Colonial Times to 1970*, 2 vols. Washington, D.C.: GPO.

———, Twentieth Census [1980]. *1980 Census of Population*. Vol. 1, "Characteristics of the Population." Chap. D, pt. 1, sec. A. Washington, D.C.: GPO.

U.S. Census Office, Ninth Census [1870]. *The Statistics of the Wealth and Industry of the United States, Compiled from the Original Returns of the Ninth Census (1870)*. Washington, D.C.: GPO.

———, Tenth Census [1880]. *Statistics of the Population of the United States at the Tenth Census (June 1, 1880)*. Washington, D.C.: GPO.

U.S. Commissioner of Labor. 1890. *Sixth Annual Report of the Commissioner of Labor; 1890*. Washington, D.C.: GPO.

———. 1891. *Seventh Annual Report of the Commissioner of Labor; 1891*. Washington, D.C.: GPO.

U.S. Immigration Commission. 1911. *Reports of the Immigration Commission*. Vol. 20, "Immigrants in Industries." Pt. 23, "Summary Report on Immigrants in Manufacturing and Mining," 2 vols. Washington, D.C.: GPO.

U.S. National Center for Health Statistics. 1978. *Vital Statistics of the United States: 1978*. Vol. 2, "Mortality." Pt. A. Bethesda, Md.: NCHS.

Vinovskis, Maris A. 1972. "Mortality Rates and Trends in Massachusetts Before 1860." *Journal of Economic History* 32:184–213.

Yasuba, Yasukichi. 1962. *Birth Rates of the White Population in the United States, 1800–1860: An Economic Study*. Baltimore, Md.: Johns Hopkins University Press.

2

TRENDS IN THE LABOR FORCE ACTIVITY OF THE ELDERLY IN THE UNITED STATES, 1940–1980

Nancy Brandon Tuma and Gary D. Sandefur

In recent years there has been considerable research on the social and economic behavior of aged Americans but much less research on how their behavior has changed over time. In this paper, we examine basic trends in the labor force activity of aged individuals (those 55–80 years old) during the period 1940–1980. We focus on various measures of labor force activity rather than on retirement specifically because retirement is difficult to measure, especially when analyzing data from widely differing time points. We include the "young" elderly, those 55–64 years old, because withdrawal from the labor force is increasingly occurring in this age group. For the most part we exclude the "old" elderly, those over age 80, because our preliminary analyses indicated that few of those over age 80 were economically

This research was supported by grant HD21738 to Nancy Brandon Tuma and grant HD19473 to Gary D. Sandefur from the National Institute for Child Health and Human Development. Additional research support and facilities were provided to Tuma by the Hoover Institution on War, Revolution and Peace and the Stanford Center for the Study of Families, Children and Youth and to Sandefur by the Institute for Research on Poverty and the Center for Demography and Ecology at the University of Wisconsin at Madison. We thank Jiwon Jeon, Cheryl Knobeloch, Raymond Mirikitani, Joanne Pearson, and Martin Schulz for their able research assistance. We also thank Sheldon Danziger for helpful comments on an earlier draft.

active at any point during the 1940–1980 period and because the economic behavior of very old workers may differ from that of the more typical group of aged individuals, who leave the labor force by age 80. We begin with 1940 primarily because the initial federal social legislation directed toward the elderly was formulated and enacted in the 1930s; hence, 1940 serves as a good point to begin a study of changes in labor force activity of aged Americans.

Previous research has found that the proportion of aged men who work has declined dramatically in recent years. According to Parsons (1980), the labor force participation (LFP) rate of men aged 55–64 fell from 89 percent in 1948 to 74 percent in 1976; Ellwood (1985) reported that the LFP rate of men aged 65 and over decreased from 35 percent in 1960 to 20 percent in 1980. In view of these trends, it is not surprising that the fraction of the income of the elderly that is earned has declined (Hurd and Shoven 1982).

These declines are often attributed to the expansion of public trans-fers—Social Security, Supplemental Security Income (SSI), Food Stamps, Medicare, and Medicaid—which have reduced the dependence of the elderly on their current earnings (Duggan 1984; Parsons 1980). Still other research has indicated that retirement decisions of the elderly are responsive to incentives other than social programs: those with greater wealth retire earlier, and those who expect to gain more by deferring retirement do, in fact, retire later (Fields and Mitchell 1981).

In addition, changes in the U.S. economy over the 1940–1980 period have undoubtedly influenced trends in LFP rates of the elderly. The beginning of this period was at the end of the Great Depression. At that time, many Americans were still in public service employment or out of work. The period from 1940 to 1970 was one of relatively sustained growth in the economy but little inflation until the late 1960s. The recession of 1969–70 saw the end of this growth. In contrast to the previous 30 years, the 1970s were characterized by little real economic growth, high inflation, and comparatively high unemployment. Consequently, individuals contemplating retirement at the beginning and end of the period we examine were operating under much different labor market conditions than those in the middle of the period. These changes in the economy, as well as the more often noted growth in availability of nonwage income for the elderly, need to be kept in mind when examining labor force activity of aged Americans during 1940–1980.

In contrast to the findings for aged men, it has been reported that the LFP rates of women aged 55–64 and 65 and over were relatively stable during 1960–1980 (Ellwood 1985); indeed, Duggan (1984) suggests that they may have increased slightly during 1974–1980. Still, LFP rates are so much lower for aged women than for aged men that the declines for men are understandably viewed as the more important trend, especially insofar as demands on the Social Security trust fund are concerned.

The declining work efforts of aged American men—combined with an expanding elderly population,[1] more generous benefits of public transfers to the elderly, and maturation of the Social Security system—have generated considerable interest in the trends in the labor force activity of the elderly and in the factors behind them. There have been several excellent studies of this topic based on data collected in the past two decades, including those cited above.[2] Investigations of the economic behavior of aged Americans over a long historical period have been rare. One notable example is Ransom and Sutch's (1986) examination of labor force patterns of American men between 1870 and 1940, including also Chapter 1 in this volume.[3]

Our primary goal in this paper is to examine labor force activity of aged American men and women from 1940 to 1980 using data from the Public Use Microdata Samples (PUMS), which were collected at the decennial censuses in these years. These data provide large, nationally representative samples but rather scanty information on individuals, especially on their past behavior. One advantage of these data, which we believe has not previously been recognized, is that they permit the study of changes in an individual's economic activity. That is, there is a small amount of longitudinal information on each sample member. In particular, each of these five censuses gathered reports on the number of weeks worked by the individual in the year *before* the census as well as a report of his or her employment status *at* the census. Thus, we can examine both departure from the labor force of those who worked the previous year and entry into the labor force of those who did not work the previous year. For the elderly, the former transition is often equivalent to entering retirement. The latter transition, which should be particularly infrequent among retired individuals, provides information on the extent to which labor force departure among the elderly is temporary.

The plan of this paper is as follows. Given the consensus on the importance of nonwage income for the decision to retire, we begin by reviewing what is known about changes in nonwage income available to elderly Americans in 1940–1980. We then discuss the specific hypotheses that we test in our analyses. Our results are presented in the next section. We conclude with a summary and a few comments on the implications of our findings.

SOURCES OF NONWAGE INCOME FOR AGED AMERICANS

As noted above, previous research on declines in LFP rates of aged men attributes much of the decline to the increased availability of nonwage income for the elderly. The major sources of nonwage income, in addition to public transfers, are private pensions and assets (cash savings and property).

We have varying amounts of information about the growth in assets, private pensions, and public transfers from 1940 to 1980. Least is known about changes in assets. Our own analyses (Sandefur and Tuma 1987), however, indicate that the percentage of those aged 55 and over who live in their own homes or in homes owned by other occupants (such as a son or daughter) has increased considerably between 1940 and 1980: from 61.8 percent in 1940 to 80.4 percent in 1980. Although a home is not a liquid asset, and although not all of the elderly own the home they live in, this trend suggests that assets of the elderly have grown over this period.

We know somewhat more about the growth in pensions. The first private pension program was put into operation by the American Express Company in 1875. Other railroad companies soon started pension programs, and by 1920 there were nearly 400 private pension programs in the United States (Nalebuff and Zeckhauser 1985). Ippolito (1986) argues that pensions became particularly popular with employers and employees during the post–World War II era, when people realized that high income-tax rates on earned income were permanent. In addition, the Revenue Act of 1942 provided tax incentives for employers to establish pension plans. In 1950, 25 percent of American workers had some pension coverage; by 1980, this had grown to approximately 50 percent (Ellwood 1985). The biggest expansion in pension coverage occurred during the 1950s and 1960s. Growth in pension receipt continues as those who acquired coverage in the 1950s and 1960s begin to retire. Of those aged 55 and over, some pension income was received by only 4 percent in 1940 but by about 30 percent in 1980 (ibid.). Still further increases are likely for those retiring in the next few decades.

We have the most information about changes in public transfers. Currently, the main source of post-retirement income is benefits obtained through the Social Security program (U.S. Department of Health and Human Services [USDHHS] 1986, 75). The Social Security Act of 1935 initiated Social Security coverage for all workers in commerce and industry with the exception of railroad workers, most of whom were already covered by pensions. Over the years, coverage has been broadened to include most types of employment. The percentage of workers who were insured under Social Security was 56 percent in 1940 and 1950, 74 percent in 1960, and 87 percent in 1980 (ibid., 97). The percentage of workers aged 65 and over who received Social Security benefits grew from 20 percent in 1940 to 59 percent in 1950 to 85 percent in 1960 to 94 percent in 1980 (ibid., 99). In short, the importance of Social Security benefits for the average aged American was slight in 1940 but had become great by 1960.

Undoubtedly, the *level* of benefits provided by public transfers is also a factor in retirement decisions. One indicator of this level is the average Social Security benefit to a retired man expressed as a percentage of the median earnings of all male workers.[4] In 1940 this percentage was 30 percent, but, as indicated above, only 20 percent of those aged 65 and over received such benefits. Although the percentage of those aged 65 and over receiving benefits rose to 59 percent in 1950, the level of the benefits fell dramatically: the average Social Security benefit to a retired male worker in 1950 was only 14 percent of median male earnings. Consequently, it seems likely that the impact of Social Security benefits on retirement decisions was still small in 1950. During the 1950s, growth in the level of benefits was substantial. The average level of benefits for retired men was 28.5 percent of median male earnings in 1960 and only slightly less, 26.6 percent, in 1970. Legislation in the early 1970s (in particular, indexing of benefits to the cost of living) led to still further increases. By 1980, the average benefit to retired men had risen to 37.5 percent of median male earnings. In view of this growth, it is not surprising that by 1984 the percentage of all income of the noninstitutionalized elderly coming from Social Security benefits was 31 percent for those aged 65–69 and 43 percent for those aged 70 and over (USDHHS 1986, v). Thus, we would expect Social Security benefits to be an important factor in the retirement decisions of aged Americans in the 1980s.

Over the years there have been a number of other changes in the Social Security system that are likely to have affected trends in the labor force activity of those aged 55 and over.[5] First, beginning in 1956, women could retire and receive benefits at 62. In 1961 this change was extended to men. Second, beginning in 1975, Social Security benefits became automatically adjusted for the cost of living. Third, beginning in 1950, there was a series of legislative changes pertaining to the exemption from the earnings test on Social Security benefits for workers over a certain age. In 1950 the exempt ages were 75 and over, but in 1954 they were altered to 72 and over. In 1977 the exempt ages were changed to 70 and over; however, this change did not go into effect until 1982. Consequently, this latter change is probably not relevant to behavior observed in the data gathered at the 1980 census, which we analyze below. In sum, at the 1960 through 1980 censuses, Social Security benefits of workers aged 72 and over are not reduced, whatever the level of earnings. This should act as a work incentive for persons in this age group.

An additional change in the Social Security system that may be relevant to labor force activity of the young elderly is the establishment in 1956 of benefits for workers aged 50–64 who suffer a permanent disability that prevents them from working. In 1958 benefits for the dependents of disabled workers began. The effects of these changes should not be apparent in the data we analyze until 1960.[6]

One should not assume that Social Security completely eliminates either the need for earnings or the desire to work. Beneficiaries of all ages are permitted to work to a certain extent, and recent evidence indicates that a sizable fraction of new beneficiaries of Social Security continue some involvement in the labor force. Overall, approximately half of those individuals who entered the Social Security rolls in recent years continued to work some (Fox 1984). Roughly one-fifth of women still work 18–30 months after they first received retirement-worker benefits from Social Security, based on the 1982 New Beneficiary Survey (Iams 1986). Partial retirement is relatively common among white men aged 58–69, particularly partial retirement into a job different from the full-time job held at age 55 (Gustman and Steinmeier 1984).

Other public transfers that may influence the elderly's labor force participation are Medicare, Medicaid, and SSI. Medicare and Medicaid were initiated in 1965. Medicare has always been available to Social Security recipients, and after 1972 Medicare coverage could be purchased by those with insufficient earnings credits to receive Social Security benefits. Medicaid, a means-tested medical assistance program, is often used to provide Medicare coverage to the impoverished elderly (USDHHS 1986, 40). The average Medicare benefit per person served rose from $592 in 1967 to $1,055 in 1975 to $1,791 in 1980 (ibid., 232). Thus, Medicare is likely to be perceived by the elderly as a significant source of nonwage income, especially if they or a dependent have a health problem. SSI, which was initiated in 1972, provides cash assistance to those who are blind, disabled, or elderly (defined as 65 and over) and whose other income is insufficient. The automatic cost-of-living adjustments begun for Social Security benefits in 1975 are also used with SSI benefits. Prior to the legislation establishing SSI, assistance to the elderly was handled by states, which had widely varying programs. The existence under SSI of uniform eligibility criteria and a minimum benefit probably enables a higher proportion of the elderly with very small financial resources to retire in 1980 than in 1970.

Food Stamps are another public transfer likely to affect labor force decisions of aged Americans. Although Food Stamps were available in many states in 1970, this program became mandatory in all states only in 1973. During the 1970s, eligibility requirements were loosened and the number of recipients expanded greatly (ibid., 284). Moreover, the removal in 1977 of the requirement that some stamps be purchased with cash may have made it easier for some of the elderly to participate in the Food Stamp program.

Sources and levels of nonwage income are likely to vary for men and women and for whites and nonwhites; therefore, the retirement patterns of these groups are likely to differ. Asset and pension income is much more likely to be available to men than to women and to whites than to nonwhites due to differences in labor force activity at younger ages. Moreover, Social Security benefits received by whites and men are much higher than those received by nonwhites and women due to differences in prior earnings histories. On the other hand, a much higher proportion of women and nonwhites than of men and whites receive SSI (Root and Tropman 1984). Since SSI was not instituted until 1972 and states were not required to participate in the Food Stamp program until 1973, public transfers are likely to have affected retirement decisions of whites and men more than those of nonwhites and women in 1960 and 1970—the first census years that Social Security benefits were widely available and replaced earnings to an appreciable degree. By 1980, racial and gender differences in nonwage income of the elderly may have decreased due to the availability of SSI and Food Stamps for those who were impoverished.

HYPOTHESES

From the viewpoint of economic theory, the decision of an elderly individual to retire (or not) is just an instance of the usual labor-leisure choice faced by everyone and is governed by the same principles. This theoretical perspective is so highly developed and familiar as to require minimal explanation. It assumes that everyone prefers leisure to work, ceteris paribus; the wage received by a worker compensates for the loss of leisure. Viewed differently, the wage rate is the price of leisure, and, other things being equal, a higher wage rate (more costly leisure) increases labor supply. The other side of the coin is that wages received for working generate income, and income enables a person to "purchase" leisure. Thus, other things being equal, a higher income (whether earned or not) decreases labor supply. Important issues for the labor supply decisions of the elderly are therefore the factors affecting wage rates and income.

By law, the wage rates of aged individuals may not legally depend on age, only on performance. Still, energy, stamina, and health status—and therefore performance—are likely to decline as age increases, even if there is no age discrimination in the setting of wage rates. Hence, ceteris paribus, the relationship between age and wages is probably negative at sufficiently high ages. Moreover, as an individual ages, the time available to achieve long-deferred personal goals (for example, travel) visibly begins to shrink; consequently, the elderly seem likely to value their remaining potential leisure more than others do. For these reasons we expect labor supply to decline as age increases, and at an accelerating rate.

At all ages, education is a key indicator of performance and therefore of wages. This leads to the hypothesis that the labor supplied by elderly individuals increases with educational level, ceteris paribus. There is another reason why individuals are more likely to be in the labor force if they are more educated—namely, the kind of work that people perform tends to be less physically demanding as education rises. Hence, aging probably affects job performance adversely more for those with low education than for those with high education. Moreover, occupations of those with low education tend to have a higher risk of disability than the occupations of those with high education. The more demanding nature of work and the greater risks of disability clearly support the hypothesis that the labor supply of the elderly is lower for those with less education. This factor is probably more important for men than for women, but we believe that the argument applies to both.

For various reasons not pertinent to our discussion, wage rates of nonwhites, especially of men, have historically been significantly lower than for seemingly comparable whites. Although this wage gap has narrowed in recent years (Smith and Welch 1986), nonwhites at risk of retiring between 1940 and 1980 can safely be assumed to have appreciably poorer opportunities as an aged worker than comparable whites. Moreover, among those covered by Social Security, retired-worker benefits replace a higher fraction of earnings for those with a history of low wages and underemployment (for example, nonwhites) because these benefits rise with the level of past contributions, but at a decreasing rate. These facts could imply a larger impact of public transfers on the retirement decisions of nonwhites than of whites. However, lower earnings in the past means smaller past contributions to Social Security and, hence, smaller Social Security benefits as a retired worker. Indeed, a smaller fraction of nonwhite than white men are likely to be fully insured. Consequently, nonwage income from public transfers is likely to be lower for nonwhites, especially prior to initiation of the SSI program in 1972. Therefore, the impact of Social Security on labor force activity of the elderly may have been smaller for nonwhites than for whites prior to 1980. In sum, there are good reasons to expect nonwhites to differ from whites in their retirement decisions, but it is unclear a priori if elderly whites or nonwhites are likely to supply more labor.

Although white women and nonwhite men are alike in having lower wages than otherwise comparable white men, there are important differences between gender and race that are relevant to our study. Most important, although women (like nonwhite men) typically have lower wages and smaller potential Social Security benefits as retired workers than men do, most women are married at typical ages when retirement occurs. The level of their Social Security benefits usually depends more on their husband's work history than on their own. Therefore, relative to unmarried women, we expect married women to be less likely to be in the labor force. Since the ratio of a husband's earnings to his wife's tends to be smaller for nonwhites than whites, we hypothesize that the effect of marital status on labor force activity is smaller for nonwhites than for whites. For men, neither the wife's earnings nor her Social Security benefits as a former worker are likely to be an important source of nonwage income during retirement. (This may change in future decades when today's more career-oriented women begin to retire.) Indeed, aged men who are married appear more likely than those who are unmarried to view themselves as the family breadwinner and to be less likely to retire. The effect of marital status for nonwhite men is expected to be smaller than for white men since nonwhite wives are more likely to have been significant contributors to family income throughout a couple's married life.

The differences in the typical work patterns of whites and nonwhites brought another individual characteristic to our attention—place of birth. Prior to 1950, a large fraction of the labor force in the South worked in agriculture, where wages are especially low and retirement has traditionally occurred at older ages. Moreover, Social Security coverage of employed farm (and domestic) workers did not begin until 1950. Since the available data do not tell where individuals worked most of their lives or what their former occupations were, being born in the South may serve as a crude indicator of agricultural employment. Since Southern nonwhites were especially likely to be in agriculture and other forms of employment not originally covered by Social Security, we hypothesized that the effect of being born in the South might be particularly evident for nonwhites.

Another aspect of nativity—being foreign born—may also be relevant to labor force activity in the elderly. Those born abroad are likely to have less access to private sources of nonwage income (including savings and earnings of kin) and lower average Social Security benefits because fewer will have participated in the Social Security program long enough to be fully insured. Consequently, we expect the labor supply of the elderly to be higher for the foreign born than for the native born.

Finally, the growth in nonwage income due to the expansion of public transfers and private pensions seems likely to be a major reason why the effects of individual attributes, including those listed above, change over this period. Since entitlements to public transfers are linked to age, the effects of age are especially likely to have changed over time.

As we indicated in the previous section, insofar as the elderly are concerned, neither public transfers nor private pensions nor even assets appear to have been appreciable in the 1940s. We therefore expected the economic activity of the elderly in 1940 to be high, though decreasing with age as poor health and disability exacted their toll. We thought that the situation of the elderly in 1950 should be very similar because average Social Security benefits of the eligible elderly were such a small fraction of typical earnings (14 percent) and because only 60 percent of those aged 65 and over were even eligible. By 1960, however, most of the elderly were eligible for Social Security benefits, and the average benefit was a reasonable fraction of median earnings (nearly 30 percent, as we noted earlier). Thus, in 1960 we expected Social Security rules to begin affecting the economic activity of aged Americans.

The fact that in 1960 women could receive partial Social Security benefits at age 62, but men could not receive any benefits until age 65, provides a way of detecting the impact of the Social Security system. We hypothesized that in 1960 labor force withdrawals jumped at age 62 for women (as well as at 65 when full benefits became available) but only at age 65 for men. In 1970 and 1980, when both men and women could receive partial Social Security benefits at age 62 and full benefits at 65, we expected both men and women to show sharp increases in labor force withdrawals at these specific ages as well as upward shifts in the relationship between age and the probability of leaving the labor force at these ages.

Another age-related "benefit" of the Social Security system concerns the earnings test on benefits, which stops at age 72, following legislation in 1954. To us, this program characteristic seemed unlikely to have much influence on leaving the work force—after all, roughly half of aged men retired by this age, even before Social Security began (see Ransom and Sutch, Chapter 1 in this volume). However, the removal of the earnings test may increase the likelihood of labor force entry of those aged 72 and over.

RESULTS

The data that we analyze come from the 1940, 1950, 1960, 1970, and 1980 PUMS, which are based on responses of samples of the U.S. population to questions asked during the decennial censuses. These data have the advantage of providing large samples of aged individuals over a 40-year period. They are not without disadvantages, however. First, as is well known, the range of information is much more limited than in surveys of small samples, and it tells extremely little about respondents' past experiences as contrasted with their current situations. This fact makes it impossible to estimate realistic behavioral models from these data. At best we can estimate models that, we hope, have some value as descriptive tools. Second, the U.S. Bureau of the Census (USBC) has altered its questions and procedures over the years, which limits the comparability over time. In the Appendix we summarize the changes that we consider to be the most relevant to our analyses. Despite the limitations of the PUMS data, we believe they are exceedingly valuable for what they do suggest about the labor force activity of aged Americans.

Before turning to labor force activity, however, we give a detailed picture of the age composition over time in Figure 2.1. This figure shows the percentage of the total population that is each exact age, except at age 85, which is the percentage of those 85 and over. The percentage of those who are a given age tends to rise from 1940 to 1980, with the increases especially large at the oldest ages. Thus, the percentage of the U.S. population that is potentially retired is large and growing. Notice also that there are prominent peaks at ages ending in 0 and 5 (heaping) in 1940 and 1950, followed by troughs at ages ending in 1 and 6. This and other aspects of age misreporting were particularly prevalent in these decades; for further discussion, see the Appendix.

General Patterns of Labor Force Activity

Although Ellwood (1985) and Parsons (1980) have reported that LFP of aged men in the United States has declined over much of the period we consider, we begin by examining cross-sectional pictures of the labor force activity of American men and women aged 55 and over. Given the large samples available in the PUMS data, we can look at variations in labor force activity by single years of age rather than for age groups, as did previous investigators referenced above.

In Figure 2.2 we show the percentage of individuals who reported zero weeks of work in the year before the census and who were out of the labor force during the census referent period (usually the week of the census; see the Appendix). For convenience, we refer to such individuals as "consistently not working." Most elderly people in this category would be considered "retired," although some (especially women) may never have worked. It excludes recent retirees—those who are out of the labor force at the census but who worked the previous year.

Despite previous research cited earlier that young aged men (those 55–64) have been working less in recent decades, Figure 2.2 gives little hint of this for the 1940–1970 period until age 62. But above this age, it is clear that a higher fraction of men were consistently not working in 1960–1970 than in 1940–1950. More striking, in 1980 there is a sharp rise in the percentage who were consistently not working at every age, including ages 55–59. In contrast, the percentages for ages 55–59 are virtually indistin-

FIGURE 2.1
PERCENTAGE OF THE U.S. POPULATION OF A GIVEN AGE

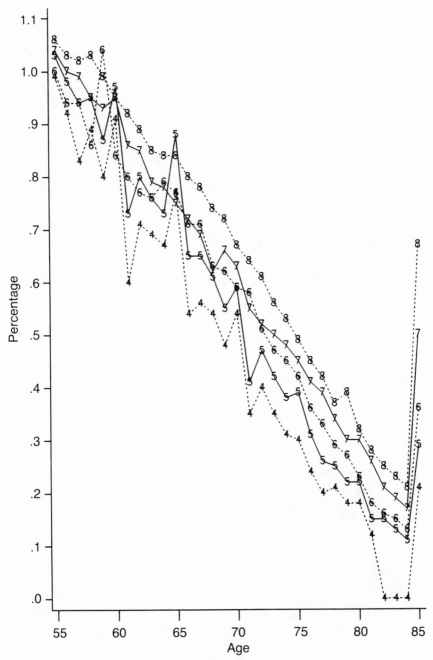

NOTE: 4=1940; 5=1950; 6=1960; 7=1970; 8=1980

FIGURE 2.2

PERCENTAGE OF THE U.S. ELDERLY CONSISTENTLY
NOT WORKING, BY AGE, SEX, AND YEAR

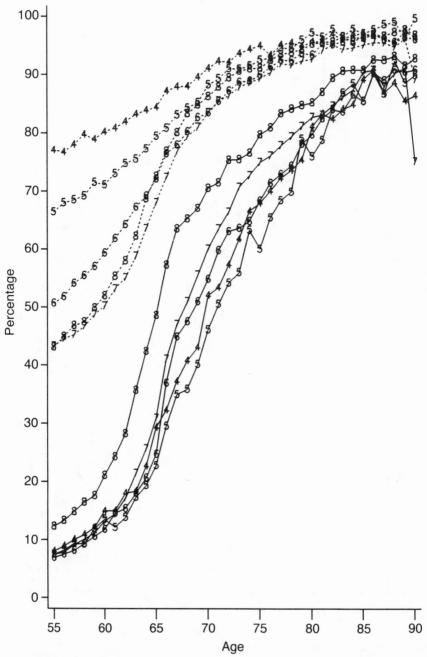

NOTE: Solid=men; dots=women;
4=1940; 5=1950; 6=1960; 7=1970; 8=1980

guishable for the other four decades. We know of no change in the definition of variables between 1970 and 1980 that accounts for this. It seems to be a genuine change. Lastly, note that in all five censuses, the percentage of those who were consistently not working rises substantially between ages 60–69 and is relatively flat both for ages 55–59 and above age 70. This supports conventional wisdom: most people leave the labor force in their sixties.

The picture for women is quite different. At almost every age, the percentage of those who were consistently not working is highest in 1940, somewhat lower in 1950, still lower in 1960, and lowest in 1970. The curves for 1970 and 1980 are similar for ages 55–62, but then diverge, with the percentage of those consistently not working higher in 1980 than in 1970. These curves vividly demonstrate that movement of women into the labor market in these decades affected older as well as younger women. Only at ages over 62 in 1980 do we see a reversal of this trend, with older women, like older men, less likely to be working.

We next examine the reverse of the behavior depicted in Figure 2.2—the percentage of those who were consistently working. This term is an abbreviation for working at least 48 weeks in the year before the census and being employed during the census referent period. Those in this category seemed to be firmly attached to the labor market. (The percentage of those consistently working plus the percentage consistently not working does not equal 100 percent. We discuss this further below.)

In Figure 2.3 we show the percentage of aged individuals who were consistently working by age, sex, and year. Although there is little variation between 1940 and 1970 for men aged 55–62 in Figure 2.2, there is considerable variability across years at every age for men in Figure 2.3. At the younger ages, 55–62, the percentage of men consistently working is lowest in 1940 and next lowest in 1950; it is highest in 1970. The values for 1940 and 1950 may partly be low because of misreporting of labor force variables (see the Appendix). In addition, these variations may partly reflect variations in economic conditions affecting workers of all ages. In 1940, effects of the Great Depression were still apparent. Though the U.S. economy was in a recession in 1970, elderly workers probably could hold onto their jobs due to their seniority.

Although the percentage of men who were consistently working at ages 55–62 is smallest in 1940 and 1950, the reverse is true at older ages. For example, for ages 65–69, the percentage of men consistently working is largest in 1940 and smallest in 1980, with regular drops from decade to decade. Age misreporting in the 1940 and 1950 censuses, which is believed to involve overreporting of ages 65–69 and underreporting of ages 55–64 (see the Appendix), may partially account for the high levels in 1940 and

FIGURE 2.3

PERCENTAGE OF THE U.S. ELDERLY
CONSISTENTLY WORKING, BY AGE, SEX, AND YEAR

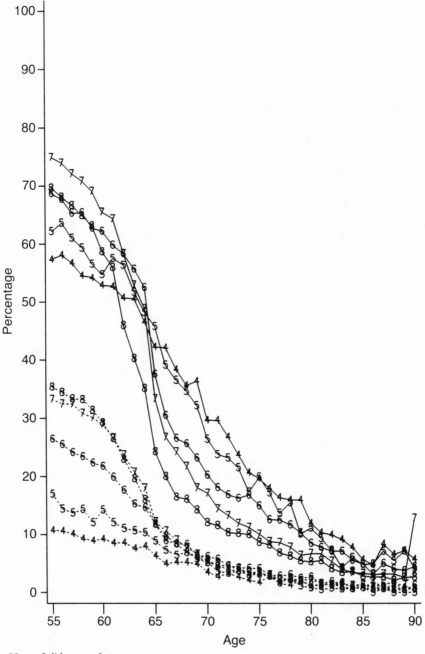

NOTE: Solid=men; dots=women;
4=1940; 5=1950; 6=1960; 7=1970; 8=1980

1950. Still, the trend seems clear: the fraction of men aged 65 and over who were consistently working fell throughout this period.

The patterns for women in Figure 2.3 are quite different from those for men. Above age 65, variations across the decades in the percentage of those who were consistently working are small; under 15 percent are in this category at any age in any year. In contrast, variations across the decades are substantial for the young elderly, 55–64. The percentage of women who were consistently working is highest (and about the same) in 1970 and in 1980; it is smallest in 1940, next smallest in 1950, and at an intermediary level in 1960. Whereas in 1940 roughly 8–10 percent of women were consistently working at ages 55–64, in 1970 and 1980 about 35 percent were consistently working at age 55 but only about 20 percent at age 64, with most of the decline occurring at ages 60–64. Thus, although more young-aged women work consistently now than in the past, like aged men, they mainly stop working during this decade of life.

As mentioned earlier, not everyone falls into the category of either consistently working or consistently not working. Rather than examine the residual as a group, we make further distinctions that we consider to be quite enlightening insofar as the decision to retire is concerned. Since the PUMS data contain information on weeks worked in the previous year and on labor force status during the census referent period (usually the week of the census; see the Appendix), it is possible to examine labor force transitions: departure from the labor force and entrance into it.

In Figure 2.4 we show the percentage of those aged 55–80 with positive weeks of work in the previous year who are out of the labor force at the census by age, sex, and year. This percentage divided by 100 approximates the age-specific probability of retiring for aged individuals, though it will overstate it if an appreciable fraction of those out of the labor force later re-enter the work force. Below we examine the reverse transition, labor force entrance, to check for this possibility.

The curves for men suggest that the probability of leaving the work force is small but increasing between ages 55 and 61. Moreover, the slope in this age range is noticeably steeper in 1970 and 1980 than in earlier years, perhaps because of the greater availability of disability benefits, as Parsons (1980) has suggested. Above age 61, the percentage leaving the labor force rises steadily with a nearly constant slope in 1940 and in 1950, though the slope is steeper in 1950 than in 1940. In 1960, the percentage rises steadily until age 65, when it jumps sharply; thereafter, it rises slowly—less rapidly than in 1940 and 1950. The peak at age 65 in 1960 reflects, we believe, the impact of Social Security, which made benefits available to eligible men aged 65 and over in 1960. Legislation in 1961 made partial Social Security benefits available to eligible men at age 62 and full benefits available at age 65.

FIGURE 2.4

PERCENTAGE OF THE U.S. ELDERLY LEAVING
THE LABOR FORCE, BY AGE, SEX, AND YEAR

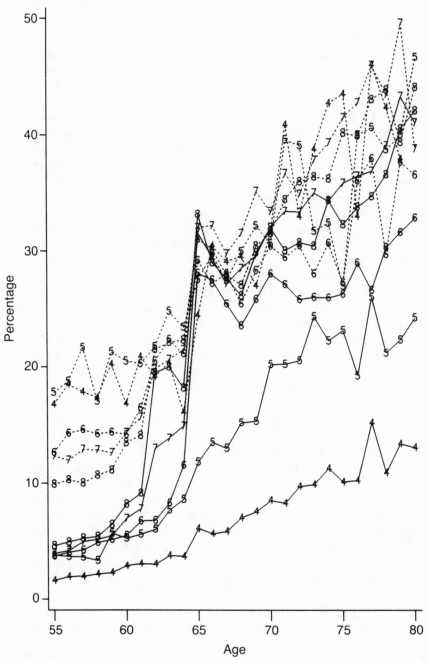

NOTE: Solid=men; dots=women;
4=1940; 5=1950; 6=1960; 7=1970; 8=1980

Reflecting this legislative change, the percentage leaving the labor force jumps at age 62 in 1970 and 1980 and again at age 65. Above 65 (the age of full entitlement), the slope in 1970 and 1980 is roughly the same as in earlier years. The removal of the earnings test on Social Security benefits at age 72, which has been in effect since 1954, has no visible impact. Since the jumps at ages 62 and 65 are not followed by compensating changes in the opposite direction at slightly older ages, the percentage leaving the labor force at ages over 65 are markedly higher in 1970 and 1980, and to a lesser extent in 1960, than in 1940 and 1950.

In Figure 2.4 we also show that labor force behavior of aged men and women differs appreciably, especially among the young elderly. The percentage of working women who leave the labor force is relatively flat between ages 55 and 64 in 1940 and 1950 and noticeably higher than in more recent decades until age 62. In 1960, when Social Security benefits were available at age 62 for women (but not for men), the percentage leaving the work force jumps at age 62. Similar jumps recur in 1970 and 1980. The percentage at ages 63–64 is about the same in all five years, except for a dip at age 64 in 1940. Another jump occurs at age 65 in all five years. Thereafter, the percentage of those who leave the work force rises gradually as age increases. Again, there is relatively little consistent variation across the years in the percentage leaving the work force at ages over 65. Of course, a much smaller fraction of aged women than of aged men are at risk of leaving the work force above age 65, so the curves for women at these ages are much more erratic than those for men. Still, it is clear that in 1970–1980, the probability of leaving the labor force for men and women over age 65 was not only much more similar than for the younger elderly but also much more similar than in 1940–1950.

In Figure 2.5 we display the percentage of those aged 55–80 who reported zero weeks of work in the year before the census who are in the labor force during the census referent period by age, sex, and year. These curves give some indication of the extent to which withdrawal from the labor force among the elderly is transitory.

The curves in Figure 2.5 suggest that the patterns of aged men's entry into the work force are rather similar in 1940 and 1950 and also in 1960 through 1980, but the patterns in more recent decades are sharply different from those in the earlier decades. There are no noteworthy peaks or changes in slopes that can plausibly be associated with the Social Security program. In particular, the removal of the earnings test on Social Security benefits at age 72 in 1960–1980 does not noticeably increase entry into employment. Moreover, since 1960, aged men's entry into the work force has been quite uncommon, ranging from less than 15 percent at age 55 to under 5 percent at ages 65 and over. Withdrawal from employment seems permanent for

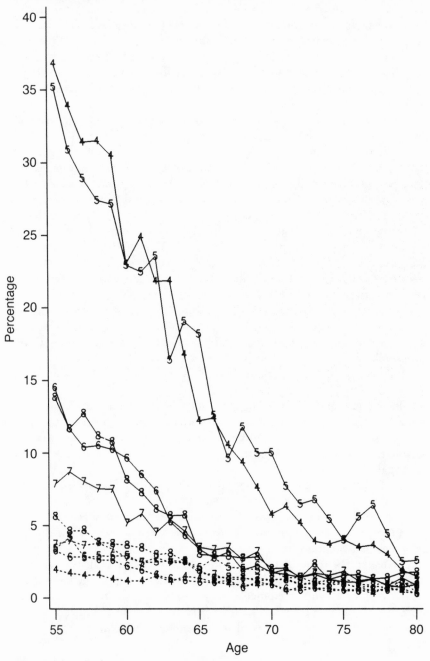

FIGURE 2.5

PERCENTAGE OF THE U.S. ELDERLY ENTERING
THE LABOR FORCE, BY AGE, SEX, AND YEAR

NOTE: Solid=men; dots=women;
4=1940; 5=1950; 6=1960; 7=1970; 8=1980

most men. Entry into the work force is appreciably higher in 1940 and 1950 at every age, ranging from about 35 percent at age 55 to roughly 15 percent at age 65. Problems with age misreporting and labor force definitions in 1940 and 1950 (see the Appendix) explain an unknown portion of the differences by year.

The curves for women require little discussion since variation both with age and across years is slight. The maximum percentage of women who enter the work force, about 5 percent, occurs at age 55 in 1960. The overall average is about 2 percent. Again, there are no peaks or shifts in slope at particular ages that appear to be due to the Social Security program.

It is interesting to note that during 1960–1980, the patterns of men and women in Figure 2.5 are quite similar for ages 65 and over but noticeably different for ages 55–64. In 1940 and 1950, the patterns for men and women are quite different at all ages.

In Figures 2.2. through 2.5 we display various aspects of the labor force activity of aged Americans for men and women separately. We thought that there might also be important differences between whites and nonwhites. Consequently, we examined the same sorts of displays for white and nonwhite men and for white and nonwhite women. Given the voluminous literature on differences in the labor force behavior of *non*aged whites and nonwhites during this historical period, we were surprised to discover that the plots for whites and nonwhites of the same sex were remarkably similar. The only notable differences occurred for white and nonwhite women in 1940 and 1950, when the tendency of nonwhite women to work more than white women was very apparent. Given the relatively small differences overall, we do not show these more detailed figures.

Multivariate Analyses

Although the displays in Figures 2.2–2.5 strongly suggest that labor force activity of aged men and women differs and that Social Security programs affect work decisions of aged Americans between 1960 and 1980, a graphical approach is not very useful for testing hypotheses about a wide range of variables. For this purpose we estimated logistic regression models of a dichotomous (0–1) variable indicating whether the individual was in or out of the labor force during the census reference period, conditional on whether weeks worked in the year before the census exceeded zero. Being *out* of the labor force (OLF) at the census when weeks worked in the previous year exceeded zero indicates labor force departure; this is the quantity displayed in Figure 2.4. Being *in* the labor force (ILF) at the census when weeks worked in the previous year was zero indicates labor force entry; this is the quantity shown in Figure 2.5. As in the case of the corresponding graphs, we analyzed data only on those aged 55–80. We excluded those over age 80 because we thought effects of covariates on their labor force transitions might have somewhat different patterns. We begin with the multivariate results for labor force departure and then turn to those for labor force entry. Descriptive statistics on the variables in the samples analyzed (and sample sizes) are given in Tables 2.1 and 2.2 for reference. Trends in the distribution of the covariates over time are essentially what one expects.

Labor Force Departure. In Tables 2.3 and 2.4 we report the maximum likelihood estimates of the parameters in a logistic regression model of labor force departure by year for men and women, respectively.[7] For both men and women, likelihood ratio tests of the reported model against one with no covariates are statistically significant at a very low probability level. Moreover, for both men and women, a likelihood ratio test of the reported model against one with the same variables but identical effects across the years is also statistically significant at a very low probability level. This means that the effects of the covariates vary significantly over time.

Although the magnitude of estimated effects of covariates differ for men and women, in most instances effects for men and women have the same sign. Therefore, we discuss these results together, noting first whether our hypotheses are supported generally and then indicating gender differences.

First consider variation across the years in the intercepts, which indicate the probability that an unmarried 55-year-old, native-born white with twelve years of schooling leaves the labor force. The graphical displays in Figure 2.4 indicate that for men, labor force departure at age 55 varies little across the years (except in 1940), but that for women, it differs in 1940–1950 from 1960–1980. Not surprisingly, for men the estimated intercepts are quite similar, except for 1940. But for women, the estimated intercepts are also within two standard deviations of one another, suggesting that some of the variation seen in Figure 2.4 is attributable to shifts in the distribution of women across these covariates.

As hypothesized, those with less than twelve years of schooling are significantly more likely to leave the work force than those with exactly twelve years of schooling, except in the case of women in 1950, and even here the sign is positive. The estimated effect of low education shows no particular pattern of variation across the years for men, but it tends to decline for women. This may reflect shifts in the kinds of occupations held by less-educated women over time. Also as hypothesized, those with more than twelve years of schooling are significantly less likely to leave the labor force than those with exactly twelve years of schooling in 1950–1980 for men and in 1940–1960 for women. The effect of high education for men

TABLE 2.1

PERCENTAGE OF MEN AND WOMEN AGED 55–80 WITH NONZERO WEEKS OF WORK

	MEN					WOMEN				
	1940	1950	1960	1970	1980	1940	1950	1960	1970	1980
Education < 12 years	84.1	79.3	75.5	62.4	42.6	76.1	69.7	65.0	53.4	37.4
Education > 12 years	8.3	10.4	13.3	18.1	28.0	11.5	14.7	18.0	20.3	24.3
Nonwhite	7.8	7.3	8.1	8.5	9.4	12.6	10.7	10.4	10.0	11.4
Married	80.1	81.3	85.0	86.5	87.8	33.0	38.5	45.8	51.3	57.2
Married nonwhite	6.1	5.8	6.4	6.8	7.6	4.6	4.7	5.0	5.1	6.0
Southern born	26.7	25.0	26.6	28.1	29.3	27.6	25.2	26.8	28.3	30.7
Southern born nonwhite	6.6	6.0	6.0	5.8	5.8	10.9	9.1	8.2	7.1	7.5
Foreign born	23.2	22.5	16.5	9.9	7.8	16.3	16.2	12.5	8.7	7.7
Age < 62	48.3	45.6	46.6	48.6	51.8	52.2	52.1	51.3	51.9	54.1
Age = 62	5.8	6.3	5.7	6.3	6.3	5.8	5.9	5.7	6.4	6.3
Age = 63, 64	10.9	10.8	11.2	10.8	10.2	10.0	10.0	10.2	10.2	10.0
Age = 65	5.4	5.5	5.1	4.7	4.1	5.7	5.4	4.4	4.2	4.0
Age = 66–71	18.8	19.2	18.4	16.9	15.1	16.4	15.9	16.7	15.1	14.0
Age = 72	1.7	1.8	1.6	1.4	1.3	1.4	1.2	1.4	1.2	1.1
Age > 72	4.3	5.2	5.4	4.8	4.3	3.9	3.7	4.2	4.3	3.8
Leaving the LF	4.1	8.8	12.2	14.1	14.4	21.8	23.1	19.3	19.7	17.8
Sample size	61,625	24,480	95,034	104,451	103,334	13,213	7,457	44,435	62,390	68,725

TABLE 2.2

PERCENTAGE OF MEN AND WOMEN AGED 55–80 WITH ZERO WEEKS OF WORK

	MEN					WOMEN				
	1940	1950	1960	1970	1980	1940	1950	1960	1970	1980
Education < 12 years	89.1	85.9	85.9	78.8	63.3	84.8	80.5	79.0	69.6	55.8
Education > 12 years	5.4	6.5	6.9	9.8	15.8	5.5	7.4	8.7	11.8	16.3
Nonwhite	6.5	7.7	9.7	11.0	12.4	5.9	6.3	7.5	8.5	10.9
Married	60.1	62.7	67.4	70.9	76.8	55.1	56.2	57.3	55.9	55.9
Married nonwhite	3.7	4.6	6.2	6.8	8.2	2.7	2.7	3.5	3.9	4.8
Southern born	22.0	26.9	28.1	29.9	32.8	24.4	26.2	28.0	29.4	32.3
Southern born nonwhite	5.4	6.3	7.3	7.5	8.7	5.0	5.4	6.0	6.2	7.6
Foreign born	28.2	23.4	21.9	14.5	9.9	23.0	20.6	17.2	12.0	9.7
Age < 62	17.7	16.1	10.8	10.3	13.2	34.5	31.4	25.6	22.6	21.3
Age = 62	3.4	3.1	2.4	2.5	3.2	4.8	4.7	4.2	3.9	3.8
Age = 63, 64	7.4	6.8	5.9	6.4	8.5	9.3	8.8	8.8	8.0	8.3
Age = 65	5.4	4.7	3.6	4.0	4.9	5.7	5.6	4.6	4.5	4.5
Age = 66–71	34.7	34.3	40.2	37.9	38.2	25.8	26.6	30.1	30.9	31.6
Age = 72	5.3	5.4	5.8	5.3	5.0	3.1	3.4	3.8	4.0	4.2
Age > 72	24.2	27.6	29.3	31.1	24.5	13.2	15.8	18.8	22.4	22.8
Entering the LF	12.6	12.8	3.2	2.9	3.9	1.2	2.2	1.4	1.9	2.1
Sample Size	30,772	11,101	45,824	57,597	87,641	78,069	30,802	113,983	133,076	170,680

seems relatively stable in 1950–1980 but shows no particular pattern for women. The very small and insignificant effects of high education for women in 1970 and 1980 surprised us, and we have no plausible explanation for this finding.

Although we argued that there were good reasons for expecting labor supply to vary for aged whites and nonwhites, the results in Tables 2.3 and 2.4 offer little support to this hypothesis. Nonwhite men and women were significantly less likely than whites to leave the labor force in 1980. In addition, nonwhite women were significantly more likely to leave the labor force in 1950, which is also the one year in which the effect of being nonwhite for men is positive (although not significant). But, our overall conclusion is that being nonwhite has had relatively little effect on labor force departure of elderly Americans until 1980, when its effect is negative. We think that this is worth noting since labor force behavior of nonwhites and whites among the *non*-aged (especially men) is usually found to differ significantly.

Marital status is one covariate that we hypothesized would affect labor force behavior of men and women differently, and our results support this hypothesis. The effect of being married is statistically significant for both men and women; however, its effect is large and negative for men but large and positive for women, as we expected. Moreover, the estimated effect in a given year is much larger in magnitude for women than for men. This is consistent with the usual finding that labor supply of married and unmarried individuals differs less for men than for women. Over time, the effect of marital status appears to decline for both men and women. This trend is quite plausible since both growth in nonwage income and in women's *own* earnings over this period tend to reduce a couple's dependency on the husband's earnings.

We hypothesized that marital status might affect the labor force activity of nonwhites less than of whites due to the greater balance in the labor supplied by nonwhite men and women over their work histories. For men, the effect of the interaction between being married and nonwhite is in the expected direction, but not statistically significant. For women, it is also in the expected direction and, in this case, is significant. The magnitude of the interaction for women seems to decrease over the period 1940–1980, which is also plausible in view of the trend toward increasing similarity of *non*aged white and nonwhite women's work behavior.

We hypothesized that nativity would also affect the labor supply of the elderly, not directly but as an indicator of access to nonwage income. In particular, we hypothesized that foreign- and Southern-born individuals would have lower access to nonwage income and would be less likely to leave the labor force. The estimates in Tables 2.3 and 2.4 indeed show that foreign-born men and women are significantly less likely to withdraw from the labor

TABLE 2.3

ESTIMATED COEFFICIENTS IN A LOGISTIC REGRESSION MODEL OF THE
TRANSITION FROM WORKING TO OLF, MEN BY YEAR

	1940	1950	1960	1970	1980
Intercept	−3.933***	−3.120***	−3.253***	−3.135***	−3.010***
	(0.116)	(0.120)	(0.057)	(0.047)	(0.044)
Education < 12 years	0.328***	0.178*	0.386***	0.351***	0.219***
	(0.089)	(0.083)	(0.038)	(0.027)	(0.023)
Education > 12 years	−0.069	−0.279*	−0.240***	−0.205***	−0.242***
	(0.119)	(0.118)	(0.050)	(0.036)	(0.027)
Nonwhite	−0.452	0.116	−0.140	−0.104	−0.278**
	(0.247)	(0.231)	(0.100)	(0.079)	(0.089)
Married	−0.471***	−0.454***	−0.328***	−0.315***	−0.150***
	(0.047)	(0.055)	(0.028)	(0.027)	(0.029)
Married nonwhite	0.216	0.163	0.064	0.019	0.155
	(0.187)	(0.192)	(0.089)	(0.078)	(0.083)
Foreign born	−0.121*	−0.050	−0.073*	−0.213***	−0.263***
	(0.053)	(0.060)	(0.029)	(0.032)	(0.038)
Southern born	−0.093	0.140*	0.107***	0.070**	0.045*
	(0.055)	(0.061)	(0.027)	(0.023)	(0.023)
Southern born nonwhite	0.042	−0.260	0.086	0.031	0.037
	(0.237)	(0.217)	(0.092)	(0.073)	(0.071)
Age	0.105***	0.085***	0.078***	0.116***	0.136***
	(0.019)	(0.022)	(0.010)	(0.009)	(0.008)
Age 62 Spline	−0.007	0.085	0.277***	0.233***	0.219***
	(0.045)	(0.052)	(0.024)	(0.021)	(0.020)
Age 65 Spline	0.027	−0.029	−0.229***	−0.225***	−0.288***
	(0.041)	(0.046)	(0.020)	(0.018)	(0.017)
Age 72 Spline	−0.088***	−0.137***	−0.151***	−0.109***	−0.041***
	(0.025)	(0.028)	(0.012)	(0.012)	(0.012)
Age = 62	−0.116	−0.096	−0.209***	0.260***	0.523***
	(0.108)	(0.119)	(0.059)	(0.042)	(0.037)
Age = 65	0.300***	0.134	0.630***	0.571***	0.464***
	(0.088)	(0.101)	(0.039)	(0.037)	(0.039)
Age = 72	−0.005	−0.096	−0.237***	−0.129*	−0.084
	(0.115)	(0.130)	(0.064)	(0.060)	(0.064)

*p < .05   ** p < .01   *** p < .001

TABLE 2.4

ESTIMATED COEFFICIENTS IN A LOGISTIC REGRESSION MODEL OF THE
TRANSITION FROM WORKING TO OLF, WOMEN BY YEAR

	1940	1950	1960	1970	1980
Intercept	−2.662***	−2.298***	−2.540***	−2.470***	−2.556***
	(0.092)	(0.107)	(0.047)	(0.037)	(0.036)
Education < 12 years	0.486***	0.160	0.273***	0.246***	0.096***
	(0.076)	(0.083)	(0.036)	(0.026)	(0.025)
Education > 12 years	−0.315**	−0.433***	−0.206***	−0.001	0.008
	(0.109)	(0.114)	(0.046)	(0.032)	(0.027)
Nonwhite	−0.195	0.472*	0.069	0.036	−0.168*
	(0.197)	(0.236)	(0.096)	(0.072)	(0.072)
Married	1.482***	1.137***	0.704***	0.457***	0.372***
	(0.050)	(0.064)	(0.028)	(0.023)	(0.023)
Married nonwhite	−0.612***	−0.460**	−0.260***	−0.150*	−0.162*
	(0.138)	(0.169)	(0.076)	(0.069)	(0.069)
Foreign born	−0.385***	−0.175*	−0.094*	−0.119**	−0.193***
	(0.067)	(0.085)	(0.039)	(0.038)	(0.042)
Southern born	0.424***	0.451***	0.166***	0.077**	0.058*
	(0.059)	(0.077)	(0.032)	(0.026)	(0.025)
Southern born nonwhite	−0.274	−0.206	0.161	−0.015	0.034
	(0.206)	(0.248)	(0.100)	(0.077)	(0.076)
Age	0.044**	0.053**	0.048***	0.052***	0.078***
	(0.016)	(0.020)	(0.009)	(0.008)	(0.008)
Age 62 Spline	−0.013	0.032	0.144***	0.164***	0.172***
	(0.044)	(0.055)	(0.024)	(0.020)	(0.020)
Age 65 Spline	0.120*	0.013	−0.128***	−0.109***	−0.178***
	(0.047)	(0.059)	(0.024)	(0.020)	(0.020)
Age 72 Spline	−0.095**	−0.063	−0.032	−0.067***	−0.010
	(0.035)	(0.049)	(0.018)	(0.015)	(0.015)
Age = 62	−0.004	0.047	0.170**	0.157***	0.306***
	(0.107)	(0.132)	(0.055)	(0.045)	(0.042)
Age = 65	0.134	0.090	0.243***	0.308***	0.262***
	(0.109)	(0.137)	(0.059)	(0.049)	(0.048)
Age = 72	−0.266	0.126	−0.025	−0.153	0.060
	(0.179)	(0.247)	(0.096)	(0.082)	(0.081)

* p < .05   ** p < .01   *** p < .001

force, except for men in 1950, where the effect is negative but insignificant. For both men and women, there seems to be a U-shaped pattern to the effects over time, with the largest effects in 1940 and 1980 and the smallest in 1960. Since we have no post hoc explanation for this pattern, we cannot conjecture whether it is genuine or due to chance variations.

Being born in the South does have a significant effect on the probability of leaving the labor force (except for men in 1940), but the sign is opposite that of our hypothesis. Those born in the South are *more* likely to withdraw from the labor force than otherwise comparable native-born individuals. We have no ready explanation for this finding. We also hypothesized that the effect of being born in the South would be even greater for nonwhites. However, the interaction between nonwhite and being born in the South is statistically insignificant (and varying in sign over time) for both men and women. We conclude that aged Southern-born nonwhites and whites are about equally likely to withdraw from the labor force, ceteris paribus.

Finally, we included a variety of representations of a person's age in our model in order to assess the effects of age-specific entitlements under Social Security (and also private pensions available to some workers).[8] We expected the probability of labor force departure to increase with age in all years, and the significant positive coefficient of age for men and women in each year supports this hypothesis. To capture the effects of Social Security entitlements beginning at ages 62 and 65 and of the removal of the earnings test at age 72, we included linear splines at these ages[9] (which permit the effect of age to shift at these ages) as well as dummy variables indicating these exact ages (which permit transitory shifts at these ages). As we explained in the discussion of our hypotheses, we expected effects of the Social Security program to begin only in 1960. Moreover, in 1960 men could not receive Social Security benefits until age 65, so in 1960 we expected the age 62 spline and the age 62 dummy variable to have effects only for women, not men. Results in Tables 2.3 and 2.4 largely support these hypotheses.

As hypothesized, the additional age variables have smaller and mainly insignificant effects in 1940 and 1950 for both men and women, in contrast to larger and mainly significant effects from 1960 onward.[10] The effect of the age 62 spline variable is small and insignificant in 1940 and 1950 for both sexes, but it is large and positive in 1960–1980. This mainly supports our hypothesis. The only surprise is this variable's positive effect for men in 1960, a year before legislation providing partial Social Security benefits for men at age 62 was enacted. The effect of the age 65 spline is significant and negative for men and women from 1960 to 1980; moreover, the magnitude is roughly the same, though opposite in sign, to that of the age 62 spline. This implies a brief acceleration in the age-specific rate of labor force departure at ages 62–65, and then a decline. Although the age 65 spline has a significant effect for women in 1940, the sign is opposite that in 1960–1980. Perhaps it reflects age misreporting in 1940 (see the Appendix).

The effect of the age 72 spline is negative for men and women in all years; however, it is statistically significant for women only in 1940 and 1970. This negative effect implies that the effect of age on those still in the labor force at age 72 declines still further. Summing the effects of age and the age splines in a given year gives the net effect of age on the probability of labor force departure at ages 72 and older. Doing this shows that the net effect of age for those aged 72–80 is close to the effect of age for those aged 55–61 for women in all years and for men in 1940–1970. The net effect of age for those aged 72–80 is actually noticeably negative for men in 1980 (−0.193). In short, those still in the labor force at age 72 are about as likely to leave the labor force as those aged 55–61. These die-hard workers probably differ in some important unobserved ways from the typical group of workers who retire in their mid- to late sixties.

Finally, the dummy variables indicating exact age 62 and exact age 65 have significant positive effects for women in 1960–1980 but not in 1940 and 1950. For men, the effect of the age 62 dummy is significantly positive in 1970 and 1980, and the effect of the age 65 dummy is significantly positive in 1960–1980. We believe that these effects indicate people's response to the start of entitlements to Social Security benefits (and perhaps also private pensions). The age 65 dummy is also positive for men in 1940. Since we can think of no substantive reason for its effect in 1940, we wonder if it reflects problems with age misreporting in 1940 (in particular, heaping on digits ending in 0 and 5). The age 62 dummy has a significant effect for men, but its sign is negative—opposite its sign in 1970 and 1980. It is also about the same magnitude as the effect of the age 62 spline for men in 1960, so the net effect at age 62 for men in 1960 is about the same as for those aged 55–61. Hence, the age 62 spline for men in 1960 really differs from zero only for those aged 63 and 64. We doubt that this is of substantive significance.

These results may appear complicated because there are five years, two sexes, and seven variables representing age. A brief summary of our interpretations may help. To us, the results for the age variables indicate that in 1940 and 1950, before the Social Security program was likely to be an important source of nonwage income, elderly men and women were increasingly likely to leave the labor force as they aged, but the increase with age was slow and gradual. From 1960 onward, the Social Security program was an important source of nonwage income for aged Americans, and its rules pertaining to the age of entitlements had substantial impact on the probability that aged men and women departed from the labor force. At the age when entitlements to benefits begin, there are one-year jumps in the probability of leaving the labor force. In addition, at the age of the first entitlement, there is an upward shift in the net effect of age. At the age of the second entitlement (that is, age 65 for women in 1960–1980 and for men in 1970–1980), there is a downward shift in the effect of age. But, until age 72, the net effect of age still exceeds that at the ages before these entitlements began. At age 72 there is another downward shift in the effect of age, and in most instances the effect of age on the probability of labor force withdrawal is about the same as it is at ages 55–61. Since rather small fractions of the elderly are still in the labor force in their seventies, it is hard to be certain whether the shift at age 72 is attributable to the removal of the earnings test. We suspect that differences in the intrinsic value of work and leisure for older workers are more salient than the earnings test but, admittedly, this is just our guess.

Entry into the Labor Force. In Tables 2.5 and 2.6 we give the maximum likelihood estimates for men and women, respectively, of a logistic regression model of a dichotomous (0–1) variable that indicates if a person who reported zero weeks of work in the year before the census was in the labor force during the census referent period. We hypothesized that the effects of most covariates on labor force entry would be opposite their effects on labor force departure. This, indeed, seems to be the case.

For both men and women, those with less than twelve years of schooling seem generally less likely to enter the labor force than those with twelve years of schooling. However, though the effects of low education are negative in every year for both groups, they are statistically insignificant except for women in 1960 and 1970. Having more than twelve years of schooling rather than exactly twelve tends to raise the probability of entering the labor force, except for women in 1970. However, the effects of high education are not significant for men in 1950 or for each sex in 1960. That low education deters labor force entry less than it enhances labor force departure (compare Table 2.3 with Table 2.5 and Table 2.4 with Table 2.6) suggests that some labor force departures were involuntary and/or transitory and therefore not what is usually considered to be retirement.

The results in Tables 2.5 and 2.6 also provide partial support for our hypothesis that labor force behavior of whites and nonwhites differs, especially in the case of women. Overall, nonwhites appear to be more likely than whites to enter the labor force, except in the case of nonwhite men in 1940. The estimated positive effect of the nonwhite variable is, however, statistically significant only in 1970 and 1980 for men and in 1940, 1950, and 1970 for women. Still, the generally positive effect suggests that nonwage income of nonwhites is often inadequate relative to their needs, encouraging them to enter the work force.

Being married has large, significant effects on labor force entry, as it did

TABLE 2.5

ESTIMATED COEFFICIENTS IN A LOGISTIC REGRESSION MODEL OF THE
TRANSITION FROM NOT WORKING TO ILF, MEN BY YEAR

	1940	1950	1960	1970	1980
Intercept	−0.852***	−1.083***	−2.107***	−2.557	−1.997***
	(0.093)	(0.144)	(0.128)	(0.116)	(0.071)
Education < 12 years	−0.026	−0.118	−0.015	−0.032	−0.065
	(0.076)	(0.106)	(0.101)	(0.077)	(0.045)
Education > 12 years	0.209*	0.048	0.163	0.272**	0.201***
	(0.102)	(0.147)	(0.134)	(0.100)	(0.055)
Nonwhite	−0.135	0.215	0.336	0.504***	0.235*
	(0.201)	(0.286)	(0.172)	(0.145)	(0.109)
Married	0.477***	0.679***	0.262***	0.302***	0.107*
	(0.041)	(0.072)	(0.066)	(0.065)	(0.049)
Married nonwhite	−0.071	−0.182	−0.078	−0.107	0.248*
	(0.161)	(0.245)	(0.164)	(0.149)	(0.104)
Foreign born	0.102*	−0.125	0.003	0.232**	0.479***
	(0.042)	(0.078)	(0.076)	(0.075)	(0.060)
Southern born	−0.131*	0.167*	0.017	−0.194**	0.016
	(0.053)	(0.075)	(0.070)	(0.066)	(0.045)
Southern born nonwhite	0.140	−0.306	0.009	0.028	−0.042
	(0.196)	(0.277)	(0.175)	(0.147)	(0.098)
Age	−0.097***	−0.099***	−0.081***	−0.078***	−0.111***
	(0.014)	(0.025)	(0.021)	(0.023)	(0.014)
Age 62 Spline	−0.041	−0.019	−0.189***	−0.007	−0.049
	(0.036)	(0.063)	(0.053)	(0.055)	(0.035)
Age 65 Spline	−0.050	0.004	0.136*	−0.043	0.012
	(0.035)	(0.060)	(0.054)	(0.049)	(0.034)
Age 72 Spline	0.089***	0.012	0.065	0.052	0.120***
	(0.026)	(0.037)	(0.036)	(0.029)	(0.023)
Age = 62	−0.006	0.208	0.102	−0.183	−0.092
	(0.083)	(0.145)	(0.128)	(0.139)	(0.087)
Age = 65	−0.239**	0.275*	−0.063	−0.186	−0.366***
	(0.087)	(0.137)	(0.154)	(0.128)	(0.099)
Age = 72	0.079	−0.124	−0.045	−0.260	−0.234
	(0.123)	(0.181)	(0.177)	(0.162)	(0.136)

* p < .05   ** p < .01   *** p < .001

TABLE 2.6 _____

Estimated Coefficients in a Logistic Regression Model of the Transition from Not Working to ILF, Women by Year

	1940	1950	1960	1970	1980
Intercept	−2.862***	−2.349***	−2.702***	−2.773***	−2.618***
	(0.130)	(0.150)	(0.095)	(0.073)	(0.059)
Education < 12 years	−0.079	−0.111	−0.202**	−0.148**	−0.012
	(0.112)	(0.120)	(0.073)	(0.050)	(0.041)
Education > 12 years	0.448**	0.426**	0.060	−0.045	0.190***
	(0.153)	(0.158)	(0.101)	(0.071)	(0.051)
Nonwhite	0.661**	0.649*	0.297	0.332**	0.154
	(0.245)	(0.277)	(0.174)	(0.120)	(0.093)
Married	−1.670***	−1.190***	−0.684***	−0.382***	−0.458***
	(0.083)	(0.088)	(0.058)	(0.047)	(0.040)
Married nonwhite	0.697**	0.552*	0.386*	0.396**	0.326***
	(0.228)	(0.252)	(0.150)	(0.120)	(0.090)
Foreign born	−0.117	−0.203	−0.224**	0.188**	0.288***
	(0.088)	(0.109)	(0.079)	(0.063)	(0.058)
Southern born	−0.281**	−0.213*	−0.153*	−0.147**	−0.140**
	(0.095)	(0.105)	(0.066)	(0.052)	(0.044)
Southern born nonwhite	−0.081	−0.199	0.174	−0.065	0.255*
	(0.270)	(0.301)	(0.183)	(0.129)	(0.100)
Age	−0.130***	−0.094***	−0.094***	−0.074***	−0.081***
	(0.024)	(0.028)	(0.017)	(0.015)	(0.012)
Age 62 Spline	0.162*	0.093	−0.096	−0.026	−0.064
	(0.067)	(0.076)	(0.049)	(0.040)	(0.033)
Age 65 Spline	−0.179**	−0.108	0.108*	−0.009	0.014
	(0.069)	(0.078)	(0.053)	(0.041)	(0.034)
Age 72 Spline	0.071	−0.040	−0.001	0.091***	0.087***
	(0.052)	(0.059)	(0.038)	(0.026)	(0.024)
Age = 62	0.245	0.006	−0.077	0.086	0.008
	(0.151)	(0.187)	(0.126)	(0.094)	(0.080)
Age = 65	−0.012	−0.232	−0.055	−0.133	−0.095
	(0.156)	(0.195)	(0.151)	(0.113)	(0.095)
Age = 72	0.208	0.005	−0.335	−0.112	−0.077
	(0.254)	(0.283)	(0.222)	(0.151)	(0.133)

$* \ p < .05$ $** \ p < .01$ $*** \ p < .001$

on labor force exit. As we hypothesized, the signs for men and women are opposite. It is interesting to note that the effects of marital status on labor force entry are roughly equal in magnitude (though opposite in sign) to those on labor force exit. Again, the magnitude of the effect of marital status declines steadily from 1940 to 1980 for both men and women. It is also again the case that the effect of marital status for whites and nonwhites does not differ significantly for men (except in 1980), but it does differ significantly for women. Aged married nonwhite women are much more likely to enter the labor force than otherwise comparable married white women.

The results on labor force exit in Tables 2.3 and 2.4 indicate that foreign-born individuals are less likely to leave the labor force than the native born. The results in Tables 2.5 and 2.6 show that the foreign born are also more likely to enter the labor force, especially in 1970 and 1980. However, labor force entry of foreign-born women was less likely in 1940–1960, significantly so in 1960. It is not obvious what caused this change. Still, the effects for 1970 and 1980 agree with our hypothesis that the foreign-born elderly supply more labor due to lower nonwage income.

The effect of being born in the South on labor force entry of men varies across the years in sign, magnitude, and statistical significance. These variations suggest that we should not look hard for any single explanation of the effects for men. Being born in the South has a consistently negative (and significant) effect on labor force entry of women. This negative effect may reflect the more traditional sex roles of men and women in the South; the declining magnitude of the effect over time may reflect declines in the South's distinctiveness in this respect over time. As in Tables 2.3. and 2.4, the interaction of Southern birth with race is not statistically significant for either men or women, except for women in 1980.

We hypothesized that the probability of entering the labor force would decline as age increases and that the effect of the timing of the Social Security entitlements on labor force entry would be smaller than on labor force exit, except possibly for the removal of the earnings test at age 72. These hypotheses are largely borne out by the results in Tables 2.5 and 2.6.[11] The effect of age is indeed significantly negative for both men and women in each year. Its effect appears to be fairly stable across time for men but to decline over time for women.

For men, the effect of the age 62 spline is negative in every year; however, it is small except in 1960, when it is significant. For women, the effect of the age 62 spline is significant only in 1940, when it is positive. In more recent decades it is negative, though not significant. The effects of the age 65 spline are quite variable across the years both in sign, magnitude, and significance. In view of this, we think these effects do not call for a substantive interpretation. The effect of the age 72 spline is positive for both men and women, except for women in 1950 and 1960; however, it is only significant in two years for each sex. As in the case of the effects of this variable on labor force departure, we are reluctant to attribute these effects to the removal of the earnings test on Social Security benefits, especially because this variable's positive effects are about as large before Social Security became an important source of nonwage income as afterward.

None of the dummy variables for specific ages associated with changes in Social Security benefits (62, 65, and 72) is statistically significant for women. Only the dummy variable indicating age 65 is significant for men, but its sign is negative twice (1940 and 1980) and positive once (1950). Its effects in 1940 and 1950 may reflect age misreporting (heaping on digits ending in 0 and 5).

In sum, the probability of entering the labor force among elderly men and women declines as their age increases, and there do not appear to be any particular ages at which this overall trend undergoes marked and consistent changes that can plausibly be attributed to age-specific entitlements to nonwage income. A final change that is perhaps worth noting is changes over time in the intercept, which declines over this period for men but not for women. This indicates, ceteris paribus, a declining probability of entering the labor force for 55-year-old men and rather little variation for women. The latter is, of course, what the results in Figure 2.5 suggested.

CONCLUSION

Much attention has been given to the declining labor force participation of aged American men in recent years. Our research has largely confirmed this picture for the period 1940–1980; however, we have also pointed out that the labor force participation of aged American women has risen over this same period, except for slight downturns for women in their sixties in 1980. It therefore cannot be claimed simply that all elderly Americans are working less than in the past. Another view of the same data is that labor force activity of aged Americans is becoming increasingly similar for men and women. This is especially apparent for those aged 65 and older.

Related to this, we noted that the effects of marital status on labor force behavior, which are opposite for men and women, have decreased steadily over this period. We think that this trend reflects declines over time in an elderly couple's dependence on the husband's earnings. This decline is, of course, only partly due to increased earnings of wives; growth in nonwage income is surely another important factor.

The major source of nonwage income of aged Americans is public transfers, especially Social Security benefits to retired workers and to their dependents and survivors. Our review of the expansion of public transfers indicated that Social Security became an important source of income to the elderly between 1950 and 1960. Private pensions also grew substantially during this same period. We hypothesized—and our results corroborated—that the age-specific entitlements to Social Security benefits (and perhaps also to some private pensions) affect labor force departure of aged workers and, to a much lesser extent, labor force entry of those not working.

In 1940 and 1950, before Social Security benefits were large enough and widespread enough to affect most of the elderly, labor force withdrawal became increasingly likely as workers got older, but the likelihood of leaving the labor force increased only gradually with age. In contrast, from 1960 onward there have been large jumps in labor force withdrawals at the ages associated with entitlements to Social Security benefits. Moreover, these are not just one-year jumps, but upward shifts in the likelihood of leaving the labor force as a worker ages. These statements apply to women as well as men; however, the impacts appear to be larger for men, perhaps because the timing of labor force withdrawal for married women depends partly on their husbands' age. It is also worth noting that for men, the impacts of these age-related entitlements seem to have increased between 1960 and 1980.

Not all elderly Americans leave the labor force before their 70th birthday. We found that for those still working at ages 72 and over, getting still older had relatively little impact on the likelihood that they would leave the labor force. The removal of the earnings test on Social Security benefits, which is thought to be a work incentive, seems to have had little effect either on labor force departure of those still working or on labor force entry of those not working. Work by the very old may be due to nonfinancial factors (for example, actually liking to work or at least being strongly committed to work) or to wanting more income than nonwage income can supply. For some, the latter means having much higher earnings than Social Security and pensions would provide; for others, it means having little nonwage income but high needs for cash.

We also found evidence that several other attributes of the elderly are associated with working more. Labor force departure is more likely for those lacking a high school degree and less likely for those who attended college. The opposite pattern tends to hold for labor force entrance. Foreign-born men and women are also less likely to leave the labor force and, except for women in the early decades of the period, more likely to enter it. In contrast, men and women born in the South tend to leave the labor force sooner. Finally, although differences between whites and nonwhites tend to be surprisingly small, the differences that do exist mainly indicate greater work efforts by nonwhites than by whites. Lower nonwage income of non-whites is a plausible explanation.

Some people are likely to view the trends we found for 1940–1980 positively, believing that elderly Americans now have the opportunity to rest from their labors after years of work. Others are likely to view them nega-tively, believing that elderly Americans should keep on working as they did in the past. We do not want to take sides in this debate. If one takes the latter view, however, our research shows the importance of age-specific entitle-ments to nonwage income. It also shows that elderly Americans over age 65 who have been out of work for at least a year are unlikely to enter the labor force. To encourage elderly Americans to work, they need to be discouraged from leaving the labor force in the first place.

Appendix

We analyze data from the 1940, 1950, 1960, 1970, and 1980 PUMS, which are based on responses of samples of the U.S. population to questions asked during the decennial censuses. The sampling fractions were 0.0098 in 1940, 0.00303 in 1950, and 0.010 in 1960–1980. The number of individuals aged 55 and over in these samples is 192,812 in 1940, 78,095 in 1950, 318,611 in 1960, 389,470 in 1970, and 474,503 in 1980. Of those aged 55 and over, the percentage over age 80 ranges from about 5 percent in 1940 to nearly 10 percent in 1980.

Although these data have the advantage of large samples covering a relatively long period, they are not completely comparable over time, be-cause the USBC has altered its questions and procedures over the years. One major change occurred in 1960 when the decennial census began to be collected through self-enumeration rather than through a personal inter-view. This change was especially consequential for some items. For example, a person's race was assigned by the interviewer in 1940 and 1950 but was chosen by the respondent in 1960–1980. In addition to this general change, there have been a variety of changes pertaining to specific variables used in our analyses.

Age

Age misreporting is a problem in each of the censuses, but it is a greater problem in 1940 and 1950 than in the other years. In 1940 and 1950, heaping on ages ending in 0 and 5, and to a lesser extent those ending in 2 and 8, is apparent. The heaping occurs because the question used to elicit age asked individuals to report their age in complete years (USBC 1943, 1953). Beginning in 1960, individuals were asked to report their month and year of birth, and age was then computed from this information (USBC 1964). This new procedure greatly reduced the amount of heaping; however, some heaping of ages ending in 4 and 9 still occurs due to a tendency of people to overreport birth years ending in 0 or 5. The extent of heaping seems to have declined considerably since 1960 (USBC 1973, 1983). Indeed, in Figure 2.1 heaping is scarcely apparent for 1960–1980 (except for a peak at age 59 in 1960), but it is quite evident in 1940 and 1950.

Another problem is more extensive misreporting of older ages than of younger ages. Reporting of ages 85 and over is generally suspect in the decennial censuses (Shryock and Siegel 1976); however, this problem probably has little effect on our analyses since our analyses concentrate on those aged 55–80. Of more relevance to our analyses is overreporting of ages 65–74 and underreporting of ages 55–64, which is thought to have occurred especially in 1940 and to a lesser extent in 1950. (The USBC believes that this resulted from the 1935 Social Security Act.) When the USBC compared the age distributions in 1930 and 1940, taking into consideration age-specific mortality rates in the 1930–1940 period, it concluded that there had been a net overcount of those aged 65–74 and a net undercount of those aged 55–64 in the 1940 census (USBC 1943). This phenomenon recurred in 1950 and 1960, but by 1960 the USBC concluded that it was probably not due to systematic and deliberate misreporting of age as 65 or over. Still, some fraction of those claiming to be over 65 were probably under 65, especially in 1940 and 1950. This could mean that the labor force activity of those over 65 in 1940 and 1950 is overstated since some fraction of these individuals were probably under 65 and younger individuals are more likely to be in the labor force.

Race

We compare whites and nonwhites in our study. "Whites" are individuals identified by census enumerators as white in 1940 and 1950 and self-identified as white in 1960–1980. Nonwhites include blacks, Native Americans, and Asians. Hispanics may be of any race. Individuals who were of mixed race and who were unsure of their race were assigned to the race of their nonwhite parent in 1940–1960, the race of their father in 1970, and the race of their mother in 1980.

A potentially more serious problem concerns changes in the treatment of the race of Hispanics in 1980. Prior to 1980, most Hispanics were classified as white. For example, 93 percent of Hispanics were classified as white in 1970. Due to changes in enumeration procedures, only 58 percent of Hispanics were classified as white in 1980 (USBC 1983). Hence, white and nonwhite categories in 1980 are not completely comparable to the same categories in earlier years. We do not think that this jeopardizes our analyses since in every year most nonwhites are black. For example, roughly 70 percent of nonwhites in 1980 were black, and approximately 89 percent of the nonwhites in 1970 were black. The percentage of nonwhites who were black is even higher in previous years. The percentage of Asian and Hispanic nonwhites increased over the 1940–1980 period due to the high level of immigration of Asians and Hispanics, especially after the 1965 Immigration Act.

Labor Force Characteristics

Our analyses of labor force activity are based on two variables: weeks worked during the year before the census, and labor force status during a referent week during the census year. The reporting of both variables has changed over time. Durand (1968) has discussed the changes that occurred between 1940 and 1960; the changes are also discussed in the published reports on each decennial census. The USBC claims that the quality of measurement of these variables has improved substantially over time.

In 1940 enumerators were instructed to convert weeks of part-time work into full-time equivalents. Beginning in 1950, no distinctions between full-time and part-time work were made. Beginning in 1960, individuals were asked if they had worked at all during the preceding year before they were asked to report weeks of work. Consequently, the weeks worked variables are strictly comparable for 1960–1980, but only approximately for 1940 and 1950. These differences probably have a comparatively small effect on our analyses because we mainly distinguish between those who did not work at all and those who worked some, and only to a lesser extent between those who worked a full year (48 years or more) and those who worked a part year (1–47 weeks).

Labor force status was based on activity during March 24–30 for all respondents in 1940. In 1950 the referent week was the week preceding completion of the census form; this week varied across people. In 1960 no particular time period was specified as the referent. In 1970 and 1980, the reference period was the four weeks preceding the time of completing the census form. Moreover, beginning in 1970, individuals had to indicate that they were currently available for work in order to be considered unemployed.

The changes described above were made to improve the quality of labor force data. Most of the improvements occurred between 1950 and 1960 as a result of the development of the Current Population Survey (CPS). When estimates of labor force indicators based on the 1950 census were compared with those based on the 1950 CPS, substantial discrepancies were discovered. As a result of these discrepancies, the USBC eliminated a question concerning a person's main activity ("What was this person doing most of last week: working, at home, or in school?"). It was suspected that enumerators might not have asked a person's labor force status if the main activity was "at home" or "in school." Due to these and other unspecified "improvements," the discrepancies between census and CPS estimates were much smaller in 1960 than in 1950. For example, the census undercount of those in the civilian labor force (using the CPS as the standard) was 5 percent in 1950 but only 2 percent in 1960. The census undercount of the unemployed fell from 19 percent in 1950 to 4 percent in 1960. And, the census undercount of those who worked in the previous year went from 10 percent for 1949 to 1 percent in 1959. Thus, it is important to keep in mind that labor force participation is underestimated to a greater extent in the 1940 and 1950 censuses than in the later censuses.

Other Variables

The other major variables used in our analyses are education, gender, marital status, and place of birth. Fortunately, there are no comparability problems with these variables, except that categories of education were finer in some years than in others. However, in our analyses we distinguish between less than twelve years of schooling, exactly twelve years, and more than twelve years, and these distinctions occurred in all five censuses. We also use much cruder categories for marital status and place of birth than the USBC collected. In the case of the former, we distinguish between currently married and not currently married (which includes those divorced, widowed, and never married). In the case of the latter, we distinguish those born outside the United States and those born in the South from other native-born Americans.

DISCUSSION

Olivia S. Mitchell

Researchers in many of the social sciences have decried the budget cutbacks recently sustained by data-gathering agencies around the nation. Indeed, many invaluable time series that were once produced by the federal government have now been discontinued, probably forever. Along these lines, it is unfortunate that the Longitudinal Retirement History Survey is no longer being fielded, as it is a data set of significant interest to most researchers at conferences such as this.

Although it is more difficult to look at ourselves currently and probably in the future as well, it does seem that looking into our past is now easier— or at least more informative. One of the potentially most exciting developments for social scientists who use individual and household data is the computerization of all the U.S. decennial censuses between 1940 and 1980. In previous years, researchers seeking explanations for behavioral patterns and trends were forced to limit their focus to single cross-sectional surveys, or occasionally they followed a handful of respondents for a decade or so at most. When I was in graduate school, even the best of the number crunchers could pull data from only three sets of census tapes. Hence, the advent of five censuses in computer-readable format offers a host of new opportunities for social scientists interested in longer-term behavioral patterns.

It is informative to review what these new opportunities are, and what potential pitfalls may await us when dealing with five decades of census data, before turning to a closer examination of Nancy Brandon Tuma and Gary Sandefur's contribution. First let me list the opportunities.

    1. The vastness of the census samples offers researchers the opportunity to focus on statistically rare demographic groups that cannot otherwise be studied with smaller surveys. For instance, only census

data sets are large enough to permit statistically powerful tests of hypotheses about specific age, sex, and ethnic groups' behavior.

2. Because of the long time period covered, it will be possible to trace long-term changes in some interesting variables. For example, to the extent that census questions are comparable over time, it will now be possible to identify more clearly where our parents and grandparents worked, where they lived, and what they earned.

3. Also because of the long time period covered, those researchers interested in causal analysis may be better able to examine how changes in the social and economic environment alter behavior. As an example, it would be useful to know how much labor supply over time has responded to the availability and amount of income transfers such as Social Security payments.

4. The long time period in the census also offers an opportunity to tease out sources of differences in behavior. This is especially important for those who wish to explain why behavior varies both within and across cohorts. Explanations for the upward trend in women's work and the downward trend in men's labor force attachment fall into this category.

These points give a flavor of the opportunities now available for research with the new census data sets. It is also useful to point out some of the pitfalls:

1. The dangers of working with five different censuses should not be downplayed. Variables are frequently defined differently, questions change through time, and answers to identical questions will also change across years. For instance, missing data on income was said to be more problematic in the 1980 census than in previous years, and the systematic nonreporting evidently imparts bias to income and earnings data across years.

2. Statistical tests become questionable when several hundred thousand observations are used in analysis.

3. Some of the variables that we as researchers tend to think we cannot live without are not available on the census files, or they are not directly comparable with similar variables from panel data sets. For instance, the censuses typically contain little in the way of event histories regarding education, marriage and fertility, labor market experience, and work patterns.

4. There are limits on the complexity of cohort analysis given only five observations per cohort through time (one for each census).

Having spelled out a few of the opportunities and pitfalls of the new census data sets, let me now comment directly on the paper by Tuma and Sandefur. The authors' objective is to identify patterns of labor force activity among the population aged 55–80, for the period 1940–1980. The paper begins with a general discussion of this group's work-force attachment and offers several descriptive hypotheses regarding anticipated patterns in the data. Next, the authors provide graphical summaries of time trends in labor force activity by age and sex. Finally, multivariate Logit models are estimated using the underlying micro data segregated by sex and year.

The object of the Logit models is to identify correlates of changing labor force status. Two dependent variables are used, one of which is associated with retirement and is measured by finding people who worked in the year prior to the census but were not in the labor force during the week prior to the survey. The second dependent variable is an "unretirement" variable, measuring movement between nonemployment in the previous year and employment in the previous week. The authors' use of these retrospective labor market attachment questions in the census is certainly original and is to be applauded. Unfortunately, it is not clear whether and how this particular definition of retirement is comparable with those examined previously by researchers using cross-sectional and panel data sets.

The authors have evidently devoted a great deal of effort to developing and understanding this new census data. Their tables and figures are particularly instructive in this regard, indicating careful attention to problems of changing variable definitions and measurement over time. Along these lines, it might have been interesting to explore further whether individual variables had different behavioral impacts through time as their definitions and measurements changed. (The authors test and reject the hypothesis that the entire vector of coefficients remained unchanged through the period, but they do not examine whether individual coefficients or subsets thereof were stable. It is recognized that statistical tests are questionable when several hundred thousand observations are used in analysis.)

As noted above, this data set offers the unique opportunity to find out how much labor supply has responded to the availability and amount of Social Security (and pension) payments over time. The authors take on the task by entering into the Logit models a complicated set of age dummy variables, age splines, and a continuous age term, arguing that these represent Social Security entitlement effects and benefit amounts. (No pension variables are used in the analysis.) The authors note that results for the age variables are often "as hypothesized": for example, 62-year-old men were more likely to leave the labor force in 1970 and 1980, when they were eligible for Social Security, than in previous years. Nevertheless, the results are just as often contradictory. For example, age 62 was also significant for men in 1960, when they were not eligible for early retirement benefits. Also puzzling is the age 65 dummy for men in 1950, which is statistically significant but should not be, according to the authors' predictions, since Social Security benefits were not yet being paid. It is probably premature to concur with the authors' conclusion that "the Social Security program . . . rules pertaining to the age of entitlements had substantial impact on the probability that aged men and women departed from the labor force."

In overview, Tuma and Sandefur's research drawn from the new census data offers a host of interesting insights for analysts of older Americans' labor market behavior. Their paper also points to many new research questions that other users of this data must confront. Future efforts to look into our past will undoubtedly benefit from their pathfinding work.

NOTES

1. Based on the 1980 census (U.S. Bureau of the Census [USBC], 1983), the total U.S. population increased by 71 percent between 1940 and 1980; however, the population aged 55 and over grew by 141 percent, and the population aged 85 and over increased by 450 percent. Naturally, this implies that the elderly were an increasing fraction of the total U.S. population. The percentage of Americans who are aged 55 and over rose from 14.9 percent in 1940 to 20.9 percent in 1980.

2. Although many of these investigations have been based on analyses of cross-sectional data, there have also been several longitudinal studies of the economic behavior of aged individuals. The 1982 Social Security New Beneficiary Survey and the 1969–1979 Retirement History Survey are two of the better known longitudinal surveys used for this purpose. Previous research using the New Beneficiary Survey to study retirement include Iams (1986) and Maxfield and Reno (1985). Among recent research based on the Retirement History Survey are studies by Fox (1984) and Hausman and Wise (1985).

3. When this research was nearly complete, we found an unpublished Ph.D. thesis by Ross (1986), who also analyzed the labor force activity of aged Americans using data from the 1940–1980 Public Use Microdata Samples (PUMS). Ross's study differed from ours in several ways. Most important, she focused on changes over time in the LFP rate and in weeks worked but did not examine transitions into and out of the labor force, as we have done. She also investigated only men and used age groups rather than single years of age.

4. Information on median earnings of male workers and on average benefits of retired men comes from tables 23 and 37, respectively, in USDHHS (1986).

5. For an excellent summary of changes in Social Security rules, see USDHHS (1986, 2–23).

6. Parsons (1980) has suggested that disability benefits are important in explaining the downward trend in LFP rates of young aged men. Danziger, Haveman, and Plotnick (1981) and Haveman and Wolfe (1982) have argued that their impact is less than suggested by Parsons.

7. At the outset, we also tested whether data on men and women could be pooled in a given year, allowing only for an intercept shift due to gender. This model was also rejected at a low probability level. Given the visible differences between men and women in Figure 2.2–2.5, we did not really expect a model with common effects for men and women to fit acceptably. Consequently, we decided to focus on separate analyses of the data on men and women.

8. Undoubtedly entitlements to private pensions as well as to Social Security affect retirement decisions of the elderly. Entitlements to private pensions are sometimes based on length of service (which leads to high variability in the age of entitlement) and sometimes on the worker's age. The latter type of pensions often follow

the Social Security program in setting the age at which entitlements begin. Since we have no data on which individuals are covered by private pensions, we cannot assess the extent to which the age-specific patterns discussed below are due to private pensions rather than to Social Security.

9. The linear spline for age X was constructed by subtracting X from exact age and setting the result to zero if it was negative.

10. Likelihood ratio test statistics for the deletion of the three age splines and three age dummies, which have a chi-square distribution with six degrees of freedom under the null hypothesis that these six variables have no effect, are as follows: 39.1 (men, 1940); 60.0 (men, 1950); 1562.8 (men, 1960); 1489.6 (men, 1970); 1735.9 (men, 1980); 25.9 (women, 1940); 4.2 (women, 1950); 132.5 (women, 1960); 235.8 (women, 1970); and 322.85 (women, 1980). Although all of these values are statistically significant at the .05 level except that for women in 1950, the values for 1960–1980 are strikingly larger than those for 1940–1950.

11. Likelihood ratio test statistics for the deletion of the three age splines and three age dummies, which have a chi-square distribution with six degrees of freedom under the null hypothesis that these six variables have no effect, are as follows: 32.0 (men, 1940); 8.9 (men, 1950); 34.4 (men, 1960); 45.5 (men, 1970); 91.8 (men, 1980); 10.4 (women, 1940); 8.0 (women, 1950); 13.0 (women, 1960); 30.0 (women, 1970); and 34.6 (women, 1980). These values are statistically significant at the .05 level, except for women in 1940 and 1950 and men in 1950. But even the significant values are much smaller than in the case of the models of leaving the labor force (see Note 10). This suggests that the age splines and age dummies help to explain labor force entry of the elderly much less than labor force departure.

REFERENCES

Danziger, Sheldon, Robert H. Haveman, and Robert Plotnick. 1981. "How Income Transfer Programs Affect Work, Savings, and the Income Distribution: A Critical Review." *Journal of Economic Literature* 19: 975–1028.

Duggan, James E. 1984. "The Labor Force Participation of Older Workers." *Industrial and Labor Relations Review* 37:415–30.

Durand, John D. 1968. *The Labor Force in the United States, 1890–1960.* New York: Gordon and Breach Science Publishers.

Ellwood, David T. 1985. "Pensions and the Labor Market: A Starting Point (The Mouse Can Roar)." In David A. Wise, ed., *Pensions, Labor and Individual Choice.* Chicago: University of Chicago Press.

Fields, Gary S., and Olivia S. Mitchell. 1981. "Economic Determinants of the Optimal Retirement Age." *Journal of Human Resources* 19:245–62.

Fox, Alan. 1984. "Income Changes at and after Social Security Benefit Receipt: Evidence from the Retirement History Study." *Social Security Bulletin* 47:3–23.

Gustman, Alan C., and Thomas L. Steinmeier. 1984. "Partial Retirement and the Analysis of Retirement Behavior." *Industrial and Labor Relations Review* 37:403–15.

Hausman, Jerry A., and David A. Wise. 1985. "Social Security, Health Status, and Retirement." In David A. Wise, ed., *Pensions, Labor and Individual Choice.* Chicago: University of Chicago Press.

Haveman, Robert H., and Barbara Wolfe. 1982. "Disability Transfers and the Work Effort Response of Older Males: A Reconciliation." Cambridge, Mass.: National Bureau of Economic Research.

Hurd, Michael, and John B. Shoven. 1982. "Real Income and Wealth of the Elderly." *American Economic Review* 72:314–18.

Iams, Howard M. 1986. "Employment of Retired-Worker Women." *Social Security Bulletin* 49:5–13.

Ippolito, Richard A. 1986. *Pensions, Economics, and Public Policy.* Homewood, Ill.: Dow Jones-Irwin.

Maxfield, Linda D., and Virginia P. Reno. 1985. "Distribution of Income Sources of Recent Retirees: Findings from the New Beneficiary Survey." *Social Security Bulletin* 48:7–13.

Nalebuff, Barry, and Richard J. Zeckhauser. 1985. "Pensions and the Retirement Decision." In David A. Wise, ed., *Pensions, Labor and Individual Choice.* Chicago: University of Chicago Press.

Parsons, Donald O. 1980. "The Decline in Male Labor Participation." *Journal of Political Economy* 88:117–34.

Ransom, Roger L., and Richard Sutch. 1986. "The Labor of Older Americans: Retirement of Men on and off the Job, 1870–1937." *Journal of Economic History* 46:1–30.

Root, Lawrence S., and John E. Tropman. 1984. "Income Sources of the Elderly." *Social Service Review* 58:384–403.

Ross, Christine M. 1986. "The Change in the Labor Supply and Well-being of the Elderly, 1940–1980." Ph.D. dissertation, Department of Economics, University of Wisconsin at Madison.

Sandefur, Gary D., and Nancy Brandon Tuma. 1987. "Social and Economic Trends Among the Aged in the United States, 1940–1985." Working Paper no. 849-87, Institute for Research on Poverty, University of Wisconsin at Madison.

Shryock, Henry S., Jacob S. Siegel, and associates. 1976. *The Methods and Materials of Demography.* Condensed edition by Edward G. Stockwell. New York: Academic Press.

Smith, James P., and Finus R. Welch. 1986. *Closing the Gap: Forty Years of Economic Progress for Blacks.* Santa Monica, Calif.: Rand Corporation.

U.S. Bureau of the Census. 1943. *Census of Population: 1940.* Vol. 4, "Characteristics by Age." Pt. 1, "U.S. Summary." Washington, D.C.: GPO.

———. 1953. *Census of Population: 1950.* Vol. 2, "Characteristics of the Population." Pt. 1, "U.S. Summary." Washington, D.C.: GPO.

————. 1964. *Census of Population: 1960.* Vol. 1, "Characteristics of the Population." Pt. 1, "U.S. Summary." Washington, D.C.: GPO.

————. 1973. *Census of Population: 1970.* Vol. 1, "Characteristics of the Population." Pt. 1, "U.S. Summary," sec. 2. Washington, D.C.: GPO.

————. 1983. *Census of the Population: 1980.* Vol. 1, "Characteristics of the Population." Pt. 1, "U.S. Summary," PC 80-1-B1. Chap. C1, "General Social and Economic Characteristics, U.S. Summary," PC 80-1-C1. Washington, D.C.: GPO.

U.S. Department of Health and Human Services. 1986. *Social Security Bulletin, Annual Statistical Supplement, 1986.* Washington, D.C.: GPO.

3

WOMEN: RETIREES AND WIDOWS

Rita Ricardo-Campbell

This is an initial exploratory paper concerned with women's retirement decisions and the financial status of older women. The familiar economic modeling of retirement decisions—involving such issues as value of time (whether in the labor force or the home), value of assets, anticipated income streams after retirement, and health—is the same for women as for men. However, women may have different preferences and work histories than men. Sociologists deal with preferences, whereas economists deal with harder data. Such data about women's retirement are sparse. Data on the financial status of older women are changing rapidly.

Despite the large increase in the labor force by women, there are few studies and little data about currently working women's plans for retirement. This is understandable since the surge of women aged sixteen and over entering the labor force has been fairly recent: from about 32 percent in 1950 to 55 percent in 1985. In 1986, women made up 44 percent of the total U.S. labor force. Although of this number many work part-time, it is still true that 34 million women aged twenty and over are working full time (U.S. Bureau of the Census 1985, 395) and others work year-round at part-time jobs.

Among middle-aged women, 40 years and older, the increase in labor force participation has been extraordinary. These are the women who will start retiring 15–20 years from now. Will their decisions on when to retire be made on the same basis as men's? Will their decisions on when to retire be similar to such decisions being made by older women today who, on the average, have been in the work force far fewer years than women who are 40–50 years of age today?

The existing economic and sociological literature has limitations. For example, in an article on "Joint Retirement in the Dual Worker Family," all employees of "private business" are omitted (O'Rand and Henretta 1983, 511). In paring down further the broad Longitudinal Retirement History Survey data, the authors include for their analysis only those couples where the man stayed married to the same woman from 1969 to 1975 and in which husband and wife each worked in the survey years 1969, 1971, 1973, and 1975. Also omitted are nonwhites. Further, 15 percent of the final 1,868 cases were dropped because husbands and wives were *both* still working, that is, not retired. Thus the study covers only government workers, the self-employed, and (strangely) unpaid workers in a family business. Government workers have an exceedingly favorable pension system that encourages early retirement: an indexed-to-cost-of-living full pension at age 55 after 30 years of service. Do women employees in private industry differ from government women workers in their retirement decisions? Do women employed in for-profit business differ from those in nonprofit employment in their retirement decisions? What are the variables that induced 15 percent of O'Rand and Henretta's sample to work while the remaining 85 percent decided to retire?

Another study using national data reports that in 1982, working women aged 45–59, the majority of whom were nonwhite, were planning to retire as follows: 22 percent before age 62; 20 percent at age 62; 1 percent at ages 63–64; 20 percent at age 65; and 11 percent at 66 and over or "never." Twenty-seven percent said that they did not know when they would retire.

White women in the study intended to retire somewhat later: 12 percent before age 62; 20 percent at age 62; less than 1 percent at ages 63–64; and 24 percent at age 65. Fifteen percent would retire past age 65 or "never"; and 29 percent did not know when they would retire (Shaw 1986, 123). Among the older white women, the intrinsic interest of their jobs was an important factor in delaying retirement. The most important predictor for retirement before age 62 for all subgroups of women—married and unmarried, white and nonwhite—was eligibility for a pension.

Table 3.1 summarizes the sources of income for women aged 65 and over in 1984.

In an attempt to find out something more about retirement decisions by women in private industry, a pilot study was initiated. The Hewlett-Packard (H-P) company supplied demographic data for 5,014 of their women employees aged 40–50 in 1986. Similar data was supplied for 903 of their recent (last ten years) women retirees.

TABLE 3.1 _____

TYPE OF INCOME FOR WOMEN AGED 65 AND OVER, 1984

Type of income	Women Aged 65 and over with income (percentages)	Median (in dollars)	Mean (in dollars)
Total money income		6,020	8,800
Wage or salary income	9.4	10,640	13,082
Property income, total[a]	67.5	7,698	10,724
Social Security or railroad retirement income	93.4	6,072	8,769
Retirement income, total[b]	20.8	10,601	13,739
Private pensions or annuities only	11.3	9,344	12,319
Federal employee pensions only	2.5	13,353	15,846
State or local employee pensions only	5.6	11,869	14,441
Combinations of income types:			
Earnings	10.6	10,458	13,713
Earnings and property income	8.1	11,855	15,288

SOURCE: U.S. Bureau of the Census (1986a).

NOTE: Excludes approximately 220,000 women who receive no income (1.4 percent of sample of women aged 65 and over).

a. Includes interest, dividends, net rent, and estates or trusts.

b. Includes private pensions, annuities, military retirement pensions, and federal, state, and local pensions.

An advertisement in H-P's employee and retiree newsletters in 1986 asked for "volunteers . . . to answer a brief questionnaire" with assurances of confidentiality. The questionnaire was mailed to self-selected respondents of women workers aged 40–50 at H-P and aged 40–55 at the Hoover Institution, asking them about their demographic and economic status, employment history, and anticipated age at retirement. Additionally asked were the number of hours a week worked on the job, broad occupation classifications, and some attitude questions about retirement.

The pilot questionnaire was answered by only 30 currently working women: sixteen divorced or separated, eleven married, and three never married or widowed. This self-selected sample of workers had a disproportionate percentage (62 percent) of college graduates, including 38 percent with graduate degrees. As would be expected, a high proportion (two-thirds) are in professional, technical, managerial, or administrative positions. By age 22, 80 percent had been in paid employment; by age 25, 90 percent. Only 40 percent had no years out of the work force. One-fourth had never worked part-time. The median number of years of their employment is 21.

The most frequent age of intended retirement of the 30 currently working is 65, but this age is heavily weighted by the nonprofit, Hoover employees. One-fourth of the combined group stated that they do not intend to retire; one-third stated that they might retire to pursue other careers; and one woman intends to retire at age 70. Of the combined 30 women respondents, 58.6 percent would prefer part-time work. Two of the 30 have part-time jobs. Forty percent report working more than 40 hours per week.

Seventeen percent of all respondents did not report salary; the same percentage earned $3,000–$4,000 monthly, and 13 percent earned more than $4,000. Just over one-fourth are vested in pension plans other than their current employer's.

Over 75 percent disagree with the statement that "people who do not retire when they are financially able to are foolish," and 80 percent disagree that "older workers should retire early." Although 63 percent think more of people who work, only 31 percent agree that "work is the most meaningful part of life."

In order to compare the intended age of retirement of current women workers with the actual retirement age of recent women retirees, the pilot study of the fifteen H-P, self-selected, women workers aged 40–50 is examined separately and then compared to the 900 already retired women employees of H-P. This is followed by a comparison of the demographic data of H-P's 5,000 active women workers with their already retired women workers.

Hewlett-Packard Pilot

Sixty percent of these employed women (N = 15) are divorced or separated and only 33 percent are married. Fifty-seven percent have college degrees and, of these, four women have graduate degrees. Sixty-seven percent are in professional/technical jobs, and 20 percent in managerial/administrative jobs. Thus, far fewer (13 percent) work in clerical/secretarial positions at H-P than in the nonprofit Hoover group (47 percent). The H-P pilot group had far fewer years out of the labor force than the Hoover pilot group: 67 percent of active women workers at H-P had no years out, as compared to only 13 percent at Hoover. Forty percent of H-P women employees had never worked part-time and 7 percent had worked part-time for five years or more. All the H-P worker respondents had worked full time for nine years or more; however, 47 percent would prefer part-time work (H-P offers flex-time but not part-time work). Fifty-three percent worked more than 40 hours a week. Their median number of years worked is twenty.

Fifty-seven percent of the H-P pilot group intend to retire by age 55 or younger; 86 percent by age 60; 93 percent by age 62; and all by age 65. However, two persons (13.3 percent) checked that they "never" intend to retire. Forty percent would take early retirement to pursue other careers.

Twenty-seven percent did not report salary; 20 percent earned $3,000–$4,000 monthly and 27 percent more than $4,000 monthly. This is a highly educated, well-paid group. Twenty percent are vested in pension plans other than H-P's.

H-P's pension plan provides for retirement at age 55 and fifteen years of service, with 10 percent of vesting at five years and 25 percent between five and six years; vesting gradually increases to 100 percent after twelve years. The new tax regulations will change this plan toward earlier vesting.

Sixty-six percent disagree with the statement that "people who do not retire when they are financially able to are foolish," and nearly 90 percent disagree that "older workers should retire when they can, so as to give younger people more of a chance on the job." Although 60 percent believe that "most people think more of someone who works than someone who does not work," only 27 percent agree that "work is the most meaningful part of life."

It is difficult to compare the retirees with currently active workers, because only three retirees asked for[1] and returned the questionnaire, and the demographic data supplied by H-P is limited.

H-P Pilot and H-P Recently Retired Women

Among the recently retired 903 women, the most common age of retirement was 62, when 15 percent retired. By that age, however, 47 percent had already retired: 7 percent at age 55, 9 percent at age 60, and lesser percentages until age 63, when 11 percent retired. Eight percent retired at age 64 and 10 percent at age 65. Eight percent worked beyond age 65.

In comparison, the most common age of intended retirement of active women workers (pilot sample, N = 15) at H-P is 55, when 29 percent intend to retire. Fifty-five is the median age of their intended retirement, as compared to age 62 for H-P retirees. By age 60, 86 percent of the H-P pilot currently employed women intend to retire, more than double the percentage (41 percent) of those who have actually retired by age 60 during the last 10 years.[2]

H-P also supplied demographic data on its 5,014 active women employees aged 40–50. Thirty-five percent were hired before age 35 and about 60 percent between ages 35 and 44. Among retired women, 15 percent were hired before age 35 and 60 percent at ages 35–44. Almost one-fourth were age 45 or older when hired. The overwhelming majority of currently working women at H-P work full time.

The female labor force of H-P is stable: 42 percent of the currently working women aged 40–50 have H-P seniority of 5–9 years; 23 percent have 10–14 years; and 10.7 percent have 15–19 years. Moreover, nearly 90 percent of these women had no break in their service at H-P and only 3 percent had taken a leave of seven months or more. Among recent retirees, 62 percent had twenty years or more of seniority, but only 72 percent had no break in service and nearly 13 percent had taken leaves of seven months or more. The comparative data give a picture of what is generally known about the two broad age cohorts: older women started to work later in life and were more likely to take time from paid work to bear and nurture children. Thus, older women may have retired later than younger women will, because even so their labor force participation as a percentage of their adult life is no higher.

A comparison of the work histories of the two H-P groups—current workers and recent retirees with fifteen years of service—shows clearly several differences that all point to the more favorable financial status of currently working women; the comparison also indicates that this more favorable financial status will continue after they, too, retire. Although 38 percent of H-P's current women employees earned under $20,000 in 1986, 40 percent earned $20,000–30,000; 13.4 percent earned $30,000–40,000; 8.6 percent $40,000–75,000; and 0.3 percent, or 15 women, earned $75,000–99,000. No H-P woman employee in 1986 earned more than $100,000.

In comparison, 53.4 percent of the retirees earned, during their last year of work, less than $20,000; 33.5 percent earned $20,000–30,000; 11 percent earned $30,000–40,000; and 2.1 percent, or nineteen women, earned $40,000–75,000. The higher salary levels of the currently working women reflect their higher average level of education attained. Although 84 percent have no college degree, 3 percent have an associate of arts degree and 13 percent graduated from four-year colleges. Of the latter, nearly 200 women have advanced degrees. In contrast, among the recently retired women 97 percent have no college degree and 3 percent have an associate of arts degree or graduated from college, including one woman with a master's degree.

From this pilot study it is a viable hypothesis that currently working women will retire at younger ages than have recently retired women. This is because working women today will have longer work histories and thus be influenced in making retirement decisions by the greater availability of higher pensions. In general, men have been retiring earlier because it has become economically feasible for society to support them as GNP per capita increased and the number of children per capita shrank. However, in recent years U.S. real per capita income has not been increasing. This, plus national policy to encourage later retirement, may restrain the growing tendency to retire ever earlier. The latter may be influenced by an increasing number of jobs having less intrinsic interest—that is, they are boring—than many people are willing to admit.

The shift from an agricultural to a manufacturing economy has encouraged early retirement. The current and future growth in importance of the service sector, especially in the computer and other informational industries, may eventually reverse this trend. Initially, the advent of computers probably hastened early retirement of some older individuals because they did not adjust. But among midlife workers these skills are now common. In 1980, women constituted 48 percent of the labor force in the computer industry and computer-related occupations (Strober and Arnold 1986, 148). The transitional phase to the computer age has required many older workers to retrain for new jobs at a higher technological level, resulting in some retiring earlier than planned. Although the transition is virtually complete, unforeseen technological demand shocks could occur later.

That women are proportionally overrepresented in the nonprofit and government sectors can, if averages across all industry are used, distort the perception of when currently working women in private industry intend to retire. It is probable that women are not unlike men in being "reasonably accurate in predicting their actual age of retirement over the next decade" (Burkhauser and Quinn 1985, 147). However, only 45 percent of men in that study retired within a year of their intended retirement age. For men who started their current job prior to age 50, 60 percent retired "on time" (ibid., 153). Although women in my sample are on the average probably more than one decade away from retiring, they are all at least 40 years old. By the year 2000, 49-year-olds today will be age 62.

It is probable that most workers are unaware that in 1990 an individual's Social Security benefits are scheduled gradually to increase beyond the current 3 percent for each year of retirement delayed after he or she reaches age 65. By 2000, the annual compounded gain for delaying receipt of a Social Security retirement benefit will be 6 percent, and by 2008, 8 percent for each year of work at age 65 and over.[3]

At 8 percent the lifetime return is higher, assuming current average life expectancies and plausible economic trends, than the foregone benefits. Because Social Security benefits are indexed to rises in the cost of living, inflation predictions are especially important.

It is unknown to what degree Social Security's financial incentive to continue to work at later ages will act to induce later-than-planned retirement. However, some effect is anticipated.

Women workers will be better off at retirement 15–20 years from now than earlier cohorts of working women because they will have earned more and worked for a greater number of years, which will entitle them to larger private pensions. Additionally, the 1986 change in the tax law requires 100 percent vesting in graded pension plans at seven years and in nongraded plans at five years. Moreover, the Employee Retirement Income Security Act (ERISA) does not generally allow plans to recognize leaves of less than one year to count as a "break in service." These regulations will help at retirement especially those women who have had a pattern of interruptions, such as for childbirth, during their worklives. It has been estimated that there will be a 10 percent increase in the number of women with vested pensions (Woods 1986b, 34). In addition, the growth in two-worker families—to over 60 percent of all families—has increased family private pension coverage. Women workers and their spouses become entitled to pensions in the same fashion as do men and their spouses. Two-worker families become two-pension families.

Although men have been increasingly retiring earlier, this is not true for women. Women aged 55–64 have increased their labor force participation rate from 27 percent in 1950 to slightly over 40 percent in 1965–1983. Although that rate has been fairly stable during the last twenty years, the percentage of women aged 65 and over who are working has fallen slightly, from about 10 to 8 percent. Older women, of 65 years or more, are increasingly working part-time: from 43 percent of those still working at age 65 and over in 1960, to 61 percent in 1984 (U.S. Department of Health and Human Services [USDHHS] 1986, 77, 79). Among all workers aged 25–64 who work at least half time —1,000 hours or more— 61 percent are covered by a pension plan (Woods 1986a, 23). Although overall private pension coverage has been dropping, from 61 to 56 percent (1979–1983), possibly as a result of higher costs imposed by new government regulations, the gap between women's and men's coverage has diminished and a greater percentage of those covered are vested. The growth in two-worker families lessens the effect of the slightly lesser individual coverage. Policy for portability of pensions, rather than new regulations increasing employer costs, has resurfaced.

Among men aged 65 and over there has been a continuous drop in labor force participation, from 32 percent in 1960 to less than 20 percent in 1984. However, their level of participation is still far higher than that of women of comparable ages (Figure 3.1).

Whereas retirement used to be considered a luxury, it is now accepted to be a normal phase of a man's life cycle: school, work, and then retirement. It is claimed that by 1980, the average man spent 20 percent of his average 69.3 years of life in retirement (USDHHS 1986, 71). But 20 percent of 70 years is 14, and this would imply that the common age of male retirement is 56 when in fact it is 62.

Many women, but not all, have experienced different life-cycle phases than men: school, work, bearing children and not working outside the home, then work again and, finally, retirement. Women have a longer life expectancy than men: at age 65, an additional 18.8 years of life compared to men's additional 14.4 years. Many women have already spent 20 percent of their longer lives at home bearing and nurturing children and not working for pay, and it may be that it is primarily these women who today are choosing to retire somewhat later than men do. For example, "a study of aerospace workers' attitudes toward retirement . . . finds the women particularly opposed to mandatory retirement on the grounds that having started work at ages forty or forty-five, they are not ready to retire as long as they feel themselves capable of working" (Campbell 1979, 258).[4]

FIGURE 3.1
LABOR FORCE PARTICIPATION RATES OF
OLDER MEN AND WOMEN, 1960–1985

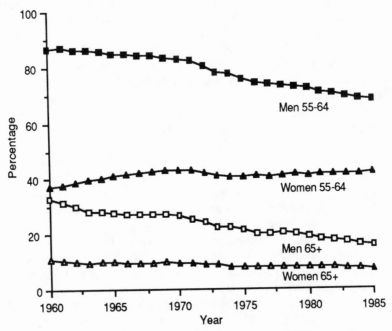

SOURCES: U.S. Department of Labor (1985); U.S. Census Bureau (1986).
NOTE: Civilian labor force participation rates.

In recent years younger working women have *not* been leaving the labor force to bear children but rather are choosing to stay in the labor force while bearing and nurturing children. Will these women choose to retire at increasingly younger ages as men have been doing? Will two-worker families increasingly make joint decisions to retire simultaneously, or will the usual age gap between spouses result in the husband retiring first and his younger wife retiring somewhat later? At least one research study found that the latter pattern was more common than the former; the younger wife continues to work after her husband retires (Haug 1985). A few comparative studies of the social and psychological characteristics of older men and women also lend support to this thesis (Atchley 1976, 204–11) of a "new family form of wife working and husband retired" (Haug 1985, 7).

Will women, because of their longer life expectancy and increasingly single status (widowed, divorced, or never married), continue to increase their total lifetime number of work years to levels closer to men's? Future higher levels of real earned incomes of women and the impending Social Security change that more substantially rewards work after age 65 could delay women's retirement age because of the higher opportunity cost of retiring. By 2009 entitlement to a full Social Security benefit will require reaching age 66, not 65. Corresponding reductions will be made in the percentages of the full benefit awarded as early retirement benefits at ages 62 through 65. Offsetting these inducements to continue working will be women's entitlements to higher private pensions, higher Social Security benefits, and generally improved financial status.

WIDOWS

Working women may become widows before or after retirement, and their anticipated financial status in the event of becoming a widow can affect their retirement decision. Therefore, I will say a few words separately about widows, a category that cuts across workers and nonworkers, full-time and part-time. Some policy analysts view widows as a category without past history. They emphasize the poverty that exists today among the low-income one-third of all widows. Widows today as a group are poorer than aged married women, of whom about 15 percent are poor. However, the future financial status of all older women including widows will be greatly increased over that of older women today.

Widows include two extremes of financial status: the very poor, usually women aged 80 and older, and the very well off, concentrated mostly among younger widows. New widows may suffer a substantial drop in their standard of living. Using 1969–1971 data, economists Auerbach and Kotlikoff found that "more than a third" of new widows in this period had a 25 percent drop in their standard of living, whereas only 2 percent of husbands "could expect to suffer a 25 percent drop in their standard of living if their wives died suddenly" (Burtless 1987, 18; see also Auerbach and Kotlikoff 1987, 229–67).

Among "unrelated females"—that is, those living alone who are age 65 and over—31 percent were in poverty in 1981 as compared to 63 percent in 1959 and 50 percent in 1970 (U.S. Bureau of the Census 1984, 120). This downward trend in poverty is likely to continue because of the increasing percentage of women who work and become entitled to pensions and Social Security benefits.

Most older women today do not have private pensions because they either did not work, worked part-time, or worked in industries where pensions were not common. By May 1983, 41 percent of full-time women workers in private employment were covered by pension plans and 44 percent of this group were entitled to benefits (Andrews 1985, 21). The assets of all funded pension plans, including insurance-managed plans, grew from $203 billion in 1973 to $863 billion in 1983 (ibid., 23) and are much higher in 1987.

The lack of past involvement in the work force does not, however, diminish the Social Security income of most widows, because that income derives from their husbands' work status. Widows—whether they have worked or never worked outside the home—may at age 60 receive a surviving spouse's Social Security benefit upon the death of their "entitled" spouse.[5] The level of benefit is reduced for ages prior to 65. The level of future surviving widows' benefits will be based largely on the higher earnings of their spouses from 1970 on, compared to the lower benefit level paid to many older widows today, whose benefits are based on the lesser earnings of their husbands during the 1950s and 1960s.

In addition, the 1984 Retirement Equity Act (P.L. 98–397) reversed the entitlement choice under private pensions that assumed that the retiring worker (who until recently has usually been male) preferred a higher pension while he was alive without a continuing survivor benefit above a smaller annuity continuing over the lifetime of the surviving spouse. Today, unless there is a written refusal of the continuing spouse's benefit by both husband and wife, the assumption of preference is for the annuity to be spread over the longer period of time to include the surviving spouse. Two-worker families can greatly increase family pension coverage.

Widows who have worked will have had higher lifetime earnings, which would enable many to accumulate some savings, such as IRAs, and also to receive a private pension in their own right. Widows who have never worked may be entirely dependent on their share of the family wealth and

Social Security benefits. The more fortunate widows may receive sizable life insurance benefits and valuable homes. Eighty percent of older individuals own their own homes, 75 percent free of mortgage. These large assets can be converted into annuities. Recent experiments with reverse annuity mort-gages make these assets liquid and enable some widows to live in their own homes while receiving an annuity. For example, six Massachusetts banks have a trial five-year "annuity" plan, based on home equity. The children as potential heirs are the primary objectors to such plans. Substantial private life insurance benefits can also increase the incomes of those widows who convert the lump sum to an annuity.

Recent research supports what the public has always believed: it is generally true that those who are poor over their working lifetime remain poor in their old age (see Boskin and Shoven 1986). Within the larger demographic picture, older women will—like older men—grow in numbers. As society's real income has increased, the elderly have been receiving a larger share, and older women have participated in this shift of resources. Although many factors will continue to improve older women's financial status, the increasing number of women aged 80 and over will weight the income data for widows to continue to show them to be disproportionately poorer than other segments of society.

DISCUSSION

John Shoven

This paper is best thought of as a pilot study or a research proposal. The most striking aspect of the paper is how little statistical information we have regarding women's retirement plans and even women's actual retirement circumstances. The government public-use tapes are both out of date and inadequate. The retirement history study began almost twenty years ago sampling people aged 54–64. In terms of the role of women in the work force, twenty years ago is a different era.

Rita Ricardo-Campbell tried to gather some information herself to learn about retirement plans of currently working women. She contrasts those plans with the actual retirement behavior of those who have retired in the last ten years.

The most discouraging (and perhaps revealing) fact about her study is the terrible response rate. As I understand it, Hewlett-Packard supplied some demographic information for 5,014 women employees between the ages of 40 and 50. However, Ricardo-Campbell only managed to come up with fifteen completed questionnaires in response to an advertisement in Hewlett-Packard's employee newspaper about the survey. I think it is impossible to reach any conclusions with a self-selected response by less than one-third of 1 percent of the sample. Presumably, those responding are quite nonrepresentative in their attitudes toward retirement.

The response at the Hoover Institution was better, but Hoover is quite an unrepresentative employer in the economy. Even with this better response, Ricardo-Campbell only has a combined 30 questionnaires to evaluate.

With such small samples, I think most people would have thrown in the towel. Ricardo-Campbell looks at the answers to the questionnaires to formulate some initial hypotheses about women's retirement, but all of her numerical evidence is subject to extremely large standard errors and selection biases. I doubt whether any of the results are statistically significant.

The findings, if verified by larger and more scientific samples, are interesting. It is important for such programs as Social Security to forecast when people will retire. Ricardo-Campbell's preliminary evidence tends to suggest that there will be a reversal, in that women may begin to retire at younger ages. Recently, the labor force participation of older women has been on the increase, so if her results stand up, they forecast a major shift in behavior.

My main conclusion from the paper is that we need more data to address important issues such as this. I also think that government participation and sponsorship is probably necessary to the data-gathering question. What is needed is a new Retirement History Survey—a panel data set assembled over the next ten to twenty years. Although this would be costly, the effort would almost certainly have a high social payoff.

NOTES

1. H-P printed in part the following in their December 1986 issue of *For Your Health*, a newsletter for retirees participating in H-P's health plan. "Dr. Rita Ricardo-Campbell, a Senior Fellow and health economist at Stanford University, is seeking women volunteers who retired from Hewlett-Packard within the last ten years to answer a brief questionnaire regarding retirement."

2. The nonprofit employee data, however, does not show this strong contrast, with age 65 being the most common (57 percent) intended age of retirement. Self-selection by women into nonprofit and government jobs with lesser daily intensity of work than in for-profit jobs may increase statistically the average intended retirement age. Existing pension plans in large companies, such as the one used here, are also usually more favorable than the pension plans for the nonteaching staff of nonprofit educational institutions. Also, the salaries in for-profit industry are often higher for comparable jobs and ability than in nonprofit industry and government jobs.

3. The schedule of the phase-in is in part: 1990–91, 3.5 percent; 1992–93, 4 percent; 1996–97, 5 percent; 2000–2001, 6 percent; 2004–5, 7 percent; and 2008 and later, 8 percent. From U.S. Department of Health and Human Services (1984, 101).

4. Shirley Campbell is referring to Kasschau (1976).

5. An individual may receive only one Social Security benefit: his or her own earned benefit or a derivative spousal benefit. The latter is half the worker's benefit, but upon the death of the worker it is equal to the worker's benefit. Because men on the average earn more than women, the widow's 100 percent spousal benefit is usually higher than her earned benefit.

REFERENCES

Andrews, Emily S. 1985. *The Changing Profile of Pensions in America*. Washington, D.C.: Employee Benefit Research Institute.

Atchley, Robert C. 1976. "Selected Social and Psychological Differences Between Men and Women in Later Life." *Journal of Gerontology* 31: 204–11.

Auerbach, Alan, and Laurence Kotlikoff. 1987. "Life Insurance of the Elderly: Its Adequacy and Determinant." In Gary Burtless, ed., *Work, Health, and Income Among the Elderly*. Washington, D.C.: Brookings Institution.

Boskin, Michael J., and John B. Shoven. 1986. "Poverty Among the Elderly: Where Are the Holes in the Safety Net?" NBER Working Paper no. 1923. Cambridge, Mass.: National Bureau of Economic Research.

Burkhauser, Richard V., and Joseph P. Quinn. 1985. "Planned and Actual Retirement: An Empirical Analysis." In Zena Smith Blau, ed., *Current Perspectives on Aging and the Life Cycle*, vol. 1. Greenwich, Conn.: Jai Press.

Burtless, Gary. 1987. "Introduction and Summary." In Gary Burtless, ed., *Work, Health, and Income Among the Elderly*. Washington, D.C.: Brookings Institution.

Campbell, Shirley. 1979. "Delayed Mandatory Retirement and the Working Woman." *Gerontologist* 19: 257–63.

Haug, Marie R. 1985. "Husband's Retirement Status and Wife's Labor Force Participation." Paper presented at the eightieth annual conference of the American Sociological Association, Washington, D.C.

Kasschau, P. L. 1976. "Perceived Age Discrimination in a Sample of Aerospace Employees." *Gerontologist* 18:166–73.

O'Rand, Angela M., and John C. Henretta. 1983. "Joint Retirement in the Dual Worker Family." *Social Forces* 62: 504–20.

Shaw, Lois B. 1986. "Looking Toward Retirement: Plans and Prospects." In Lois B. Shaw, ed., *Midlife Women at Work: A Fifteen Year Perspective*. Lexington, Mass.: Lexington Books.

Strober, Myra H., and Carolyn L. Arnold. 1986. "Integrated Circuits/Segregated Labor: Women in Computer-Related Occupations and High-Tech Industries." In Heidi I. Hartmann, Robert E. Kraut, and Louise A. Tilly, eds., *Computer Chips and Paper Clips: Technology and Women's Employment*. Washington, D.C.: National Academy Press.

U.S. Bureau of the Census. 1984. *Demographic and Socioeconomic Aspects of Aging in the United States*. Current Population Reports, series P-23, no. 138. Washington, D.C.: GPO.

———. 1985. *Statistical Abstract of the United States 1986*. Washington, D.C.: GPO.

———. 1986a. *Money Income of Households, Families, and Persons in the United States: 1984*. Current Population Reports, table 36, series P-60, no. 151. Washington, D.C.: GPO.

———. 1986b. *Statistical Abstract of the United States, 1987*. Washington, D.C.: GPO.

U.S. Department of Health and Human Services. Social Security Administration. 1984. *Social Security Handbook 1984*. SSA Pub. No. 05-10135. Washington, D.C.: GPO.

———. U.S. Senate Special Committee on Aging in conjunction with the American Association of Retired Persons, the Federal Council on Aging, and the Administration on Aging. 1986. *Aging America Trends and Projections 1985–1986*. Washington, D.C.: GPO.

U.S. Department of Labor. Bureau of Labor Statistics. 1985. *Handbook of Labor Statistics*. Bulletin 2217. Washington, D.C.: GPO.

Woods, John. 1986a. "The Changing Profile of Pensions." *Social Security Bulletin* 49: 22–25.

———. 1986b. "Working Women and Pensions." *Social Security Bulletin* 49: 33–34.

4

THE RELATIONSHIP OF PRODUCTIVITY TO AGE

Laurence J. Kotlikoff

Public policy toward employment of the elderly has shifted markedly in recent years. The federal government has virtually eliminated mandatory retirement; it has legislated a gradual increase in Social Security's age of retirement from 65 to 67; it has reduced Social Security's post–age 65 work disincentive by raising the post-65 actuarial benefit increase for delaying retirement; and it has reduced somewhat the earnings testing of Social Security benefits. These changes have occurred against a backdrop of increases in longevity and projections of significant difficulties in financing Social Security in the next century.

The success of the new public policy toward employment of the elderly is predicated on two ifs. The first is that the elderly will choose to remain employed, the second is that they will remain employable. There is little evidence at the moment that the trend toward increasingly earlier retirement has slowed, let alone reversed. Although much of the postwar increase in early retirement may reflect a response to Social Security and private retirement incentives, much appears to reflect a strong desire of the elderly for significant leisure. But, even if the often substantial retirement incentives

I am grateful to the Hoover Institution and the National Institute of Aging grant #1P01AG)582-01 for research support. Jagadeesh Gokhale and Jinyong Cai provided excellent research assistance. I thank Edward Lazear, Jagadeesh Gokhale, Kevin Lang, Chris Ruhm, and Larry Katz for helpful comments.

were eliminated and preferences shifted in the direction of more old-age labor supply, the question of the productivity of the elderly would remain.

This paper summarizes the findings of two recent studies that bear on the issue of the productivity of the elderly. The first study, Kotlikoff and Wise (1987), examines the age-accrual profile of private pension plans. Knowledge of the age-accrual profile of pensions as well as the age profile of nonpension compensation permits inferences concerning the relationship of the age-productivity profile to the age–total compensation profile. The second study, Kotlikoff (1987), uses information about the age–total compensation profile to directly estimate the age-productivity profile.

The results of the first study strongly contradict the view that workers are paid annually an amount equal to that year's productivity. Unlike the age profile of nonpension compensation, the profile of pension compensation is highly irregular, with sharp spikes at the ages of vesting and early retirement. Since pension compensation at particular ages is substantial, the highly irregular age-pension compensation implies a highly irregular age–total compensation profile. Hence, to believe that workers are paid annually their marginal product, we would need to believe that their productivity changes with age in precisely the highly irregular pattern of the age–total compensation profile. Even though these findings persuasively reject the notion of a perfect spot market, knowledge of the age–total compensation profile may still be important for understanding the age-productivity relationship. It could be, for example, that although productivity and compensation are not exactly equal at each age, they are roughly equal. Stated differently, it could be that there is no systematic age-related difference in compensation and productivity.

The results of the second study suggest, however, that there is a systematic difference. The second study indicates that workers are paid less than they produce when young and more than they produce when old. It also indicates that productivity declines with age. These results are, however, based only on the data of a single firm, albeit quite a large Fortune 500 firm. They are also predicated on several assumptions that may be questioned. The findings reported here—that productivity declines with age—must be viewed as tentative, but they do suggest that those elderly who wish to continue to work may need to accept substantial reductions in their compensation.

The two studies together also help distinguish alternative theories of the labor market. They support Becker and Stigler's (1974) and Edward Lazear's (1979, 1981) bonding contract models in which workers are paid less than they are worth when young and more than they are worth when old. This upward tilting of the age–total compensation profile relative to the age-productivity profile provides workers an added incentive not to shirk—that is, shirking, if discovered, will cost workers not only their jobs but also their opportunities in the future to earn more than they produce.

The results of the two studies appear to contradict both the conventional spot-market theory of the labor market in which workers are paid, at least annually, their marginal products, and the efficiency wage models of Harris and Todaro (1970), Stofft (1984), Yellen (1984), Stiglitz and Shapiro (1984), and Bulow and Summers (1986). These efficiency-wage models suggest that above-market clearing wages, rather than the shape of the age–total compensation, will be used as an incentive device. Although workers in these models receive above-market wages, they are paid their marginal products at each point in time. Hence, these efficiency-wage models, like the spot-market theory, predict that the age-productivity profile equals the age–total compensation profile. A third theory that receives negative support is the Mincer (1974) and Becker (1975) specific human-capital models. This theory suggests that if firms are free to fire older workers, the age–total compensation profile will be structured such that earnings exceed productivity when young and vice versa when old.

The relationship of the age-productivity profile to the age–total compensation profile described here accords with the findings of Medoff and Abraham (1981) and Lazear and Moore (1984). Medoff and Abraham compared the pay increases of older workers with their productivity evaluations. They found that pay rises late in the work span, although indexes of productivity decline. Lazear and Moore report that earnings profiles of the self-employed are flatter than those of employees, which also suggests earnings in excess of productivity among older workers. Kahn and Lang (1986), in contrast, examine responses to questions concerning desired hours of work; they point out that older workers, with earnings in excess of their marginal products, are likely to be hours-constrained by their employers and, therefore, should want to work more. The opposite would be true if earnings of older workers are below their marginal products. Kahn and Lang's empirical findings support the view that marginal productivity exceeds earnings for older workers.

The paper proceeds as follows. The next section summarizes briefly the methodology used in Kotlikoff and Wise (1987) to construct age–pension accrual profiles. It then presents specific examples of age–pension accrual profiles as well as the average age-accrual profile of defined benefit pension plans that determine benefits as a percentage of a specified earnings base. This analysis is based on the Bureau of Labor Statistics 1979 Level of Benefits Survey. The percentage of earnings plans considered in this section account for over half of participants in defined benefit plans. The third section summarizes the methodology used in Kotlikoff (1987) to infer the age-productivity profile and discusses the data used in that analysis; the fourth presents findings on the shape of the age-productivity profile and its relationship to the age–total compensation profile; and the final section summarizes the results of the two studies and suggests additional research.

PENSION BENEFIT ACCRUAL PROFILES

Pension Benefit Accrual Formulas

Equation (1) presents the formula for vested pension benefit accrual at age a, $I(a)$. $I(a)$ is simply the difference between pension wealth at age $a+1$, $Pw(a+1)$, and pension wealth at age a, $Pw(a)$, accumulated to age $a+1$ at the nominal interest rate r.

$$I(a) = Pw(a+1) - Pw(a)(1+r) \tag{1}$$

Pension wealth at age a is defined as the expected value of vested pension benefits discounted to age a. Intuitively, $Pw(a)$ can be thought of as the worker's pension bank account. If $I(a)$ equals zero, the worker continuing employment with the plan sponsor at age a has exactly the same pension wealth at age $a+1$ as an identically situated worker who terminates employment at age a. Pension accrual is thus the increment to pension wealth in excess of the return on the previously accumulated pension bank account.

If the labor market exhibits spot-market equilibrium, $I(a)$ plus the worker's nonpension compensation at age a, $W(a)$, equals the worker's marginal product at age a, $M(a)$:

$$M(a) = W(a) + I(a) \tag{2}$$

Obviously, if $W(a)$ is a smooth function of age and $I(a)$ exhibits sharp discontinuities, $M(a)$ must exhibit sharp discontinuities at these same ages to satisfy equation (2).

There are two principal discontinuities in age-accrual profiles of standard earnings-related defined benefit plans. The first occurs at the age of vesting, and the second occurs at the age of early retirement. Clearly, $I(a)$ is zero prior to the age of vesting and then jumps to the value $Pw(a^*)$ at the vesting age a^*. At age a^*+1, in contrast, the value of $I(a^*+1)$ will equal $Pw(a^*+1) - Pw(a^*)(1+r)$, which will typically be much smaller than $Pw(a^*)$. Hence, there is a spike in the accrual profile at age a^*. At early retirement the accrual profile of most firms also exhibits a sharp spike. The reason is that staying with the firm through the age of early retirement often provides enhanced benefits. For example, many firms reduce benefits for those who retire early, but the extent to which benefits are reduced depends on when the worker retires. If the worker stays beyond the age of early retirement, the benefit reduction is often much less severe than if he leaves prior to the age of early retirement. In addition, many firms provide supplemental benefits to workers if they stay with the firm through early retire-

ment. These supplemental benefits may take the form of an explicitly designated additional benefit, or they may take the form of a provision that
benefits will not be offset for Social Security prior to the firm's normal
retirement age.

Pension Accrual Profiles: Some Examples

In Figure 4.1 I depict three accrual profiles normalized by the worker's
wage for a worker who begins participating at age 30 in a defined benefit
plan with 100 percent vesting at ten years of service. The plan calculates
normal retirement benefits as 1 percent of average earnings over the last five
years of service times the number of years of service. If the worker leaves the
plan prior to the early retirement age of 55, his benefits are actuarially
reduced. If he leaves after age 55 but prior to age 65, the age of normal
retirement, his benefits are reduced, but by only 3 percent per year, an
amount that is less than is actuarially fair according to the interest rates
assumed in the diagram. Besides the different reduction in benefits for those
who retire prior to and after the early retirement age, there is no additional
advantage assumed in the diagram to postponing retirement until the early
retirement age. The diagram assumes that wages grow over the work span at
the rate of wage inflation plus an adjustment for the cross-section profile of
wages by age.

The three profiles differ because of differences in assumed interest rates
and rates of wage inflation. However, each exhibits a sharp spike at the age
of vesting and another sharp spike at the age of early retirement. For example, in the case of a 2 percent rate of wage inflation and a 5 percent nominal
interest rate, pension accrual at age 40, the age of vesting, represents over a
third of that year's wages. At age 55 the accrual is roughly 15 percent of the
wage. All three profiles indicate reductions in the accrual rate of about 8
percentage points at age 56. In order to reconcile these profiles with the
dictates of spot-market equilibrium, we must believe that marginal products
rise abruptly by an additional 5–37 percent exactly at age 40 and then fall
by an additional 3–31 percent exactly at age 41. In addition, an abrupt
decline in the worker's marginal product of close to 8 percentage points
exactly at age 56 that occurs neither prior to nor after age 56 is required for
the theory of spot equilibrium.

One response to these profiles is that straight wage compensation,
rather than increasing smoothly through time, could adjust to meet the spot-
market condition. In Figure 4.2 I suggest the implausibility of this view.
Here accrual rate profiles for three workers joining the pension plan at ages
31, 41, and 51 are presented based on the intermediate wage and interest-

FIGURE 4.1

PENSION INCREMENTS AS A PERCENTAGE OF SALARY, BY AGE, FOR WAGE INFLATION OF 2, 6, AND 10 PERCENT

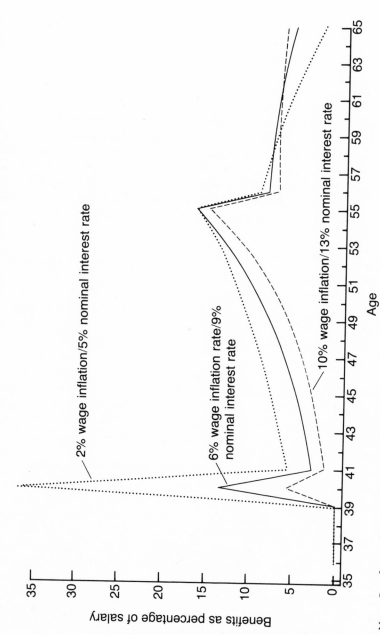

NOTE: Benefits are discounted at a 3 percent real interest rate.

rate assumptions of Figure 4.1. The vesting spikes for the three profiles are 14 percent, 36 percent, and 66 percent of the corresponding wage at ages 40, 50, and 60. Hence, for the spot-market theory to hold, wages would have to fall by 14, 36, and 66 percent for the three workers at the ages of 40, 50, and 60, respectively. Such dramatic worker-specific reductions in wages at particular ages certainly do not characterize the U.S. labor market.

The profiles depicted in Figures 4.1 and 4.2 may appear to be special cases, but they are actually quite typical. The large firm whose data is used to estimate age-productivity profiles does, in contrast, have a somewhat atypical pension plan. In Figure 4.3, based on similar assumptions as those in Figure 4.2, I display in absolute 1985 dollars the pension accrual projected at each age for male managers hired at age 20 in 1985 by this firm, together with estimates of their Social Security accrual and their wage compensation. The early retirement pension accrual spike is much larger in this diagram, which reflects the firm's policy of providing a special early retirement benefit for those who stay with the firm through age 55, the early retirement age; at age 55 the accrual is over one and a half times the annual wage.

Average accrual profiles for defined benefit plans that determine benefits as a specified percentage of a specified earnings base and that have ten-year cliff vesting are shown in Table 4.1 by early and normal retirement ages. Three of these average profiles, corresponding to plans with the respective early and normal retirement ages 55/55, 55/65, 65/65, are graphed in Figure 4.4. In this and subsequent accrual profiles, annual accrued pension benefits are expressed as a ratio of the wage. The graphs show substantial declines in the rate of pension wealth accrual at several critical ages. First, the age of normal retirement equals the age of early retirement for plans with no early retirement option. Second, there is a sharp decline in the rate of accrual at the age of early retirement, but this decline is substantially smaller than the decline at the normal retirement age. Third, there is a substantial decline between ages 65 and 66 in the average accrual rate no matter what the ages of early and normal retirement.

There is also a wide variation across plans in accrual rates at specific ages. In Table 4.2 I present average accrual rates for the 513 plans of Table 4.1 that specify early retirement at age 55 and normal retirement at age 65, together with median, maximum, minimum, and upper and lower 5th percentile accrual-rate levels. Consider the accrual rate at vesting. Although the average rate at vesting for this sample is 0.071, the median is 0.021, the maximum is 0.383, and the minimum is 0. The ratio at the lowest 5th percentile is 0, while it is 0.201 for the highest 5th percentile. A similarly larger dispersion is indicated at each of the ages 40 through 70.

FIGURE 4.2

PENSION INCREMENTS AS A PERCENTAGE OF SALARY BY AGE, FOR AN EMPLOYEE BEGINNING WORK AT AGE 31, 41, OR 51

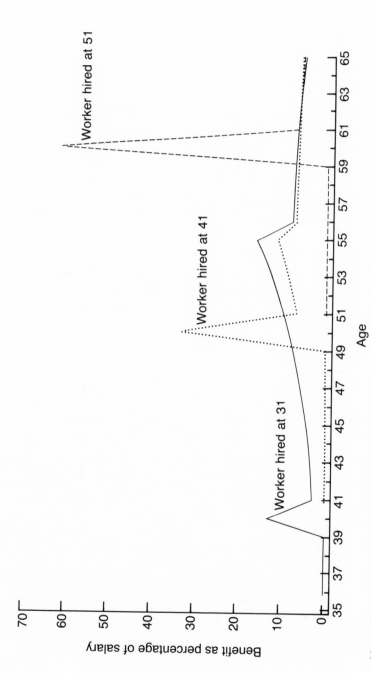

NOTE: Wage inflation is 6 percent, real interest rate is 3 percent.

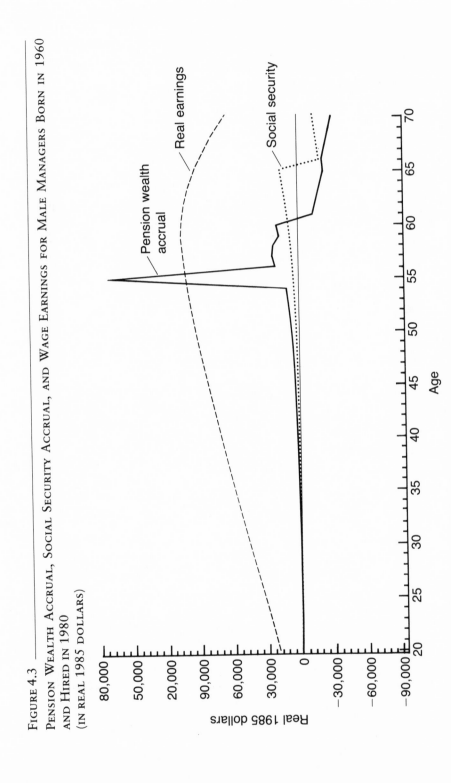

FIGURE 4.3

PENSION WEALTH ACCRUAL, SOCIAL SECURITY ACCRUAL, AND WAGE EARNINGS FOR MALE MANAGERS BORN IN 1960 AND HIRED IN 1980

(IN REAL 1985 DOLLARS)

FIGURE 4.4

WEIGHTED AVERAGE ACCRUAL RATES FOR PERCENTAGE OF EARNINGS PLANS WITH TEN-YEAR CLIFF VESTING, FOR SELECTED EARLY AND NORMAL RETIREMENT AGES

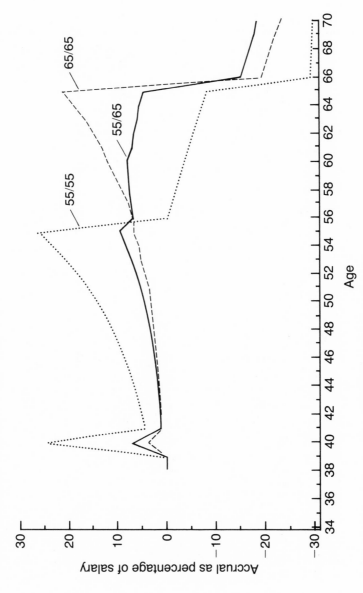

NOTE: Plans with early or normal retirement supplements are excluded.

TABLE 4.1

WEIGHTED AVERAGE ACCRUAL RATES FOR PERCENTAGE OF EARNINGS PLANS
WITH TEN-YEAR CLIFF VESTING, BY EARLY AND NORMAL RETIREMENT AGE

	EARLY RETIREMENT/NORMAL RETIREMENT							
	55/55	55/60	55/65	60/60	60/65	62/62	62/65	65/65
Number of plans	152	115	513	78	53	19	8	50
Age								
40	.244	.111	.071	.034	.047	.038	.054	.036
41	.045	.022	.013	.007	.010	.016	.009	.010
42	.051	.026	.016	.008	.011	.017	.010	.011
43	.058	.029	.018	.010	.013	.120	.011	.012
44	.066	.033	.020	.011	.015	.029	.013	.014
45	.075	.036	.023	.013	.017	.036	.013	.016
46	.085	.043	.026	.016	.019	.042	.015	.018
47	.097	.050	.031	.028	.022	.047	.017	.021
48	.110	.057	.035	.039	.025	.054	.019	.024
49	.124	.064	.040	.056	.029	.060	.021	.027
50	.141	.077	.046	.065	.034	.068	.023	.031
51	.159	.072	.052	.084	.040	.077	.026	.033
52	.180	.087	.062	.091	.050	.090	.028	.043
53	.204	.099	.072	.105	.060	.101	.032	.050
54	.231	.113	.083	.117	.068	.114	.035	.055
55	.261	.130	.097	.149	.082	.128	.039	.065

Age								
56	−.003	.100	.068	.170	.094	.144	.036	.068
57	−.012	.111	.072	.192	.107	.162	.039	.076
58	−.020	.118	.076	.224	.127	.184	.044	.089
59	−.028	.129	.077	.241	.146	.208	.048	.105
60	−.038	.143	.079	.269	.167	.241	.054	.118
61	−.048	−.090	.068	−.061	.113	.220	.059	.128
62	−.058	−.091	.064	−.091	.115	.248	.066	.145
63	−.067	−.091	.056	−.114	.114	−.130	.017	.163
64	−.076	−.092	.053	−.121	.114	−.136	.012	.186
65	−.085	−.094	.044	−.121	.112	−.144	.006	.211
66	−.292	−.169	−.152	−.138	−.088	−.266	−.081	−.194
67	−.294	−.174	−.162	−.155	−.115	−.263	−.080	−.204
68	−.295	−.179	−.171	−.171	−.142	−.260	−.079	−.213
69	−.296	−.182	−.179	−.184	−.162	−.258	−.078	−.221
70	−.297	−.184	−.186	−.196	−.182	−.255	−.077	−.234

SOURCE: Kotlikoff and Wise (1987).

NOTE: Plans with early or normal retirement supplements are excluded.

TABLE 4.2

DISPERSION OF ACCRUAL RATIOS FOR TABLE 4.1 PLANS WITH AGE 55 EARLY RETIREMENT AND AGE 65 NORMAL RETIREMENT

	Weighted average accrual ratios	Median accrual ratios	Minimum accrual ratios	Maximum accrual ratios	Lowest 5th percentile	Largest 5th percentile
Number of plans	513	513	513	513	513	513
Age 40	.071	.021	0	.383	0	.201
41	.013	.012	−.025	.071	0	.036
42	.016	.013	−.025	.080	0	.041
43	.018	.014	−.027	.091	0	.046
44	.020	.016	−.026	.103	0	.052
45	.023	.019	−.029	.116	0	.058
46	.026	.023	−.028	.131	0	.066
47	.031	.028	−.024	.162	0	.076
48	.034	.032	−.020	.167	0	.083
49	.040	.039	−.020	.188	0	.093
50	.046	.046	−.011	.212	0	.106
51	.052	.052	−.020	.240	0	.119
52	.062	.061	−.019	.270	0	.140
53	.072	.072	−.015	.305	0	.157
54	.083	.083	−.015	.344	0	.180
55	.097	.100	−.005	.405	0	.208
56	.068	.075	−.065	.424	0	.165
57	.072	.079	−.063	.363	0	.171
58	.076	.083	−.051	.248	0	.183
59	.077	.083	−.046	.286	−.0006	.190
60	.079	.086	−.064	.345	−.014	.204
61	.068	.074	−.156	.339	−.038	.181
62	.064	.068	−.154	.325	−.050	.190
63	.056	.062	−.192	.310	−.115	.191
64	.053	.060	−.221	.460	−.119	.210
65	.044	.052	−.323	.326	−.148	.205
66	−.152	−.136	−.558	.121	−.203	0
67	−.162	−.159	−.550	.060	−.406	0
68	−.171	−.179	−.541	.043	−.412	0
69	−.179	−.190	−.534	.029	−.414	0
70	−.186	−.197	−.618	.014	−.424	0

SOURCE: Kotlikoff and Wise (1987).

ESTIMATING THE AGE PRODUCTIVITY PROFILE

Methodology

Certainly the diagrams just presented strongly rule out an annual equality between productivity and total compensation. But is there no relationship whatsoever between productivity and compensation over the work span? The answer provided by contract theories of the labor market is that productivity and compensation, though not necessarily equal at any age, will be related over the course of the work span. More precisely, if we assume risk-neutral employers, the present expected value of compensation over the work span will be equal to the present expected value of productivity. This profit-maximizing condition in the contract model is the analogue to the static spot-market profit-maximizing condition that compensation equals productivity at each point in time.

The strategy adopted in Kotlikoff (1987) to estimate the age-productivity profile makes use of this present value profit-maximizing condition. Specifically, I parameterize the age-productivity relationship, write the present value profit-maximizing condition in terms of these parameters, and then estimate the parameters nonlinearly using information on the present expected value of compensation. Equation (3) presents the present value profit-maximizing condition under the assumptions that the structure of the labor contract and the probability of staying with the firm are time invariant.

$$w(a, t) \sum_{s=t}^{t+75-a} \mu(a+s-t, a)q(a+s-t, a)R^{s-t} = \tag{3}$$
$$\sum_{s=t}^{t+75-a} E_t\, \theta_s q(a+s-t, a)h(a+s-t, a)R^{s-t}$$

In this equation, $w(a, t)$ stands for the initial wage of a worker hired at age a in year t. The term $\mu(a+s-t, a)$ stands for the growth rate of wages at age $a+s-t$ for workers who join the firm at age a. The term $q(a+s-t, a)$ stands for the probability a worker who joins the firm at age a will still be with the firm at age $a+s-t$. The term R stands for one divided by one plus the interest rate. The term $E_t\, \theta_s$ gives the expected value of labor productivity in year s. Finally, the term $h(a+s-t, a)$ is the productivity of a worker age $a+s-t$ who was hired at age a measured per unit of total labor input.

The values of each of the terms on the left side of equation (3) are available or can be directly constructed from the data. Since I have no data on the values of expected labor productivity, I make the simplifying assumption that expectations are static and write $E_t\, \theta_s = \theta_t$. The term θ_t is estimated as one of the parameters of the model. Next I parameterize the age-productivity relationship, $h(\ ,\ )$ as a cubic polynomial in age. Although we could, in principal, parameterize $h(\ ,\ )$ as a function both of age and age of hire, in practice the resulting variables are too colinear to secure independent parameter estimates. Rather than treat $h(\ ,\ )$ as a continuous function of both age and age of hire, I attempt to circumvent the colinearity problem by estimating equation (3) both for the entire sample and for the samples of workers hired prior to age 35 and workers hired after age 35.

The Large-Firm Data

The large-firm data used in this study are earnings histories covering the period 1969–1983 of workers employed in the firm at some time during the period 1980–1983. The workers are classified into rather broad occupation and sex groups: male office workers, female office workers, salesmen, saleswomen, and male managers. There are too few female managers to warrant their analysis. Unfortunately, there are no additional demographic variables that could be included in the analysis.

The firm has a defined benefit plan with a fairly complex set of age- and service-related benefits. The benefit formula is a percentage-of-earnings formula in which the basic retirement annuity equals a percentage rate times the number of years of service for workers with fewer than 26 years of service. For those with more service, the formula equals 25 times the former percentage rate, plus the additional service beyond 25 times a lower percentage rate. The basic benefit is offset by the amount of Social Security benefits the firm predicts the worker will receive. The predicted Social Security benefit is derived from another age- and service-related formula unique to the firm.

The pension plan's normal retirement age is 65, and its early retirement age is 55. For workers who retire after the early retirement age but before the normal retirement age, there is a special early retirement benefit reduction table that is based on the workers' age and service. Workers who terminate employment before age 55 are not eligible for the quite generous early retirement benefit reduction rates and face instead actuarially reduced benefits. As mentioned, another important penalty for terminating before the early retirement age is that workers retiring after the early retirement age have their Social Security offset deferred until they reach age 65. As indicated in Figure 4.3, these provisions of the firm's pension can produce substantial vested pension accrual at age 55 but rather modest accrual prior to age 55. After age 55 the accrual is much smaller and, indeed, can become negative.

The $q(\ ,\ )$s used in constructing $w(a, t)$ and the variables in equation (3) were calculated separately for each of the five sex-occupation groups in the following manner. First, the fraction of workers at a given age and initial age of hire who remain in the firm from one year to the next was calculated. Next, these annual survival hazards were smoothed using a third order polynomial in age, age of hire, and interaction terms. Finally, the cumulative survival probabilities, the $q(\ ,\ )$s, were computed based on the smoothed annual survival probabilities.

The $\mu(\ ,\ )$s in the above discussion have stood for the growth in total compensation, including pension compensation; but in order to determine the course of pension compensation, we need first to know the course of nonpension compensation. Hence, the function $\mu^*(\ ,\ )$, which gives the growth in nonpension compensation, was first estimated by regressing observed growth rates in earnings, excluding pension compensation, against a third order polynomial in age, age of hire, and interaction terms. The initial wage together with the smoothed $\mu^*(\ ,\ )$s provide a path of nonpension compensation that can be used to calculate the path of pension accrual. The path of nonpension plus pension compensation is then used to form the present expected value of total compensation.

The Age-Productivity and
Age–Total Compensation Profiles

In Figures 4.5 through 4.9 I present for each sex-occupation group the age-productivity and age–total compensation profiles arising from estimating equation (3) assuming a 6 percent interest rate. The diagrams consider a worker who begins work at age 35. The age 35 initial levels of productivity and compensation are chosen to ensure that both the present expected value of compensation and the present expected value of margin product equal $500,000.

Productivity initially rises with age in each diagram, but it eventually starts declining with age. For male office workers, productivity peaks at age 45 and declines thereafter; age 65 productivity for this group is less than one-third of peak productivity. The female office workers' productivity profile is quite similar to that of the male office workers. Both the salesmen and saleswomen productivity profiles peak a few years later than those of office workers, but their rate of decline with age is quite similar. Productivity for male managers peaks at age 43; by age 60 productivity is less than one-third of peak productivity, and productivity actually becomes negative after age 62.

In four of the diagrams, productivity exceeds total compensation when the worker is young and then falls below total compensation; in the remaining case, that of salesmen, the relationship of compensation and productivity is quite similar to the other four groups, except after age 61 when productivity again exceeds compensation. Except for the kinks in the age-compensation

FIGURE 4.5
TOTAL COMPENSATION AND PRODUCTIVITY FOR MALE OFFICE WORKERS

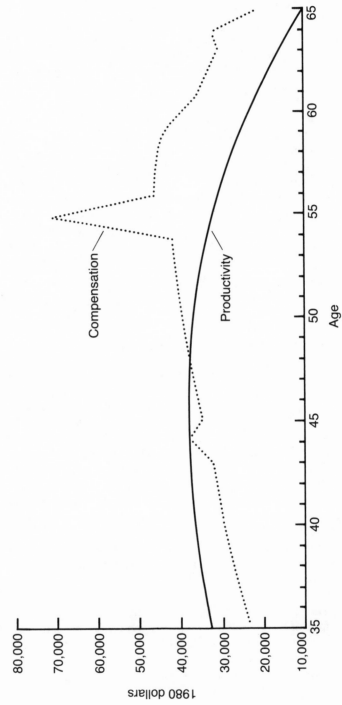

NOTE: Age of hire = 35; r = 6 percent; PV = $500,000.

FIGURE 4.6

TOTAL COMPENSATION AND PRODUCTIVITY FOR FEMALE OFFICE WORKERS

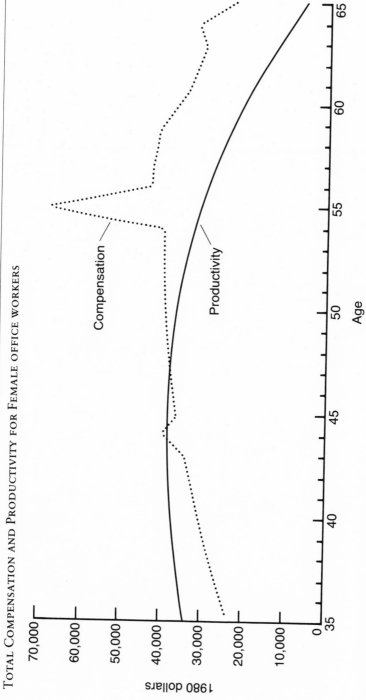

NOTE: Age of hire = 35; r = 6 percent; PV = $500,000.

FIGURE 4.7
TOTAL COMPENSATION AND PRODUCTIVITY FOR SALESMEN

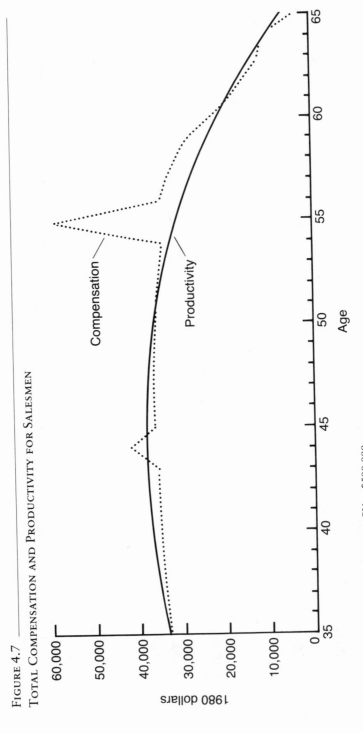

NOTE: Age of hire = 35; r = 6 percent; PV = \$500,000.

FIGURE 4.8
TOTAL COMPENSATION AND PRODUCTIVITY FOR SALESWOMEN

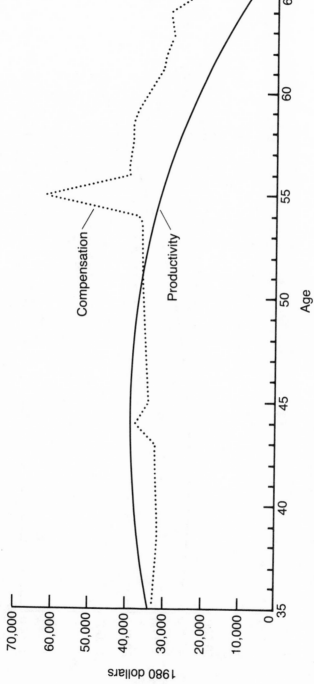

NOTE: Age of hire = 35; r = 6 percent; PV = $500,000.

FIGURE 4.9

TOTAL COMPENSATION AND PRODUCTIVITY FOR MALE MANAGERS

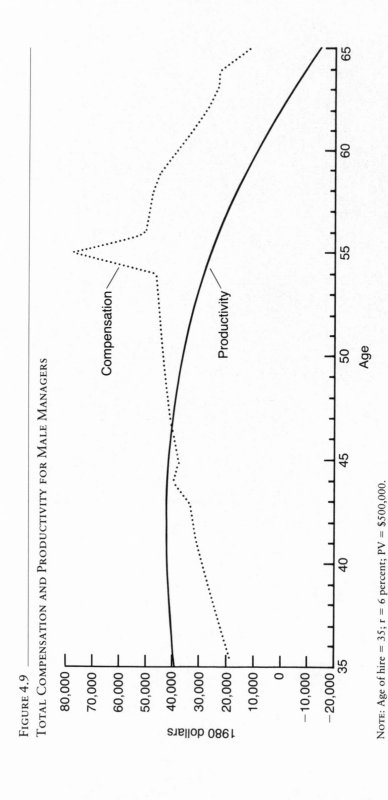

NOTE: Age of hire = 35; r = 6 percent; PV = $500,000.

profiles associated with pension accrual, the age-compensation profiles and age-productivity profiles for salesmen and saleswomen are close to one another at each age. This is to be expected, since salesworkers in this firm are paid largely on a commission basis.

In contrast to the results for salesworkers, we might expect the weakest connection between annual earnings and annual productivity among male managers. In Figure 4.9 I indicate that this is indeed the case. At age 35 productivity for male managers exceeds total compensation by more than a factor of two, whereas compensation is over twice as high as productivity by age 57. The discrepancies between total compensation and productivity at these ages are somewhat smaller for office workers but still quite important. For example, age 35 total compensation for female office workers is $22,616, whereas age 35 productivity is $33,604. In contrast, age 57 total compensation is $42,526, although productivity is only $28,117.

The results depicted in Figures 4.5–4.9 are not sensitive to the inclusion of pension accrual in total compensation; if we ignore pension accrual in the estimation, the age-earnings and age-productivity profiles have the same relative shapes as those presented. Of course, the age-earnings profile does not exhibit the kinks of the age–total compensation profile, since these kinks arise from pension accrual. In the absence of considering pension accrual, we can also use the data on workers hired prior to 1970. Although the initial wage of those hired prior to 1969 is not reported, this wage can be inferred based on the wage observed in 1969 and the $\mu($, $)$s; that is, we can impute backward the wage at the initial age of hire. The results based on this larger data set are again extremely similar to those presented in Figures 4.5–4.9.

The general shapes of the age–total compensation profiles and age-productivity profiles are also insensitive to the choice of interest rate. For example, compare the 3 percent and 9 percent compensation and productivity profiles of female office workers in Figures 4.10 and 4.11. Since the present value of these profiles always equals $500,000, the profiles assuming a 9 percent interest rate are initially higher than those assuming a 3 percent interest rate. The percentage differences between the two profiles are slightly larger at early and late ages, assuming a 9 percent rather than a 3 percent interest rate; but since the initial levels of the profiles in Figure 4.11 are higher, the absolute differences between compensation and productivity are considerably larger. The age at which productivity of female office workers falls below compensation also depends on the interest rate. The cross-over age is roughly 50 assuming a 3 percent interest rate; it is roughly 48 assuming a 6 percent interest rate; and it is roughly 45 (ignoring the vesting kink in the compensation profile) assuming a 9 percent interest rate.

Another concern is the extent to which the profiles described here as age-productivity profiles confound service-productivity effects. Unfortu-

FIGURE 4.10

COMPENSATION AND PRODUCTIVITY FOR FEMALE OFFICE WORKERS (R = 3 PERCENT)

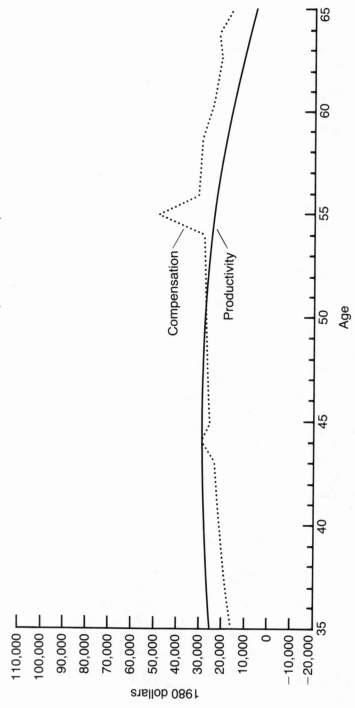

NOTE: Age of hire = 35; PV = $500,000.

FIGURE 4.11

COMPENSATION AND PRODUCTIVITY FOR FEMALE OFFICE WORKERS (R = 9 PERCENT)

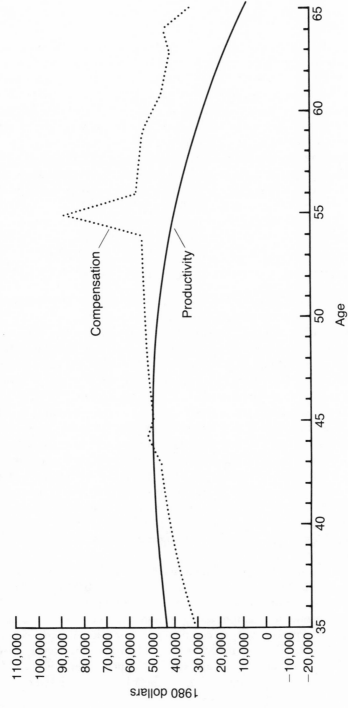

NOTE: Age of hire = 35; PV = $500,000.

nately, the colinearity between cumulated service and age variables precludes modeling the $h(,)$ function as a continuous function both of age and age of hire. An alternative way to explore this issue is to model $h(,)$ as depending only on age, but to estimate the model separately for workers hired at different ages. If one estimates the model separately for those hired prior to age 35 and those after age 35, the resulting general shapes of the productivity profiles are quite similar to those based on the entire sample. The post–age 35 profiles are indeed similar, whereas the pre–age 35 profiles exhibit a steeper decline in productivity with age, with negative predicted productivity roughly after age 55. This prediction of negative productivity late in the work span may simply represent a poor fit in the tail of the estimated polynomial.

Conclusions and Suggestions for Additional Research

The findings that productivity decreases with age must be viewed cautiously. Contrary to what has been assumed, it may be that some workers within a sex-occupation category receive different contracts than others. Suppose that within a sex-occupation category there are type A and type B workers and that type A workers receive contracts with steeper compensation profiles than type B workers. Also assume that type A workers have smaller values of $q(,)$ than type B workers. If the composition of workers remaining with the firm changes, the estimated $\mu(,)$ and $q(,)$ functions would differ from those for either A or B separately or from those that would arise if the separate $\mu(,)$s and $q(,)$s for A and B were averaged using constant weights. As a consequence, the age-productivity profile derived using the method presented here could differ from either the profile for group A workers or the profile for group B workers. Similar biases may arise if the composition of type A and type B workers among new hires changes as the age of hire increases. These potential biases need to be explored more formally as does the possible bias arising from assuming static expectations of overall worker productivity.

These concerns notwithstanding, the results are fairly striking. Productivity falls with age, compensation at first lies below and then exceeds productivity, and the discrepancy between compensation and productivity can be substantial. It is interesting to note that there is much closer correspondence of productivity to compensation for salesworkers, who are compensated more on a spot-market basis, than for other types of workers. Also, the relationship of productivity to compensation is weakest for male managers, who, we would expect, are most likely to be hired on a contract rather than a spot-market basis.

In addition to confirming contract theory, the results lend support to the bonding wage models of Becker and Stigler (1974) and Lazear (1979, 1981). In contrast, the results contradict the predictions of the standard Mincer (1974) and Becker (1975) human capital models in which workers receive more than they are worth when young and less than they are worth when old. The results are also at odds with the assertion of some efficiency wage models that workers receive their marginal product on an annual basis.

DISCUSSION

Edward P. Lazear

Larry Kotlikoff has demonstrated his cleverness once again. He has tackled an extremely important problem and made headway on providing empirical evidence. The relation of the age-productivity profile to the age-earnings profile is of great significance to a number of theories. Naturally, I am pleased with his results since they support my hypothesis that the age-earnings profile is an incentive device, where young workers are paid less than they are worth and old workers are paid more than they are worth. Although I think that his findings are suggestive, they are less than conclusive for a number of reasons.

Kotlikoff summarizes his pension work as well as the more original work on age-productivity profiles that comes from the one firm sample. I will first make a few remarks on the pension argument and then turn to the direct age-productivity analysis.

It is well known that pension formulas create spikes at certain years, primarily because of vesting and early retirement benefits. These spikes and the general shape of the accrual profile were documented many years ago by Bulow (1981) and by Lazear (1982, 1983a, 1983b) as well as in earlier papers by Kotlikoff and Wise (1987). I find these spikes less troubling than does Kotlikoff for two reasons.

First, almost all economic data have discontinuities. For example, prices change infrequently and by discrete amounts, even over a product's life cycle. Quantity discounts are rarely smooth. Sales occur for short periods of time with prices being much higher at either end. Although it is true that some extremely competitive markets have smoother price movements—for example, the New York Stock Exchange—many competitive products do experience jumps. Explaining when something happens in time and why the magnitude is what it is takes us beyond the current power of economic analysis. Thus, I believe Kotlikoff's concern to be somewhat exaggerated.

Second, and perhaps more compelling, it is inappropriate to think of the entire value of a vested pension as accruing in the vesting year. Instead, working the first year gives a worker the option to work a second year, which entitles him to work the third, and so forth. Eventually, he works the year during which his pension vests. But the first year, second year, and every year of employment have pension accrual as well. The accrual is the option value of working that year. The option value, which is the correct value to focus on, has spikes as well, but they tend to be less pronounced than those for the pension value itself. It is essential to consider the option value, or it would be impossible to explain why soldiers never quit in year 17 when their pension vests in year 20. The option value of the pension in year 17 is close to that of year 20, even though the actual accrual is zero. (See Lazear and Moore [1987] for a detailed discussion.)

The new evidence from the Fortune 500 firm is more interesting. There, Kotlikoff uses data on age-earnings profiles to infer age-productivity profiles in an ingenious fashion. The basic argument is that by observing a worker's total earnings from, say, age 55 to age 65, we obtain an estimate of his total productivity over those years. By comparing total earnings of that individual with one who works from age 54 to age 65, we can estimate productivity at age 54 as the difference between the two totals.

The idea is clever, but it hinges on a hidden identifying assumption. In order to infer that differences across ages are due to differences in productivity, it must be assumed that age-productivity profiles do not differ systematically by starting age. If, for example, individuals who started at age 54 had steeper age-productivity profiles with higher present values than those who started at age 55, the difference between them would overstate the productivity at age 54. Human capital provides a reason for these differences. Younger starters are more likely to invest in firm-specific human capital than older individuals. Thus, those who start young have higher lifetime productivity than those who start old. This tends to cause age-earnings profiles to appear flatter than they actually are.

The argument is not especially troubling, however. Since differences in investment behavior are most likely to result from differences in time horizons, finite life is what makes the assumption suspect. But for most workers, especially the young, this is not an important consideration. It is unreasonable to argue that 27 year olds invest a great deal more than 28 year olds because they have a longer period over which to recoup the returns to the human capital investment.

Additionally, the differential investment argument also implies differences in age-earnings profiles. If young workers invest more, their age-earnings profiles are steeper and higher. This means that in a cross section, estimates of age-earnings profile slopes are biased down. Thus, if it is the difference between age-earnings profiles and age-productivity profiles that is relevant, it is not clear that the human capital investment bias has any effect whatsoever.

A similar criticism relates to cohort effects. Productivity increases over time so that an individual who starts at age twenty in 1960 has lower expected lifetime productivity than an individual who starts at age twenty in 1987. The reason this is a problem is because, in a cross section, the older individuals are those who are from earlier cohorts. This, too, flattens both age-earnings profiles and age-productivity profiles. In theory, this can be repaired. A panel data set, which has twenty year olds who start in different years and work during the same ages, permits estimation of the cohort effect. An examination of differences in lifetime earnings, holding constant starting age and years of work, provides an estimate of the cohort effect.

Working in the opposite direction is selectivity on health. Those older workers who start new jobs may be in better health than the average individual of the same age. As such, productivity and earnings are likely to be higher for these individuals. This tends to overstate the productivity of those who begin jobs later, which causes the Kotlikoff estimates of the age-productivity profile to be too steep.

Despite these potential biases, there are a number of factors that suggest that the analysis is more than merely suggestive. First, the age-earnings profiles that are obtained, and on which all subsequent analysis is based, are reasonable. They have shapes that have been observed in other data and square well with most theories of life-cycle earnings. The only exception to this is that pension spikes make the profile less continuous than would be expected.

Second, the basic point is consistent with evidence found in the industrial psychology literature. There are two kinds of studies there: one group examines the ability of individuals of different ages to perform tasks in a laboratory setting; another group examines actual work environments where productivity can be measured and relates productivity to age. Most studies find that productivity declines once workers go beyond some age, although the decline differs by type of task. Since earnings tend to level off but do not decline in any dramatic way, this literature suggests that the Kotlikoff results are on the mark.

Third, as I have argued elsewhere (Lazear 1979), the desire by firms to retire older workers forcibly is prima facie evidence that workers are paid more than their output when old. Otherwise, mandatory retirement would be desired by neither firms nor workers.

Finally, and most convincing, Kotlikoff's results make a great deal of sense when workers are disaggregated by occupation. He finds that the age-earnings profile and age-productivity profile are almost identical for salesmen, who are paid on the basis of output. He also finds that managers and office workers have the steepest age-earnings profile relative to age-productivity profile. Since managers' output is not as easily observed, it is sensible to use upward-sloping age-earnings profiles as incentive devices for these workers.

Thus, the Kotlikoff analysis sheds new light on an important question. Although the data come from only one firm and the technique is not immune from criticism, the results are the most direct evidence available on the relation of the age-earnings profile to the age-productivity profile. Since that relation is of significant importance, this paper is to be applauded.

References

Becker, Gary S. 1975. *Human Capital,* 2d ed. New York: Columbia University Press.

Becker, Gary S., and George Stigler. 1974. "Law Enforcement, Malfeasance, and Compensation of Enforcers." *Journal of Legal Studies* 3:1–18.

Bulow, Jeremy. 1981. "Early Retirement Pension Benefits." Working Paper no. 654, National Bureau of Economic Research, Cambridge, Mass.

Bulow, Jeremy, and Lawrence H. Summers. 1986. "A Theory of Dual Labor Markets with Application to Industrial Policy, Discrimination, and Keynesian Unemployment." *Journal of Labor Economics* 4:376–414.

Harris, John, and Michael P. Todaro. 1970. "Migration, Unemployment, and Development: A Two-Sector Analysis." *American Economic Review* 60:126–42.

Kahn, Shulamit, and Kevin Lang. 1986. "Constraints on the Choice of Work Hours." Mimeo, University of California at Irvine.

Kotlikoff, Laurence J. 1987. "Estimating the Age Productivity Profile Using Lifetime Earnings." Mimeo.

Kotlikoff, Laurence J., and David A. Wise. 1987. "The Incentive Effects of Private Pension Plans." In Zvi Bodie, John Shoven, and David A. Wise, eds., *Issues in Pension Economics.* Chicago: University of Chicago Press.

Lazear, Edward P. 1979. "Why Is There Mandatory Retirement?" *Journal of Political Economy* 87:1261–64.

———. 1981. "Agency, Earnings Profiles, Productivity, and Hours Restrictions." *American Economic Review* 71:606–20.

———. 1982. "Severance Pay, Pensions and Efficient Mobility." Working Paper no. 854, National Bureau of Economic Research, Cambridge, Mass.

———. 1983a. "Incentive Effects of Pensions." Working Paper no. 1126, National Bureau of Economic Research, Cambridge, Mass.

———. 1983b. "Pensions and Severance Pay." In Zvi Bodie and John Shoven, eds., *Financial Aspects of the U.S. Pension System.* Chicago: University of Chicago Press.

Lazear, Edward P., and Robert L. Moore. 1984. "Incentives, Productivity, and Labor Contracts." *Quarterly Journal of Economics* 74:275–96.

Lazear, Edward P., and Robert L. Moore. 1987. "Pensions and Turnover." In Zvi Bodie, John Shoven, and David A. Wise, eds., *Issues in Pension Economics.* Chicago: University of Chicago Press.

Medoff, James L., and Katherine G. Abraham. 1981. "Are Those Paid More Really More Productive? The Case of Experience." *Journal of Human Resources* 16:186–216.

Mincer, Jacob. 1974. *Schooling Experience and Earnings.* New York: Columbia University Press.

Stiglitz, Carl, and Joseph Shapiro. 1984. "Equilibrium Unemployment as a Worker Discipline Device." *American Economic Review* 74:433–44.

Stofft, Steven. 1984. "Cheat-Threat Theory." Mimeo, Boston University.

Yellen, Janet. 1984. "Efficiency Wage Models of Unemployment." *American Economic Review* 74:200–205.

5

CHANGING HEALTH OF THE OLDER WORKING-AGE POPULATION AND RETIREMENT PATTERNS OVER TIME

Eileen M. Crimmins
and Maria T. Pramaggiore

In recent years we have witnessed dramatic increases in the rate of labor force withdrawal among men below the age of 65. Cross-sectional studies suggest that poor health is a determinant of labor force withdrawal among the older working-age population, but it is not clear if trends in the health of this age group have contributed to the increase in labor force withdrawal below age 65. This paper will examine trends in the reported health among the male population aged 55–64 between 1969 and 1981 to investigate the possibility that changing health may have contributed to the downward trend in labor force participation.

The central issue we investigate is whether or not health among men in this age group actually deteriorated between 1970 and 1980. An alternative explanation offered by some economists is that men were increasingly taking advantage of benefit programs such as Social Security Disability Insurance. Reasons for people increasingly to claim health-related benefits include the possibility that benefits were easier to obtain during the mid-1970s than in earlier periods, the likelihood that individuals became better informed about benefit programs in the early 1970s, the fact that health is a more acceptable reason for retirement than simply wishing to stop working, and the fact that the earnings-replacement ratio increased.

CHANGING HEALTH

Health change over time as an explanation for the declining trend in labor force participation in this age group is certainly a reasonable avenue of investigation. Mortality declines among the older ages since 1968 have been significant (Crimmins 1981). However, the nature of the relationship between mortality decline and morbidity change is far from being resolved; there are arguments that claim morbidity and mortality should move together and some that expect them to move in opposite directions.

Morbidity from the chronic diseases that are prevalent in the older working-age population may increase with a mortality decline, because death may be prevented and treatment of a disease may occur at a stage of the disease where the individual is left disabled. This possibility has been called the "failure of success" by Gruenberg (1977). But health may also improve if declining mortality is due to medical and life-style changes that postpone the onset of disease, prevent the development of disease, or at least prevent the most disabling effects of chronic disease. This would result in what Fries (1980) calls the rectangularization of the morbidity curve, whereby people experience more years in good health and mortality and morbidity are compressed into a few years at the end of the life span. Another possibility, as suggested by Manton (1982), is that disease prevalence has been increasing but the severity of diseases has been decreasing.

Three studies have addressed the question of changes in health among the older working-age population. Verbrugge (1984) and Colvez and Blanchet (1981) both report a deterioration in health in the population aged 45–64 during the 1960s and 1970s. Each of these authors allows for the possibility that the change could also be related to the increased use of medical care and a growing accommodation to disease. Ycas (1987) reports that health did deteriorate among people aged 55–70 from 1969 to 1975 and then either stabilized or reversed, depending on which health measure is used.

THE DECLINE IN LABOR FORCE PARTICIPATION

Researchers who have attempted to explain the time trend in labor force participation have concluded that generosity of benefits and improved access to program benefits are the primary causes of nonparticipation, but Parsons (1980a) finds that the effects are of greater magnitude than those found by Haveman, Wolfe, and Warlick (1984, 65–93). Both of these studies agree that individuals who leave the labor market in response to increased Social Security Disability Insurance are those with the lowest earning potential—the elderly, the disabled, and the unemployed.

Some researchers have addressed the role of changing health in affecting the time trend in labor force participation. Sunshine (1981) examines the possibility that health could have worsened, but he rejects this thesis based on an examination of data on the proportion of new disability awardees in the Federal Civil Service Retirement Program who are disabled by heart disease. He concludes, like Parsons, that the rise in men leaving the labor force and claiming disability benefits is the result of the profusion of benefit programs and the availability of better benefits within programs. Sunshine also notes that dissemination of knowledge about these programs has been relatively slow and increased usage could be a result of the realization among a growing proportion of disabled people that an alternative to working exists.

Chirikos (1986) reaches conclusions that are quite different from Sunshine's. Chirikos observes the increase in the proportion of older men claiming that they have a work-limiting health condition. After noting that there are numerous possible explanations for such a trend, he concludes that the increase in not working is due to an increase in ill health. Specifically, Chirikos identifies increases in the prevalence of physical-sensory impairments and of chronic diseases.

These studies of declining labor force participation have either ignored the possibility of increasing morbidity as a cause of early labor force withdrawal (Parsons 1980a) or have neglected to investigate changes in health thoroughly (Sunshine 1981). On the other hand, studies focused on changes in health (Verbrugge 1984; Colvez and Blanchet 1981; Chirikos 1986) do not account for possible confounding effects of changing labor force status.

Our study will thoroughly investigate the possibility of declining health as a factor in declining labor force participation by examining changes over time in a variety of health indicators for men aged 55–64. Indicators of morbidity include the prevalence of work-limiting conditions and the number of restricted-activity days, bed disability days, and work-loss days for men in various activity status groups. In addition, we will examine the conditions or diseases causing disability and the changes, if any, in these causes over time.

If health did deteriorate over the period, we expect to find an increase in the proportion of men retired because of their health and no change over time in the average health of workers and retirees. Measures of health for workers and retirees would remain constant. Men should be retiring at about the same level of ill health as they did previously, but more of them should attain that level of ill health.

If men did not become more unhealthy over time, and if they accepted benefits because these were available and not because of poorer health, we expect that the health of both workers and retirees would improve. Over time the men who retire would be less sick, which should leave the work force on average in better health. Similarly, the men who report they are retired because of their health should show improvements in health over time because the new entrants into this category would not be as sick as they were in the past.

We will return to these two scenarios in examining the data for health and labor force trends among older working-age men, and we will attempt to discern the relative likelihood of each one, given the evidence presented in the data.

DATA

The data used in this study come from the microdata tapes of the National Health Interview Survey (NHIS) from 1969 through 1981. This survey is taken continuously in order to monitor the health and medical care usage of the U.S. population. Each year interview schedules are completed for approximately 120,000 individuals. About 5,000 of these are men between the ages of 55 and 65.

Before beginning our analysis of health trends in this population, we document in Table 5.1 that the well-known increase over time in retirement or labor force withdrawal rates among men aged 55–64 is observed in this data set. The variable closest to labor force participation is a report of "usual activity during most of the past year." Choices for men include working, retired because of health, retired for other reasons, going to school, and a residual category for those doing something else that represents primarily unemployment.

In this table we show that the number of men identifying themselves as retired increases from 11 percent in 1969 to 24 percent in 1981. This results from a 14 percent drop in the percentage working. The total nonparticipation rate in the sample ranges from 16 percent in 1969 to 30 percent in 1981. Data based on the Current Population Survey (CPS) for the same years give comparable figures of 17 and 29 percent (Parsons 1980a, 118; U.S. Bureau of the Census 1984, 392). From these figures it appears that the percentage of men working declined by 14 percent from 1970 through 1981. At the same time the percentage retired because of health increased 4 percent and retired/other increased 6.5 percent. These figures alone would lead us to conclude that declining health has played a major role in promoting withdrawal from the labor force. Parsons (1980a, 126; 1982, 81) identifies an important problem in accepting these data at face value, namely that most health data are self-reported. People may report poor health as a

TABLE 5.1 ——
USUAL ACTIVITY STATUS OF MEN AGED 55–64, 1969–1981
(PERCENTAGES)

| | | RETIRED | | |
Year	Working	Due to health	Other reasons	Other
1969	84.0	*	10.9	5.1
1970	82.6	8.8	5.0	3.6
1971	81.2	8.8	5.6	4.5
1972	80.4	8.3	5.9	5.4
1973	78.3	10.9	6.9	3.9
1974	77.4	10.8	7.5	4.3
1975	75.1	10.9	8.0	5.9
1976	73.6	11.5	9.3	5.7
1977	71.7	13.0	10.4	4.9
1978	73.3	12.3	9.3	5.1
1979	71.4	13.3	10.2	5.1
1980	71.3	13.3	10.3	5.1
1981	70.1	13.0	11.5	5.4

* This category did not exist in 1969. All retirees are included in the category retired/other.

reason for retirement *ex post* because it is more acceptable to use health as a reason for retirement than admit to simply wanting to leave the labor force.

It is possible that this tendency could have changed over time as people have become more knowledgeable about benefits and as benefits have become more generous. It is also possible that people have become more knowledgeable about diseases and have used more medical care. It has been suggested that changing attitudes toward ill health may have resulted in accommodation to disease and a restriction of activities at an earlier stage of the disease (Chapman, LaPlante, and Wilensky 1986; Verbrugge 1984, 509). Any of these factors could have resulted in more people declaring themselves unable to work.

RESULTS

The analysis that follows divides the group into 55–61 year olds and 62–64 year olds. The reason for this relates to the differing availability of Social Security benefits for nonworkers by age. Program rules require ill health or the inability to work in order to participate before age 62 in the disability part of Social Security, but the rules permit anyone eligible who wishes to participate in the retired workers' program at age 62. Therefore, it seems reasonable to separate the group at that age.

Trends in Health Status

Operational definitions of health are all imperfect. There is no generally agreed-on best measure. An analysis of time trends must be based on what is available. One of the major indicators of health from the NHIS is limitation of activity:

> Limitation of activity is a measure of long-term reduction in activity result-
> ing from chronic disease or impairment and is defined as the inability to
> carry on the usual activity for one's age group [in this case working] or
> restriction in the amount or kind of usual activity or restriction in other
> activities (e.g., civic, church, or recreation). (U.S. Department of Health,
> Education, and Welfare 1973, 4)

Thus, men in this age group who are limited can be classified as limited in secondary activities or limited in work ability. Those limited in work ability include those unable to work and those limited in the amount or kind of work they can do.

The measure is appropriate for this study because its referent is work ability, which is our interest, and because it is based on impairment from a chronic or long-term condition rather than from short-term conditions. Its major drawback is that it is self-reported.

From the data in Table 5.2 we show that reported limitation of activity generally increases from 1969 through 1981 among men in both age groups. Although there were increases in both components of activity limitation (that is, limitation in work activity and limitation in secondary activities), most of the increase occurred in the limitation in ability to work category. In this table we provide a further breakdown of the reported limitation in work ability into those limited in the amount or kind of work and those who are unable to work. There is little consistent change in those reporting that they are limited in the amount or kind of work that they can perform, with perhaps a small decrease among those aged 62–64. The percentage report-ing themselves unable to work because of health, however, appears to have risen dramatically in both of these age groups over this period. Reporting oneself unable to work increases 60 percent among the younger men and almost 50 percent among the older men.

In 1981 one out of seven men aged 55–61 said he was unable to work because of his health. This was an increase from one out of eleven in 1969. Among men aged 62–64, self-perceived inability to work increased from one in six in 1969 to one in four in 1981. Changes in activity limitation

TABLE 5.2

LIMITED IN ACTIVITY, BY TYPE OF LIMITATION,
FOR MEN AGED 55–61 AND 62–64, 1969–1981
(PERCENTAGES)

Year	(1) Limited in activity	(2) Limited in secondary activity	(3) Limited in work ability	(4) Limited in amount or kind of work	(5) Unable to work
55–61					
1969	23.4	3.4	20.0	11.1	8.9
1970	25.7	4.8	20.9	11.7	9.2
1971	24.8	4.5	20.3	10.7	9.6
1972	26.1	5.0	21.1	11.8	9.3
1973	27.7	5.5	22.2	12.3	9.9
1974	30.3	6.0	24.3	12.4	11.9
1975	29.8	5.0	24.8	11.9	12.9
1976	28.5	5.4	23.1	11.1	12.0
1977	29.2	4.3	24.9	11.4	13.5
1978	28.7	4.8	23.9	10.4	13.5
1979	29.8	5.7	24.1	10.1	14.0
1980	30.6	5.3	25.3	11.1	14.2
1981	28.9	4.7	24.2	10.3	13.9
62–64					
1969	32.2	3.4	28.8	13.2	15.6
1970	34.4	3.8	30.6	13.6	17.0
1971	33.9	4.1	29.8	13.5	16.3
1972	33.4	4.1	29.3	13.4	15.9
1973	37.7	3.7	34.0	13.2	20.8
1974	37.8	4.7	33.1	13.3	19.8
1975	34.1	5.0	29.1	11.0	18.1
1976	39.8	4.6	35.2	14.5	20.7
1977	39.7	4.6	35.1	13.6	21.5
1978	37.3	5.0	32.3	12.9	19.4
1979	37.5	4.8	32.7	10.8	21.9
1980	36.5	4.4	32.1	12.8	19.3
1981	38.4	4.4	34.0	10.8	23.2

NOTE: Column 1 = Column 2 + Column 3;
　　　Column 3 = Column 4 + Column 5.

indicate a worsening of health among men aged 55–64. The overall worsening of health is due almost entirely to an increase in being unable to work, not an increase in limitation in the amount or kind of work. Only a small portion is due to an increase in limitation of secondary activities.

We have already noted that limitation of activity has flaws as a measure of health. Because of this we examine an additional indicator of health from the NHIS that should not be as affected by job and income availability. Annual restricted-activity days are estimated from the number of days in the last two weeks that a person had to cut down on his usual activities for the whole day because of illness or injury. Restricted-activity days can be subdivided into bed disability days and other days of restricted activity. Bed disability days are the subset of restricted-activity days on which a person stayed in bed all or most of the day. Thus, for this measure, a person's usual activities are whatever he would normally do during the two weeks preceding the survey. If he had previously cut back on work activities because of his health, he would respond relative to the new set of activities. Unlike limitation of activity, restricted-activity days can be due to both chronic and acute conditions.

In Table 5.3 we demonstrate that restricted-activity days increased by over 20 percent among men aged 62–64 and by 45 percent among men aged 55–61. Bed disability days did not show any clear trend in either age group. Over time there appears to be a small increase in the younger group and a small decrease in the older group. The overall increase in restricted-activity days was due to the increases in other restricted days, which increased approximately 60 percent from 1969 to 1981 in each age group.

Our data do not confirm the conclusion by Yeas (1987, 28), which was based on an analysis of similar data, that "there has been a real change in trend from worsening to improving health at some point roughly midway between 1969 and 1981 among persons aged 55–70." Like Colvez and Blanchet (1981) and Verbrugge (1984), we find indicators of deteriorating health across this period: an increase in retirement due to health, an increase in limitation of activity due to an inability to work, and an increase in nonbedridden restricted-activity days.

We remain reluctant to conclude that health worsened in this age group, however, because it is possible that all of these reported increases in ill health are due to changes in factors other than health. These factors include an increasing knowledge of alternatives to working when in poor health and an increase in sick men defining themselves as unable to work.

Health Among Usual-Activity Groups

At this point, we disaggregate men into their usual-activity categories and examine changes in health status within these categories. Examining

TABLE 5.3

ANNUAL RESTRICTED-ACTIVITY DAYS
AMONG MEN AGED 55–61 AND 62–64, 1969–1981

Year	Days of restricted activity	Bed disability days	Other restricted-activity days
	55–61		
1969	21.4	7.3	14.1
1970	19.9	6.0	13.9
1971	22.8	7.9	14.9
1972	25.0	7.9	17.1
1973	23.4	7.5	15.9
1974	25.8	8.8	17.0
1975	27.4	8.0	19.4
1976	27.2	8.5	18.7
1977	25.2	8.5	16.7
1978	27.9	8.1	19.8
1979	27.1	6.9	20.2
1980	30.9	8.4	22.5
1981	31.1	8.7	22.4
	62–64		
1969	25.2	12.2	13.0
1970	29.2	8.9	20.3
1971	26.3	8.4	17.9
1972	28.9	10.5	18.4
1973	28.6	11.4	17.2
1974	28.4	9.6	18.8
1975	28.3	9.8	18.5
1976	32.9	12.5	20.4
1977	26.5	8.8	17.7
1978	25.9	8.5	17.4
1979	32.0	11.4	20.6
1980	30.2	9.0	21.2
1981	30.5	8.7	21.8

health trends within these categories, together with the redistribution of individuals over the categories, will help to clarify the reasons for the apparent deterioration in health.

Because change has been fairly regular over the twelve years studied here, we group our data into three-year periods surrounding the census year and examine change over ten years. This results in a sample of about 15,000 for each of the three-year periods centered on 1970 and 1980. For most of the analysis presented, only the years 1970 and 1971 are used to represent 1970, because retired men were not classified into retired/health and retired/other in 1969. Before beginning our analysis of the separate groups, we present the breakdown by age and usual-activity status for data grouped as just described (Table 5.4).

We observe differences by age in Table 5.4 that were not evident in Table 5.1. Among those aged 55–61, the decrease in working was due more to the increase in the retired/health than the retired/other category. Among the older men, the increase among those who retired for other reasons was twice as great as among those who retired due to health.

Now we examine health change over time for men divided by usual-activity status. As noted above, both a deterioration in health and a greater availability of benefits could result in an increase in the percentage of men who say they are not working because of health. However, our expectations for the direction of change within activity groups differs depending on the direction of change in health over the period.

If there were no change in average health status and men were retiring from work to take advantage of more easily available or newly discovered benefits, we would expect that over time the men leaving the labor force, though they might meet the eligibility criteria for disability, would be on average healthier than those retiring in the past. The sickest men in either 1970 or 1980 would not work no matter what the alternative benefit level. If disability benefits had gradually become easier to qualify for* and benefit amounts were higher, more of those whose health conditions were of lesser severity would withdraw, resulting in a somewhat healthier group of working men over time. Additionally, those who retired because of health would be healthier, because entrants into this category would be healthier.

If health actually deteriorated and men were not withdrawing from the labor force because of the easier availability of somewhat higher benefits, then those men who retired in 1970 and 1980 would be at the same level of unhealthiness. There would be no change in the health level of either workers or those who retired because of ill health, but a higher proportion of the total population would be in the retired/health category. Men in the retired/other groups are responding primarily to factors other than health. For this reason we do not expect any change in the health of this group.

---

*Editor's note: Legislative debate prior to the passage of the 1980 Disability Amendments made clear the tremendous growth in disability benefits ($3–15 billion in 1970–1980) and the great disparity in the rate of disability awards per 100,000 population among the states.

TABLE 5.4
USUAL-ACTIVITY STATUS OF MEN
AGED 55–61 AND 62–64, 1970 AND 1980
(PERCENTAGES)

	1970	1980	1980 – 1970
		55–61	
Working	86.6	78.1	−8.5
Retired/Health	6.7	10.8	4.1
Retired/Other	2.5	5.4	2.9
Other	4.2	5.7	1.5
N	7,389	10,873	
		62–64	
Working	68.5	51.6	−16.9
Retired/Health	14.6	19.8	5.2
Retired/Other	13.2	25.0	11.8
Other	3.7	3.6	−0.1
N	2,794	3,992	

NOTE: The 1970 data are from 1970 and 1971; 1980 data are from 1979, 1980, and 1981.

Most of the data in Table 5.5 indicate that the health of men in the work force did not change between 1970 and 1980. There is no significant change in the percentage limited in activity, the annual number of restricted-activity days, or the number of bed disability days. There is, however, a significant drop in the work-loss days—from 11.5 to 8.1 days, a 30 percent decrease—occurring among working men aged 62–64. The change in this measure indicates that older *working* men could have been healthier in 1980 than they were in 1970.

The data in Table 5.5 show no significant change in the health status of men who continued to work with a limitation. Even the nine-day reduction in work-loss days, from 30.0 to 21.1 for the older group, is not statistically significant.

In Table 5.6 we present indicators of the health of the retired male population, divided into those who report that they retired because of their health and those who retired for other reasons. For both of these groups there is a statistically significant increase in restricted-activity days among 55–61 year olds in 1980 as compared to 1970. There is no statistically significant change in this indicator among those aged 62 and over. There is also no statistically significant change in the number of bed disability days in

TABLE 5.5

INDICATORS OF HEALTH AMONG WORKING MEN
AGED 55–61 AND 62–64, 1970 AND 1980

	LIMITED IN ACTIVITY (PERCENTAGES)		RESTRICTED-ACTIVITY DAYS		BED DISABILITY DAYS		WORK-LOSS DAYS	
	1970	1980	1970	1980	1970	1980	1970	1980
All working men								
55–61	16.8	17.6	13.6	15.4	4.2	3.6	7.3	6.5
62–64	20.2	19.4	19.0	17.2	5.0	5.5	11.5	8.1[a]
Working men with limitation of activity								
55–61	—	—	41.2	46.2	9.4	8.6	20.1	18.5
62–64	—	—	55.3	48.8	11.2	12.2	30.0	21.1

NOTE: The 1970 data are from 1970 and 1971 except "limited in activity" data, which are from 1969, 1970, and 1971; 1980 data are from 1979, 1980, and 1981.
a. Difference between 1980 and 1970 is statistically significant at the .05 level.

TABLE 5.6

INDICATORS OF HEALTH AMONG RETIRED MEN
AGED 55–61 AND 62–64, 1970 AND 1980

	RESTRICTED-ACTIVITY DAYS		BED DISABILITY DAYS	
	1970	1980	1970	1980
Retired/health				
55–61	89.9	108.7[a]	30.2	32.3
62–64	70.1	75.9	26.1	24.5
Retired/other				
55–61	11.0	23.2[a]	3.9	4.2
62–64	15.1	16.7	5.2	4.2
Retired/other with limitation of activity				
55–61	21.6	55.8[a]	5.7	11.0
62–64	33.1	35.7	11.2	6.8

NOTE: The 1970 data are from 1970 and 1971; 1980 data are from 1979, 1980, and 1981.
a. Difference between 1970 and 1980 is significant at .05 level.

these groups. For those men who retired for reasons other than health and who report a limitation of activity, restricted-activity days are statistically significantly higher for those aged 55–61, but not for the older group. Changes in bed disability days are not statistically significant in either age group among these retirees.

These results seem to indicate a worsening of health both among those retired because of health and among those retired for other reasons. The deterioration is greater among those who report that they are limited but retired for other reasons. With respect to our two scenarios, we hypothesized that the health of both groups of retirees would have remained the same even if the health of the total age group worsened over the period. Overall, the data suggest that men who are withdrawing from the labor force for health and/or other reasons are less healthy—or perceive themselves as less healthy—than their counterparts in past periods. There is no suggestion of an increase in malingerers withdrawing from the labor force.

Causes of Disability

The causes of disability provide additional insight into the evaluation of change over time in the indicators of health. The cause of a disability or impairment may serve as some indication of the severity of ill health.

Sunshine (1981, 20), in his analysis of the causes of rising disability, examines changes in disablement from heart disease. Heart disease was chosen to test the evidence supporting the notion that decreased death rates from heart disease could be accompanied by increasing disability from heart disease. Using published data from the NHIS, Sunshine points out that the proportion of persons unable to carry out normal activities because of heart disease stayed stable for 45–64 year olds for 1966 and 1976. He also notes that the proportion of new disability awardees having cardiovascular disease among federal pension recipients declined from 40 percent in 1960 to 30 percent in the mid-1970s. From this and other evidence, Sunshine concludes that it "seems extremely improbable that the increased use of disability programs results from poorer health" (ibid.).

Chirikos (1986, 287) examines change over time in disability by dividing causes into physical and sensory impairments, rising and falling mortality conditions, and other diseases. He finds an average annual rate of increase in the prevalence of work disability from most of these conditions of about 2 percent. He attributes the majority of the rise in disability over this period to an increasing prevalence, of diseases and impairments rather than to other causes, such as sociodemographic or economic factors. Data indicating a greater increase in heart disease prevalence, despite evidence that the incidence of heart disease is falling, lead Chirikos to suggest the possibility of future increases in disability due to heart disease (ibid., 289).

Our analysis by disease and/or disabling impairment divides men according to their reported main cause of activity limitation. The analysis was completed using seventeen specific cause categories, including the major causes of death and morbidity for this age group. For brevity of presentation, however, we display results using nine cause categories. Each of seven individual categories accounts for at least 5 percent of all limitation, and there are two residual categories. The specific categories are heart disease, arteriosclerosis and cerebrovascular disease, bronchitis and emphysema, arthritis, musculoskeletal impairments, vision and hearing losses, and paralysis. The residual categories are all other mortal and all other morbid conditions. These categories consist of individual causes other than those listed above, grouped into those from which a person could die and those very unlikely to play a role in causing death.

From the data in Table 5.7 we show that in 1980, for men aged 55–61, 30 percent were limited, and for those aged 62–64, 37.5 percent were limited. The most prevalent limiting condition, which accounted for approximately one out of four or five limitations in these age groups was heart disease. Musculoskeletal impairments, which would include back, shoulder, and limb injuries, are usually next in importance as a cause of morbidity. Arthritis, arteriosclerosis and cerebrovascular conditions, and paralysis are the other major causes of morbidity.

Causes of morbidity that are also causes of mortality account for just over half of the limitation in these age groups. This fact alone should weaken the relationship between mortality and morbidity change. Over time there is little change in the distribution of the causes of limitation. Certainly there is no dramatic shift in the pattern of causation, nor does one category clearly account for the increase in limitation.

Heart disease is the major condition causing limitation among men in each usual-activity category (Appendix A). Across usual-activity status, the ranking of other conditions is roughly similar as well.

Over time, those suffering from heart disease constitute a smaller proportion among those limited in each of the usual-activity groups. The one exception is among men aged 55–61 who retired because of poor health. In this group those suffering from heart disease increased from 22 to 25 percent of those limited.

The decline in the percentage of people disabled by heart disease is more than offset in most groups by the increase in the percentage suffering paralysis. In the case of those retired for reasons of health, there is an increase in both heart disease and paralysis categories.

TABLE 5.7

PERCENTAGE OF MEN AGED 55–61 AND 62–64
LIMITED BY SPECIFIC CAUSES, 1970 AND 1980

| | 55–61 | | 62–64 | |
	1970	1980	1970	1980
Heart disease	5.4	6.1	7.8	7.5
Arteriosclerosis and				
cerebrovascular diseases	2.3	2.9	3.1	4.4
Bronchitis and emphysema	1.6	1.7	2.7	3.1
Other mortal diseases	4.3	5.1	6.0	7.1
Arthritis	2.1	3.2	3.7	4.1
Musculoskeletal				
impairments	4.5	4.8	4.6	4.2
Vision and hearing loss	1.0	1.3	1.5	1.4
Paralysis	1.8	3.0	1.9	3.6
Other morbid conditions	2.1	1.8	2.8	2.2
No limitation	74.8	70.2	65.9	62.5

Among the older group, for all three activity groups, we find a decrease in the proportion of people with heart disease and an increase in the proportion with paralysis. We believe it is difficult to say anything more conclusive about the changing health conditions of men who cite limitations of usual activities. Certainly there is no clear-cut indication in the data that some subgroups are either healthier or less healthy.

Among those reporting limitations, the likelihood that they continue working does not vary much by the disease or disability condition causing the limitation. Our data (shown in Appendix B) repeat the finding of Chirikos (1986, 289) that the disability risk for heart disease is roughly equivalent to that of other chronic diseases.

There are some striking decreases over the decade in the likelihood that a man continued to work with a limiting condition. Among younger men in 1970, at least 50 percent of limited men worked in all of the cause categories. By 1980, the figure was 50 percent or more in only three out of the nine categories. Among older men, the pattern of change was the same but the levels of working were lower. The decline in percentage working in each cause category is generally fairly similar in magnitude to the increase in the retired/health category among those aged 55–61 and to the increase in both categories of retired for those aged 62–64.

Discussion

The data in Appendix B strongly suggest that, over the decade, accommodation to diseases by limiting activity and early retirement increased. Men disabled with the same conditions in 1970 and 1980 were more likely to have withdrawn from the labor force in 1980 for all disease categories. This finding suggests that men were perhaps more aware of the possibility of controlling the severity of a given disease by reducing activities in the early stages. For example, individuals who were diagnosed as having high blood pressure may have retired earlier, rather than prolonging work and its possible stressful side effects.

One reason why individuals might be less likely to work with a diagnosed health condition is that they are more knowledgeable about diseases and their progression. Data from the NHIS (not shown) indicate that more men in both the working and retired groups reported in 1980 having seen a doctor during the past year than reported having done so ten years earlier: 72 percent as compared to 66 percent. If older men were more likely to receive medical attention in 1980 than in 1970, it is possible that they had a better understanding of diseases and their ability to control the severity of symptoms or halt disease progress by actions such as early retirement.

It is also possible that there was a more complicated set of interactions. Individuals are becoming more knowledgeable about diseases and are learning to accommodate their illnesses. Verbrugge (1984, 509) has suggested increased accommodation to disease as an explanation of the increase in overall morbidity. To test this idea, we postulated that if accommodation were taking place increasingly between 1970 and 1980, then the average duration of limitation would decrease over that period. That is, men would be leaving the work force after fewer months with a condition in 1980 than in 1970.

Our results do not confirm this hypothesis. For retired men, the average duration of limitation for those limited for five years or less did not change significantly. For those retired because of their health, the average duration of limitation was approximately 31 months at both dates for both the younger and older men. Thus, these data on duration of illness do not support the idea that accommodation in the form of leaving the work force earlier after being diagnosed was taking place. However, the data in Appendix B do suggest that some form of accommodation was increasingly taking place. Being diagnosed with any chronic health condition meant that a person was more likely to leave the labor force in 1980 than in 1970. It is possible that doctors and social workers have been instrumental in disseminating information about the availability of disability program benefits to people they view as eligible.

Summary and Conclusions

The evidence does not provide a clear-cut answer to the question of whether or not men actually became less healthy over time or if improved access and more generous benefits led to a withdrawal of increasing numbers of less unhealthy men. There is no indication that health improved between 1970 and 1980 among men aged 55–64. This is true for men in all activity-status categories. Indeed, there are signs of deteriorating health: an increase in limitation of activity and restricted-activity days among all men aged 55–64, an increase in restricted-activity days among retired men, and a lack of improvement in health among working men when more men retired for health reasons.

Our evidence on whether the reported deterioration in health results from real deterioration in health, perceived deterioration in health, or no change in real or perceived health but an increase only in reported ill health because of a desire not to work is less clear cut. We cannot distinguish between changes in real and perceived health. The lack of improvement in health among workers and the deterioration in health among retired men are consistent with either a deterioration in real or perceived health. There is also some evidence that could be viewed as supporting the idea that neither real nor perceived health changed, but instead people increasingly reported ill health to justify not working. This includes the concentration of the deterioration of health in work ability, rather than the other categories of activity limitation (Table 5.2) and the decrease in the proportion of men working with an activity-limiting condition no matter which disease they suffered from (Appendix B).

We view these two changes as consistent with an increasing accommodation to disease by withdrawing from work rather than an increase in reported ill health to justify gaining benefits. The evidence that leads us to this conclusion is that people are not accommodating to disease at an earlier stage. Men who retired because of their health in 1980 had been sick just as long as men who retired in 1970. In addition, men who are retired report more restricted-activity days in 1980 than in 1970. Thus, we do not think the evidence supports the idea that relatively healthy men were dropping out of the labor force to collect easily available benefits. In our view, the evidence supports the idea that sick men became more aware over the decade of alternatives to working with a disease.

We therefore conclude that the overall pattern of changes in the proportion of men working and in the health of both workers and retirees is consistent with some deterioration in health as well as an increasing tendency to withdraw from the labor force when a health condition is diagnosed.

Appendix A

Specified Cause of Limitation by Usual Activity For Men Aged 55–61 and 62–64, 1970 and 1980 (Percentages)

Cause	TOTAL		WORKING		RETIRED/HEALTH		RETIRED/OTHER	
	1970	1980	1970	1980	1970	1980	1970	1980
			55–61					
Heart disease	21.6	20.4	23.4	19.2	22.0	25.0	18.5	14.2
Arteriosclerosis and cerebrovascular diseases	9.1	9.7	8.0	8.3	12.3	10.7	8.8	8.6
Bronchitis and emphysema	6.3	5.7	5.7	5.4	9.0	6.8	6.1	6.7
Other mortal diseases	17.2	16.8	15.2	17.7	18.7	15.9	18.9	20.8
Arthritis	8.5	10.7	8.6	10.5	7.5	11.1	12.3	15.3
Musculoskeletal impairments	17.7	16.2	19.7	18.4	14.6	12.2	12.8	15.4
Vision and hearing loss	4.0	4.4	3.9	5.1	2.4	3.1	7.9	4.9
Paralysis	7.2	9.9	8.4	11.2	5.2	8.5	3.0	11.0
Other morbid conditions	8.1	6.1	7.0	4.3	8.3	6.9	11.8	3.2

APPENDIX A (continued)

Cause	TOTAL		WORKING		RETIRED/HEALTH		RETIRED/OTHER	
	1970	1980	1970	1980	1970	1980	1970	1980
			62–64					
Heart disease	23.0	19.9	21.6	19.7	26.1	22.4	20.1	12.1
Arteriosclerosis and								
cerebrovascular diseases	8.9	11.9	7.9	10.5	8.8	13.1	11.2	13.1
Bronchitis and emphysema	8.0	8.2	8.6	5.7	8.3	8.9	7.6	8.9
Other mortal diseases	17.7	18.6	15.7	20.1	18.4	17.0	17.8	23.1
Arthritis	10.7	11.0	10.6	13.3	12.1	9.5	9.1	10.7
Musculoskeletal impairments	13.3	11.2	15.7	12.0	10.1	10.0	14.1	10.6
Vision and hearing loss	4.4	3.8	5.6	5.0	4.0	2.8	4.4	5.1
Paralysis	5.7	9.6	4.8	7.4	5.4	10.4	6.8	10.3
Other morbid conditions	8.1	5.9	9.2	6.2	6.8	5.9	9.1	6.0

NOTE: The 1970 data are from 1970 and 1971; 1980 data are from 1979, 1980, and 1981.

Usual Activity Status Among Men Aged 55–61 and 62–64 Who Are Limited by Specific Causes, 1970 and 1980 (Percentages)

55–61

Cause	WORKING			RETIRED/HEALTH			RETIRED/OTHER		
	1970	1980	1980 – 1970	1970	1980	1980 – 1970	1970	1980	1980 – 1970
Heart disease	63.5	43.6	–19.9	26.6	43.2	16.6	2.5	3.9	1.4
Arteriosclerosis and cerebrovascular diseases	54.1	39.7	–14.4	34.3	39.2	4.9	2.8	5.0	2.2
Bronchitis and emphysema	52.4	43.9	–8.5	36.9	41.8	4.9	2.8	6.6	3.8
Other mortal diseases	51.9	48.5	–3.4	28.3	33.2	4.9	3.1	6.9	3.8
Arthritis	59.6	45.1	–14.5	23.1	36.6	13.5	4.2	8.0	3.8
Musculoskeletal impairments	65.2	52.6	–12.6	21.4	26.5	5.1	2.1	5.3	3.2
Vision and hearing loss	57.6	54.4	–3.2	16.0	25.1	9.1	5.7	6.3	0.6
Paralysis	68.6	52.0	–16.6	18.7	30.2	11.5	1.2	6.2	5.0
Other morbid conditions	50.5	32.1	–18.4	26.8	39.8	13.0	3.6	2.9	–0.7
All causes	58.7	46.3	–12.4	26.1	35.4	9.3	2.9	5.6	2.7

APPENDIX B (*continued*)

Cause	WORKING			RETIRED/HEALTH			RETIRED/OTHER		
	1970	1980	1980 – 1970	1970	1980	1980 – 1970	1970	1980	1980 – 1970
				62–64					
Heart disease	37.5	26.3	–11.2	47.1	57.1	10.0	10.1	10.1	0.0
Arteriosclerosis and cerebrovascular diseases	35.7	23.6	–12.1	41.1	56.3	15.2	14.6	18.3	3.7
Bronchitis and emphysema	43.3	18.6	–24.7	43.1	55.1	12.0	11.0	18.2	7.2
Other mortal diseases	35.7	28.9	–6.8	43.9	46.7	2.8	11.5	20.7	9.2
Arthritis	39.6	32.2	–7.4	46.5	44.0	2.5	9.7	16.3	6.6
Musculoskeletal impairments	47.2	28.6	–18.6	31.3	45.7	14.4	12.1	15.8	3.7
Vision and hearing loss	50.7	34.8	–15.9	37.9	37.9	0.0	11.4	22.3	10.9
Paralysis	33.7	20.6	–13.1	39.5	54.9	15.4	13.7	17.9	4.2
Other morbid conditions	45.5	28.3	–17.2	34.5	51.3	16.8	11.7	17.1	5.4
All causes	40.0	26.6	–13.4	41.5	50.9	9.4	11.5	16.7	5.2

DISCUSSION

Donald O. Parsons

The attachment of adult men to the labor force has declined substantially in the postwar period in the United States. Among men aged 45–54, the non-participation rate (the percentage of the population neither working nor looking for work) has more than doubled, from 4.2 percent in 1948 to 8.8 percent in 1982. Among black men in this age group, the nonparticipation rate is approaching 20 percent (17.8 percent in 1982). Similar trends have occurred among other (older) male age groups. The identification of the source or sources of these trends is clearly of considerable social interest.

The Social Security Disability Insurance program has been identified as one major factor in the decline in adult male labor force participation in the United States (Parsons 1980a, 1980b; Leonard 1979, 1986). The Social Security program first paid cash benefits in 1957 to cover workers who were aged 50–64 years and were no longer capable of "substantial gainful activity." In 1960 the program was extended to cover workers under age 50. The program expanded rapidly in the subsequent twenty years, so that by 1982 approximately 2.6 million disabled workers were receiving $14.8 billion in cash benefits. The empirical evidence is overwhelming that the older working population is sensitive to the incentive structure of the Social Security Disability Insurance system; this benefit sensitivity has been established on time-series data, individual cross-section data, and state cross-section data.[1]

The magnitude of the disincentive effect, however, remains imprecisely measured. Eileen Crimmins and Maria Pramaggiore raise the important issue of whether the observed upward trend in nonparticipation in the labor force could in part have been induced by a decline in actual health conditions for this population. An affirmative answer to this question has implications beyond disability insurance policy, most obviously for health care policy.

On the surface, the deteriorating health hypothesis proposed by Crimmins and Pramaggiore seems implausible. Mortality rates, an easily measured attribute of population health conditions, have declined substantially for this group in the postwar period, particularly in the 1970s when labor force withdrawal was rapid. Crimmins and Pramaggiore, however, make the point that this large decrease in mortality may itself reduce the average health of those living. If, for example, an accident victim were spared death by a newly developed life support system and instead spent his or her life in a coma, the fraction of the population out of the labor force and the fraction of the population disabled would both increase, not in spite of the health care advances but because of them.

The major empirical difficulty in confronting the deteriorating health hypothesis is the absence of time series data on "objectively" measured health conditions among older men after World War II. All the measures available to the authors are socially conditioned, and the most abundant and accessible measures are self-reported. Clearly, in an environment in which individuals receive transfer payments only if they are disabled, self-reporting of health problems may be strategically biased (Parsons 1982b; Anderson and Burkhauser 1983).

Crimmins and Pramaggiore recognize this problem and propose a creative and indirect approach to the use of self-reported health data. Their approach is more limited and their results more imprecise than they recognize, however. The structure of change in health technology is central to the discussion, so it will be useful to develop the possibilities more explicitly. The model reveals the conditions under which it is invalid to use population mortality measures as (positive) indicators of population morbidity and disability. This is done in the next section below. The model is then used in the third section to organize and interpret Crimmins and Pramaggiore's empirical findings. An implicit model of self-reported health status employed by the authors is briefly discussed at that point since it affects one, but not all, of their proposed tests. In the final section I comment briefly on the general usefulness of self-reported health in the estimation of actual health trends.

MORTALITY RATES AS INDICATORS OF DISABILITY AND MORBIDITY RATES

The absence of an objective measure of health conditions has led several investigators to use mortality rates as an indicator of ill health (for example, Parsons 1980a, 1980b, 1982; Anderson and Burkhauser 1983). To what extent does a change in population mortality rates accurately index a change in disability rates?

At any point in time, an individual in a given birth cohort of working age can be found in one of four states: dead, disabled, working but restricted, and working with no restrictions. Assume that a health-improving shift in technology or behavior reduces mortality rates. If the individuals whose lives are spared are disabled by the life-threatening condition, then the fraction disabled in the new environment will rise, other things being constant. There is, of course, little reason to assume that all lives saved result in a disabled individual; neither is there reason to assume that health technology advances that save lives do not also improve less severe health conditions. This will shift individuals from the disabled state to one of the working states. If these advances are large enough, and if the population becoming disabled is large relative to the population that dies in any given time interval, then the proportion of disabled individuals among the living will fall as a result of improved medical technology.

As Crimmins and Pramaggiore note, the validity of the population mortality-rate trend as an indicator of the trend in morbidity rates is, in the end, an empirical issue. First, have recent advances in medical technology been primarily mortality specific, or have they been more evenly spread across health conditions? Second, have the individuals saved been primarily relegated to disability status, or have they been restored to less restricted functional statuses? At one extreme, if mortality rates are small relative to disability rates, and if reductions in impairments among the previously disabled population parallel reductions in mortality rates, then the mortality rates will be a good proxy for disability. At the other extreme, if none of the technological advances that reduce mortality rates are reflected in reduced disability rates, and if all the people saved are disabled, then the change in mortality rates will be negatively correlated with the change in the proportion disabled, a poor proxy indeed.

SELF-REPORTED HEALTH BY WORK STATUS

Crimmins and Pramaggiore attack the question of secular trends in the health conditions of older working-age men through a clever use of the self-reported health data. They do not assume, as others have, that self-reported health measures are universally valid, but instead they define subpopulations for whom misreporting should not be a problem and explore the self-reported health trends in these subgroups. In particular, the authors ask whether or not it might be possible to test the two hypotheses— the work disincentive hypothesis and the deteriorating health hypothesis— by looking at the trends in self-reported health of the population *partitioned by work status*.

Consider the self-reported health status of the working population. If the work disincentive hypothesis were the sole source of the upward trend in reported disability, then the growth in generosity of the disability system that induced some workers out of the labor force would also have induced those individuals to change their self-reported health status from "working but limited" to "disabled."[2] If this were the case, Crimmins and Pramaggiore correctly argue, the reported health of the working population should have improved as more of the workers with health problems were drawn out of the labor force. The alternative hypothesis of deteriorating health implies no change in the average health of the working population; if health conditions change but the work decision conditional on health does not, then the health conditions of the working population should be unchanged.

Crimmins and Pramaggiore also propose a second test, based on the reported health of those out of the labor force. Specifically, they argue that self-reported health of the nonworking population should have improved under the work disincentive hypothesis. The intuitive notion is that the new group of disabled include the previously "working but limited" group, who are on average healthier than those who had previously classified themselves as disabled in the earlier, less generous environment. Here I believe that Crimmins and Pramaggiore confuse actual and self-reported health. Certainly the *actual* health of the nonworking population should improve when the disability program became more generous; whether *self-reported* health for this group improves, however, is not known without additional and not necessarily plausible assumptions on reporting behavior. If, for some reason, individuals who are marginally unhealthy report themselves as less severely impaired than those who are severely disabled, then the conjecture is true. If, however, the marginally disabled strategically exaggerate their health difficulties to make themselves indistinguishable from the truly disabled, the conjecture is false.[3]

It would seem, then, that only the test proposed on the self-reported health of the working population is valid, at least without strong ancillary assumptions. If the self-reported health of the working population improved from 1970 to 1980, then the economic disincentive model would be favored; if the health condition of the working group was unchanged, the deteriorating health model would be accepted. What is the evidence on trends in the health condition of the working population? Unfortunately, the evidence appears to be mixed. In terms of *severe* self-reported problems, the answer seems generally consistent with the disincentive hypothesis, since the self-reported health of the male working population has improved in this period. In Table 5.5, Crimmins and Pramaggiore report that among working men aged 55–61, the number of bed disability days dropped from 4.2 to 3.6 between 1970 and 1980 and the number of work-loss days dropped from 7.3 to 6.5. Neither of these declines are statistically significant, however.[4] Among men aged 62–64, the number of work-loss days declined significantly, whereas the number of bed disability days increased, though the increase was not statistically significant. The result would seem to be that severe health problems for the working population became less common, although the imprecision of the estimates makes this conclusion quite tentative.

The authors also attempt a slightly different attack on the problem: exploration of the claimed type of disability. In a mode of argument that was apparently first utilized by Sunshine (1981), Crimmins and Pramaggiore ask whether or not a shift in the specific source of the claimed health problem may signal that the claims are legitimate. If the claimed health problem is an "elastic," hard-to-define condition (for example, musculoskeletal problems), it is plausible that the shift in self-reported health is strategic. If, however, the problem is concrete (for example, cancer), the strategic argument is less plausible. Sunshine, based on his analysis of heart disease, argues that the observed health shift is a reporting phenomenon. Crimmins and Pramaggiore consider a wider range of maladies and conclude that the evidence is more ambiguous. They report that the disease categories with the largest increases (among men aged 55–61) between 1970 and 1980 are arthritis and paralysis (Table 5.7). The same patterns are observed when the sample is conditioned on work status. This sort of argument is naturally limited in precision, since it is difficult to structure the argument formally in a way that would permit rigorous testing. I am not sure, for example, whether arthritis or even paralysis, if less than complete, are flexible categories or rigid ones.

ACTUAL HEALTH TRENDS AND SELF-REPORTED HEALTH TRENDS

It seems intuitively plausible that health improvements in the postwar period have not been mortality specific but have been more general, given that average wealth has increased and technological advances have been made along a variety of fronts. The evidence that Crimmins and Pramaggiore present does not convince me that the intuitive view is incorrect; indeed, the evidence would seem mildly supportive of the intuitive view. This conclusion is quite tentative, however, since the indirect approach they employ, based on self-reported health status, is dependent for its interpretation on models of technology change and labor force behavior.

A practical difficulty in measuring the health deterioration (or improvement) trend after World War II is twofold: the hypothesis is not mutually exclusive with the major competing hypothesis (the work disincentive model), and the structural changes in the work-disincentive structure have been so large in this period that it is difficult to isolate less dramatic processes. In the early 1970s, disability benefit levels were increased sharply in real terms; the benefit waiting period was reduced from six to five months; the low-income "safety-net" program was federalized (Supplemental Security Income); and the Social Security disabled were given access to medicare after a two-year waiting period. This major restructuring and improvement in the system induced a large increase in applications for Social Security Disability Insurance and, given the crudeness of the disability screen, a large increase in the percentage of the population certified as disabled. As a consequence of these structural changes, the disability system approached a funding crisis in 1977 that led to a major tightening of the screening system.[5] The Social Security Administration pressured state agencies to increase the rigor of the

FIGURE 5.1

INABILITY TO WORK AMONG MEN AGED 55–61, 1969–1981

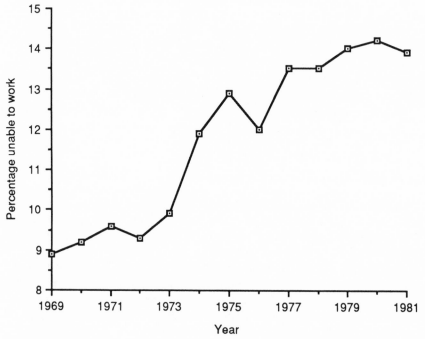

SOURCE: See Table 5.2.

screening process; within one year initial allowance rates dropped by 20 percent and within two years by 30 percent. This had predictable, positive effects on labor force participation for older men.

The rapid changes in the self-reported health measure in the 1970s are fully consistent with the changes in the Social Security disability structure (Figure 5.1). The sharp increase in the number of people who claimed to be unable to work around 1974 and the flattening of that profile in 1978 follow closely the improvement in the program and the subsequent tightening of eligibility. Given these large structural shifts in the system, the attempt to isolate what is surely a less dramatic shift in health conditions is unlikely to be successful. The general methodology proposed by Crimmins and Pramaggiore is an interesting one, however, and in a more stable economic environment it may well be a valuable approach to the problem of using readily available self-reported health data to monitor health trends.

Notes

1. See Leonard (1986) for an excellent review of this literature.

2. It is unlikely that the robustly healthy portion of the working population would successfully secure eligibility for disability benefits, given the rigorous, if inaccurate, health screening required in the disability program.

3. If the affected group did show such restraint as to maintain the ordering between themselves and the severely disabled, the disability system could use reported health problem orderings to screen applicants for eligibility.

4. In terms of measures more inclusive of milder conditions, reported poor health among working men has apparently increased, although again not significantly; the percentage reporting limited activity increased from 16.8 to 17.6 percent and the number reporting restricted-activity days increased from 13.6 to 15.4 percent.

5. For a discussion of the disability funding crisis, see Meyer (1979). Parsons (1984) provides an analysis of the screening response and its labor market consequences.

References

Anderson, Kathryn H., and Richard V. Burkhauser. 1983. "The Effect of Actual Mortality Experience Within a Retirement Decision Model." Working Paper no. 83-W08, Vanderbilt University.

Chapman, Stephen H., Mitchell LaPlante, and Gail Wilensky. 1986. "Life Expectancy and the Health Status of the Aged." *Social Security Bulletin* 49: 24–48.

Chirikos, Thomas. 1986. "Accounting for the Historical Rise in Work-Disability Prevalence." *Milbank Memorial Fund Quarterly* 64:271–301.

Colvez, Alain, and Madelaine Blanchet. 1981. "Disability Trends in the United States Population 1966–76: Analysis of Reported Causes." *American Journal of Public Health* 71:464–71.

Crimmins, Eileen M. 1981. "The Changing Pattern of American Mortality Decline, 1940–1977, and Its Implications for the Future." *Population and Development Review* 7:229–54.

Fries, James F. 1980. "Aging, Natural Death and the Compression of Morbidity." *New England Journal of Medicine* 303:130–35.

Gruenberg, E. M. 1977. "The Failure of Success." *Milbank Memorial Fund Quarterly/Health and Society* 55:3–24.

Haveman, R., B. Wolfe, and J. Warlick. 1984. "Disability Transfers, Early Retirement, and Retrenchment." In Henry J. Aaron and Gary T. Burtless, eds., *Retirement and Economic Behavior*. Washington, D.C.: Brookings Institution.

Leonard, J. S. 1979. "The Social Security Disability Program and Labor Force Participation." Working Paper no. 392, National Bureau of Economic Research.

———. 1986. "Labor Supply Incentives and the Disincentives for Disabled Persons." In Monroe Berkowitz and M. Anne Hill, eds., *Disability and the Labor Market*. Ithaca, N.Y.: ILR Press.

Manton, Kenneth G. 1982. "Changing Concepts of Morbidity and Mortality in the Elderly Population." *Milbank Memorial Fund Quarterly/Health and Society* 60:183–244.

Meyer, C. W. 1979. *Social Security Disability Insurance: The Problems of Unexpected Growth*. Washington, D.C.: American Enterprise Institute.

Parsons, Donald. 1980a. "The Decline in Male Labor Force Participation." *Journal of Political Economy* 88:117–34.

———. 1980b. "Racial Trends in Male Labor Force Participation." *American Economic Review* 70:911–20.

———. 1982. "The Male Labour Force Participation Decision: Health, Reported Health, and Economic Incentives." *Economica* 49:81–91.

———. 1984. "Social Insurance with Imperfect State Verification: Income Insurance for the Disabled." Working Paper Series, Economics Department, Ohio State University.

Sunshine, Jonathan. 1981. "Disability Payments Stabilizing After Era of Accelerating Growth." *Monthly Labor Review* 104:17–22.

U.S. Bureau of the Census. 1984. *Statistical Abstract of the United States: 1985*. Washington, D.C.: GPO.

U.S. Department of Health, Education, and Welfare. 1973. *Current Estimates from the Health Interview Survey, 1971*. Series 10, no. 70. Hyattsville, Md.: National Center for Health Statistics.

Verbrugge, Lois. 1984. "Longer Life But Worsening Health?: Trends in Health and Mortality of Middle-Aged and Older Persons." *Milbank Memorial Fund Quarterly/Health and Society* 62:475–519.

Ycas, Martynas. 1987. "Recent Trends in Health Near the Age of Retirement: New Findings from the Health Interview Survey." *Social Security Bulletin* 50:5–30.

6

AGE-SPECIFIC DEATH RATES

Jere R. Behrman, Robin Sickles, and Paul Taubman

Good knowledge of why variations in mortality occur is important. Such variations might underlie behavioral differences in labor force, retirement, health, medical care use, and saving patterns; they might also influence public policy decisions such as what transfer payments should be made and to whom these payments should be made.

Economists lately have investigated in detail the determinants of age of retirement.[1] Economists and other social scientists also have analyzed the determinants of mortality.[2] The mortality studies are generally based on a single cross-section or a short panel. In these studies, the probability of dying in a given time period is related to variables such as the person's education and age.

Recently, however, demographers and statisticians have developed and improved alternative statistical models to estimate baseline survivor distributions (that is, what percentage of the sample is alive at a given age), which can shift with covariates over time.[3] A major problem, which these methods are designed to overcome, is that in most samples not everyone has died by

This work has been supported by grants from the National Institute on Aging and from the Hoover Institution. The authors would like to thank Abdo Yazbeck for his valuable computational assistance and Jennifer Green for her editorial help. Special thanks go to Richard Burkhauser for his many suggestions.

the end of the sample frame. This right censoring is generally dealt with by making distributional assumptions about the form of the survivor function, using an unobserved baseline and employing a partial likelihood estimator, or using nonparametric techniques. Another major problem is the potential bias caused by unobserved heterogeneity in individual frailties that appears less severe as the number of explanatory variables is increased.

Previous related studies by demographers have generally been based on small samples and short periods of time. In this paper we make use of two large samples with data on death by month for ten and sixteen years, respectively. After presenting these data sets, we discuss the models we estimate and the construction of our variables, and we present results based on several estimators and different distributional assumptions.

THE DATA

The first of our two data sets is the Retirement History Survey (RHS), which has been used extensively by economists. The RHS is a large random sample with relatively rich information and with about ten years of death data. A large proportion of its observations are censored, which may make our results sensitive to the distributional assumptions used. We also consider a second data set, the Dorn sample, which is unknown to (or at least has not been used by) most economists. This is quite a large sample of white men who were generally born before 1900 and for whom censoring is less of a problem than for the RHS. However, with the exception of smoking and occupational data, less covariate information is available in the Dorn sample. Finally, the Dorn sample contains a nonrandom element that we discuss below.

The Retirement History Survey

The Retirement History Survey was started in 1969 with about 11,000 men and women. At that time it was a nationwide random sample of heads of households aged 58–63. The sample members were reinterviewed every two years through 1979. We have constructed a longitudinal file from the interviews through 1977 (and shortly we will be able to extend coverage through 1979). Death information has been collected from two sources. The RHS records death as a reason for non-reinterview when they know this to be the case, generally through interviewing the widow. This source is incomplete. The other source is the Social Security files, which record death reported to them by month and year as part of the process of issuing death benefits (such as burial grants and survivor benefits for dependent children) and making necessary adjustments in Old Age, Survivor and Disability Insurance benefits. We currently have this death information through 1977 (with incomplete data into 1979).[4] We have compared these two sources, and there are only two cases of deaths recorded in the RHS that are not in the Social Security files. Moreover, the Social Security files' date of death is in accord with the RHS in that the individual does not give interviews after Social Security files. Moreover, the Social Security files' date of death is in accord with the RHS in that the individual does not give interviews after Social Security records his or her death. Duleep (1986), following up on the earlier work of Rosen and Taubman (1984), has indicated that in comparison to national death rates the Social Security files now record nearly all deaths.

The RHS contains substantial information on the respondents and their spouses, including age, education, wealth, current earnings, pensions, Social Security benefits, earnings covered by Social Security annually for the period 1951–1976, number of children, current and previous occupation, marital history, spouse's earnings, health status, medical usage, retirement status and plans, nutrition, and some aspects of life style including contact with children.

The advantages of the RHS include: (1) the RHS contains substantial information on respondents and spouses; (2) it is a random draw of the population of heads of households in 1969; and (3) it is of manageable size to experiment with various hazard functions employing different techniques and assumptions with a relatively large number of covariates. The major disadvantage of the RHS is that currently we can only look at the survivor curve over at most a fifteen-year age-time period and, when we wish to study each age group separately, a ten-year period. In addition, a large proportion (about 80 percent of the sample was still alive in 1977 and is thus censored in an analysis of survival. Below we report how sensitive our estimates are to alternative treatments of the censoring problem.

The Dorn Sample

The sample was originally constructed by Dorn (1958), whose pioneering effort was extended by Kahn (1966), by Rogot (1974)—who is our source for the following description—and by Rogot and Murray (1980); it has recently been updated through 1980 by Hrubec, Norman, and Rogot.[5] Dorn was interested in studying the relationship of tobacco use to mortality experience in general and to specific causes of death. With the cooperation of the Veterans Administration (V.A.), he mailed a short questionnaire to 293,958 U.S. veterans who in December 1953 held U.S. government life insurance policies and who had served in the armed forces between 1917 and 1940. The questionnaire, which can be found in Kahn (appendix E), asked how many times a day a person smoked cigarettes, cigars, and/or a pipe, how long ago he had stopped, his occupation, his industry, and his age. About 200,000 veterans responded in 1954. Another 49,000 responded to a second mailing in January 1957, and 46,000 did not reply. The V.A. recorded deaths by month as well as by year and by causes.

Rogot (1974, 192) presents the age distribution for 1954 and 1957 as:

Age	Respondents in 1954	Respondents in 1957	No reply	Total
30–34	7,421	43	2,148	9,612
35–44	16,735	7,156	4,037	27,928
45–54	10,317	1,242	2,232	13,791
55–64	137,820	26,579	31,468	195,867
65–74	25,002	13,683	5,603	44,288
75–84	1,525	523	424	2,472
30–84	198,820	49,226	45,912	293,958

People of different ages may have had different environmental exposures and different medical technology available when ill. Thus, it is possible that survivor functions vary by age cohort. This sample is large enough to allow the estimation of separate survivor functions for different age groups. Those in the 55–64 cohort can eventually be divided into single-year intervals. For other ages we can combine several adjacent groups. Currently we subdivide those born before 1891 from those born between 1891 and 1900.

We have excluded from the analysis those people who have no information on any of the variables studied. This left us with a sample of nearly 200,000. We have examined the plots of the age-specific death rates for the 200,000 and for the full sample. They are nearly identical.

The Dorn sample has cause-of-death data taken from death certificates. The cause-of-death data will be aggregated into heart disease, stroke, all forms of cancer, accidents, and all other. Although we realize that the information on cause of death is noisy, in part because of the difficulty in distinguishing immediate primary from underlying and contributory causes, the categories given are fairly broad and the first four categories include the causes of most deaths. We will eventually modify our hazard analysis to treat each cause as a distinct outcome, just as economists have treated employment, unemployment, and out of the labor force as separate states.[6]

The Dorn veteran sample includes only those veterans whose V.A. life insurance was still in force in December 1953. A questionnaire administered at that time collected information on occupation. As shown by Dorn (1958) and by Kahn (1966), the sample has disproportionally fewer unskilled workers than the corresponding white male cohort.[7]

During the last several decades, epidemiologists have investigated the accuracy of the V.A.'s information on date of death (see DeBakey and Beebe 1952; Beebe and Simon 1969; Cohen 1953). Procedural details differ across these studies, but basically the researchers took death certificates of men in the appropriate age range, matched them to military records to obtain military serial numbers, and then gave the names and numbers to the V.A. Roughly 95 percent of the deaths were recorded in the V.A. files, with many of those not listed having been dishonorably discharged or in the army no more than four days during World War I. This high rate of coverage occurs because veterans draw pension benefits that cease at death and other benefits that commence at death, such as burial plots, a flag, and a burial allowance. In the Dorn sample the economic incentives to keep in touch with the V.A. were particularly strong, since all participants had V.A. life insurance in force in 1954. Although some 75,000 terminated their insurance between 1963 and 1969, they were still eligible for the death benefits. For the Dorn sample, Rogot (1974, 190) reports that special efforts were made to check these 75,000 cases, and he says, "The overall mortality follow-up, with respect to the fact of death and year of death, is considered to be almost 100 percent complete."

The data on death have been updated periodically. The data for 1969–1980 have been collected and added to the file. However, we only received the post-1969 data in early 1987. Our current analysis is therefore based on death records through 1969. Moreover, we currently are limited by computer memory size to using about 85,628 individuals.

Sample means and standard deviations (S.D.) are given for the Dorn and RHS samples in Appendixes A and B, respectively.

MODELS AND VARIABLES

In this section we provide a brief overview of our models and variable construction. A detailed treatment of the statistical models is given in Appendix C.

We estimate both proportional and accelerated hazard models. The hazard rate is defined to be the probability of dying in a year divided by the probability of being alive at the beginning of the year. (More formally this is the ratio of the density function to one minus the cumulative density function.) In the proportional hazard model covariates act multiplicatively on the baseline hazard, whereas in the accelerated hazard model the covariates act multiplicatively on the baseline failure time. Although the potential for individual specific heterogeneity exists in both data sets, we do not deal with the problems by introducing flexible parametric distributions for the heterogeneity (Manton, Stallard, and Vaupel 1986) or by estimating the distribution function for heterogeneity (Heckman and Singer 1984a, 1984b). Rather, as a first attempt at examining the patterns of covariate effects in both data sets, we deal with the potential for omitted variable bias as one typically does in any nonlinear modeling environment—that is, by including a rather exhaustive set of individual specific explanatory variables, or covariates in the terminology of the demographers; and by experimenting with different functional forms. The proportional hazard estimates are based on maximizing the Cox partial likelihood. The accelerated hazard estimates are based on maximum likelihood using several flexible parametric baseline survivor distributions: exponential, Weibull, lognormal, loglogistic, and gamma. A more detailed discussion of the statistical models is given in Appendix C.

We should point out that, due to the construction of the Dorn sample, all sample covariate information is fixed. This is not the case in the RHS, and thus time-varying covariates are considered in our estimates. Furthermore, both samples are right censored, since not all individuals die by the end of the sample period. We do not, however, deal with the issue of left censoring. In both samples, respondents are not followed from birth, but rather are on average 57 years old when they enter the Dorn sample in 1954 and are no younger than 58 when they enter the RHS in 1969. Thus, inferences drawn on the effects of the covariates for individuals at all age groups would most likely be biased. Dealing with this potential shortcoming by truncating the densities of failure times (which truncated densities would be censored for those with incomplete spells) is a computational complication that we hope to deal with in future research.

The economic model that justifies inclusion of our covariates is quite well known and is outlined in Sickles and Taubman (1986). Although it is a static model, it does explain the role of the explanatory variables in the reduced form for the hazard function. An individual maximizes a utility function whose arguments are consumption, leisure, and health, subject to a budget constraint and a health production function. First-order conditions for utility maximization are then used to solve for the reduced form demand for consumption, hours of work, and health. Here we consider only health in isolation. The general specification of the health augmentation equation is based on the work of Anderson and Burkhauser (1983), Grossman (1972), and Taubman and Rosen (1982). The unobservable health stock is endogenously determined and can be augmented by investment in health services or depreciated by the environment of the home and work place. The health stock differs across individuals and families and is determined in part by social and demographic factors such as education, occupation, race, and age. Other important variables include access to health information and the ability to pay for health services as well as life style and genetic factors.

We use as an index of healthiness the hazard of dying. In earlier work with the RHS, the index of heathiness was self-reported health status relative to others the same age. Our proxies for the determinants of health are somewhat limited in the Dorn sample. Occupation is represented by an index for the riskiness of the work place. In the Dorn sample we have industry and occupation at the three-digit level. With the use of the *Underwriters' Handbook* used by the life insurance industry, we can replicate the risk class attached to these industry and occupation classifications when insurance premiums are set. The index ranges from 1 to 7 as the riskiness of the occupation rises and has a mean of 2.2 with some variation across age cohorts. The riskiest occupations are jobs such as firefighting and police work, whereas the least risky are jobs such as teaching. Another index was developed to control for the physical activity of the occupation. The index ranges from 1 for sedentary to 4 for heavy construction jobs. Life style is represented by information on tobacco use. The Dorn sample contains this information in the form of how much tobacco the respondent used, how many years he used it, and the manner in which he used it. At this stage we have constructed variables that indicate the number of years of occasional usage (an average of 3 percent of the years individuals were over ten years old) and the number of years of regular usage (an average of 54 percent of the years individuals were over ten years old). Since the questionnaire was administered in the mid-1950s when the respondent ages differed, it is possible that younger men who smoked regularly throughout their lives would still be able to report fewer years they smoked regularly than comparable older men. To account for this, we have divided the years-smoked variables by "age ten" at the survey data. These normalized variables have noticeably higher "t"-test statistics in otherwise identical equations. This adjustment may not be perfect; hence, the tables based on narrower age cohorts may be more appropriate for these variables. It is possible to distinguish type of tobacco use, but we have not yet done so. Nor have we made use of all information on past versus current habits. Factors such as regional differences in access to health care and exposure to health-depreciating environments are controlled for by four regional dummy variables with the West the omitted category.

There is a more extensive list of variables in the RHS that can be constructed to represent determinants of health than in the Dorn sample. Many of the variables we use are the same as those used in Sickles and Taubman (1986). We have socioeconomic data on race and marital status (we have omitted women from the study), number of years of education, longest occupation at the two-digit level, number of dependents, and genetic proxies such as the number of surviving parents of the respondent heads of households. We also have economic data such as initial wealth holdings, Social Security benefits, wage and nonwage income, income from assets, and Supplemental Security Income (SSI). A few words are in order about why we included some and excluded other economic variables, in particular earnings. Earnings, retirement, and health are intercorrelated, probably in a causal way.[8] Therefore, inclusion of earnings would probably lead to simultaneous equation estimation problems that we are not yet in a position to examine. To avoid this problem with Social Security benefits, we calculated the benefits that a person would expect to receive if retirement began in the respective year on the basis of earnings histories before 1969. They are computed using covered earnings taken from each person's Social Security record, which is part of the RHS, and then replicating Social Security's rules. By using benefits available rather than those actually paid to retirees, we avoid an obvious selection problem.

SSI, which began in 1974, was based on eligibility criteria as of 1969. The time-varying covariates in the analysis are number of dependents, number of surviving parents, potential Social Security benefits, and SSI. The remaining covariates are fixed throughout the sample period.

RESULTS

We turn first to results based on the Dorn sample. Table 6.1 contains the maximum likelihood estimates of the accelerated hazard model for the period 1954–1970 using a sample of 85,628 persons. In these estimates the baseline hazard is the gamma function, which is often our best fitting model. We present the results in terms of elasticities of the time to death with respect to selected covariates.

About 65 percent of the Dorn sample was still alive by the end of 1969. Thus, the treatment of censoring may be important. We have also estimated the accelerated hazard model with the four other distributions discussed in Appendix C. It should be noted that the empirical distribution is known to be rising; hence, the exponential, which has a constant hazard, is a misspecification. The results using the other baseline hazards are quite similar. The four other distributions permit nonconstant hazards. These four functional forms have similar log likelihood values and likelihood ratios, though the loglogistic has a marginally better fit than the gamma with respect to the empirical hazard.

The normalized number of years of tobacco use has highly significant negative effects whose magnitudes are about 7 and 2 percent reduction in

Table 6.1 ————————————————————————————
Dorn Sample: Accelerated Time Models,
Whole Sample and Two Cohorts

Variable	All cohorts (t-statistic)	Cohort born before 1890 (t-statistic)	Cohort born 1891–1900 (t-statistic)
Intercept	6.92 (2572.)	6.88 (1313.)	6.83 (1753.)
Proportion of years used tobacco occasionally	−.0214 (−4.36)	−.0260 (−3.29)	−.00975 (−1.88)
Proportion of years used tobacco regularly	−.0688 (−34.8)	−.0393 (−11.4)	−.0515 (−24.2)
Region			
South	−.00886 (−4.54)	−.00630 (−1.95)	−.00661 (−2.98)
Northeast	−.00390 (−2.07)	−.00386 (−.123)	−.00455 (−2.14)
North central	−.00434 (−2.27)	−.00545 (−1.70)	−.00423 (−1.98)
Activity index	.00237 (2.42)	.000133 (.0792)	.00220 (1.97)
Risk index	−.00288 (−5.65)	−.00163 (−1.83)	−.0000279 (−.047)
Scale	.125 (115.)	.107 (107.)	.164 (178.)
Shape	0.506 (31.1)	−0.774 (−13.6)	−1.06 (−26.7)
LogL	−210299.	−42175.	−152951.

life span for regular smoking and occasional smoking, respectively. Thus, changing from not smoking to regular smoking would shorten a person's life noticeably. Information about the region where a person lived as of the mid-1950s generally indicates that life expectancies in the South, the Northeast, and the north central region were worse than in the West, but the magnitudes of the differences were small.

The physical activity index is also significant. Moving from an inactive 1 to an active 4 increases the time to death by about 0.7 to 1 percent. The occupational risk variable is highly significant though of small magnitude. The difference between a 1 and a 7, the lowest and highest risk groups, is about 1.4 to 2 percent shorter life.

In Figure 6.1 we present the actual and estimated hazard based on the gamma function. The estimated hazard fits the data well with an R^2 of 0.892 and captures the increase in the hazard with age.

In the columns of Table 6.1 we present the accelerated hazard results with the Dorn sample divided into two age groups.[9] One is for 10,794 persons in the cohort born before 1891. (Normalized) regular tobacco use is highly significant and negative with a point estimate of about 4 percent per year used, whereas occasional use has a significant negative coefficient of about −2.5 percent. The southern inhabitants in the mid-1950s had significantly shorter life spans than western residents, but the differential is small.

Both the risk index and the physical activity index are based on the person's occupation in the mid-1950s when these men were in their mid-fifties or older. In these indexes a larger number means more activity and risk. The activity index is not significant. The risk index is almost significant in the gamma column; but the difference between 1 and 7 on this index is

FIGURE 6.1 _____

DORN SAMPLE: ALL AGES, HAZARD FUNCTIONS, TIME-TO-FAILURE
GAMMA FUNCTION

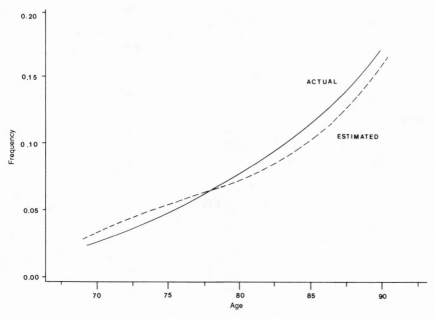

about 1 percent, so the effect is small. As risk increases, time to death is shortened.

The last column contains the results for the 59,151 sample members born between 1891 and 1900. The gamma distribution fits the data best and is the focus of our discussion. Each additional year of regular smoking reduces time to failure by a significant 5 percent (with the other specifications indicating slightly bigger impacts). The occasional smoking variable has a coefficient of about −1 percent, which is not significant.

Those from the South, the Northeast, and the north central region live less long than those from the West, though the differences are still not large. Increased physical activity associated with certain occupations leads to a significantly longer life (only for the gamma case), but the risk index is insignificant. All in all, the coefficients in the two right-hand columns of Table 6.1 are similar to each other and to those in the left-hand column, even though there are more truncated observations in the last column.

Table 6.2 contains the estimates using Cox's partial likelihood model,

TABLE 6.2

DORN SAMPLE: COX PARTIAL LIKELIHOOD ESTIMATES
FOR HAZARD FUNCTION FOR DIFFERENT COHORTS

Variable	Cohort born before 1890, estimate (t-statistic)	Cohort born 1890–1899, estimate (t-statistic)	All cohorts, estimate (t-statistic)
Proportion of years used tobacco occasionally	0.287 (2.91)	0.157 (2.30)	0.212 (4.44)
Proportion of years used tobacco regularly	0.550 (12.6)	0.632 (28.2)	0.655 (33.4)
Region			
South	0.112 (2.91)	0.0853 (3.84)	0.0872 (4.69)
Northeast	0.0759 (2.01)	0.0674 (3.16)	0.0461 (2.57)
North central	0.0717 (1.84)	0.0626 (2.91)	0.0474 (2.61)
Activity index	0.0135 (0.67)	−.0141 (−1.28)	−.0173 (−1.85)
Risk index	0.0108 (1.01)	0.0107 (1.87)	0.0234 (4.87)
LogL	−55972.	−226841.	−311672.

which has an unknown baseline hazard and which estimates the effects of covariates on shifts in this baseline. The parameters shown indicate the percentage shift in the hazard rate with respect to a change in X. In this model an increase in the hazard rate is considered bad. Here we see that cigarette smoking occasionally and regularly are both associated with a higher hazard, with regular use about three times as bad.

The residents of the West have better hazards than denizens of other areas, with the worst area being the South; this set of results is roughly consistent with those in Table 6.1. The risk index is highly significant, with those in riskier occupations having a higher hazard. The physical activity index indicates that the more active have lower hazards though the coefficient is not significant at conventional levels.

In Figure 6.2 we present the actual and estimated proportional hazard. The baseline hazard is the one for the people who are in the West and do not smoke (the omitted categories). Normally the baseline category cannot be calculated, but we have a large enough sample to do so. Again the model fits the data well with an R^2 of 0.93.

The two right-hand columns of Table 6.2 contain the Cox estimates for the aforementioned cohorts. These estimates can be described quickly, since

FIGURE 6.2

DORN SAMPLE: ALL AGES, PROPORTIONAL HAZARD

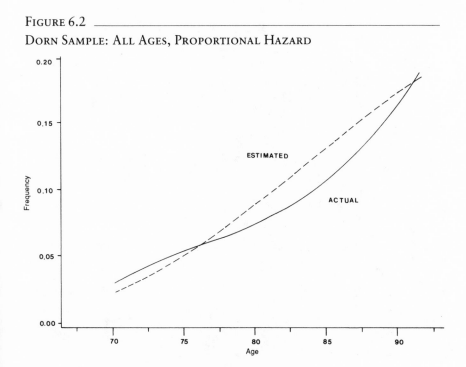

TABLE 6.3

RHS Sample:
Accelerated Time-to-Failure Models

Variable	Exponential, Estimate (T-Statistic)		Weibull, Estimate (T-Statistic)		Lognormal, Estimate (T-Statistic)		Loglogistic, Estimate (T-Statistic)		Gamma, Estimate (T-Statistic)	
Intercept	7.48 (84.7)	7.42 (84.1)	6.75 (1525)	6.74 (1456)	6.72 (1544.7)	6.72 (1522)	6.72 (1497.)	6.72 (1463.)	6.71 (1283.)	6.70 (1344.)
Black	-.136 (-1.61)	-.115 (-1.39)	-.0112 (2.69)	-.00930 (-2.14)	-.0124 (-2.98)	-.0114 (-2.69)	-.0133 (-3.09)	-.0124 (-2.80)	-.0118 (-2.91)	-.0102 (-2.58)
Married	1.99 (24.2)	1.601 (22.2)	.124 (26.8)	.0914 (22.1)	.105 (27.9)	.0837 (26.6)	.112 (26.9)	.0855 (24.4)	.0984 (26.5)	.0829 (29.9)
Widowed	-.477 (-8.14)	-.668 (-12.2)	-.0354 (-12.1)	-.0509 (-17.1)	-.0369 (-11.8)	-.0478 (-15.6)	-.0371 (-12.0)	-.0517 (-17.1)	-.0353 (-10.9)	-.0384 (-11.2)
Divorced/ separated	1.233 (5.65)	1.24 (5.70)	.0742 (6.78)	.0781 (6.79)	.0755 (8.93)	.0765 (8.95)	.0745 (7.96)	.0769 (7.97)	.0766 (9.94)	.0779 (10.9)
Education	.0115 (1.47)	.0110 (1.45)	.000331 (.895)	.00394 (.985)	.000352 (.951)	.000367 (.973)	.000381 (1.00)	.000435 (1.12)	.00031 (.858)	.000213 (.609)
Social Security benefits (thousands)	.113 (6.66)	.113 (6.66)	.0124 (14.1)	.0127 (13.8)	.0123 (16.0)	.0122 (15.6)	.0132 (15.8)	.0132 (15.2)	.0118 (16.4)	.012 (16.7)
Spouse working	-.579 (-10.2)	— (—)	-.0512 (-17.5)	— (—)	-.0345 (-11.6)	— (—)	-.0410 (-13.3)	— (—)	-.0261 (-7.70)	— (—)
Supplemental Security income (thousands)	.860 (3.34)	.977 (3.74)	.0652 (4.63)	.0811 (5.32)	.0559 (5.70)	.0605 (5.98)	.0624 (5.01)	.0715 (5.40)	.0518 (5.95)	.0488 (6.03)

Number of dependents	-.0460 (-1.30)	-.0686 (-1.95)	-.00589 (-3.56)	-.00747 (-4.32)	-.00557 (-2.87)	-.00660 (-3.36)	-.00527 (-2.76)	-.00662 (-3.47)	-.00536 (-2.68)	-.00572 (-2.82)
Pension income (thousands)	.0829 (4.32)	.0841 (4.31)	.00614 (6.46)	.00720 (6.80)	.00615 (7.16)	.00539 (6.72)	.00639 (6.86)	.00639 (6.51)	.00572 (7.33)	.00491 (7.01)
Longest occupation										
Professional	.0935 (1.31)	.0927 (1.30)	.00683 (1.91)	.00536 (1.42)	.00683 (2.01)	.00679 (1.97)	.00731 (1.98)	.00746 (2.05)	.00639 (1.97)	.00611 (1.96)
Management	.0536 (.751)	.0669 (.934)	.00431 (1.12)	.00515 (1.37)	.00781 (2.25)	.00819 (2.32)	.00706 (1.98)	.00753 (2.06)	.00853 (2.54)	.00894 (2.75)
Scale	1.0 (—)	1.0 (—)	.0499 (49.7)	.0524 (49.3)	.0697 (53.1)	.0712 (52.9)	.0394 (49.3)	.0407 (49.0)	.0761 (40.3)	.0802 (51.4)
Shape	—	(—)	—	—	—	—	—	—	.466 (4.07)	-.912 (-8.74)
LogL	-3516.6	-3567.87	387.0	239.9	501.24	431.56	455.24	364.64	510.59	475.41

the parameters are similar to those obtained in the full sample in each cohort except that the activity and risk indexes are no longer significant (and in one case change signs). The results in this table are in qualitative accord with those in Table 6.1.

We now turn to the RHS sample. Table 6.3 contains the results for men in the RHS for the period 1969–1977 using accelerated hazard models. There are two covariate specifications for each distribution, with spouse working excluded in the second version. Note that in this sample, the censoring rate is nearly 80 percent. Nevertheless, all but the exponential distribution fit the data about equally well, but the gamma fits best. It appears that in this random sample blacks (about 9 percent of the sample) die about 1 percent younger. In comparison with single men, married and divorced men live somewhat longer, with coefficients about seven to twelve times as large as the black coefficient. Widowers have a shorter life span. Both the divorced and widower results are surprising given previous results on health (see, for example, Rosen and Taubman 1984).

Perhaps most interesting is that income greatly matters, with Social Security and pension benefits having about the same effect of 1 to 0.5 percent, though the former is somewhat larger. Social Security benefits are a function of an average of monthly earnings generally calculated over 20–25 years. The Social Security's transformation is highly regressive. Pension benefits are a function of plan used, with some plans based on lifetime contributions and pension earnings and others based on earnings in the last one to five years. Pensions are either proportional to the earnings base used or are progressive when a company integrates its pension plan with Social Security benefits. Although it is possible that chronic health problems affect earnings throughout a person's lifetime, it is difficult to believe that our findings on the two-income sources represent the common effect of poor health on income, given the huge differences in the way earnings are translated into Social Security and pension benefits. Supplemental Security Income also matters to a similar extent. This in some ways is surprising, since the variable is zero until we first measure it in 1975 and since some people who would have been eligible if they had lived until 1975 are classified as not eligible because they died earlier.

A working spouse has a negative effect of 3 percent in the gamma column, and this effect ranges up to 5 percent. This variable is statistically significant for all four distributional assumptions. It is possible that a wife at work cannot urge a husband to see a doctor, keep him out of bars and away from unhealthly consumption, or provide regular meals. However, it is also possible that having a chronically ill husband induces a wife to work. Thus, we also present equations omitting this variable; changes in other coefficients are minor.

The coefficient on dependents at home (who are present in only 7 percent of the cases) is a highly significant −0.6 percent. Perhaps such dependents require time and emotional resources that could otherwise be used to lengthen the caretaker's life. Alternatively, dependents may more likely be at home in cases in which morbidity experience suggests a higher hazard rate.

The RHS also records the longest occupation. We use this information directly in dummy variable form. (We omit the physical activity transformation that is highly colinear with the dummies used.) Compared to everyone else, managers and professionals live 0.6 to 0.9 percent longer.

In Figure 6.3 we present the actual and estimated hazards using the gamma distribution. The model fits the data very closely with an R^2 of 0.981.

Table 6.4 contains the hazard function estimates for the RHS sample based on Cox's (1975) partial likelihood model. In this model the married and widowed variables have opposite signs and are highly significant. Pen-

FIGURE 6.3 _____

RHS HAZARD FUNCTIONS: TIME-TO-FAILURE GAMMA FUNCTION

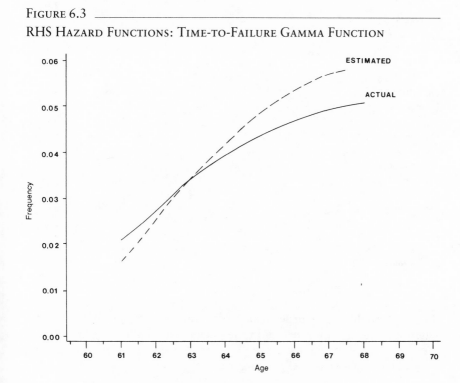

TABLE 6.4 ──

RHS SAMPLE: PROPORTIONAL HAZARD MODEL
(COX'S PARTIAL LIKELIHOOD)

VARIABLE	PROPORTIONAL HAZARD, ESTIMATE (T-STATISTIC)	
Intercept	—	—
	(—)	(—)
Black	.211	.165
	(2.53)	(1.99)
Married	−2.42	−1.74
	(−29.2)	(−24.3)
Widowed	.695	.952
	(11.9)	(17.3)
Divorced/separated	−1.46	−1.46
	(−6.71)	(−6.70)
Education	−.0066	−.0075
	(−.884)	(−1.01)
Social Security benefits	−.238	−.229
(thousands)	(−13.4)	(−13.0)
Spouse working	.960	—
	(16.6)	(—)
Supplemental Security income	−1.25	−1.47
(thousands)[a]	(−4.50)	(−5.14)
Number of dependents	.110	.137
	(3.30)	(4.15)
Pension income	−117.	−.128
	(−6.15)	(−6.4)
Longest occupation		
Professional	−.121	−.092
	(−1.69)	(−1.2)
Management	−.0909	−.09
	(−1.27)	(1.35)
LogL	−13533.2	−13663.6

a. Measured in 1975.

sion and Social Security benefits are of roughly the same size and are highly significant and negative, as are the supplemental security benefits. Dependents at home raise the hazard rate. Figure 6.4 displays the observed and estimated hazards. The fit is good with an $R^2 = 0.822$.

Conclusion

In this paper we have used the RHS and the Dorn samples to examine the relationship between mortality and various sociodemographic and life-style measures. We do so using time-to-failure and hazard models. These models are made more complicated because 60–80 percent of the people were still alive at the end of the sample frames.

To surmount censoring we have used a variety of assumptions in our time-to-failure models. We find that these models can be fit to the data even with the large amount of censoring and a relatively large number of covariates, some of which vary over the sample period.

In the time-to-failure models, the exponential function implies a constant hazard rate that is inappropriate for mortality data. The other four distributions usually yield similar results among them, but in a few cases the impact of a variable differs depending on the distributional assumption used. In terms of goodness of fit, the gamma and loglogistic seem best for the baseline hazard.

FIGURE 6.4

RHS Proportional Hazard

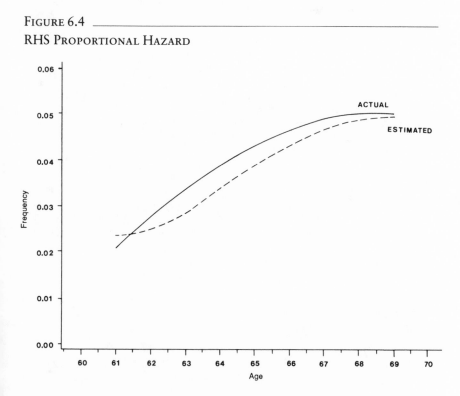

We find that regular tobacco users have shorter lives and that there are regional variations and occupational differences. In the RHS, married and divorced men live longer than those widowed or never married. We also find that pensions and Social Security benefits, both of which are related to preretirement work, have strong effects on life expectancy with Social Security having somewhat stronger effects. We also find that having a child at home or a working spouse when a man is in his sixties is associated with shorter life spans, though in both cases the direction of causality is questionable. Those in the professional and managerial occupations live longer. Education, however, is not statistically significant.

These are preliminary results based on fewer observations and more limited assumptions than we will eventually be able to utilize. It will be of interest to see how robust these findings are in our future analyses.

APPENDIX A _____

DORN SAMPLE:

SUMMARY STATISTICS FOR DIFFERENT COHORTS

Variable	COHORT BORN BEFORE 1890		COHORT BORN 1890–1899		ALL COHORTS	
	Mean	S.D.	Mean	S.D.	Mean	S.D.
Proportion of years used tobacco occasionally[a]	.0330	.142	.0318	.143	.0307	.138
Proportion of years used tobacco regularly[a]	.495	.327	.546	.353	.543	.343
Region						
South	.258	.438	.240	.425	.249	.430
Northeast	.300	.458	.307	.461	.290	.452
North central	.264	.441	.289	.452	.271	.442
Activity index	2.17	.848	2.13	.830	2.19	.841
Risk index	2.01	.158	.199	.156	2.20	1.70
Number of observations	10784		59147		85627	
Percentage censored	40.04		63.7		65.5	

a. Number of years of tobacco use divided by age at survey date minus ten.

APPENDIX B _____

RHS SAMPLE: SUMMARY STATISTICS

Variable	Mean	S.D.
Black	0.874	.284
Married	0.585	.493
Widowed	0.131	.338
Education	9.84	3.52
Social Security benefits (thousands)	1.29	1.28
Spouse's earnings (thousands)	1.47	3.08
Supplementary Security income (thousands)	.0245	.168
Dependents	.143	.560
Pension income (thousands)	1.31	2.52
Professional	.179	.383
Management	.161	.367
Number of observations	7915	
Percentage censored	78.3	

In the proportional hazard model, covariates act multiplicatively on the hazard. If t is the random variable denoting failure time, then

$$\lambda(t;x) = \lambda_o(t) \, e^{\{x\beta\}}$$

where $\lambda_o(t)$ is the baseline hazard with an unspecified distribution. The survivor function is given by:

$$S(t;x) = [exp\{-\int_o^t \lambda_o(\xi)d\xi\}]^{e^{\{x\beta\}}}$$

where exp is the exponential function.

The accelerated hazard model specifies $\log T$ as a linear function of the covariates, that is, $y = \log T = x\beta + \sigma\varepsilon$ where ε is a random disturbance. Alternatively, failure time can be expressed as $T = exp\{x\beta\}T_o^{\sigma}$ where $T_o = exp\{\sigma\varepsilon\} > 0$ has a baseline hazard function $\lambda_o(t)$ that is independent of β. The baseline hazard function depends on $te^{\{-x\beta\}}$. In terms of the baseline hazard, the hazard for T is:

$$\lambda(t;x) = \lambda_o e\{-x\beta\}$$

with survivor function

$$S(t;x) = exp[-\int_o^t e^{\{-x\beta\}} \lambda_o(\xi)d\xi].$$

The covariates act multiplicatively on failure time rather than on the hazard. That is, they change the rate at which an observation moves along the baseline hazard over time and thus accelerate or decelerate the time to failure.

Our estimates of the proportional hazard model are based on the maximization of the partial likelihood function (Cox 1975). The nuisance baseline hazard function is not specified. However, the resulting estimates of the covariate effects are still consistent and asymptotically normal. Because of the relatively large data bases we are examining, we are able to use observations from the omitted categories in the covariate list to estimate the baseline hazard with the Kaplan and Meier (1958) product-limit estimator. We use the same estimator when examining the degree to which the alternative models of failure time fit the underlying observed sample hazards.

Maximum likelihood estimates of the accelerated-failure-time model are based on five different specifications for the distribution of the baseline failure time: exponential, Weibull, lognormal, loglogistic, and gamma. The hazard functions for these different baseline distributions in the log-linear regression models are:

(exponential) $\quad \lambda(t;x) = e^{\{-x\beta\}}$;

(Weibull) $\quad \lambda(t;x) = \sigma^{-1}e^{\{-x\beta/\sigma\}}t^{(\sigma^{-1}-1)}$;

(lognormal) $\quad \lambda(t;x) = [\ exp\{\ -(log(t)-x\beta)^2/2\sigma^2\}/(\sigma\ t\sqrt{2n})]/$

$$[\int^\infty f(\xi)d\xi\,]$$

$$(ln(t)-x\beta)/\sigma$$

where $f(\xi)$ is the standard normal density function;

(loglogistic) $\quad \lambda(t;x) = e^{\{-x\beta/\sigma\}}\sigma^{-1}t^{(\sigma^{-1}-1)}/(1\ +\ e^{\{-x\beta/\sigma\}}t^{-\sigma})$;

(gamma) $\quad \lambda(t;x) = [|\gamma|(t^\gamma/\gamma^2)^{(1/\gamma^2)}e^{\{-t^{\gamma}/\gamma^2\}}\ (t\Gamma(1/\gamma^2))]/$

$$[\delta + (-1)^\delta\Gamma(1/\gamma^2,\ t^\gamma/\gamma^2/\Gamma(1/\gamma^2)]$$

where $\delta = [\begin{smallmatrix}1\ \text{if}\ \gamma<0\\0\ \text{if}\ \gamma>0\end{smallmatrix}]$ and where $\Gamma(\alpha_1)$ is the incomplete gamma function, $\Gamma(\alpha_1, \alpha_2)$ is the incomplete gamma function, and γ is the gamma distribution shape parameter.

DISCUSSION

Richard V. Burkhauser

This interesting paper provides the first results from a relatively new data set, new at least for economists—the Dorn Sample of Veterans. The paper uses hazard modeling to estimate a baseline survivor distribution for both the Dorn sample and for men in the Retirement History Survey. This technique allows us to measure the risk of death over time for an age cohort while estimating covariates that control for cohort heterogeneity.

The paper is of interest both as an attempt to use a relatively new statistical technique—hazard modeling—and because it introduces economists to a new and potentially important data set. Several specific issues can be raised with respect to the limits of the data and the inferences of the model. However, they should be prefaced by the old saying that: "Upon seeing a talking horse with a Southern accent, the wonder is not how he got the accent but that he talks at all." Particularly in discussing the limits of the Dorn data, it must be recognized that the authors have taken on an enormous task in analyzing this data set, and I look forward to how additional economic inferences will be drawn from its limited variables.

As the authors recognize, researchers in demography, statistics, and engineering among other disciplines use hazard modeling to a much greater extent that economists. They are usually interested in the timing of events like death, the breakdown of a machine, or the movement of a star. For the most part, it is only to control for heterogeneity that covariates are introduced. Hence, they spend little time or effort on developing a behavioral model linked to such covariates or in making inferences about their values. To this point, most economists who have used hazard models have also emphasized the time parameters and the problem of separating true time dependence from observed or unobserved heterogeneity. Heckman and Singer (1984b), for instance, offer one solution to this problem. Flinn and Heckman (1983) in their early work model the hazard of return to work and see if people who say they are out of the labor force do, in fact, stay out of work longer than those who say they are unemployed. Little is made of the covariates used in the model.

A simple example of the separation problem can be found in Holden, Burkhauser, and Feaster (1987). Workers are observed at the start of retirement and followed thereafter so that their risk of falling into poverty can be estimated over time. A hazard model is used to see if this risk increases or decreases. If we simply follow the experience of this cohort, a strong negative time dependence is found. That is, the risk of falling into poverty falls over time. But this may be caused by heterogeneity within the cohort. The amount of wealth held at retirement will also affect the speed of falls into poverty. The negative time dependence may simply be an artifact. It may simply be the case that in the first period those closest to the poverty line are more likely to become poor and hence leave the sample. In the second period, the survivors who were initially wealthier and hence less likely to fall into poverty remain. This wealthier cohort will have a lower risk of falling into poverty in the next period. Unless this cohort heterogeneity is controlled, it will be confused with negative time dependence.

Depending on the question asked, we may or may not need to control for heterogeneity within the cohort. A more subtle issue concerns controlling for unobserved heterogeneity, or the so-called nuisance parameter, and separating its effects from true time dependence. Unobserved variation within the cohort may effect the timing of the risk. For instance, in the unemployment literature is it "scaring"—that is, time in unemployment—that decreases the likelihood of finding employment, or is it "unobserved heterogeneity"—that is, that people with a strong but unobserved work ethic quickly get jobs, leaving the "loafers" behind? In this paper, issues of unobserved heterogeneity are not considered. Rather, the model is fitted to various specific functional forms and the major discussion is on the value of the covariates. There is little discussion of the economic model these covariates are testing.

The authors point out a major advantage of a hazard model—it addresses the problem of incomplete spells or right censoring. That is, a hazard model allows the use of information on individuals in a sample who have not encountered the hazard—such as death, poverty, or retirement—by the time the sampling period ends. Hence their spell of life, nonpoverty, or work is incomplete. Because most people have not died in both the data sets tested, this is a compelling reason for using such models. There is little discussion, however, of left censoring. That is, both data sets first observe people in the middle of a spell (in the middle of life). The RHS first follows men at ages 58–63. In the Dorn study, the ages vary but anyone not alive in 1954 is excluded from the sample. Again, this may or may not be a problem, depending on the specific questions the researchers are addressing. For instance, if they are interested in how occupations affect mortality rates but pick up their sample at advanced ages, they select out those who have died previously. If the risk associated with the disease is quick and fatal (for example, working the night shift at a 7–11 store), this is a major problem. If it is slow and only shows up at much older ages (such as black lung), it is less of a problem. But it is still a problem to the degree that people who work in hazardous jobs have adjusted investment in health to compensate for the reduction in health associated with a specific occupation.

The major finding in the Dorn study is that positive time dependence exists. That is, the risk of dying increases over time. In addition, smoking increases the risk of death at any age. This seems perfectly reasonable. It is in measuring the magnitudes of the effect that a fuller discussion of the problem of left censoring must be undertaken. This is particularly true of the region variables and the occupation variables. How useful are measures of region or occupation at advanced ages in discussions of mortality? This must greatly depend on the mobility of people across regions and their occupations at younger ages. This is particularly a problem in the subsample of veterans who in 1953 were aged 60 and over. At these ages it is likely that many of the veterans are already retired from their career jobs.

The RHS data is far richer in socioeconomic variables than the Dorn data, although the data are for a much shorter time period, 1969–1979. The findings here are once again reasonable. The risk of dying increases over time. The authors recognize the endogeneity of labor supply decisions and have developed a model elsewhere; see Sickles and Taubman 1986, in which health and work decisions are considered simultaneously. Butler, Anderson, and Burkhauser (1987) test a bivariate hazard model which shows that health decisions and decisions about re-entry into the labor market after retirement are made simultaneously.

Here the authors attempt to avoid the issue by explicitly excluding labor supply variables. This strategy is not fully successful, however. The authors calculate the earnings record of workers only up to 1969. But they then estimate benefits available in each year thereafter. These yearly benefits are positively correlated with age and time. The actuarial adjustment of Social Security between ages 62 and 65 increases the yearly benefit by 25 percent and hence is highly sensitive to age. In addition, the benefits themselves were increased by congressional action over this time period. Hence, there is a built-in positive correlation between the size of benefits and survival that confounds the results. Depending on what the Social Security variable is supposed to be measuring—that is, past earnings or current wealth—a better measure might be the Average Indexed-Monthly Earnings (AIME), a good proxy of lifetime earnings used by the Social Security Administration to calculate benefits. It is less sensitive to the age at which benefits are taken.

The next surprising finding is that SSI receipt means a lower risk of death. Since recipients of SSI are clearly at the lower end of the wealth distribution, this is a rather odd finding. Again this may be simply an artifact of the data. Since a person has to be age 65 to get SSI and the program was not started until 1974, when workers in this sample were aged 63–68, it may simply be picking up the fact that a worker could only get an SSI value in this data if he lived until the 1975 sample. A final caveat is in regard to the authors' use of R^2 to choose between the various models presented. Since the equations are nonnested, the R^2 statistic is inappropriate. A more appropriate measure is the Kolmegorov-Smirnov test.

Despite these reservations, this paper provides an interesting first run through the data. More time and effort by economists should go into considerations of the importance of covariates as well as into the difference in time dependence across groups. The preliminary results are not enormously surprising, but we would have less faith in the data if they were. The risk of death does increase over time. Cigarette smoking is a sure way of avoiding the problems of old age. The authors are well aware of most of the issues raised here, and I suspect the next time out this horse will not only talk but maybe even tap dance.

Notes

1. See Sickles and Taubman (1986) and references therein.

2. See, for example, Rosen and Taubman (1984), Kitagawa and Hauser (1973), and Duleep (1986) and references therein.

3. See, for example, Cox (1972), Manton, Stallard, and Vaupel (1986), Kalbfleisch and Prentice (1980), and Vaupel, Manton, and Stallard (1979). These techniques have been used by economists on different problems such as the duration of unemployment. See, for example, Heckman and Singer (1984) and Lancaster (1979).

4. This information on date and cause of death has recently been assembled through 1983, but we have not yet had access to information for years after 1979.

5. For details, contact Z. Hrubec, Radiation Epidemiology Branch, National Cancer Institute, Landow Building, Room 3A22, Bethesda, Maryland 20892.

6. Separation by cause has a number of advantages. First, we can determine the influence of expenditures in various National Endowment for the Humanities research programs on specific diseases and determine their separate price responsiveness. Such information should help in allocating research budgets. Second, the data on death may yield biased results that arise because of aggregation, especially if functions are not linear. Third, better decisions on both research and treatment facilities can be made if we have advance knowledge on what diseases are likely to strike the elderly, who will be a much larger share of the population in the future. Fourth, the hazard functions by cause of death may more confidently be extrapolated to older ages to predict what will happen to currently elderly people, though it is possible that this is offset by negatively correlated misclassification error.

7. The sample has only a small number of nonwhites.

8. We thank Richard Burkhauser and Laurence Kotlikoff for these suggestions.

9. We do not include separate results for the youngest age group since only 5 percent died by 1969. This age group is included in all the cohort groups.

References

Anderson, K., and R. Burkhauser. 1983. "The Effect of Actual Mortality Experience Within a Retirement Decision Model." Mimeo. Nashville, Tenn.: Vanderbilt University.

Beebe, G., and A. Simon. 1969. "Ascertainment of Mortality in the U.S. Veteran Population." *American Journal of Epidemiology* 89:636–43.

Butler, T., K. Anderson, and R. Burkhauser. 1987. "Work and Health After Retirement: A Bivariate Interval Hazard Model Approach." Working Paper, Vanderbilt University.

Cohen, B. 1953. "Methodology of Record Follow-up Studies on Veterans." *American Journal of Public Health* 43:1292–98.

Cox, D. 1972. "Regression Models and Life Tables." *Journal of the Royal Statistical Society* (Series B) 33:187–202.

———. 1975. "Partial Likelihood." *Biometrika* 62:269–76.

DeBakey, M., and G. Beebe. 1952. "Medical Follow-up Studies on Veterans." *Journal of the American Medical Association* 182:1103–9.

Dorn, H. 1958. "The Mortality of Smokers and Non-Smokers." In *Proceedings, Social Statistics Section, American Statistical Associations*, pp. 34–71.

Duleep, H. 1986. "The Socioeconomic Determinants of Mortality: The Role of Income." *Journal of Human Resources* 21:238–51.

Flinn, C., and J. Heckman. 1983. "Are Unemployment and Out of the Labor Force Behaviorally Distinct Labor Force States?" *Journal of Labor Economics* 1:28–42.

Grossman, M. 1972. "On the Concept of Health Capital and the Demand for Health." *Journal of Political Economy* 80:223–55.

Heckman, J., and B. Singer. 1984a. "Econometric Duration Analysis." *Journal of Econometrics* 24:63–132.

———. 1984b. "A Method for Minimizing the Impact of Distributional Assumptions in Econometric Models for Duration Data." *Econometrica* 52:271–320.

Holden, K., R. Burkhauser, and D. Feaster. 1987. "The Timing of Fall into Poverty After Retirement: An Event History Approach." Working Paper, Vanderbilt University.

Kahn, H. 1966. "The Dorn Study of Smoking and Mortality Among U.S. Veterans: Report of 8 1/2 Years of Observation." In W. Haenszel, ed., *Epidemiological Approaches to the Study of Cancer and Other Diseases*. Monograph 19. Bethesda, Md.: U.S. Public Health Services, National Cancer Institute.

Kalbfleisch, J., and R. Prentice. 1980. *Statistical Analysis of Failure Time Data*. New York: Wiley.

Kaplan, E. L., and P. Meier. 1958. "Nonparametric Estimation from Incomplete Observations." *Journal of the American Statistical Association* 53:457–81.

Kitagawa, E., and P. Hauser. 1973. *Differential Mortality in the United States of America: A Study in Socioeconomic Epidemiology*. Cambridge, Mass.: Harvard University Press.

Lancaster, T. 1979. "Econometric Methods for the Duration of Unemployment." *Econometrica* 47:939–56.

Manton, K. G., E. Stallard, and J. W. Vaupel. 1985. "Alternative Models for the Heterogeneity of Mortality Risks Among the Aged." *Journal of the American Statistical Association* 81:635–44.

Rogot, E. 1974. *Smoking and General Mortality Among U.S. Veterans 1954–1969.*

DHEW Publication (NIH) 74-544. Washington, D.C.: Department of Health, Education and Welfare.

Rogot, E., and J. Murray. 1980. "Smoking and Causes of Death Among U.S. Veterans: 16 Years of Observation." *Public Health Reports* 95:213–22.

Rosen, S., and P. Taubman. 1984. "Changes in Impact of Education and Income on Mortality in the U.S." In *Statistical Uses of Administrative Records with Emphasis on Mortality and Disability Research.* Washington, D.C.: U.S. Department of Health, Education and Welfare.

Sickles, R., and P. Taubman. 1986. "An Analysis of the Health and Retirement Status of the Elderly." *Econometrica* 54:1339–56.

Taubman, P., and S. Rosen. 1982. "Healthiness, Education and Marital Status." In V. Fuchs, ed., *Economic Aspects of Health.* Chicago: University of Chicago Press.

Vaupel, J., K. Manton, and E. Stallard. 1979. "The Impact of Heterogeneity in Individual Frailty on the Dynamics of Mortality." *Demography* 16:439–54.

7

RETIREMENT AS A DUBIOUS PARADISE— ANOTHER POINT OF VIEW

Kingsley Davis

Taken by itself, the word "retirement" is confusing. It can refer to withdrawal from all labor-market activity or only from a particular job. The withdrawal can be voluntary or involuntary; it can be based on age, length of service, health, or disability; it can provide access to a public or private pension; and it may or may not be limited to old age. About the only general meaning of the term is withdrawal from previous employment, but this hardly distinguishes it from resignation or dismissal. The confusion is made worse by the fact that an individual not only retires *from* an activity but also must retire *into* something else, whether paid, volunteer, or leisure activity. Unless the various meanings of the term are kept in mind, questions about retirement can be misleading.

In this brief speech I shall deal with the fundamental question of work versus nonwork for elderly men and women. I shall try to avoid the ambiguities of the word retirement by examining actual paths of the elderly, regardless of the words used. Let me begin with the pattern most familiar to us, which I shall call the "Western Standard Path." This pattern assumes that the individual has been employed for a number of years and that suddenly, as of the retirement date, the employment ceases, leaving him with reduced income. What does he do then?

Assuming that his basic needs are taken care of by his pension, Social Security, Medicare, and investments, he lives in what is by implication a perpetual paradise of leisure and recreation. Although he has a budget constraint, it is typically not rigorous, and he has no time constraint. He can fish all day if he wants to, or play golf every afternoon. He can buy or rent a "recreation vehicle" and go wherever he thinks he would like to be. He is probably the freest man who ever lived, and if his health holds up, he can enjoy this status for fifteen to twenty years.

Problems of the Western Standard Path

Although this utopian pattern is the ideal pursued by the United States and several other industrial countries, it has some major problems. One problem is that most human beings fare poorly under conditions of perpetual recreation. Since their job has normally been their main preoccupation as well as their main source of income, total retirement entails loss not only of money but of self-esteem, status, purpose, and friends. Above all, it takes away their guidelines, without which they are aimless, indecisive, and overly cautious. In other words, a policy of universal retirement of the elderly overlooks a frequently observed truth—namely, that work organizes people's lives.

A second problem with total retirement as a policy is that it conspicuously disregards the singular contribution of women and therefore causes inequity and social disorganization. According to the Western Standard Path, if women have been in the labor market they are entitled to retirement benefits just like men; but many older women have either not been in the labor market or have been there only a short time. In that case, how are they affected by a policy of total retirement of the elderly?

A third problem of the Western Standard path is that it is frightfully expensive—so much so that its cost, especially the Social Security portion, is the chief criticism of the retirement system.

The high cost of retirement derives from production foregone as well as payments to those retired. Insofar as people cease to work because of their age, the economy suffers the loss of what they otherwise would have produced. Inevitably there are people beyond any set age who are still productive and whose contribution would be lost by retirement.

Admittedly, age is a better proxy for productive capacity than traits such as sex, race, or religion. Further, it is precise, and insofar as we all grow older, it treats everybody alike. Nevertheless, from an economic point of view, age is at best only a very rough proxy for competence. As is well known, there are wide differences in ability among the elderly. By divorcing all old people from employment, a retirement policy based exclusively on age throws away much productive capacity. A better basis for retention or retirement would be individual competence, measured by relevant tests or employer judgment. Inevitably a sizable portion of the older population will prove to be unable to work, and the inescapable costs of caring for this group will be huge enough; but to add the support of the able elderly to that for the disabled elderly is to create an enormous and in part unnecessary burden.

According to the 1984 life table for the United States, the average person retiring at age 63 still has eighteen years to live (for men, sixteen years). This number, which is equivalent to 42 percent of the average working life, is not only a long time to spend in perpetual recreation but also a long time to spend in dependency on others. If the average person goes to school until age 20 and quits work at 63, the total period of dependency is almost as long (88 percent) as the working life.

So far, the loss of production due to increased retirement has been more than made up by the entry of working-age married women into the labor force, but this bonanza will not last long. In 1960 in the United States, women made up 33.4 percent of the civilian labor force; by 1986, they made up 43.8 percent. During the same period, despite the increase of the older population, workers aged 65 and over declined from 4.6 percent of the civilian labor force to only 2.5 percent. If these trends continue, the share of women in the labor force will soon become static at around 50 percent, and the share of the elderly will have vanished. As of 1990, there will be approximately 32 million older adults in the United States whose contribution to economic production will be nil. Short of drastic change in the retirement system or of massive immigration, the downward trend in the ratio of workers to nonworkers will continue.

It should not be assumed that the exodus of the elderly from the labor force is all due to policy. As of 1982 in the United States, only 59.3 percent of people aged 65 and over had no activity limitation due to chronic ailments. If we confine our accounting to these healthy individuals, we find that the total production of about 17.5 million older workers is lost through the policy of complete retirement. This is about 14 percent of the total civilian labor force.

A critic of elderly employment can of course raise the question, "Why do people need to work so hard? Even if we lose the labor of seventeen million able and qualified seniors, what difference does this make? Industrial technology can provide enough for everybody." One response is that reduction in a nation's total output by shortening the number of hours the workers spend working (such as hours per week) might be competitively disadvantageous, but it would be fair because it would apply to all potential workers. If, on the other hand, production is reduced by retirement of the elderly, a special group is being given what some consider the greatest gift of all—life without work. Ironically, the work ethic is so strong that it even offers a justification of retirement for the elderly. The seniors, it is said,

"have worked hard all their lives and now deserve to be free from work."
This argument, and the fact that all individuals expect to be part of this
privileged group at some point in their lives, rationalizes the extension of
retirement to even younger ages.

Transfer Costs

So far we have been talking about production lost through retirement.
However, to the extent that the elderly are idle and do not have income,
they must be supported by the rest of the society or past savings. Since
transfer payments are highly visible (more so than production foregone),
and since they have been rising alarmingly, it is not surprising that critics
of the major public retirement system have seized upon transfer costs as
their chief objection.

In 1985, U.S. federal benefits for the elderly amounted to $263.6 bil-
lion, or 27.5 percent of all federal government expenditures, including de-
fense. With 87 percent of men and 93 percent of women aged 65 and over
not working, the U.S. economy is paying a high price for retiree heaven. In
the near future, as the elderly population grows in proportion to the total
population, the burden on the labor force will be enormous. In 1970 there
were four workers for every nonworking oldster; by 1995 there will be only
three.

Chances of Reform

There are four solutions to this looming problem: first, increase the
labor force participation of old people; second, reduce their benefits, especially the benefits of those able but unwilling to work; third, increase productivity; and fourth, increase fertility rates. These policies can be mutually
reinforcing but at best are difficult to implement. In respect to the first
solution, greater employment of the elderly would add substantially to the
national income. In respect to the second, the basic needs for welfare, medical care, housing, and so forth could continue to be met, but not so gener-
ously as to beggar the economy. The third and fourth policies would be so
difficult to implement that we do not consider them here.

Of the two possible solutions, a reduction of benefits is probably the
harder. Once the support of the elderly has become impersonal—a charge
on the general public rather than on grown children and other kin—there is
no moral constraint on old people's economic demands. Further, the elderly
are so numerous, so articulate and experienced, and so possessed of free
time (since they are not working) that they can and do lobby powerfully for
their own interests.

The other approach—keeping the elderly in the labor force—is not easy either. Once people have tasted the privilege of living well without working, they are not likely to give it up unless forced to by circumstances. If total retirement is a just reward for a lifetime of work, it is the ultimate "benefit" that can be given the elderly. There is also the popular notion that if the elderly remain in the labor force, they will deprive the young of opportunities for employment and promotion. They will, it is claimed, slow the progress of technology and create a stifling gerontocracy in business and industry.

Although dubious, such allegations provide a justification for policies encouraging early and total retirement—policies that often serve covert purposes (such as getting rid of elderly personnel whose skills are obsolete but whose wages, due to seniority, are needlessly high). Against these antiwork doctrines and motives, current efforts to keep able-bodied seniors in the labor force are likely to be feeble. Such measures as abolishing mandatory retirement (already legislated), raising the minimum age for retirement, retraining senior workers, and helping the elderly to find employment are not likely to succeed unless strong sanctions (most of them on employers) are adopted.

When we look at actual trends, we find no evidence of reform. The elderly continue to abandon work but also receive generous old-age benefits. In 1970, 26.8 percent of U.S. men aged 65 and over were in the labor force; in 1984, only 16.3 percent were so occupied. Worse yet, the movement into retirement is extending down into younger age groups. Of men aged 55–64, 83 percent were in the labor force in 1970, but only 68.5 percent were there in 1984.

The main reason for the exodus of the elderly, one suspects, is that their economic security has risen so bountifully that they feel the extra income from working is not worth the effort. By common definition, work is something that one does for pay. If pay is not needed, why work? Besides, people stand up better under the stress of employment when they are young than when they are old.

In sum, policymakers in countries with the Standard Western Path face a major dilemma. On the one hand, they believe that if the elderly retire from work, this will free jobs for younger people who are raising families and utilizing up-to-date skills. On the other hand, they fear that if the elderly do not work, the costs of maintaining them in idleness will bankrupt the nation. In my view, the first horn of the dilemma is the weaker. The alleged disadvantages of keeping old people at work are either imaginary or remediable; hence, measures taken to keep them there (such as later age at retirement, more part-time jobs, retraining programs, modification of the seniority system, and employment centers and exchanges) could conceivably succeed.

As noted already, however, the U.S. trend has been overwhelmingly in the opposite direction. There was an exodus of approximately 11.2 million people aged 55 and over from the labor force between 1970 and 1984. The ultimate consequence of such a trend is hard to visualize, but one possibility is a revolt of the working young against their idle elders. If so, it promises to be an unequal struggle, because the ever-rising proportion of the elderly in the population makes them a powerful lobbying group. They want freedom of employment, to be sure, but above all they want generous benefits.

The Japanese Path

For a comparative perspective, let us turn to another industrial country— Japan—which has a different public and private retirement system. As in other countries, the Japanese system is a patchwork created by historical upheavals (world wars, depressions, and booms), but the general outline seems clear enough (for detailed accounts, see Palmore and Maeda 1985, chap. 5; Kii 1984, chap. 3). The chief difference from the Western path is that, for the average Japanese worker, retirement from his primary job does not usually mean departure from the labor force. It means, rather, a change in the work situation. Japanese workers change employers less often than their American counterparts do. Accordingly, when old age sets in, the Japanese worker has normally been employed by the same firm or agency for decades. When he retires from his position in this firm (usually before 60 years of age), it is what we might call his first retirement, because it does not mean that he quits working. On the contrary, and in contrast to the American pattern, he usually gets another job. Although the first retirement is not the only one he will experience, it is usually the most important because it marks the end of his upward mobility and initiates a cycle of downward mobility. He loses his seniority, his normal salary, and his usual authority, but he does not ordinarily lose his chance to work.

There are several options his firm can take, and two or three he himself can take, that will keep him in the labor force. A frequently used option is re-employment in the same company but at a lower salary and a tenure usually limited to five or fewer years (Kii 1984, 61). Alternatively, for key employees, the company may simply waive its mandatory retirement age; but again the salary will be reduced and the arrangement short-lived. Another frequently used option is employment in a different firm. Usually, smaller firms have a later mandatory retirement age than do big firms, with the consequence that the worker can remain employed by moving down the ladder of company size and prestige (ibid., 75). The worker's former employer often helps him to get a job in a lesser company. Finally, the worker may be self-employed and hence privileged to work as long as he is able and willing.

As a result of these options, "the majority of Japanese elders . . . continue to work at paid employment" (Palmore and Maeda 1985, 50–51). Japan has a higher proportion of men aged 65 and over in the labor force than any other industrial country. Even among Japanese aged 80 and over, 18 percent are employed, as compared to almost none in the United States, Great Britain, and France. In fact, at all ages over 60 Japan has a much higher rate of male participation in the labor force than do other industrial countries, especially those of European origin. For example, in 1980, 65 percent of Japanese men aged 65–69 worked, as compared to just under 30 percent in the United States and 14 percent in Sweden. If we keep in mind that a sizable proportion of the elderly are involuntarily incapacitated for work, we see that, for those who do have the capacity, Japan achieves a remarkable level of employment. For example, if two-fifths of men aged 70–74 are incapacitated, this leaves three-fifths able to work. Of the three-fifths, Japan manages to get 72 percent into the labor force. Helping in this success is the fact that a higher percentage of elderly Japanese workers (about two-thirds, as compared to one-third in the United States) are managers or at least self-employed. Elderly workers in Japan are also more prone to work full time and to put in longer hours. In retiring from their long-run or main job, the Japanese do so early, usually in their fifties. The custom of early retirement from one's primary job fits with the system. It increases the chance that the retiree will be young enough to adapt to new vocational circumstances.

Although Japanese elders are typically employed, and employed in jobs that are less important and less remunerative than the jobs that they left, they do very well at maintaining economic and political control in the nation at large. In fact, state Palmore and Maeda (1985, 50), "most Japanese businesses, the legislatures, educational and religious organizations, etc., are largely controlled by elders." There is also great public respect for elderly intellectuals. "As a symbol of this respect, several outstanding elder artisans, actors, writers, etc., are designated as 'living national treasures' each year by the national government and are given a pension to support their continued occupation" (ibid., 52).

In sum, the Japanese retirement system differs fundamentally from that in the United States, for it assumes that the individual will continue to work as long as he is able. Japan thus escapes the financial burden of a vast army of able but unproductive citizens. For this reason, in both theory and practice, the Japanese system seems better than that in the United States. However, like the U.S. system, Japan's is undergoing constant change. At present it depends on informal understandings and special opportunities to such an extent that it could crumble in a prolonged recession. Driven by necessity, employers might take advantage of the customarily low age at first retirement to rid themselves of expensive senior workers. The rehiring of persons aged 60 and over, if it is to be productive, requires an increasing amount of retraining, and in hard times this may prove to be too expensive. But despite these reservations about the future, the Japanese path seems superior.

Retirement Paths for Women

My discussion thus far has been largely confined to men. When we take gender into account, the retirement problem becomes more complex. The reason, as often noted, is that women have two roles. First, like men, they are economic producers; second, unlike men, they are also often wives, mothers, cooks, chauffeurs, and housekeepers. As producers they can presumably retire like men, but as mothers and wives they cannot do so, at least not in the ordinary sense of the term.

It is often assumed that the first role, the economic role, is quite new for women, but this assumption reflects historical ignorance. It rests on the observation that until recently in the noncommunist industrial countries, married women seldom entered the labor market. In the long view, however, the recent entry of wives into the labor force is not a new development but rather a return to the abiding condition of humankind. What is really new, or at least unprecedented, was their prior exclusion from economic production in the nineteenth and early twentieth centuries in the industrial countries. Throughout human history, until the industrial revolution, women were important economic producers. In hunting and gathering societies, for example, judging by present-day examples, women normally produced over half and sometimes a much larger share of the calories consumed by the social group.[1] To feed herself and her offspring, a woman had to do the foraging, food processing, and hunting of small game herself, since there was little sharing of food except from mother to child.

The advent of agriculture made the division of labor between the sexes more complex and arbitrary, but it certainly did not free women from hard labor. Reporting on studies of shifting cultivation in sub-Saharan Africa, Boserup (1970, 22) writes: "The joint result of women's high participation in agricultural work and their generally longer working hours was that women, in nearly all cases recorded, were found to do more than half of the agricultural work; in some cases . . . around 70 percent and in one case nearly 80 percent of the total." Even after the invention of the plow, when men in many areas took over the work of cultivation, the contribution of women to subsistence was large. As population increased and food processing and handicrafts became more complex, their tasks in and around the home multiplied. Even with advanced agriculture, on the eve of industrialism, the farm wife was famous for the variety of services she provided for her family and the long hours she put in (Strasser 1982, 4–31; Boserup 1970, pt. 1).

Thus, the recent entry of married women into the labor force in industrial countries restores to wives an important economic role. The immediately preceding system—that of the nineteenth and early twentieth centuries, in which except among the poor the wife stayed at home and the husband earned the family income by work outside the home (which I call the "Breadwinner System")—was not a "traditional" arrangement, as is often carelessly assumed. It was instead a peculiar and ephemeral stage in the readjustment of sex roles under the impact of urban-industrialism (Davis 1984). It was temporary precisely because it deprived wives of their part in economic production. Gradually, in industrial countries during the twentieth century, economic production has been restored to married women, giving them the same dual roles that wives had filled for thousands of years.

In some ways, however, the recent entry of married women into the paid labor force—the so-called "Egalitarian System"—is new. First, it usually involves their working *outside* the home, just as employed men do. Second, it pays women as individuals without reference to their family status. The result is that women's dual roles are made more difficult than they were prior to the industrial age. Since time immemorial, women had specialized in those tasks that were most compatible with reproduction—namely, tasks in and close to the home. Today, because advanced economies concentrate labor in centralized facilities, wives (like their husbands) must generally leave home to work. They must combine two incompatible activities: caring for the family at home and holding a job in the workplace.

Inevitably, women's present-day dual roles must be taken into account in retirement schemes. As Ricardo-Campbell suggests in this volume (Chapter 3), female attitudes toward retirement may be changing over time due to new circumstances. Following the male model of retirement is somewhat unfair to women, because their other role (their domestic role) puts them at a disadvantage in the marketplace. They have fewer of those things—wages, promotions, seniority—that govern the size of the private retirement pension. Further, social insurance schemes do not always award benefits for being a wife. However, the unfairness of money-based retirement is slight as compared to the absence of actual retirement based upon a person's domestic role.

A principal characteristic of the domestic role is that married women do not really retire from it except when they become disabled. They enjoy some reduction in their work load when the last child has left home, when the family residence has been sold, and when the husband has died, but short of institutional care, they are nearly always doing household work of one kind or another unless they can afford to purchase substitutes. Single men have a similar but lesser problem.

Further, the rewards for domestic work are sentimental, indirect, and disproportional to the labor expended. There is no remuneration, no wage, for the amalgam of such activities. There is no point in life when her accumulated "earnings" as a housewife are recognized and incorporated in a retirement plan (except spousal benefit via Social Security). Her benefits are received through her husband, or else through a job she has held, but not as a result of her past parental and domestic "employment." She may also receive welfare as a mother, but again these payments are definitely not for retirement; they are to help her in her familial role. The only way a housewife can earn a private pension is to have an outside job where she gets retirement credits like a man (see Chapter 3).

The absence of direct monetary reward does not belie the importance of the domestic role. On the contrary, the core functions of that role—among which are childbirth, child care, socialization, and mutual care and help—are essential for human existence. Accordingly, the person assuming these tasks cannot easily abdicate. She cannot go on strike for higher wages, nor can she obtain an enforceable contract stating her precise duties. Her work does not produce a product that can be sold. The quality of her performance does not govern the rate of pay, because there is no rate of pay. Yet once she takes on the role, she is obligated (barring divorce) to see it through.

In short, the motivation for filling the domestic role is noneconomic. It is normative and sentimental. Accordingly, any attempt to thrust it into the marketplace by such measures as paying mothers a "mother wage" or giving them retirement pensions based on the value of their services would be both too revolutionary and too expensive to succeed.

The chief inequalities between men and women are not to be found in the labor market. In that market, to be sure, there may be inequities—such as in pay, promotion, and retirement—but these have their roots in a profound nonmarket difference between the two sexes, namely that men have only one basic role (production) while women have two (production and family service). The result is a structural imbalance. Men enjoy the nonmarket activities of their wives and mothers, but they do not fully reciprocate. Some are active fathers, gardeners, and tax preparers, but not as their central activity. The current situation differs from the Breadwinner System, because in that system the woman had only one role, the domestic role. For her services she received a share of the proceeds from the man's labor in the marketplace. Now, in the Egalitarian System, she continues her domestic service but also participates in the labor force. Compared to the man, she has a double burden. The imbalance may be changing as men adopt some of the domestic service roles, but it is not being eliminated.

One effect of the imbalance can be seen in retirement practice. Before his retirement, the married man has a job and need not worry about any other preoccupation. A married woman, however, job or not, has a household to take care of. Consequently, although a married man experiences a sharp transition when he retires, the transition is cushioned by the fact that his wife is still serving him in her domestic role (from which, remember, she does not retire). When a married female worker retires from her job, she has no such advantage. She not only has no one to run the household for her, but she must continue to run it for her husband. In a sense the shock of retirement from the labor force is greater for her because she has no one in the nurturing role to relieve her of her domestic obligations. On the other hand, the shock is less because she can carry on as usual in a role she knows well. The situation of single men and women without dependent children is similar. The life expectancy of single men is lower than that for married men, partly because of self selection but also because there is no one to take care of the single man.

In advanced societies, women's two roles are less compatible than they were in hunting and gathering and in agrarian societies. As a consequence, in order to maintain both roles, women try to limit their commitment to each one. In the labor market they take dead-end jobs more often than men do, withdraw more frequently, acquire less training, and do more part-time work. In their family role they postpone marriage and have fewer children. Of the two roles, participation in the labor force is probably more demanding, because it entails competition with men and a precise regimen. The working woman therefore tends to adjust her domestic role to the requirements of the job. Yet, from a societal point of view, a woman's achievement in the labor force is of less moment than her achievement in her domestic role. The simplest way for her to reduce the demands of that role is to have fewer children. As a consequence, in nearly every industrial country in the world the birthrate has dropped below replacement. In the United States, for example, the total fertility rate in 1984 was 14 percent below replacement level, and on average it had been that far below for the previous 13 years (for documentation and analysis of low fertility, see Davis, Bernstam, and Ricardo-Campbell 1987).

Retirement and Sex-Role Reform

If people in advanced countries continue their failure to replace themselves, strong reforms will likely be proposed that, if implemented, would affect work, family, and retirement. It is difficult to imagine how the government might equalize men and women both in the labor market and in domestic duties so that the double burden would be borne by men as well as women. However, such a reform might do more for sex equality than it would for the declining birthrate. There is no evidence that a readiness of men to participate in home duties raises fertility.

Another radical pronatalist reform would be the opposite—that is, to *reinforce* the division of labor by sex. Women could be excluded from work outside the home except in service, domestic-like jobs and/or only in part-time work. Reproduction and household services would then become the special female domain, but it would be oriented more toward children than toward the father.

Currently, a sizable portion of women elect to forego reproduction altogether and devote themselves to a business or professional career. A few women choose to devote themselves exclusively to reproduction and family life; they are in a sense professional mothers. Then there is a majority of women who combine both roles. A fair retirement system would not penalize women in any of the three roles, although only the latter two roles contribute to fertility.

A More Probable Future

I am not advocating or predicting any specific scheme. No scheme seems likely to be adopted or, if adopted, to raise the birthrate. As the whole world becomes "developed"—that is, urbanized, crowded, civilized, and dependent on advanced technology—its birthrate may fall below replacement. If so, this will present formidable problems in terms of an aging population and prolonged retirement, but it will not be a disaster. At present the earth is surfeited with people. It can experience birthrates below replacement for a long time before the total population falls to a size more in keeping with resources available. In the meantime, women will doubtless continue to participate in economic production just as they always have except for the brief "breadwinner" epoch. Future reform may well take the direction of reversing the trend toward nonemployment of the elderly. It may also prescribe retirement benefits for women based on their indispensable family functions as well as their labor force participation. Finally, it may provide social insurance retirement benefits directly to women as individuals, not indirectly via the husband.

NOTES

1. See the accounts by Lee, Woodburn, Watanabe, and Yengovan in Lee and DeVore (1968). See also Mason (1894, chaps. 1–7) and Lee (1979, chaps. 9–11).

REFERENCES

Boserup, Ester. 1970. *Woman's Role in Economic Development*. New York: St. Martin's Press.

Davis, Kingsley. 1984. "Wives and Work: The Sex Role Revolution and Its Consequences." *Population and Development Review* 10:397–417.

Davis, Kingsley, Mikhail S. Bernstam, and Rita Ricardo-Campbell, eds. 1987. *Below Replacement Fertility in Industrial Societies: Causes, Consequences, Policies.* New York: Cambridge University Press.

Kii, Toshi. 1984. *Aging in Japan: Policy Implications of the Aging Population*. Ann Arbor, Mich.: University Microfilms International.

Lee, Richard B. 1979. *The Kung San: Men, Women, and Work in a Foraging Society*. New York: Cambridge University Press.

Lee, Richard B., and Irven DeVore, eds. 1968. *Man the Hunter*. Chicago: Aldine.

Mason, Otis T. 1894. *Woman's Share in Primitive Cultures*. New York: Appleton.

Palmore, Erdman B., and Daisaku Maeda. 1985. *The Honorable Elders Revisited*. Durham, N.C.: Duke University Press.

Strasser, Susan. 1982. *Never Done*. New York: Pantheon Books.

PART II

SOCIAL SECURITY
AND RETIREMENT

8

THE FINANCIAL IMPACT OF SOCIAL SECURITY BY COHORT UNDER ALTERNATIVE FINANCING ASSUMPTIONS

Michael J. Boskin
and Douglas J. Puffert

For most Americans, anticipated Social Security retirement benefits have a value larger than the total value of their other financial assets.[1] Likewise, more than half of the workers in the United States pay more in Old Age, Survivors, Disability, and Hospital Insurance (OASDHI) "contributions" and/or taxes than they pay in personal income taxes. Because the program looms so large in the financial picture of so many, it is reasonable to assume that there is a significant demand for an investment evaluation of what it offers citizens. However, the program is extremely complex. A person's expected benefits depend not only on total contributions (taxes) but also on marital status, sex, age-earnings profile, length of career, number of children, and other factors.

In this paper we simplify the analysis by evaluating only the retirement portion of the program, known formally as Old Age and Survivors Insurance (OASI).[2] We examine it from the perspectives of the individual household, entire cohorts (defined by decade of birth), and aggregate system finances. Our study is partial equilibrium in the sense that we do not tackle

We wish to express our thanks to Jessica Primoff for invaluable research assistance, the Stanford University Center for Economic Policy Research for support of this research, and Dr. Mary Ross and Dr. Rita Ricardo-Campbell for valuable suggestions on an earlier draft.

the consequences of the program for labor force participation of both men and women, marital arrangements, private saving behavior, or funding the federal debt. We compute present values of taxes and benefits—including spousal benefits—using a 2 percent real discount rate.[3] We also calculate what individuals can expect to receive from Social Security as transfers— that is, the difference between the present values of benefits and taxes. A transfer is thus the surplus or gain received from participating in OASI (if the figure is positive). Finally, we compute the internal rate of return: the rate of discount that equates the expected present value of benefits with the expected present value of taxes. Throughout the analysis, we assume the participant bears the burden or effectively pays both the employer and the employee contributions to the system.[4]

The long-run financial status of Social Security is quite uncertain. First, future economic and demographic trends, which are highly uncertain, will heavily affect revenues and outlays. Second, except under the Social Security Administration's optimistic scenario, the retirement part of the system is projected to be in long-run actuarial deficit: small under the intermediate assumptions, large under the pessimistic ones. The demographic assumptions behind the optimistic scenario are higher total fertility rates (2.3 births over a woman's lifetime by the year 2011), higher immigration rates, and shorter life expectancies than in the commonly used intermediate scenario. Third, Hospital Insurance (HI) is projected to run a large deficit beginning in the 1990s. Finally, OASI and Disability Insurance (DI) together are projected to accrue (under the intermediate assumptions) a perhaps impossibly large surplus over the next 30 years. This surplus is projected to cumulate to over 25 percent of GNP (see U.S. General Accounting Office 1986), about the ratio of privately held national debt to GNP at the end of 1981. This surplus is designed to reduce the need for still larger tax increases or benefit reductions during the baby boom generation's retirement. Figure 8.1 presents estimates of these average annual (not cumulative) surpluses and deficits in Social Security, including and excluding HI, over the next 75 years to highlight this projected movement away from pay-as-you-go finance.

We have never been able to accrue a surplus this large in Social Security; the retirement surplus may well be dissipated for other purposes (such as bail out HI, fund other programs, raise benefits, or cut taxes). These possibilities involve major intercohort transfers relative to the intermediate assumptions—as do, of course, the alternative methods of dealing with the long-run deficit (see Boskin 1986). We analyze these possibilities in detail below.

The emphasis of the paper is to calculate the financial terms of Social Security's OASI for households from different birth cohorts under alternative possible futures. Our results indicate that the terms vary substantially by cohort and that trillions of (real discounted) dollars are at stake for different cohorts, both in the economic and demographic future of the United States and in the use of the projected temporary surplus in the OASI trust fund.

The remainder of the paper is as follows: the next section contains a brief survey of related literature. The third section describes our methodology and data, and the fourth presents results using intermediate assumptions for the overall financial status of the system, the situation to be faced by successive ten-year birth cohorts (from before 1912 through 1992), and the situation facing middle-income, single-earner families born in each of four years (1945, 1960, 1975, and 1990). The effects of alternative future economic and demographic patterns are analyzed in the fifth section. In addition to the standard optimistic and pessimistic Social Security Administration packages, we also present marginal changes for fertility, mortality, and real wage growth. The sixth section estimates the implications of alternative uses of the large surplus that is projected to accrue in OASI's trust fund:

FIGURE 8.1 _____

PROJECTED SOCIAL SECURITY SURPLUSES (DEFICITS) UNDER
INTERMEDIATE (II-B) ASSUMPTIONS

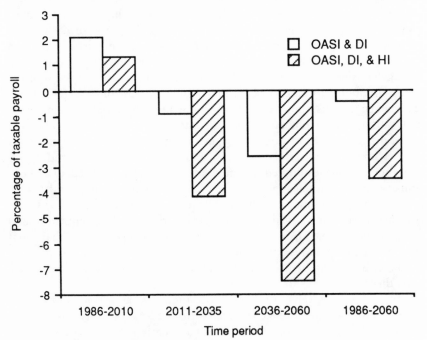

SOURCE: Social Security Administration (1986, 68, 118).

what difference it makes, in the aggregate and to specific cohorts, if the surplus is used to raise benefits or reduce taxes or if it is spent on other programs. The concluding section offers a short summary and repeats some caveats concerning interpretation of the results.

LITERATURE REVIEW

Several studies analyze the long-run financial solvency of Social Security under alternative economic and demographic assumptions. The most important, of course, are the annual Social Security trustees' reports (see, for example, Social Security Administration 1986). They present both short- and long-term actuarial projections of Social Security trust-fund finances under alternative assumptions. The reports certainly contain immensely useful information, especially given the complexities involved in generating consistent projections. However, these data are presented only as fractions of taxable payroll (except, in one table, as fractions of GNP); dollar figures (whether discounted or not) are not usually presented for long-term projections.

More important, the reports could usefully present additional information that would give a more accurate measure of the state of the retirement (OASI) trust fund at the end of each report's 75-year horizon. Each report presents the simple average, over the following 75 years, of each year's surplus or deficit (that is, tax receipts minus benefit payments) as a fraction of that year's taxable payroll as the basic information. This unweighted average considers neither the increase over time in taxable payroll nor the expected interest to be earned on the cumulated trust-fund surplus. Especially when the trust funds are projected or planned to deviate systematically and substantially from pay-as-you-go finance (approximate annual balance), it is important to supplement the information as currently presented with estimates that cumulate interest and consider how magnitudes vary over time.[5] We have adopted that methodology here and, indeed, one of our primary purposes is to supplement the information usually presented.

Boskin's (1986) estimates of the long-run financial solvency of OASI do consider annual flows of dollars and project the actual accumulation and decumulation of the OASI trust fund. He also considers what will happen if the expected cumulative surplus of the next three decades is dissipated (for example, by raising benefits) or if reforms are instituted in retirement age and other features.

Several studies have attempted to estimate what various households have received or can expect to receive from Social Security's retirement program. The general conclusion is that the early cohorts of retirees had large rates of return on their taxes and that future retirees, especially well-off ones, are likely to fare poorly, with a rate of return below that available on private assets. Hurd and Shoven (1985) document this pattern of rates of return for various cohorts and earnings levels, but their analysis was made prior to the 1983 Social Security amendments and hence does not include consideration of the increased age of eligibility for future retirees or the partial taxation of benefits.

Boskin, Avrin, and Cone (1983) report the transfer both for aggregate ten-year age cohorts and for average households in each cohort. They also present estimates of how different cohorts and the system finances as a whole would be affected by various policy changes, such as increases in the retirement age. They conclude that those retiring recently are receiving benefits that are about three times as large as the sum of their employee and employer contributions (taxes) plus 3 percent real interest—that is, about two-thirds of their benefits are transfers.[6]

These results are updated to take account of the 1983 amendments in Boskin (1986). The pattern of transfers remains qualitatively similar to that mentioned above, but attention is called to the fact that OASI and DI are unlikely to be financially solvent over the next 75 years, despite the 1983 amendments. The financial solvency issue is much worse if HI is included. Boskin emphasizes the importance for various cohorts of *how* and *when* the financial solvency issue is addressed—whether changes occur in the tax rates, benefit formulas, age of eligibility for full retirement benefits, or method of financing Social Security.

Pellechio and Goodfellow (1983) examine the net impact of the 1983 amendments on various types of households. Part of our own analysis below—that of typical households—is similar to theirs.

Boskin et al. (1987) present estimates, ignoring long-run funding issues, for alternative family types and birth cohorts. They conclude that the deal offered by Social Security has varied substantially over family structure, income, and birth year and has not always been better for poorer persons. The transfers vary by (real discounted) $200,000 per family, amounts that dwarf the redistributions debated in alternative income tax reforms. They also note that the marginal linkage between taxes paid and benefits received is quite low (sometimes zero), and thus Social Security ought to be viewed as a tax with concommitant distortions. They also note that, considering previously paid taxes, a sunk cost creates a situation in which all but very young workers expect to receive back more in benefits than they expect to pay in taxes for the remainder of their work life; thus, most people have a stake in preserving the Social Security system, even though their lifetime transfers are negative.

Methodology and Data

The results we present here are based on computer simulations of present and future American families covered by the Social Security system. Our main simulation package derives aggregate discounted figures for the taxes paid and benefits received by each of nine successive ten-year birth cohorts (for example, all those born from 1943 to 1952). It simultaneously derives figures for annual income to and expenditure from the Social Security Administration's retirement (OASI) trust fund over the next 75 years.[7]

This simulation begins with earnings records and other data concerning Social Security participants who were surveyed in 1973.[8] For subsequent years, participants' earnings are based on demographic characteristics. Benefits are derived through legislated benefit formulas, and each participant's year of death is determined through a random process based on mortality tables published by the Social Security Administration (1984).

Cohorts born beginning in 1953 are simulated differently. In considering typical male and female wage earners born each year, we derive their expected tax and benefit futures based on mortality probabilities and the proportion that can be expected to marry. We multiply by the number born each year (plus the number born that year who later immigrate as children) who will enter covered employment and thus derive figures for entire cohorts. To derive income and expenditure for the trust fund as a whole, we make a further adjustment for taxes paid and benefits received by adult immigrants; the totals for cohorts, however, considers only those covered their entire lives.[9]

Our calculation is certainly rougher than that undertaken by the actuarial staff of the Social Security Administration. As a result, we generate projections of aggregate taxes and benefits that vary from those of the 1986 trustees' report. Thus, we project small annual deficits for the trust fund in 1986 and 1987, whereas the trust fund is actually now running a small surplus.[10]

Our simulation goes beyond that of the Social Security Administration in highlighting not only the financial evolution of the trust fund but also the impact on successive cohorts of OASI, both as currently legislated and as it may have to be changed in the future in order to maintain the solvency of the trust fund.

A second simulation[11] looks at the financial impact of OASI for a variety of typical families. We use this simulation to derive the expected value (in an *ex ante* calculation that recognizes the possibility of death at any age) of a household's Social Security taxes and benefits, and thus its net transfer and real rate of return.

In the main simulation we rely on Social Security Administration projections for the proportion of Social Security benefits that are recovered for the trust fund through income taxation. These estimates are that this proportion will rise from less than 2 percent in 1986 to about 5 percent in the mid-twenty-first century. Because legislated marginal tax rates have been reduced since the Social Security Administration made its projections, we assume that, from 1988 on, 20 percent less will be collected in taxes on benefits. In 1987, the transition year, we assume that 10 percent less will be collected. In the second simulation we calculate income taxation for each case, based on the new tax law and data from the Internal Revenue Service about taxable income of the elderly (see Boskin et al. 1987).

Both of these simulations are parameterized by economic, demographic, and legal assumptions. The most important economic assumption is future growth of real wages. The chief demographic assumptions are mortality probabilities by age and fertility rates. The legal assumptions are tax rates on payroll and formulas for the calculation of benefits. In the scenarios below, we consider the alternative economic and demographic assumptions that the Social Security Administration itself uses for the scenarios in its annual trustees' reports,[12] and we consider fixed multiples of the payroll taxes and the benefits currently legislated.

The present values we derive assume a real discount rate of 2 percent. This is the rate that the Social Security Administration assumes (in its intermediate assumption) will be realized on its trust fund. We apply this rate not only to the system's finances, however, but also to participants in Social Security. Elsewhere we discuss arguments that this rate is either too low or too high when applied to individuals,[13] but we note here one advantage of this figure. When participants can expect a higher rate of return from Social Security than that received by the trust fund, it must be the case that their participation raises the trust fund's unfunded liabilities—that is, the excess of claims on the trust fund over assets. The amount of a cohort's net transfer (discounted benefits minus discounted taxes) is the amount by which the trust fund's unfunded liabilities rise. Conversely, a cohort real rate of return below 2 percent indicates a decrease in the trust fund's unfunded liabilities.

RESULTS FOR INTERMEDIATE ASSUMPTIONS

Table 8.1 presents the results of our main simulation using the trustees' report's intermediate assumptions about future economic and demographic trends (Social Security Administration 1986). Panel A shows the basic trends, well known by now, that are expected to develop in the finances of the OASI trust fund. The trust fund will run a substantial surplus over the next 25 years while the baby-boom generation is in its peak earnings years.

Table 8.1

Base Case (Intermediate Assumption)

A. Financial Flows of OASI Trust Fund
(billions of dollars discounted to 1986)

Time Period	Payroll	Taxes	Benefits	Benefit Taxes[a]	Surplus	Surplus Payroll (percent)
1986–2010	39,584	4,366	3,997	114 (141)	483	1.22
2011–2035	38,540	4,232	4,422	158 (198)	−31	−0.08
2036–2060	34,460	3,784	4,925	196 (244)	−946	−2.74
1986–2060	112,584	12,381	13,344	468 (584)	−495	−0.44

B. Financial Patterns for Birth-Year Cohorts
(1986 dollars in billions, discounted to 1986)

Year of birth	Retiree taxes[b]	Net benefits[c]	Transfer	Nonsurvivor taxes[d]	Real rate of return (percent)
Before 1912	385	3671	3286	186	11.61
1913–1922	489	1582	1093	121	5.74
1923–1932	776	1508	732	149	3.72
1933–1942	952	1446	495	193	2.75
1943–1952	1378	1695	316	340	1.96
1953–1962	1525	2040	515	350	2.31
1963–1972	1414	1809	395	325	2.17
1973–1982	1287	1660	373	283	2.22
1983–1992	1337	1751	413	282	2.28

C. Expected Values for Middle-Income Single-Earner Couples
(1986 dollars, discounted to 1986)

	YEAR OF BIRTH OF COUPLE			
	1945	1960	1975	1990
Present value benefits	161,460	140,255	133,714	122,097
Present value taxes	144,950	149,825	139,859	128,581
Present value transfer	16,510	−9,570	−6,145	−6,484
Rate of Return	2.34%	1.80%	1.87%	1.85%

a. Income taxation of benefits. Figures in parentheses refer to old tax law.
b. Payroll taxes paid by those who survive to collect benefits.
c. Benefits net of income taxation.
d. Payroll taxes paid by those who do not survive to collect benefits.

In the following 25 years (more precisely, in the mid-2020s), when the baby-boom generation retires, benefit payments will begin to exceed payroll-tax revenues. In the third 25-year period, there will be a still higher proportion of retirees to workers, and annual deficits will equal a fourth of tax receipts, or a fifth of next benefits.

For the whole 75-year period we project a deficit of nearly $500 billion in 1986 dollars discounted to 1986. This is equal to about 0.44 percent of (discounted) taxable payroll.[14] Thus, a rise in the Social Security payroll tax rate of 0.44 percent effective now, or substantially more later, would be needed to close the long-run OASI trust-fund deficit if the intermediate assumptions prove to be the case.

It is worth noting at this point why we present our figures in discounted terms. First, this enables us to consider the present value of potential futures of the OASI trust fund. This is especially valuable as we compare scenarios with different time paths of surpluses and deficits. Second, it obviates the need to give explicit consideration to the interest received (or paid out) by the trust fund on its calculated surplus (or deficit), since we assume that the interest and discount rates are identical. The present (1986) value of the surplus or deficit in 2060 will equal the sum of the present values of annual surpluses and deficits until then. As a corollary, it becomes simple to compute how taxes or benefits can or must be changed to bring the trust fund into actuarial balance.

The system finances are also presented in Figure 8.2, where the discounted surplus is shown both annually and on a cumulative basis. On a cumulative basis the system starts to run a deficit (assuming the surplus accrues and real interest is 2 percent) around 2048, and on an annual basis, around 2025. We present below some hypothetical scenarios of the surplus being dissipated or alternative economic and demographic projections that alter these conclusions substantially.

The financial patterns for successive ten-year cohorts born through 1992 are presented in panel B of Table 8.1. Retiree taxes, net benefits (that is, net of income taxation), the transfer received by those who live to retire, the taxes paid by nonsurvivors, and the real rates of return are presented. As can be seen, even those born in the immediate future may get a slightly positive transfer, computed at a 2 percent real rate of return. Thus, the rates of return that are about 2 percent or more indicate positive transfers. Were we to use 3 percent, cohorts born after 1933 would be receiving negative transfers.

Of course, since there is a long-run actuarial deficit of 0.44 percent of taxable payroll, amounting in present value to approximately $500 billion, someone will have to pay it. The base case assumes that it is paid by persons born after 1992, whose situation will be correspondingly worse.

Table 8.2 presents results from our simulation of various typical fami-

lies for four years of birth: 1945, 1960, 1975, and 1990. We consider three
different levels of earnings and two divisions of earnings between the family
members. The figures include expected present values of taxes, benefits and
transfers, and rates of return discounted both to the age when the couples
are 25 (for the purposes of comparison) and to 1986. The discounted present value of transfers (and therefore, taxes and benefits in general) varies
markedly within each age cohort for different levels of earnings (reflecting
the progressivity of the benefit formulas) and income splits (with respect to
the spousal benefit), and, to a lesser extent, the ceiling on taxable earnings.
For example, persons born in 1960 who recently entered the system have a
present value of transfers that ranges from a slight positive transfer for low-
income earners to a substantial negative transfer for high-income earners.
The rates of return for taxes paid range from 3.4 percent for the low-income
single-earner family to 0.4 percent for the high-income two-earner family.
The same pattern is repeated within each cohort. The intragenerational
redistributions are explored in much greater detail in Boskin et al. (1987).

FIGURE 8.2

DISCOUNTED SURPLUS FOR BASE CASE, ANNUAL AND CUMULATIVE

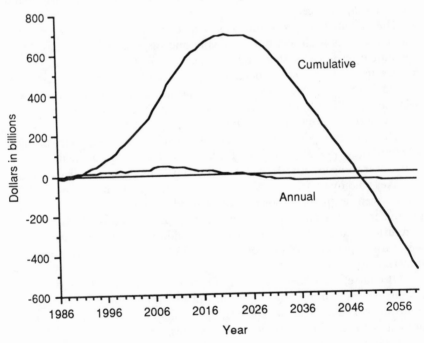

Thus, although we will primarily be dealing in the sequel with system totals and aggregates by age cohorts, substantial variation remains within each age cohort. That variation will vary systematically as we change economic and demographic assumptions and consider alternative scenarios for dissipation of the surplus.

FINANCIAL IMPACTS OF ALTERNATIVE
FUTURE ECONOMIC AND DEMOGRAPHIC PATTERNS

The Social Security Administration's intermediate economic and demographic assumptions are perhaps as reasonable as any, but we can be sure that they will not be realized with great accuracy.[15] It is thus important to consider the impacts of a range of possible futures both on the Social Security system's finances and on participants.

In Tables 8.3 and 8.4 we summarize the effects of using the Social Security Administration's optimistic and pessimistic assumptions for future wage growth, future mortality (and hence, life expectancy), future fertility, and various combinations of these parameters. In Table 8.3 we show the wide variation in results for the financial solvency of the retirement trust fund. The 1986 value of the trust-fund surplus (or deficit) in 2060 ranges from +$3.4 trillion to −$2.6 trillion for the combined optimistic and pessimistic assumptions, respectively.[16] We see in the column headed "Year annual deficit begins" that only when the optimistic assumptions are combined do tax receipts exceed benefit expenditures in each year through 2060; otherwise, current-flow deficits begin between 2014 and 2030. In the next column we see that the cumulative surplus suffices, however, to cover benefit expenditures until 2024 in the most pessimistic scenario and beyond 2060 in several of the optimistic scenarios.

In Table 8.4 we compare the rates of return realized by each of the nine ten-year birth cohorts under the alternative scenarios. We note first that, for later cohorts, the derived real rates of return vary among scenarios from about 1.5 percent to over 3 percent.

In order to understand more fully how taxes, benefits, transfers, and rates of return vary by scenario and cohort, let us now consider in detail how each of our economic and demographic assumptions affects both the finances of the Social Security retirement trust fund and the taxes and benefits of those covered by Social Security.[17]

The Social Security Administration's intermediate (II-B) assumption for growth in real wages, used in our base case, is that there will be an annual gain of 1.5 percent (with some fluctuation in the short run). The optimistic

Table 8.2

Base Case: Financial Patterns for Various Typical Families
(Expected values in 1986 dollars, discounted at real rate of 2 percent)

	LOW ($10,000)		MIDDLE ($30,000)		HIGH ($50,000)	
Division of earnings	One earner[a]	Two earner[b]	One earner[a]	Two earner[b]	One earner[a]	Two earner[b]
I. 1945 Cohort						
Discounting to 1970:						
Present value benefits	65,455	52,881	117,616	96,723	113,314	119,920
Present value taxes	37,015	36,171	105,589	108,514	112,421	178,237
Present value transfers	28,440	16,710	12,027	−11,791	893	−58,317
Discounting to 1986:						
Present value benefits	89,854	72,594	161,460	132,778	155,554	164,624
Present value taxes	50,813	49,655	144,950	148,965	154,329	244,679
Present value transfers	39,041	22,939	16,510	−16,187	1,225	−80,055
Rate of return	3.73%	3.17%	2.34%	1.64%	2.03%	0.75%
II. 1960 Cohort						
Discounting to 1985:						
Present value benefits	78,403	62,949	137,505	112,811	137,129	141,828
Present value taxes	48,963	47,833	146,888	143,499	170,004	239,165
Present value transfer	29,440	15,116	−9,383	−30,688	−32,875	−97,337
Discounting to 1986:						
Present value benefits	79,971	64,207	140,255	115,067	139,871	144,664
Present value taxes	49,942	48,790	149,825	146,369	173,404	243,949
Present value transfer	30,029	15,417	−9,570	−31,302	−33,533	−99,285
Rate of return	3.39%	2.82%	1.80%	1.27%	1.37%	0.40%

III. 1975 Cohort

Discounting to 2000:						
Present value benefits	96,616	77,388	176,432	144,978	175,842	182,174
Present value taxes	61,614	60,078	184,540	180,232	214,567	300,387
Present value transfers	35,102	17,310	−8,108	−35,254	−38,725	−118,213
Discounting to 1986:						
Present value benefits	73,224	58,651	133,714	109,876	133,267	138,066
Present value taxes	46,620	45,532	139,859	136,594	162,616	227,657
Present value transfers	26,604	13,119	−6,145	−26,718	−29,349	−89,591
Rate of return	3.31%	2.75%	1.87%	1.35%	1.43%	0.49%

IV. 1990 Cohort

Discounting to 2015:						
Present value benefits	123,218	98,859	216,823	177,840	221,189	229,261
Present value taxes	76,112	74,285	228,337	222,856	265,328	371,427
Present value transfer	47,106	24,574	−11,514	−45,016	−44,139	−142,166
Discounting to 1986:						
Present value benefits	69,387	55,669	122,097	100,145	124,556	129,102
Present value taxes	42,860	41,832	128,581	125,495	149,412	209,158
Present value transfer	26,527	13,837	−6,484	−25,350	−24,856	−80,056
Rate of return	3.40%	2.84%	1.85%	1.33%	1.48%	0.55%

a. Only husband works.
b. Husband and wife have equal wages.

TABLE 8.3

SYSTEM FINANCES AND ECONOMIC AND DEMOGRAPHIC SCENARIOS, 75-YEAR TOTALS (1986–2060)
(BILLIONS OF DOLLARS DISCOUNTED TO 1986)

Scenario	Taxes	Benefits	Benefit taxes	Surplus	Variation of surplus for base case	Surplus as percent of taxable payroll	Year annual deficit begins	Year cumulative deficit begins
Base case	12,381	13,344	468	−495	0	−0.44	2025	2048
High wage growth	18,021	17,781	639	878	+1,373	0.54	2030	By 2090
Low wage growth	10,170	11,516	398	−948	−453	−1.03	2020	2035
High mortality	12,306	12,267	429	468	+963	0.42	2027	By 2080
Low mortality	12,522	14,743	521	−1,700	−1,205	−1.49	2018	2035
High fertility	13,095	13,365	469	199	+694	0.17	2026	By 2080
Low fertility	11,516	13,315	467	−1,332	−837	−1.27	2021	2040
Overall optimistic for participants	18,235	19,757	715	−807	−312	−0.49	2025	2051
Overall pessimistic for participants	10,112	10,590	365	−113	+382	−0.12	2025	2056
Overall optimistic for trust fund	19,177	16,376	587	3,389	+3,884	1.94	*	*
Overall pessimistic for trust fund	9,644	12,653	441	−2,567	−2,072	−2.93	2014	2024

*Remains positive indefinitely.

TABLE 8.4

RATES OF RETURN FOR ECONOMIC AND DEMOGRAPHIC SCENARIOS
(PERCENTAGES)

Scenario	Before 1912	1913–1922	1923–1932	1933–1942	1943–1952	1953–1962	1963–1972	1973–1982	1983–1992
Base case	11.61	5.74	3.72	2.75	1.96	2.31	2.18	2.22	2.28
High wage growth	11.61	5.74	3.88	3.14	2.48	2.91	2.79	2.84	2.90
Low wage growth	11.61	5.74	3.60	2.48	1.65	2.00	1.87	1.92	1.98
High mortality	11.50	5.59	3.60	2.59	1.65	2.02	1.86	1.88	1.93
Low mortality	11.66	5.78	3.81	2.97	2.36	2.69	2.59	2.67	2.76
High fertility	11.61	5.74	3.72	2.75	1.96	2.31	2.18	2.22	2.28
Low fertility	11.61	5.74	3.72	2.75	1.96	2.31	2.18	2.22	2.28
Overall optimistic for participants	11.66	5.79	3.97	3.35	2.87	3.27	3.21	3.29	3.38
Overall pessimistic for participants	11.50	5.59	3.47	2.31	1.35	1.71	1.55	1.58	1.63
Overall optimistic for trust fund	11.50	5.60	3.77	2.98	2.18	2.62	2.48	2.50	2.55
Overall pessimistic for trust fund	11.66	5.78	3.69	2.70	2.06	2.37	2.29	2.37	2.46

YEAR OF BIRTH

assumption considers a gain of 2.5 percent annually; the pessimistic assumption considers a gain of 1 percent.

It is interesting to note that higher wage growth is better both for the system's finances and for participants in the system. An increase in the trust fund's annual surplus (taxes minus benefits) proves consistent with a higher ratio of benefits received to taxes paid for the participants. The reason for this is that increases in taxes, which vary with total wages, precede the increases in benefits to which wage growth leads. The wage index is used in the formula for determining benefits, and so a faster rise in this index provides a higher rate of return for participants. What "balances the books" is a growth in the unfunded liabilities of the retirement trust fund. These liabilities could become quite burdensome if wage growth slows in the future.

We see in Table 8.3 that variation in wage growth changes taxes and benefits in the same direction but that taxes change to a greater extent. High wage growth increases the long-run surplus by $1.37 trillion, more than offsetting the long-run deficit expected under the base case. Low wage growth deepens the long-run deficit by about $450 billion.

Higher (lower) wage growth increases (decreases) both taxes and benefits. It increases (decreases) annual flows of taxes more than benefits but, for a given cohort, increases (decreases) discounted benefits more than discounted taxes. Rates of return for later cohorts (also presented in Table 8.4) vary from about 2.2 percent under intermediate wage growth to about 2.8 percent under high wage growth and 1.9 percent under low wage growth.

In assumptions about mortality, what is optimistic for the solvency of the retirement trust fund is pessimistic for participants, and vice versa. The trust fund is more solvent when people die sooner and collect less in benefits. In Table 8.3 we show that under the Social Security Administration's high mortality (low life expectancy) assumption the trust fund is better off by $963 billion over the 75-year horizon, but that under the low mortality assumption the system is worse off by $1.20 trillion. In Table 8.4 we see that for later cohorts the rates of return are about 1.9 percent for high mortality and 2.7 percent for low mortality. Higher (lower) mortality reduces (raises) benefits much more than taxes for any cohort, as indeed for the trust fund's annual flow as well.

Alternative assumptions about fertility matter only for those cohorts not yet born, which are not presented in our tables. However, because Social Security participants begin paying taxes some 40 years before they receive benefits, fertility rates will have a big impact on trust-fund finances in the next century.[18] Indeed, today's low fertility rates are the most widely cited source of probable future problems in Social Security finance. Current fertility rates are below 1.9 children per woman over her child-bearing years. The

Social Security Administration's intermediate assumption is that this will rise within the next two decades to 2.0 children per woman.[19] The optimistic and pessimistic assumptions are 2.3 and 1.6, respectively.[20] The results of our simulation, shown in Table 8.3, are that high fertility would add $694 billion to the trust-fund surplus, more than eliminating what is otherwise a deficit, whereas low fertility would add $837 billion to the deficit.

We also derived results for scenarios that combine sets of optimistic and pessimistic assumptions. The assumptions that are optimistic for participants are high wage growth and low mortality (fertility being irrelevant), whereas the assumptions that are optimistic for trust-fund finances are high wage growth, high mortality, and high fertility. In the scenarios that are optimistic and pessimistic for participants, rates of return for later cohorts are about 3.3 percent and 1.6 percent, respectively.[21] The effects on system finances are offsetting and do not differ greatly from the base case.

Under the combined optimistic and pessimistic assumptions for trust-fund finances, the differences from the intermediate scenario for long-run surplus are +$3.88 trillion and −$2.07 trillion (Table 8.3). The present value of taxes differs between these extreme scenarios by a factor of nearly two, while benefits vary by a factor of about 1.3.

In Figure 8.3 we show how the size of the accumulated trust fund varies over the next 75 years for the overall optimistic, intermediate (base case), and pessimistic scenarios. Note that the continuing increase in the trust fund occurs only when the optimistic assumptions occur simultaneously. For any one of the optimistic assumptions alone, interest on the trust fund is eventually insufficient to cover the difference between current benefits and current taxes, and the principal itself is exhausted before 2090 (Table 8.3, last column).

FINANCIAL IMPACT OF ALTERNATIVE USES
OF THE POTENTIAL TRUST-FUND SURPLUS

We noted in the previous section that only under the combined optimistic assumptions for wage growth, mortality, and fertility all together can we hope that the retirement trust fund will take in at least as much each year in taxes as it pays out in benefits. In all other cases an accumulation in the trust fund is vital in order to forestall the time when taxes must be raised or benefits reduced.[22] Under intermediate assumptions, for example, an annual deficit will begin in 2025 but the accumulated surplus will keep the trust fund solvent until 2048.

Unfortunately it has always proved difficult, for political reasons, to accumulate a trust-fund surplus. It is in the interest of each session of Con-

FIGURE 8.3

DISCOUNTED CUMULATIVE SURPLUS FOR ALTERNATIVE SCENARIOS

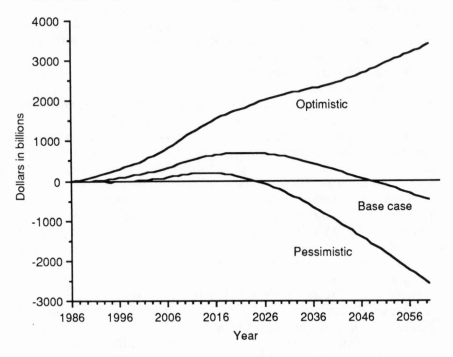

gress and of each administration to raise benefits (or perhaps to lower taxes, although that has not yet been tried) if possible. Raising benefits conveys transfers to those receiving, or soon to receive, benefits while imposing much of the cost of the action on future generations, which do not yet vote. Lowering taxes, similarly, helps a current generation of workers but requires higher taxes from future generations than would otherwise be necessary.

The situation is now particularly acute for a major demographic reason: in less than 30 years the baby-boom generation will begin to retire. If we do not preserve the accumulation of a trust-fund surplus before then, future adjustments in payroll-tax rates or in benefits will have to be much greater than would otherwise be necessary.

In Figure 8.4 we depict the combined (employer and employee) tax rates that would be required each year to fund currently legislated benefits (given intermediate assumptions) without adding to or drawing on an accumulated surplus. Until 2025[23] tax rates could be lower than those currently legislated, but thereafter they would rise drastically.

Conversely, in Figure 8.5 we show the level of benefits that could be funded by each year's tax receipts. This level is presented in the form of a ratio to benefits as provided for under current legislation. We see that benefits could be raised intermittently through 2009, to a level 30 percent higher than that now legislated, but that thereafter they must either decline or, perhaps more plausible politically, be maintained through increases in payroll tax rates. The tax rates required to finance these increased benefits are depicted in the broken line of Figure 8.4.

In Tables 8.5 and 8.6 we summarize the financial impacts of several ways of dissipating the trust-fund surplus that is projected to grow over the next 35 to 40 years. In the line for "Pay-as-you-go tax rates" we consider the scenario in which, beginning in 1990, tax rates are set each year at a level which exactly covers that year's benefit payments. Similarly, in the line for "Pay-as-you-go benefits" we consider, also for 1990 on, the adjustment of benefit levels to match projected tax receipts. The tax rates and benefit levels of these scenarios thus follow the heavy lines depicted in Figures 8.4 and 8.5, respectively.

FIGURE 8.4

TAX RATES, CURRENT LAW, AND PAY-AS-YOU-GO

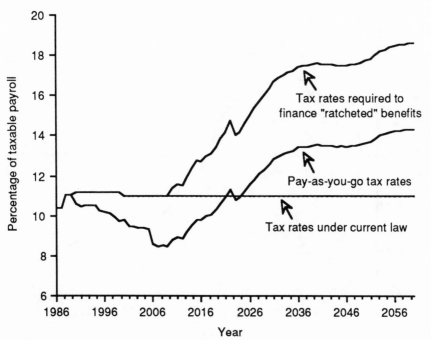

We consider 1990 a plausible starting date for these scenarios because the party that takes office in 1989 will be glad to endear itself to the voters before the 1990 congressional election. By that time the annual surplus in the trust fund will be an inviting target.

In the "benefit ratchet" scenarios we consider two cases in which benefits rise to their pay-as-you-go peak in 2009 but, like a ratchet, do not subsequently decline. The first of these scenarios illustrates the enormous deficit ($3.69 trillion cumulative by 2060) generated when the higher benefit level is not funded with taxes, whereas the second illustrates the case of taxes rising, in a pay-as-you-go fashion, to fund the increased benefits.

In the last two of these scenarios we consider what will happen if the surplus that would accumulate over the next 40 years is dissipated or directed to other purposes. Two plausible possibilities for this are that the surplus could be used to cover some of the massive deficit in Social Security HI that will (absent a major reform) develop within a few years[24] or that the surplus will, in the face of federal budget deficits, be used to fund other

FIGURE 8.5 _____

PAY-AS-YOU-GO BENEFITS AS A FRACTION OF CURRENTLY LEGISLATED
BENEFITS (HOLDING TAXES FIXED)

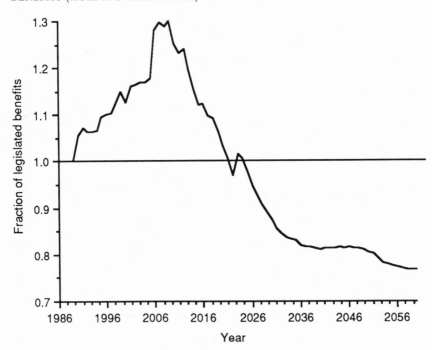

TABLE 8.5

SCENARIOS FOR TRUST-FUND SURPLUS, 75-YEAR TOTALS (1986–2060) (BILLIONS OF DOLLARS DISCOUNTED TO 1986)

Scenario	Taxes	Benefits	Benefit taxes	Surplus	Variation of surplus for base case	Surplus as percent of taxable payroll	Year annual deficit begins	Year cumulative deficit begins
Base case	12,381	13,344	468	−495	0	−0.44	2025	2048
Pay-as-you-go tax rates	12,868	13,344	468	−8	+487	0.00	n.a.	n.a.
Pay-as-you-go benefits	12,381	12,832	443	−8	+487	0.00	n.a.	n.a.
Benefit ratchet, unfunded	12,381	16,662	591	−3,690	−3195	−3.28	2010	2010
Benefit ratchet, funded by taxes	16,064	16,662	591	−8	+487	0.00	n.a.	n.a.
Surplus dissipated, funded by taxes	13,565	13,344	468	0[a]	+495	0.00	n.a.	n.a.
Surplus dissipated, adjusted benefits	12,381	12,112	420	0[a]	+495	0.00	n.a.	n.a.

a. $689 billion surplus through 2025 has been dissipated.

TABLE 8.6

RATES OF RETURN FOR TRUST-FUND SURPLUS SCENARIOS
(PERCENTAGES)

Scenario	Before 1912	1913–1922	1923–1932	1933–1942	1943–1952	1953–1962	1963–1972	1973–1982	1983–1992
Base case	11.61	5.74	3.72	2.75	1.96	2.31	2.18	2.22	2.28
Pay-as-you-go tax rates	11.61	5.74	3.73	2.84	2.17	2.56	2.37	2.26	2.09
Pay-as-you-go benefits	11.62	5.94	4.16	3.18	1.96	1.89	1.56	1.54	1.54
Benefit ratchet, unfunded	11.62	5.95	4.25	3.50	2.75	3.07	2.92	2.96	3.02
Benefit ratchet, funded by taxes	11.62	5.95	4.25	3.50	2.73	2.95	2.58	2.34	2.09
Surplus dissipated, pay-as-you-go taxes	11.61	5.74	3.72	2.75	1.96	2.31	2.11	2.04	1.96
Surplus dissipated, pay-as-you-go benefits	11.61	5.74	3.71	2.71	1.80	1.89	1.56	1.54	1.54

expenditures. In the first of these scenarios, taxes are raised in a pay-as-you-go fashion beginning in 2025, the first year in which current benefit payments exceed current tax receipts. In the second of these scenarios, benefits are reduced in a pay-as-you-go fashion from 2025 on. Thus, these scenarios are equivalent to the earlier pay-as-you-go scenarios from 2025 on; they only lack the period in which tax or benefit levels are more favorable for participants than the levels currently legislated.

The chief result for system finances (Table 8.5) under all these scenarios—except, of course, the unfunded ratcheting of benefits—is that the long-run surplus is, by construction, essentially zero.[25] The story for the successive cohorts, as we see in Table 8.6, is that some gain and some lose as a result of these changes.

Thus, under pay-as-you-go tax rates, those born before the 1980s gain; the bulk of their working lives takes place before 2025, when tax rates must rise above those currently legislated. The big losers under this scenario are those born in the next century, who will be subject to payroll tax rates of over 13 percent by 2033 (and later over 14 percent), rather than the 10.98 percent currently legislated.

Under pay-as-you-go benefits, those who receive benefits mostly before 2025 gain. Those born in the 1950s and after who collect their benefits after 2025 will do worse than projected under current legislation. Those born today can expect a benefit reduction of 23 percent, for a rate of return of only about 1.5 percent.

With a ratcheting of benefits financed by tax increases, those born before the current decade gain, as their increase in benefits more than offsets the increase in taxes that they pay during part of their working lives. But later cohorts bear the full brunt of these increased tax rates (17 percent by 2033, and higher later) and hence do substantially worse overall.

When the surplus is dissipated, there are no gaining cohorts. But those who pay taxes or collect benefits after 2025 suffer the same losses as in the first two pay-as-you-go scenarios.

CONCLUSION AND CAVEATS

The results reported in this research suggest that Social Security's retirement program offers vastly different terms to households in different circumstances and in different cohorts. More important, if we do not maintain a large OASI trust fund, the alternative scenarios for return to pay-as-you-go finance differ dramatically in the taxes, benefits, transfers, and real rates of return that can be offered to different birth cohorts.[26]

It appears that the retirement part of Social Security—but not HI—is in sound short-run financial shape and, indeed, is projected to accumulate a substantial surplus over the next 35 to 40 years under intermediate economic and demographic assumptions. However, various factors could intervene in this relatively rosy short-run scenario. We have attempted to explore some plausible alternatives to the surplus accruing: tax rates could be cut, benefits increased, or the surplus diverted to other purposes. We have traced their implications for the overall financial status of the system, the time pattern of taxes, benefits and surpluses or deficits, and therefore the treatment of different age cohorts. Under the intermediate assumptions, the Social Security surplus is projected to become two-thirds as large as today's national debt (relative to GNP). Obviously, well before this would occur, enormous pressure would be placed on financial markets as the Social Security trust funds come to hold a growing fraction of government bonds.

Since HI is scheduled to be running a substantial deficit well before the surplus peaks, one likely scenario is that the Social Security Administration will, in effect, borrow from the retirement fund to bail out the HI fund. The retirement surplus could also be a signal to fiscal authorities that additional spending could be financed on other programs, ignoring the simultaneously accruing future liabilities in Social Security. The surplus could be dissipated if the prospective increase in the retirement age is reduced, eliminated, or postponed, and/or if the tax exempt amount is indexed. In all of these situations, the short-run surplus would decrease substantially and the subsequent long-run deficit would worsen. The exact pattern of tax collections and benefit payments might take a variety of forms, but each of these would lead to a much worse deal for retirees in the distant future than for current retirees or those retiring in the near future.

The Social Security retirement system finances are quite sensitive to alternative economic and demographic events. We have presented estimates based on the Social Security Administration's pessimistic and optimistic packages, and we have also examined the marginal effect of changing mortality, fertility, and wage growth assumptions. Again, the patterns are revealing. Except in the optimistic package, the discounted value of the Social Security retirement system fund over the next 75 years is negative and is subject to substantial potential negative shocks for the reasons discussed above.

A number of caveats to our results deserve mention. First, the 1986 income tax revisions are certain to be superseded over the time horizon we examine and probably sooner rather than later. For example, marginal rates may change, Social Security benefits may be taxed fully, and some or all of the tax collections from the taxation of Social Security benefits may be diverted to general funds to help pay for deficits rather than be credited to Social Security at the time of surplus.

Second, the value of Social Security benefits may exceed their expected present value because they are paid as inflation-adjusted joint survivor life annuities. Bernheim (1986) argues that a strict adherence to the life-cycle model—at least the aspect of it that implies that one's lifetime average propensity to consume equals one—and imperfections in annuity markets imply that actuarial discounting (that is, discounting at the sum of time preference and mortality probability) is inappropriate, and he argues that simple discounting (that is, ignoring mortality probability, but with a given time horizon) may be desirable. Although we do not hold to this extreme form of the life-cycle model in this paper, and although there is substantial evidence that if individuals are given the option they refuse to annuitize their wealth (for example, college professors usually decline annuitization in favor of some years certain in their retirement pension), we do not believe that simple discounting is a sensible alternative to actuarial discounting for the whole population. However, to the extent that a fraction of the population we study is appropriately considered as pure life-cycle savers and subject to the imperfections in annuity markets, some method of aggregating heterogeneous individuals within cohorts is desirable and perhaps some convex combination of actuarial and simple discounting would be necessary. Simple discounting would alter the benefits and taxes only a few percentage points, given a real discount rate of 2 or 3 percent. Again, we would argue that these factors should be applied only to some fraction of the population, not the entire population. For the system totals, such adjustments are unnecessary; indeed, they only make sense for examining the individual cases rather than the system aggregate totals.

Related questions revolve around comparing taxes paid earlier in life and benefits received later in life. Taxes might be paid at a time in life when households are constrained in liquidity; Social Security benefits may be systematically subject to different types of risks than labor earnings or returns from assets. Hence, the taxes may be differentially risky since they are paid on realized earnings during working years relative to Social Security benefits. Again, these issues have been discussed in more detail elsewhere (see Boskin and Shoven 1987).

Thus, some risk adjustment may be necessary. Several researchers (for example, Aaron 1982) have even suggested that the appropriate discount rate should be zero because Social Security benefits are a safe asset and zero is close to the real return on government securities (safe assets) over the long term. First, adjusting for differences in risk other than mortality risk by adjusting discount rates is inappropriate. Modern finance theory teaches that a charge for risk should be assigned in the appropriate period and the appropriate measure of net adjusted benefits should then be discounted at the rate of time preference. Second, it is unclear whether Social Security benefits or earnings or the returns to other assets are differentially risky. Indeed, it is not just their inherent risk but their covariance with other components of income for households that would determine the nature of the risk charge to be applied. For persons already retired, we would expect that uncertainty would be relatively modest; for those due to retire in the distant future, there is substantial uncertainty regarding the level of such Social Security payments. This stems both from the Social Security system's problems in long-term financial solvency and from the desire of many to means-test the program fully. Thus, well-off individuals in the future may wind up getting nothing as the way to deal with the financial solvency problem. We merely point these issues out for the interested reader and refer them to the other works cited for further discussion, but these caveats should be borne in mind in interpreting the results reported here.

DISCUSSION

Mary Ross

What I find most interesting about this paper by Michael Boskin and Douglas Puffert is the clarity with which the authors describe three enormously important issues facing the Social Security program of OASI. The reader is led to the brink of several major precipices or decision points that affect the future of Social Security in the United States. These critical points are (1) the large and increasingly sensitive transfers between and within cohorts of workers/beneficiaries under Social Security; (2) the need, under various alternative financing projections, for increases in revenues or reductions in OASI benefits some 40 or 50 years from now; and (3) the prospect of large OASI trust-fund growth over the next 25 or 30 years and how that situation may be dealt with.

There are two basic points of reference that I find particularly helpful in dealing with these important issues regarding the benefit structure and the financing of Social Security in the long-range future. First, the inter- and intracohort transfers are to a substantial degree the consequences of deliberate program design. Second, apart from the question of specific financing arrangements and their effects, future OASI expenditures will be paid for on a current basis with funds raised at the time the benefits are paid.

INTER- AND INTRAGENERATIONAL TRANSFERS

This paper contains detailed measurements of the extent to which one birth cohort (or one group within a cohort) may fare better or worse in terms of the expected OASI benefits in relation to OASI taxes, as compared to others

The views expressed in these comments are solely the author's and are not necessarily those of the Social Security Administration.

or to a standard of a fair rate of return. There is extensive analysis and quantification, under various alternative assumptions, of the value of the potential Social Security benefits for retired workers, spouses, and aged survivors, using a 2 percent real interest rate and considering that the entire OASI tax (including the employer tax) is paid by the worker.

Although there are interesting variations in the internal rates of return for the various groups, the overall findings are, predictably, that the earlier cohorts fare better than do later ones, lower-paid workers fare better than those with higher earnings, and married workers with nonworking spouses fare better than single workers. The analysis also points up the higher return for the one-earner couple—as compared with the two-earner couple with the same total earnings equally divided—and the relatively low return for the earnings of the lower-paid spouse in a couple where both work.

With the exception of 1943–1952 birth cohorts (for which the real rate of return is 1.96), all cohorts have a rate of return in excess of 2 percent. However, the rate of return is less than 3 percent for all post-1932 cohorts. The obvious underlying issue is what rates of return people will find unacceptably low and what degree of variation between and within cohorts people will view as unacceptably unfair.

The question of fairness is subjective and value-laden. Obviously, from the vantage point of the program's 50-year history, absolutely equal treatment of all cohorts and groups or individuals within cohorts is not essential and not necessarily even desirable. However, if substantial numbers of Social Security taxpayers view the program as inherently unfair and as ineffective and/or irrelevant in meeting income support objectives, basic program changes may be called for.

It is useful, in this context, to recognize that Social Security serves purposes other than strict equity, as it is understood in the context of the individual annuity, and that it reflects social values that rate-of-return calculations cannot. The transfers to the early cohorts, to lower-paid workers, and to workers with families all reflect deliberate policy decisions built into the current Social Security program structure. Some of the other transfers— such as are reflected in the relative rates of return of two-earner versus one-earner couples or in the high dollar return for higher-paid workers, especially in the earlier cohorts—are the secondary results of these decisions rather than deliberate choices in themselves.

In evaluating the varying rates of return presented and explored in Boskin and Puffert's paper, it is necessary to reflect on the broad social and economic context in which the weightings in the system developed and their ongoing validity. It is also necessary to consider the possible consequences of alternative policies.

FUTURE FINANCIAL STATUS

Analysis of the future financial status of the OASI program focuses on the substantial trust-fund buildup in the next 25 years and the large deficits projected toward the latter half of the 75-year valuation period. It is useful to consider these two situations together, as Boskin and Puffert do, because the nature and extent of the long-range situation may well depend on what actions, if any, are taken to deal with the nearer-term situation.

The underlying economic and demographic assumptions and rough magnitude and shape of the cost and revenue projections reflected in this paper are generally comparable to those reflected for the OASI program in the 1986 Social Security trustees' report. However, in this analysis (as in the rate-of-return analysis) substantial reliance is placed on presentations based on discounted 1986 dollars (2 percent real interest assumption). This presentation, in the use of dollar magnitudes, provides a measure of the financing status of the program that is not present in the trustees' report. The trustees' report does not present long-range estimates in dollar terms, either nominal or discounted.[27] The trustees present long-range estimates of average annual income (excluding interest) and expenditures, expressed as a percentage of taxable payroll. The status of the trust fund (including net interest earnings) is presented as a percentage of annual outgo at five-year intervals over the 75-year long-range valuation period. Both the Boskin and Puffert paper and the trustees' report show the effects of more and less favorable economic and demographic assumptions on the future financing of the system— though the trustees' report does not show some of the variations presented in this paper.[28]

The use of discounted dollars, as presented in this paper, may facilitate consideration of the absolute size of the program and analysis of discrete program elements—revenues, expenditures, and the difference between the two. However, use of dollar figures may tend to obscure the dynamic interrelationship among the economic and demographic factors that crucially affect both OASI revenues and expenditures—an interrelationship that is inherent in estimates based primarily on percentages of taxable payroll. For example, as wage levels change, so do both the tax base (payroll) and initial benefit levels; similarly, as the size of the work force changes, so do the tax base and the potential beneficiary population.

In any event, with any reasonable projections of OASI revenues and expenditures under the current law, substantial trust-fund growth is anticipated over the next 30–35 years and a large shortfall in revenues relative to expenditures can be anticipated by the middle of the next century. As Boskin and Puffert point out, under the financing provisions now in the law, substantial reliance appears to be placed on the accumulation of sizable reserves through 2020 or so to help pay benefits thereafter until the trust fund is exhausted around the middle of the century.

Before turning to the future scenarios that are explored by Boskin and Puffert, it may be useful to reflect on the extent to which the apparent reliance on a sizable fund buildup to finance future benefits may be somewhat illusory. Whether the OASI financing schedule follows strict pay-as-you-go principles or relies on building up (and drawing down) interest-earnings reserves, future expenditures will in one way or another be financed out of revenues raised at the time the benefits are paid. Under a pay-as-you-go schedule of Social Security tax rates, future expenditures will be met from then-current Social Security tax revenues. Under a Social Security system that relies substantially on interest earnings or on drawing down trust-fund reserves, the government will have to raise taxes or borrow to redeem the U.S. obligations held by the trust funds and pay the benefits when due.

This is not to say that the timing and method of OASI financing are not significant for any number of reasons. Rather, the purpose is to suggest that the method of financing does not alter the amount or timing of the funding needed to pay OASI expenditures.

THE NEXT FEW DECADES

The projected large annual surpluses do clearly present political temptations as Boskin and Puffert describe—both in terms of spending the expected revenues and in terms of not allowing higher than currently needed funds to accumulate. Although past experience suggests that there is something inherently unstable in a situation where trust funds are projected to grow well beyond current program needs, there is little basis for predicting what actions, if any, may be taken in dealing with this situation.

In the past several decades there have been a number of situations where large trust-fund buildups were projected but—because of congressional action—such trust-fund growth did not actually occur. These situations were not entirely analogous to the present situation, however, since they occurred when current and projected payroll tax rates were considerably lower than they are today; they also occurred prior to (1) the adoption of the automatic Cost-of-Living Adjustment (COLA) provisions, (2) the use of dynamic economic assumptions in official long-range cost estimates, and (3) the explicit adoption of pay-as-you-go financing principles. For example, in the 1950s and 1960s, despite the de facto pay-as-you-go financing that occurred, the plan of financing generally called for scheduling a so-called ultimate tax rate to take effect a relatively few years after enactment. This ultimate rate was generally designed to provide for a substantial trust-fund buildup such that the program would be adequately financed over the long term without further tax-rate increases. The general practice was that Congress would act, prior to the date of a scheduled ultimate rate increase, to update benefits, make other program adjustments, and revise the tax-rate schedule.[29]

Boskin and Puffert consider a number of alternative scenarios that might develop over the next several decades:

1. One alternative outlined would be to revise the schedule to return to a more strictly pay-as-you-go basis and to schedule higher tax rates later on. This would occur, it is hoped, only after a reasonable contingency reserve had been built up, since trust funds will not reach one year's benefit payments until the early 1990s.

2. With respect to possible use of the funds for health insurance purposes, the temptation is strong and obvious. Such a use of the funds probably should not be thought of as borrowing, however, since there is virtually no anticipation of repayment of the amounts in question. A more likely approach would be a reduction in the tax rates for cash benefits and a corresponding increase in the tax rates for health purposes. It is interesting that, despite awareness of the Hospital insurance financing issue and despite current proposals relating to catastrophic health insurance, there has not yet been any congressional move toward tapping the OASI trust-fund buildup for this purpose.

3. The authors also discuss a general "benefit ratchet" alternative—that is, substantial Social Security benefit liberalizations that would reduce or eliminate the so-called surpluses and require further additional financing later on. This possibility seems somewhat less likely. Congress has tended to be very much aware of the long-range costs—and of the need to deal with them—at the times that liberalizations have been enacted. There are, however, changes that could be made that would have relatively greater short-range costs as compared to the long-range, and there is precedent for using future benefit reductions, such as the increase in retirement age, as a long-range balancing factor.

4. Consideration is also given to the potential for spending the surplus to meet other governmental costs or to reduce federal budget deficits. In a bookkeeping sense, the trust funds may now appear to reduce annual deficits in the federal budget; for example, the Gramm-Rudman-Hollings balanced budget legislation specifically provides for counting trust-fund income and outgo in determining the overall deficit/surplus status of the federal budget. There may also be a real

concern that the existence of annual trust-fund surpluses may lead to greater federal spending in non–Social Security areas than would otherwise occur.

Nevertheless, such a development would not, in itself, reduce trust-fund surpluses. Trust-fund monies not needed for current expenditures are invested in U.S. obligations and thus form part of the national debt. The revenues that the treasury receives from these trust-fund investments are used for general governmental purposes just as revenues received from U.S. obligations are held by the private sector. The treasury pays interest on these obligations and repays the principal as the obligations mature or are redeemed to pay current benefits. It seems extremely unlikely that Congress would permit the comingling of Social Security revenues with other general tax receipts in such a way that the Social Security tax revenues would not remain clearly identifiable as trust-fund assets, or that Congress would allow, in effect, the cancellation of U.S. debt held by the trust funds.

Overall, the question of how best to deal with the substantial trust-fund buildup that is projected over the next 25 years will doubtless receive considerable further review and analysis in the near future. It will be interesting to see how these issues and the interrelated issues of program fairness and transfers among and within cohorts are dealt with as the next several decades unfold.

NOTES

1. This value may very well be enhanced by the fact that the benefits are paid out as an inflation-adjusted life annuity.

2. In particular, we do not consider disability benefits or the taxes that finance them.

3. See Boskin et al. (1987) for a discussion of the choice of discount rate and sensitivity analyses.

4. Because the cost to an employer of hiring a worker includes a payroll tax contribution, and employers are presumably indifferent as to whom their labor costs are paid, the payroll tax decreases the demand for labor and causes wage rates to fall by (approximately) the amount of the tax.

5. In fact, if the reports were to present such calculations, based on the 1986 report's own assumptions and methodology, the resulting figures would be more optimistic under each of the four sets of assumptions used. A comparison of tables 10 and F2 in the 1986 report shows that taxable payroll is projected to rise at a rate slightly below the assumed interest rate (under each alternative set of assumptions). This means that the earlier positive annual balances should be given greater weight than the later negative annual balances. Thus the long-run actuarial balance would be reported as a little higher.

6. Under the present paper's use of 2 percent real interest, a still higher proportion of benefits would be transfers.

7. For further information on this simulation, or rather on an earlier version of it, see Boskin, Avrin, and Cone (1983).

8. The 1975 Social Security Exact Match File merged individual records from the 1973 Current Population Survey with records of covered earnings.

9. It will be noted that our simulation shows the 1943–1952 cohort faring rather worse than its successor, although the general pattern is that succeeding cohorts until about 1960 do progressively worse. The reason for this is that this cohort is the youngest one for which survey data are used, and many in this cohort are not yet married. It is well known that singles fare rather poorly under Social Security, since they have no option to receive a spouse or survivor benefit in addition to benefit based on their own earnings.

10. Between now and the year 2010, we derive less in annual and cumulative surpluses (due to deriving less in tax receipts) than what the 1986 trustees' report suggests is likely. Our figures are close to those of the report in the early 2010s, but thereafter until about 2040 we derive greater annual surpluses or lower deficits than those projected in the report. After 2040 we again generate higher annual deficits.

11. More extensive results from this simulation, but based on the income tax law in effect until 1986, are presented in Boskin et al. (1987) and Boskin and Puffert (1987). The former article also contains a more extensive description of our methodology.

12. We do not consider alternative assumptions for unemployment, female labor force participation, immigration, or real interest rates.

13. In previous work (Boskin et al. 1987), we and our colleagues argue for a rate of 3 percent.

14. This is slightly more than the 0.29 percent long-term actuarial deficit presented in the 1986 trustees' report. We discussed above how the latter figure is not very meaningful and how a calculation comparable to ours would yield a deficit that is lower in magnitude. A further difference is that our calculation assumes the lower marginal tax rates enacted in 1986. Under the old tax law our simulated deficit is about 0.34 percent of taxable payroll.

15. For an analysis of the inaccuracy of the economic and demographic assumptions used in the past, see U.S. General Accounting Office (1986).

16. Undiscounted, but still in 1986 dollars, the respective figures are +$14.7 trillion and −$11.1 trillion. Subsequent figures are also presented in discounted terms. To remove discounting, multiply by 4.33.

17. For each of the scenarios discussed in this section and the next, detailed results in the format of Table 8.1 are available from the authors.

18. The level of immigration, especially of young people, will have an impact for the same reason. We leave this matter for future investigation.

19. Until recently, the assumed figure was 2.1 children per woman.

20. In our simulation we use the Social Security Administration's figures for number of births each calendar year, which are derived from these fertility rates. It should be noted that the fertility rates used by the Social Security Administration refer to "the average number of children who would be born to a woman in her lifetime if she were to experience the birth rates by age observed in, or assumed for, the selected year and if she were to survive the entire child-bearing period" (Social Security Administration 1986, 35).

21. Under the combined optimistic assumptions, today's young children will pay a little more than twice as much in taxes as they would under the combined pessimistic assumptions, but they will receive nearly four times as much in benefits.

22. Of course, the consumption of the economy as a whole is limited by what is produced by those still working. Thus, in some sense Social Security benefits must always be funded at the time they are paid. Still, the method of financing Social Security determines who has what claims, and this has important implications both for equity and efficiency.

23. The higher tax rate shown for 2022 is a quirk resulting from the way our simulation handles the rise in retirement age, from 66 to 67, which occurs around that time. We simulate the change as occurring all at once rather than phased in over several years.

24. In practice, it is more likely that part of OASI's portion of payroll tax will be reallocated to HI. The analysis of OASI finances would then be similar to that of our pay-as-you-go tax-rate scenario.

25. A deficit of $8 billion appears for some scenarios due to our simulation showing a slight overall deficit between 1986 and 1989.

26. We believe that only a modest fraction of total Social Security benefit payments are offset by private intrafamily intergenerational transfers.

27. The Office of the Actuary of the Social Security Administration annually publishes a separate "Actuarial Note" entitled *Long-Range Estimates of Social Security Trust Fund Operations in Dollars,* which presents current dollar projections and various methods of converting current dollars to constant dollars. Actuarial Note no. 127 (April 1986), presents numbers underlying the 1986 trustees' report; the comparable information with respect to the 1987 trustees' report is in Actuarial Note no. 130 (April 1987).

28. Boskin and Puffert note that the averaging of the discounted dollar values (using an assumed 2 percent real interest rate) tends to give somewhat greater relative weight to the near-term surpluses. Thus, this approach may produce more favorable results than when annual percent-of-payroll figures (excluding interest) are averaged.

On the other hand, the exclusion of interest from the income rate calculations in the trustees' report is consistent with the concept of pay-as-you-go financing, which was de facto policy in Social Security throughout the 1950s and 1960s and deliberate policy beginning in the early 1970s. Also, in the present circumstances, the omission of interest from the "income rate" may serve, coincidentally, to offset some of the distortion that occurs when favorable balances in the first half of the 75-year estimating period are "averaged" with deficits later on to produce a single figure representing "average annual balance" over the entire 75-year period.

29. In the 1940s, when the OASI trust fund was relatively large in relation to annual expenditures, Congress acted several times to cancel or defer scheduled tax-rate increases, even though substantial growth in expenditures was anticipated. It is interesting to note that, throughout the 1940s and for many years thereafter, the trust fund was considerably larger in relation to then-current expenditures and in relation to GNP than has been the case in the late 1970s and the 1980s.

REFERENCES

Aaron, Henry. 1982. *The Economic Effects of Social Security.* Washington, D.C.: Brookings Institution.

Bernheim, B. D. 1986. "The Economic Effects of Social Security: A Reconciliation of the Theory and the Evidence." Mimeo, Stanford University.

Boskin, M. J. 1986. *Too Many Promises: The Uncertain Future of Social Security.* Homewood, Ill.: Dow Jones-Irwin.

Boskin, M. J., M. Avrin, and K. Cone. 1983. "Modeling Alternative Solutions to the Long-Run Social Security Funding Problem." in M. Feldstein, ed., *Behavioral Simulation Methods in Tax Policy Analysis.* Chicago: University of Chicago Press.

Boskin, M. J., L. J. Kotlikoff, D. J. Puffert, and J. B. Shoven. 1987. "Social Security: A Financial Appraisal Across and Within Generations." *National Tax Journal* 40 (March): 19–34.

Boskin, M. J., L. J. Kotlikoff, and J. B. Shoven. 1985. "Personal Security Accounts: A Proposal for Fundamental Social Security Reform." Policy Paper, Center for Economic Policy Research, Stanford University.

Boskin, M. J., and D. J. Puffert. 1987. "Social Security and the American Family." In L. Summers, ed., *Tax Policy and the Economy*. Cambridge, Mass.: MIT Press.

Boskin, M. J., and J. Shoven. 1987. "Concepts and Measures of Earnings Replacement During Retirement." In Z. Bodie, J. Shoven, and D. Wise, eds., *Issues in Pension Economics*. Chicago: University of Chicago Press.

Hurd, M. D., and J. B. Shoven. 1985. "The Distributional Impact of Social Security." In D. A. Wise, ed., *Pension, Labor, and Individual Choice*. Chicago: University of Chicago Press.

Pellechio, A. J., and G. P. Goodfellow. 1983. "Individual Gains and Losses from Social Security Before and After the 1983 Amendments." *Cato Journal* 3 (Fall): 417–42.

Social Security Administration. 1984. "Social Security Area Population Projections, 1984." Actuarial Study no. 92. Washington, D.C.

———. 1986. *Annual Report of the Board of Trustees of the Federal Old Age and Survivors and Disability Insurance Trust Funds*. Washington, D.C.: GPO.

U.S. General Accounting Office. 1986. *Social Security: Past Projections and Future Financing Concerns*. Washington, D.C.

9

A LOOK AT
VERY EARLY RETIREES

*Michael D. Packard
and Virginia P. Reno*

For men, the trend toward earlier retirement (defined here as withdrawal from the labor force) is a phenomenon that has long been recognized. As recently as 1970, the most common retirement age for men was 65. In 1985, 62 was the more common age for labor force withdrawal or for first receipt of Social Security benefits. This trend toward earlier retirement is not limited to those aged 62 and older, however. Between 1965 and 1985 the labor force participation rate of 60-year-old men fell from 86 percent to 71 percent and that for 55-year-old men fell from 93 percent to 84 percent. Obviously there are influences other than Social Security's retired-worker benefits that are causing men to stop working at ever earlier ages. This paper seeks to describe these other influences on the retirement behavior of very early retirees—that is, men who stop working at least six months before age 62, the age of eligibility for Social Security retired-worker benefits.

The data set we use is the Social Security Administration's 1982 New Beneficiary Survey (NBS). That survey interviewed 17,155 retired-worker, disabled-worker, spouse, and survivor beneficiaries who first received Social Security benefits from mid-1980 to mid-1981; it also interviewed 1,444 persons aged 65 and over who were eligible for retired-worker benefits but had not yet received those benefits by mid-1982. This study is limited to the 9,100 retired-worker respondents who represent a population of 1,214,000 new retired-worker beneficiaries. The NBS gathered detailed data on job histories from 1951 to 1982, the current job, last job, and longest job held since 1951, current health status, sources and levels of income, types and amounts of assets held, marital histories, child-care histories, and Social Security program knowledge.[1] These retirees were interviewed in late 1982, about one and a half to two and a half years after initial receipt of Social Security benefits. They represent just one cohort of retirees who were predominately aged 62–65 in 1980–81. Those who retired very early—that is, stopped working before age 61.5—did so in the late 1970s.

The first section of this paper looks at trends in retirement since 1963 using different retirement measures. The second section describes the NBS new retired-worker beneficiaries and the patterns of pension receipt, Social Security benefit level, total income, asset holdings, and reasons for leaving last job that are associated with very early retirement.

RETIREMENT TRENDS

Retirement is a seemingly straightforward concept, yet one that is defined and measured in many different ways. Retirement can mean total withdrawal from the labor force, a reduction in hours worked or level of earnings, the acceptance of Social Security or other pension benefits, the termination of a particular career, or simply a person's declaration that he or she is "retired." Each such definition would yield quite different answers to such questions as: How many people are retired? At what age do people retire? How many people retire "early"?

In spite of differences in definition and measurement, we see a clear trend over the past fifteen or twenty years in retirement behavior of men. No matter what measure is used, men seem to be retiring at earlier ages. The typical age of retirement is no longer 65; instead, 62 has become the more common age, and increasingly, labor force withdrawal or pension receipt occurs before age 62. We will briefly examine three measures of retirement that are disaggregated by single years of age to help pinpoint the timing of retirement: the labor force participation rate, the Social Security benefit receipt rate, and the pension receipt rate.

Labor Force Participation Rates

In this measure, retirees are people out of the labor force—that is, those neither employed nor looking for work. In Table 9.1 we show the proportion of men and women out of the work force by single years of age between ages 55 and 70 in 1963, 1970, and 1985. In 1963 and 1970, the sharpest increase in this measure of retirement for men occurred between ages 64 and 65. In 1985, the sharpest increase was between ages 61 and 62—almost 50

TABLE 9.1

MEN AND WOMEN AGED 55–70 OUT OF THE
LABOR FORCE IN 1963, 1970, AND 1985
(PERCENTAGE OF TOTAL POPULATION)

	MEN			WOMEN		
Age	*1963*	*1970*	*1985*	*1963*	*1970*	*1985*
55	7	8	16	52	47	47
56	7	9	18	53	52	49
57	9	11	20	55	50	53
58	9	12	23	58	52	52
59	11	12	25	57	54	56
60	12	16	29	60	56	57
61	16	19	34	64	61	62
62	20	26	49	69	64	66
63	24	31	55	71	68	72
64	28	36	58	74	72	76
65	46	50	70	80	78	81
66	57	55	74	82	81	84
67	61	61	76	84	84	85
68	67	62	80	86	85	87
69	67	66	80	87	87	89
70	73	70	84	89	88	91

SOURCES: Bureau of Labor Statistics, unpublished data; Rones (1985).

percent of 62-year-old men were out of the work force, up from about 25 percent in 1970. Withdrawal before age 62 is also increasing. Of 60-year-old men in 1985, fully 29 percent were out of the workforce, up from 16 percent in 1970. Of 55-year-old men, 16 percent were out of the labor force in 1985, twice the rate in 1970.

Social Security Receipt Rates

The Social Security receipt rate is the proportion of all persons of a given age who are receiving Social Security benefits. To receive retired-worker benefits, a person must be at least age 62, have worked enough in covered employment to be insured (as are over nine in ten men and about two in three women near retirement age today), have filed for benefits, and have earnings below the break-even point under the Social Security earnings test.[2]

Some older workers enter the Social Security benefit rolls as disabled workers, spouses of beneficiaries, or survivors of deceased workers, and they, logically, should be included in the benefit receipt rate for measuring retirement. Disabled-worker benefits are paid at any age before 65. The statutory test of disability is quite strict, and a special insured status requirement involving recent work prior to disability must be met. Surviving-spouse benefits can be received as early as age 60, earlier if minor children are present in the household.

In Figure 9.1 we show the benefit receipt rate for men in 1985 by single years of age between 61 and 70. At age 61 the receipt rate for men comprises disabled workers only and was 11 percent. At age 62, when reduced retired-worker benefits are available, the receipt rate was 43 percent, including about 11 percent who were disabled. By age 64, fully 62 percent of men received Social Security benefits. At age 65, when full benefits are paid, the

FIGURE 9.1 _____

SOCIAL SECURITY RECEIPT RATES FOR MEN
BY SINGLE YEARS OF AGE, 1985

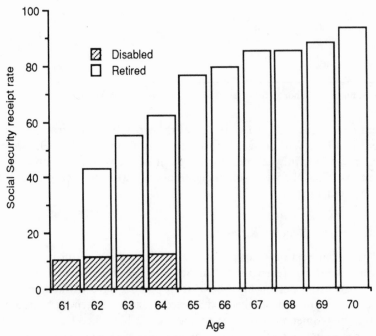

SOURCE: Numerators are in USDHHS (1988); denominators are from unpublished data at the Social Security Administration, Office of the Actuary.

NOTE: Husbands and widowers are less than 0.5 percent of population at each age.

receipt rate climbed to 79 percent and then gradually rose to about 95 percent after age 70 when virtually all insured workers received benefits whether they were retired or not.

In Figure 9.2 we show a similar pattern for women, although the beneficiaries include those receiving benefits as wives and widows in addition to those receiving benefits as retired or disabled workers. Without those receiving auxiliary benefits, the receipt rates for women would be well below the rates for men.

Over time, there has been a movement toward earlier receipt of Social Security retired-worker benefits. The percent of 62-year-old men receiving benefits increased from 25 percent in 1970 to 43 percent in 1985. The sharpest increase occurred from 1971 to 1977, when the receipt rate rose from 26 to 39 percent. The proportion of 62-year-old men receiving disabled-worker benefits has changed little over the 1970–1985 period. The growth is mainly in those receiving retired-worker benefits at the earliest

FIGURE 9.2 _____

SOCIAL SECURITY RECEIPT RATES FOR WOMEN
BY SINGLE YEARS OF AGE, 1985

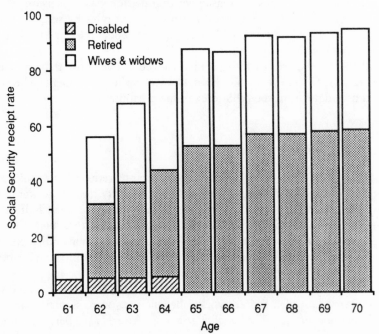

SOURCE: Numerators are in USDHHS (1988); denominators are from unpublished data at the Social Security Administration, Office of the Actuary.

eligible age. The high rate of benefit receipt at the earliest eligible age suggests that some retirement must be occurring before age 62.

Pension Receipt Rates

A recent study by the U.S. General Accounting Office (USGAO; 1986) investigates the change in early pension receipt in the general population from 1973 to 1983. It shows a significant growth in receipt of pensions before age 62. It also shows that government employee pensions are an important share of those early pensions. According to the study, the pension receipt rate for men aged 55–61 doubled between 1973 and 1983, growing from 8 to 17 percent of all noninstitutionalized men in the general population. About half the men who received pensions before age 62 had government employee pensions, including state, local, federal civilian, and military pensions. Among women, early pension receipt grew somewhat more slowly—from 4 to 7 percent of 55–61 year olds. Government pensions were not as large a share of the early pensions for women as they were for men, although government pensions—state and local, in particular—were a large share of women's pensions at age 65 and over.

Although the sharpest increase over that decade was in pension receipt before age 65, in 1983 the greatest jump in receipt rates by single years of age was between 64 and 65 (Table 9.2). Ages 65, 66, and 67 had the highest pension receipt rates.

All three measures of retirement reviewed above show that the trend over the past fifteen years has been toward earlier retirement. The next section uses data from the NBS to examine attributes of very early retirees.

VERY EARLY RETIREES IN THE NBS

The desirability of early retirement is evident among retirees in the NBS. Age 62 was the most common age at which Social Security retired-worker benefits were received by the NBS retired-worker population. Nearly half of the men and two-thirds of the women were age 62 when they first received retired-worker benefits. In fact, almost 30 percent of the men and 50 percent of the women received benefits in the month of their 62d birthday. Among new retired-worker beneficiaries, married women were the most likely to have claimed benefits at the earliest possible age (74 percent of them did so). The unmarried women retired-worker beneficiaries were similar to men in their likelihood of claiming benefits at age 62 (roughly 50 percent did so).

Many of the new retired-worker beneficiaries who became entitled to retired-worker benefits at age 62 had stopped working well before age 62.

TABLE 9.2

PENSION RECEIPT RATES FOR MEN AND WOMEN
BY SINGLE YEARS OF AGE, 1983
(PERCENTAGES OF TOTAL POPULATION)

Age	Men	Women
50	5	2
51	7	3
52	8	2
53	8	3
54	7	4
55	10	6
56	14	5
57	14	7
58	16	6
59	19	7
60	22	10
61	24	12
62	29	14
63	34	16
64	36	16
65	47	23
66	51	22
67	48	20
68	46	22
69	40	22
70	40	24

SOURCE: USGAO (1986).

Almost 50 percent of the married women and 20 percent of the men and unmarried women were very early retirees—that is, they had stopped working by age 61.5 (Table 9.3). Over 80 percent of all very early retirees claimed retired-worker benefits in the month they turned age 62, and another 10 percent claimed benefits during the following year. At the other extreme, almost 25 percent of the NBS retired-worker population were working when they were interviewed 18–30 months after they first received benefits. Unmarried women were slightly more likely than men to have been working (29 versus 25 percent). Married women were the least likely to have been working (17 percent).[3]

The remainder of this paper examines the attributes of those who stopped working before age 61.5 as compared with those who retired at

TABLE 9.3

EMPLOYMENT STATUS AT INTERVIEW AND AGE STOPPED WORKING:
RETIRED-WORKER BENEFICIARIES WITH FIRST PAYABLE BENEFIT IN JUNE 1980–MAY 1981

Employment status and age stopped working	Total	MEN			WOMEN		
		Total	Married	Not married	Total	Married	Not married
Total (in thousands)	1,214.1	689.7	579.4	110.3	524.4	364.9	159.5
Total percent	100	100	100	100	100	100	100
Stopped working	77	75	74	80	79	83	71
Before age 61.5	28	20	19	26	38	46	21
Before age 55	9	3	2	8	16	20	7
Age 55–59	10	8	8	10	13	16	7
Age 60–61.5	9	9	9	8	9	10	7
Age 61.5–62	17	19	19	22	13	14	13
Age 63 or older	29	35	36	30	22	16	36
Not reported	3	1	1	2	6	7	3
Still working	23	25	26	20	21	17	29

SOURCE: Tabulations from 1982 NBS.

older ages or who continued to work after benefit receipt. Did they have working spouses whose earnings offset their own lack of earnings? Did they receive pensions from private or government employee plans? What reasons did they give for having left their jobs? If they reported health problems as a reason for leaving, did they then receive disability pensions? Did they consider themselves totally unable to work? Did they apply for, but not receive, Social Security disability benefits? Did they lose their jobs? To what extent did they report having retired voluntarily? Was their total income substantially greater (or smaller) than that of beneficiaries who worked longer? Were their asset holdings substantially different from those who worked longer?

Spouse Work Status

For Social Security beneficiaries who are married, the earnings of a working spouse could help mitigate the loss of their own earnings. The NBS contains data on work histories of both the beneficiary and the spouse, and from these data the relative timing of retirement can be determined.

In general, the younger the beneficiary when he or she stopped working, the more likely his or her spouse was to continue working. For example, among married women who retired very early, seven in ten had husbands who kept working after they had retired (Table 9.4). Similarly, about 40 percent of the married men who retired very early had wives who worked after the husband stopped. Wives of men who retired very early and had no pensions were more likely to have worked after he retired (46 percent) than were wives of early retiring men who had pensions (35 percent). The median monthly earnings in late 1982 of working spouses of very early retirees was $650, indicating that spousal earnings were an important source of income for married retirees.

Pensions

The men who stopped working between ages 55 and 61.5 were about as likely to have pensions as men who stopped working later. Roughly six in ten men had pensions, regardless of when they stopped working after age 55 (Table 9.5).[4] The small group who stopped working before age 55 (3 percent of men) were less likely to have pensions (35 percent). The men who were still working when they were interviewed were also much less likely to have pensions 18–30 months after first receiving Social Security benefits (28 percent had pensions). But among the men who had stopped working, the very early retirees were about as likely to have pensions as those who stopped working at age 61.5 or later.

TABLE 9.4

RELATIVE TIMING OF RETIREMENT OF SPOUSES IN MARRIED COUPLES
AND MEDIAN MONTHLY EARNINGS OF WORKING SPOUSE
BY AGE LEFT LAST JOB AND SEX

| | | AGE LEFT LAST JOB | | |
Sex and timing of retirement	Total[a]	Under age 61.5	Age 61.5–62	Age 63 or older
Married men (in thousands)	431.5	109.8	109.5	208.7
Total percent	100	100	100	100
Wife never worked	10	8	11	11
Wife retired first	48	42	48	54
Both retired same year	8	10	8	7
Husband retired first	31	39	32	26
Wife not working	9	16	9	6
Wife working	22	23	23	20
Unknown	2	2	2	2
Median monthly earning of working spouse	$645	$645	$700	$640
Married women (in thousands)	301.3	167.1	50.5	59.0
Total percent	100	100	100	100
Husband retired first	29	20	42	53
Both retired same year	10	8	18	12
Wife retired first	58	70	37	32
Husband not working	30	41	8	7
Husband working	28	29	28	25
Unknown	2	2	3	4
Median monthly earnings of working spouse	$800	$650	$900	$760

SOURCE: Tabulations from 1982 NBS.
a. Includes those whose age at retirement could not be determined.

For women, the pattern of pension receipt was different. The women who waited until age 63 or later to stop working were much more likely to have pensions (53 percent) than those who stopped working between ages 55 and 61.5 (35 percent) or at ages younger than 55 (9 percent). These data corroborate earlier findings from the NBS that, among pension recipients, the men were more likely than the women to take their pensions early (Reno and Price 1985). The reasons for this difference between the sexes is not clear and may be worth further study. It is also unclear to what extent the men's earlier pension receipt reflect: 1) men's greater participation in jobs

TABLE 9.5

NEW RETIRED-WORKER BENEFICIARIES RECEIVING THEIR OWN PENSION BY AGE LEFT LAST JOB, SEX, AND MARITAL STATUS (PERCENTAGES)

| | | | | AGE LEFT LAST JOB | | | |
New beneficiaries with own pension	Total	Total[a]	Under age 55	Age 55–61.5	Age 61.5–62	Age 63 or older	Still working
Total	42	47	14	48	55	57	22
Men	51	58	35	61	61	59	28
Married	53	61	44	64	64	60	29
Unmarried	41	45	[b]	45	48	52	24
Women	29	34	9	35	44	53	13
Married	25	27	7	32	39	45	10
Unmarried	43	52	20	48	60	62	17

SOURCE: Tabulations from 1982 NBS.

a. Includes those whose age at retirement could not be determined.

b. Based on fewer than 50 cases.

that offer pensions in general or that offer very early pensions specifically; 2) men's greater likelihood of having met the plan requirements for early pension receipt; 3) men's greater preference for early retirement; or 4) some other factors.

The USGAO (1986) study reported that many workers who retired with a pension were receiving a public pension, including pensions based on federal civilian, military, state or local government, or railroad employment. Public plans were an important source of pensions for NBS pensioners as well. About 33 percent of the male pensioners and 40 percent of the female pensioners received their pensions from public employee plans. Federal civilian and military pensioners were a slightly larger share of pension recipients among male very early retirees than among other groups of retirees.

People who retire very early are not only more likely to have a public pension than those who retire later, but they are also more likely to have a pension based on a disability rather than on retirement. Overall, 5 percent of those retiring before age 61.5 had a disability pension, as compared with less than 2 percent of those retiring after that age. We suspect that one reason for this age pattern is that people who retire later, even those with disabling health problems, are more likely than younger retirees to meet the requirements for an unreduced retired-worker pension.

According to the NBS, most disability pensions were given by the public sector. Ten percent of the very early retirees who had a public pension were receiving a disability pension. About 3 percent of older public pension recipients, and less than 1 percent of private pension recipients regardless of age at retirement, were receiving a disability pension.

In some defined-benefit plans, pensions received for very early retirement are supplemented until the retiree reaches age 62 or begins receiving Social Security benefits, at which time the pension is reduced. The NBS asked a series of questions about changes in pension levels for those reporting a pension from their last job (about 80 percent of those with pensions did so). Only 5 percent of those with a pension from their last job reported having their pension benefits cut after they began receiving them.[5] However, one-third of those reporting a decrease in the pension benefits from their last job also reported that their pension benefits had inceased at some point since initial receipt. Pension reductions were most common for those leaving their last job from ages 55 to 61.5 (10 percent). About 4 percent who left their last job at other ages had their benefits from pensions on their last job reduced. One-fifth of those with a pension benefit reduction reported that their pension benefits were reduced automatically at age 62, and another fifth reported a pension benefit reduction when they began receiving Social Security benefits.

Pension increases after retirement were not uncommon. Of those who reported receiving a pension from their last job, 37 percent reported their pension had increased since they first began receiving it. Pension benefit increases were negatively correlated with the age the retired-worker beneficiary left his or her last job. More than 50 percent of those who left their last job before age 61.5 reported increases in the pensions from their last job. This percentage declined to 30 percent for those who left their last job after age 61.5. We suspect that those who retired at younger ages are more likely to have received an increase in their pension amounts for two reasons. First, younger retirees are more likely to receive public pensions, which are often indexed. Second, it is reasonable to assume that those who retired at young ages have been receiving their pensions longer than those who retired at older ages; therefore, the young retirees have had more opportunity to take advantage of any ad hoc pension benefit increases that may have been made.

When the amounts of pension income are studied (Table 9.6), we see that the very early retirees had higher pension amounts, on average, than those who stopped working at age 63 or later. Among men, the overall median monthly pension income was $465. For those who stopped working at age 61.5 or earlier, it was $575, or nearly 25 percent higher than the overall median. For those who stopped working at age 63 or later or who were still working, it was $400, or about 15 percent less than the overall median. The distribution of women's pension amounts by age at retirement is much more tightly centered on the overall median value of $225.

Although the male very early retirees had higher pensions than other retirees, they were slightly less well off by other measures of income and wealth. The differences were not great, however. The three economic measures that will be discussed briefly below are Social Security benefit amounts, total monthly income, and net worth.

Social Security Benefit Amounts

In Table 9.7 we present the median Social Security monthly benefit amount as of December 1982 (from Social Security's administrative records) for new retired-worker beneficiaries. The very early retirees are expected to have somewhat lower Social Security benefits, on average, because they generally incurred the full actuarial reduction in their Social Security benefits for having claimed them at the earliest eligible age. Among men, the median overall monthly benefit was $520. For those who stopped working at age 61.5 or younger, the median amount was roughly 80 percent as much, or $425. Among men who stopped working at age 63 or older, the median was $675, or roughly 30 percent higher than the overall median. Among women, the range in median monthly benefit levels was even greater (from $255 for those retiring before age 61.5 to $485 for those retiring at age 63

TABLE 9.6

MEDIAN PENSION AMOUNTS FOR NEW RETIRED-WORKER BENEFICIARIES
WITH PENSIONS BY AGE LEFT LAST JOB, SEX, AND MARITAL STATUS
(IN DOLLARS)

			AGE LEFT LAST JOB			
New retired-worker beneficiaries	*Total*	*Total[a]*	*Under age 61.5*	*Age 61.5–62*	*Age 63 or older*	*Still working*
Total	400	400	465	425	325	320
Men	465	475	575	500	400	395
Married	475	485	585	500	405	405
Unmarried	405	425	510	500	300	b
Women	225	235	230	250	220	145
Married	190	210	220	250	185	100
Unmarried	270	270	305	285	245	215

SOURCE: Tabulations from 1982 NBS.
a. Includes those whose age at retirement could not be determined.
b. Based on fewer than 50 cases.

TABLE 9.7

MEDIAN MONTHLY SPECIAL SECURITY BENEFIT AMOUNT
OF NEW RETIRED-WORKER BENEFICIARIES
BY AGE LEFT LAST JOB, SEX, AND MARITAL STATUS
(IN DOLLARS)

			AGE LEFT LAST JOB			
New retired-worker beneficiaries	*Total*	*Total[a]*	*Under age 61.5*	*Age 61.5–62*	*Age 63 or older*	*Still working*
Total	445	435	290	455	620	465
Men	520	515	425	505	675	540
Married	530	530	450	510	685	550
Unmarried	450	450	340	440	625	460
Women	300	300	255	330	485	320
Married	280	275	255	300	420	285
Unmarried	435	445	305	380	540	410

SOURCE: Tabulations from 1982 NBS.
a. Includes those whose age at retirement could not be determined.

or older). The difference in benefit levels between the very early retirees and others is greater than the effect of the actuarial reduction alone. It appears that those who worked to older ages had gains in their Social Security benefits owing to longer, more complete earnings records and to higher recent earnings levels.

Total Income

Income data were collected by the NBS for the three months preceding the interview and include income from earnings, Social Security, other private and public pensions, a large group of assets, public transfer programs, private transfers, and interest, rent, and dividends. The total income data used in this paper generally include the income received by both the beneficiary and his or her spouse if he or she is married.[6] Both the income and the asset data used in this section include imputed values for missing amounts.[7]

Because the total monthly incomes of the retirees include the incomes of their spouses, if married, marital status is a powerful determinant of income for both male and female retirees. Within marital status, income is similar between male and female retired workers. Among the unmarried, for example, median monthly income was $760 for the men and $765 for the women (Table 9.8). Among couples, the median monthly income was $1,460 for male retirees and their wives and $1,440 for female retirees and their husbands, almost exactly twice that of unmarried beneficiaries.

Did income vary by the age the retiree left his or her last job? It did for the unmarried. Very early retirees had much smaller total incomes, particularly among the unmarried men. Those who stopped work at least six months before age 62 had a median monthly income of $495, roughly half that of single men who stopped working at 63 or older or who were still working.

For married retirees, in contrast, the effect of very early retirement on the couple's total income seems to have been modest. Among married men, their own pensions and their spouses' retirement benefits or earnings tended to even out negative effects of very early retirement on their own Social Security income. The median monthly income of married men who stopped working six or more months before age 62 was $1,385, only about 7 percent less than that of married men who stopped working at age 63 or older.

Asset Levels

Assets listed on the survey include financial assets (banking accounts, stocks, bonds, and IRA/ Keogh accounts), commercial assets (such as business property and farms), and own home. These assets include those held by

TABLE 9.8

MEDIAN TOTAL MONTHLY INCOME, INCLUDING SPOUSES',
OF NEW RETIRED-WORKER BENEFICIARIES
BY AGE LEFT LAST JOB, SEX, AND MARITAL STATUS
(IN DOLLARS)

New retired-worker beneficiaries	Total	Total[a]	AGE LEFT LAST JOB			
			Under age 61.5	Age 61.5–62	Age 63 or older	Still working
Total	1,320	1,290	1,240	1,260	1,340	1,415
Men						
Married	1,480	1,430	1,385	1,375	1,490	1,650
Unmarried	760	710	495	665	870	[b]
Women						
Married	1,440	1,425	1,375	1,430	1,555	1,545
Unmarried	765	710	565	675	805	885

SOURCE: Tabulations from 1982 NBS.
a. Includes those whose age at retirement could not be determined.
b. Based on fewer than 50 cases.

the beneficiary's spouse, if one is present. The NBS did not obtain values for motor vehicles, consumer durables, and other miscellaneous assets, nor did it obtain data on debt other than debt secured by real property. Thus, the net worth measures used below must be viewed as rough estimates of the beneficiaries' true net worth.

Marital status is even more strongly associated with the value of assets held than it was with total income. The median total income of the married couples was about twice that of the unmarried. The median value of assets, including equity in own home, was about four times as high for married men as for unmarried men ($68,400 versus $16,600) and more than twice as high for married women as unmarried women ($64,900 versus $30,200; Table 9.9).

Among unmarried men, the very early retirees had considerably less in assets than did those who worked longer—their median total assets, including equity in a home, was $6,000, or about one-fourth of the median assets for unmarried men who worked beyond age 62. Among married men, the very early retirees had median total assets of $61,500, only slightly less than those held by married men who worked beyond age 62.

Because home ownership is concentrated in married couples (88 percent of NBS married couples owned their own home versus 58 percent of the

TABLE 9.9

MEDIAN NET WORTH INCLUDING AND EXCLUDING EQUITY IN OWN HOME OF
NEW RETIRED-WORKER BENEFICIARIES BY AGE LEFT LAST JOB, SEX, AND MARITAL STATUS
(IN DOLLARS)

New retired-worker beneficiaries	Total	AGE LEFT LAST JOB				
		Total[a]	Under age 61.5	Age 61.5–62	Age 63 or older	Still working
		Median net worth including equity in own home				
Total	58,400	57,800	55,600	56,400	60,200	60,400
Men	61,400	59,600	51,800	57,200	65,500	72,000
Married	68,400	66,100	61,500	64,000	72,000	77,200
Unmarried	16,600	14,000	6,000	19,100	24,000	24,500
Women	54,500	55,600	57,000	53,300	51,200	46,100
Married	64,900	65,000	62,000	64,200	69,600	64,200
Unmarried	30,200	31,000	27,000	28,200	35,700	28,100
		Median net worth excluding equity in own home				
Total	14,100	13,800	11,000	13,300	17,000	15,200
Men	16,500	15,500	10,400	15,300	19,400	20,200
Married	20,000	19,000	15,700	17,000	22,200	22,700
Unmarried	3,200	1,800	200	1,400	7,300	9,600
Women	11,400	12,200	11,200	12,000	12,800	8,600
Married	15,700	15,500	13,500	14,700	17,300	16,400
Unmarried	5,100	5,700	2,600	4,300	9,000	3,500

SOURCE: Tabulations from 1982 NBS.

a. Includes those whose age at retirement could not be determined.

unmarried women and 48 percent of the unmarried men), and because home equity tends to overpower the value of other assets, asset holdings excluding equity in own home is also presented in Table 9.9. The median asset level excluding home equity for this study population was $14,100. The median amount for those who retired before age 61.5 was about 20 percent lower. Married couples again had substantially greater asset levels under this measure than did unmarried persons. Married men had a median value more than six times as large as that of unmarried men ($20,000 versus $3,200) and married women three times as large as unmarried women ($15,700 versus $5,100).

Reasons Retirees Gave for Leaving Their Last Job

The new beneficiaries who had stopped working and who had been wage and salary workers on their last job were asked whether a series of factors had contributed to their decision to leave their last job (Table 9.10). They were asked which factor, if any, was the most important consideration in leaving their jobs. The reasons a retiree gives for leaving his or her job are only one component of their retirement behavior and may be influenced by their postretirement experiences. Nonetheless, the retirees' reasons for leaving their jobs provide some insights about their own perceptions of their retirement.

Studies in the 1960s and early 1970s found that poor health was the most common reason given for stopping work and claiming Social Security retirement benefits before age 65 (see, for example, Reno 1976). When the NBS was conducted in 1982, early labor force withdrawal and benefit receipt was much more common than it had been a decade earlier. Results already reported from the NBS show that voluntary reasons are more common than health problems as a reason for stopping work and claiming benefits before age 65 (Sherman 1985).

One-fourth of all new beneficiaries who had stopped working after leaving wage and salary jobs listed poor health as the primary reason for leaving.[8] (The self-employed were not asked why they retired.) Women were just as likely as men to cite health problems as the main reason for leaving their last job. Typically, whenever health problems were identified as a factor in the decision to leave a job, they were considered the main reason. The health problems, however, were not always considered totally disabling by the retiree. To discern the retiree's view of the severity of the health problem, two additional questions were asked of those who gave health as the main reason for leaving: "Would your health have allowed you to do a similar job for fewer hours a day?" and "Would your health have let you do another kind of job?" The 25 percent of men who gave health problems as

TABLE 9.10

MAIN REASON GIVEN FOR LEAVING LAST JOB BY
NEW RETIRED-WORKER BENEFICIARIES BY AGE LEFT LAST JOB

Main reason	Total[a]	AGE LEFT LAST JOB			
		Under age 55	Age 55–61.5	Age 61.5–62	Age 63 or older
Total number	934,485	107,660	231,310	203,312	357,202
Percentage responding	86	90	87	90	89
Total percentage responding	100	100	100	100	100
Involuntary	41	40	43	42	40
Health	24	24	25	27	22
Could work	9	8	9	12	9
Could not work	15	16	16	15	13
Lost job	12	15	15	11	9
Mandatory retirement	5	1	3	4	9
Voluntary	47	29	43	51	53
Retirement	38	13	30	43	48
Wanted to retire	33	9	25	37	42
Did not like job	2	4	2	1	1
To get Social Security	2	b	b	3	4
To get pension	1	b	2	1	1
Family	9	16	13	8	5
To care for others	7	14	8	5	4
Because spouse retired	3	2	5	3	1
Other reason	12	31	14	8	7

SOURCE: Tabulations from 1982 NBS.
a. Includes those whose age at retirement could not be determined.
b. Less than 0.5 percent.

the main reason included about 11 percent who agreed that their health would have permitted them to work fewer hours or at a different job and about 14 percent who said they could not have worked longer. Only 9 percent of the women indicated they could have worked in spite of their health problems.

The male beneficiaries who stopped working well before age 62 were more likely than those who worked longer to give health problems as a reason for stopping work (Table 9.11). Nearly a third of those who stopped working at least six months before their 62d birthday said health problems

TABLE 9.11

MAIN REASON GIVEN FOR LEAVING LAST JOB BY
NEW RETIRED-WORKER MALE BENEFICIARIES BY AGE LEFT LAST JOB

		AGE LEFT LAST JOB			
Main reason	Total[a]	Under age 55	Age 55–61.5	Age 61.5–62	Age 63 or older
Total number	519,542	21,554	116,991	133,564	241,438
Percentage responding	85	81	82	88	87
Total percentage responding	100	100	100	100	100
Involuntary	43	62	48	43	40
Health	25	35	30	26	21
Could work	11	14	11	12	8
Could not work	14	21	19	14	13
Lost job	11	24	13	11	8
Mandatory retirement	7	4	5	5	10
Voluntary	48	19	39	51	54
Retirement	46	15	36	47	52
Wanted to retire	40	8	31	42	45
Did not like job	1	5	2	1	1
To get Social Security	3	1	b	3	4
To get pension	2	1	3	1	1
Family	3	4	3	3	2
To care for others	2	4	3	2	2
Because spouse retired	b	0	0	1	b
Other reason	8	18	12	7	6

SOURCE: Tabulations from 1982 NBS.
a. Includes those whose age at retirement could not be determined.
b. Less than 0.5 percent.

were the main reason they left their jobs. About 60 percent of these men (19 percent of all very early male retirees) reported they were unable to work fewer hours at the same job or at a different job.

By definition, none of the new retired-worker beneficiaries in this sample had received Social Security disability benefits immediately before receiving retirement benefits. A small subset (about 5 percent), however, had previously filed for and been denied disability insurance (DI) benefits. About three-fourths of those denied disability benefits said they retired primarily for health reasons. In addition, a small group was awarded disability benefits after they began receiving retirement benefits. It appears, however, that most of those who cited health problems as the reason for leaving their jobs had not applied for Social Security disability benefits.

A larger proportion of all new retirees gave the desire to retire as the primary reason for retiring than gave health as the primary reason (33 versus 24 percent; Table 9.10). However, unlike health—which was cited as the primary retirement reason by roughly 25 percent of these retirees no matter what their age at retirement—the percentage citing a desire to retire grew rapidly with the age of retirement, from less than 10 percent for those stopping work before age 55 to over 40 percent for those stopping work at age 63 or older. Those retiring between ages 55 and 61.5 were equally likely to cite health or the desire to retire. The NBS data show clearly that a significant portion of those retiring before age 62 were retiring voluntarily.

Fifteen percent of the very early retirees retired because they "lost their job or business was bad." This response was particularly prevalent among the unmarried[9] who retired before age 55. Twenty-eight percent of these unmarried beneficiaries gave this response, as compared to only 12 percent of married beneficiaries who retired before age 55.

The last commonly cited reason given for leaving previous job by very early retirees was to care for others (10 percent). As we would expect, women who retired very early were much more likely to give this response than men (14 versus 4 percent). What is somewhat surprising is that unmarried women retiring very early gave this response more often than married women (19 versus 14 percent). The NBS did not ask who was being cared for, but we suspect it was often a family member. For currently unmarried women, it may have been for a husband who subsequently died.

Very few retirees (only 2 percent) reported that they retired primarily to get a pension or a Social Security benefit. However, these answers were each given by 8 percent of the retirees as secondary reasons for retiring.

Responses to the questions on why people retired differed by whether or not the beneficiary was receiving a pension, especially for men (Table 9.12). Men without pensions gave involuntary reasons for retirement 60 percent more often than did men with pensions; the former were 50 percent more likely to cite poor health as the major retirement reason and three times as likely to say that they lost their jobs. These differences did not vary by the age at retirement. Men with pensions were twice as likely as men without pensions to say they retired because they wanted to retire. They were four times as likely to cite this reason if they retired very early and 1.6 times as likely if they retired after age 62. These same general patterns are repeated for women but on a somewhat smaller scale.

TABLE 9.12

MAIN REASONS FOR MEN RETIRING
BY AGE LEFT LAST JOB AND PENSION RECEIPT STATUS

Reason for retirement	Total[a]	AGE LEFT LAST JOB		
		Under age 61.5	Age 61.5–62	Age 63 or older
Without a pension				
Total number	152,488	40,501	39,135	71,866
Total percentage	100	100	100	100
Involuntary	58	65	60	52
Health	31	35	33	27
Lost job	19	25	21	14
Mandatory retirement	7	4	6	10
Voluntary	32	18	32	40
Retirement	29	15	28	38
Wanted to retire	24	10	22	32
Did not like job	2	4	1	1
To get Social Security	4	1	5	5
To get pension	b	b	0	0
Family	2	3	4	2
To care for others	2	3	2	2
Because spouse retired	b	0	2	0
Other	10	18	8	8
With a pension				
Total number	290,249	73,054	77,838	137,772
Total percentage	100	100	100	100
Involuntary	36	42	34	33
Health	22	28	23	18
Lost job	6	9	7	5
Mandatory retirement	7	5	5	10
Voluntary	57	47	59	61
Retirement	54	43	57	59
Wanted to retire	48	37	51	52
Did not like job	1	2	1	1
To get Social Security	2	b	3	4
To get pension	2	4	2	2
Family	3	4	3	3
To care for others	3	4	2	2
Because spouse retired	b	0	1	b
Other	7	11	6	5

SOURCE: Tabulations from 1982 NBS.

NOTE: Sample excludes 76,805 nonworking men with missing responses for reasons for leaving last job.

a. Includes those whose age at retirement could not be determined.

b. Less than 0.5 percent.

CONCLUSION

People who stop working at least six months before they are eligible for Social Security retired-workers benefits are different, but not terribly different, from those who retire at older ages. Results from the 1982 NBS show that slightly more than 25 percent of new retirees had stopped working before age 61.5. Married women were more likely than men or unmarried women to have retired early.

Very early retirees were less likely than those who retired after age 61.5 to receive pensions. However, most of this difference in pension receipt rate by age was due to the receipt rates for women. The pension receipt rate for men was a constant 60 percent for those who stopped working at age 55 or older. A surprising finding in this paper is that pension amounts for male pensioners decreased with the age at which they stopped working. The median pension for male very early retirees was about 40 percent higher than that for men who stopped working at age 63 or older.

In contrast to their median pension levels, very early retirees tended to have lower Social Security benefit levels, lower total incomes, and lower asset levels than those who retired later or who continued to work. Very early retirees also reported that they retired for involuntary reasons more often then did later retirees.

The trend toward earlier retirement is a phenomenon that will continue to be studied by the Social Security Administration. The age at which full Social Security retired-worker benefits are paid will begin to increase in the year 2000 for those born in 1938 or later. Eventually, those born after 1959 will have to wait until they are age 67 to receive full benefits. Reduced benefits will continue to be available at age 62, but the reduction factor for those becoming entitled to benefits on their 62d birthday (and born after 1959) will be 30 percent instead of the current 20 percent. The effect of this and other changes made in the 1983 amendments to the Social Security Act should encourage later retirement. At the current time, the trend toward earlier retirement appears to be strong. The challenging question for researchers is whether, when, and how the various retirement incentives will change and interact in the future.

DISCUSSION

Richard A. Ippolito

The paper by Michael Packard and Virginia Reno is most interesting in the underlying question it poses: Why has labor force participation at older ages fallen continuously over the post–World War II period? Implicitly, their study of "very early" retirees is an attempt to better understand the reasons why workers apparently prefer to retire at ever younger ages. Their study, however, is hampered by lack of a theory of earlier retirement. This is not the fault of the authors, since a generally accepted theory of the decline of older-age labor participation has not been found.

A common measure of retirement trends is labor force participation rates of older men. These data for the years 1950–1984 are shown in Table 9.13. Participation rates over age 65, for example, have declined from 41.5 percent in 1950 to 16.3 percent in 1984.

One explanation for retirement is poor health. At some age, workers become unable to continue efficient work habits and thus withdraw from the labor force. Although this idea undoubtedly plays a role in an economic theory of retirement, it is unlikely to explain the reduction in retirement ages over time. Although measurement of health is difficult, it is unlikely that the health of American workers has been deteriorating over time, forcing progressively earlier withdrawals from the work force. Packard and Reno show that only a small minority of workers even claim this to be a factor in their retirement decisions.

A variant of the deteriorating health hypothesis is that medical advances over the past five decades have affected the mortality rate at older ages but not the morbidity rate. Simply put, more men over age 55 are living but are less likely to be capable of work. However, Baily (1987) shows that this factor cannot explain a significant portion of the reduction in reported participation rates.

Most economists have been suspicious of health arguments, but they

TABLE 9.13

RETIREMENT TRENDS, 1950–1984

(PERCENTAGES)

Year	PARTICIPATION RATE FOR MEN		Social Security rate of return	Pension assets/ total wages	Participation rate for women (all ages)
	Aged 55–64	Aged 65 and over			
1950	83.4	41.5	19.7	13	—
1955	86.4	38.5	16.5	22	34.0
1960	86.8	33.1	14.1	31	36.2
1965	84.6	27.9	11.6	41	38.0
1970	83.0	26.8	9.9	44	42.2
1975	75.6	21.6	8.5	55	45.3
1980	72.1	19.0	—	75	50.6
1984	68.5	16.3	—	79	54.0

SOURCES: *Statistical Abstract*, respective years; Moffitt (1977); Ippolito (1986).

have not ignored the role potentially played by the Social Security system. Substantial attention has been paid to the special tax on work past age 65 and to the lifetime "wealth effect" conferred especially on early retiree cohorts collecting Social Security benefits. The tax on work occurs because of the combination of the "earnings test," which offsets part of Social Security benefits against wage income, and of unfair actuarial adjustments to benefits. This combination of policies acts like a tax on work past age 65, and the magnitude of this tax is not trivial (Burkhauser and Turner 1981).[10]

The wealth effect occurs because retirees—even those retiring currently—earn an implicit rate of return on their Social Security taxes that substantially exceeds the risk-free rate of return. If this transfer is not anticipated, it may represent a net addition to cohort wealth, and workers could take this gain through earlier retirement.

Although these arguments are compelling and have undoubtedly played some—and perhaps an important—role in the reduction in labor force participation rates at older ages, there is growing evidence that the Social Security effects may be less important than commonly believed. For example, the effective Social Security tax for workers past age 65 is constraining for a progressively smaller portion of the retiring population; workers are withdrawing from the work force before reaching age 65.

Packard and Reno find that 62 percent of men received Social Security benefits before age 65. Labor force participation rates for workers aged 55–

64 have fallen from 84.6 percent in 1965 to 68.5 percent in 1984 (Table 9.13). Moreover, prior to 1977, a convincing argument could be made that the Social Security system was discouraging retirement prior to age 62. Owing to unindexed lifetime wages in the benefit formula, continued work up to age 62 resulted in disproportionate increases in benefits (Blinder, Gordon, and Wise 1980). Similar problems surround the wealth effect explanation.

Even if the Social Security wealth effects represented net wealth, the effect is clearly falling over time (Table 9.13), whereas retirement is occurring earlier. Moreover, it is not obvious that Social Security intergenerational transfers result in higher wealth at retirement. The transfers are predictable and can therefore be offset by less private saving (Feldstein 1974) and smaller transfers from children to parents (Barro 1978). For succeeding cohorts, the likelihood that the transfers are not anticipated, and therefore not offset, is remote.

Private pensions also have been implicated in the progression toward earlier retirement. The data in Table 9.13 show the impressive growth of pension assets in relation to national wages over the past 35 years. Unlike Social Security effects, which arguably are waning with time, the importance of private pensions has been growing, coincident with the acceleration toward earlier retirement. In addition, the rules in many pension plans appear to discourage late retirement (for example, Fields and Mitchell 1984; Gustman and Steinmeier 1986).

Even if pensions represent additional savings for retirement, this does not separate cause and effect. More pensions and more net savings may merely reflect a demand by workers for earlier retirement. This problem, for example, plagues the Packard-Reno finding that earlier retirees have larger pensions.

Moreover, when viewed over a lengthy time span, it is unclear that pensions represent anything more than replacement of private savings. Prior to World War II, pensions were not important forms of savings; neither were they a relatively efficient savings vehicle. Following a structural change in the income tax system during the early 1940s, pensions became a relatively efficient way to save because of their exemption from the so-called double tax on interest earnings and their income-smoothing properties. Viewed in this way, pensions may have merely replaced private accounts because they were more efficient savings vehicles for retirement.

The same tax change also made it efficient to use pension rules to reduce mobility in the firm and to regulate retirement ages. It is not clear that the existence of pension rules suggests a net lowering of retirement age, however, because alternative mechanisms otherwise could be used. For example, firms may have paid lower cash wages during early years with the firm and higher wages later, and/or they may have used mandatory retirement provisions.

Much research has been done to explain increasingly earlier retirement. Some useful results have come from this research, though we are a long way from having a general theory. I doubt that an important part of the solution lies in the ideas explored to date. Although existing time series studies of these issues have been viewed with skepticism, it is not clear that cross-section studies such as Packard and Reno's will provide the answers.

Most of the independent variables (such as income, pensions, and Social Security) used by Packard and Reno are endogenous to the retirement decision. At a minimum, we need to concentrate more on variations in such areas as type of job, industry, and work history of spouse. The authors could have made headway on this issue by comparing data in 1970 (the year of the first Newly Entitled Beneficiaries Survey) with data in 1983. It is disappointing that this was not done.

In principle, the hypothesis that pensions affect retirement age (either directly or through net saving effects) is testable. In practice, it is difficult because of selection issues and incomplete information in cross-section data and correlation problems with other variables in time series data. Nevertheless, it would have been interesting if Packard and Reno had compared the distribution of retirement ages among workers with and without pensions in 1970 and 1983. I cannot help but wonder if the temporal shifts in these distributions were similar.

If Social Security and pensions are inadequate explanations of the drift toward earlier retirement, what theories can we appeal to? One possibility is that the drift merely reflects an overall wealth effect in favor of more leisure, albeit in a new form. Until 1940 or so, hours of work decreased steadily, presumably reflecting preferences for more leisure by progressively wealthier cohorts. After 1940, hours of work have been virtually frozen; the progression toward more leisure has been reflected almost entirely in leisure at the end of the worklife (Burkhauser and Turner 1978). Although workers may prefer to spread more leisure over their entire life, productivity may be higher if workers have shorter, more intensive worklives. In short, we may have simply reached the point where it is efficient to take more leisure at the end of—rather than during—the worklife.

A similar outcome might be generated from a theory of production. For example, suppose that over time it becomes efficient to use production functions that use more specialized labor input. Because of higher disutility in these jobs, workers may want to take a significant part of the productivity gains in the form of more leisure. If efficient use of physical and human capital precludes working shorter workweeks, more leisure is taken in the form of shorter worklives. As another example, consider jobs that involve human capital. Since this capital presumably depreciates with innovation, it is inefficient for older workers to continue reinvesting in this capital because of progressively shorter "payback" periods. It is optimal for individuals to work more intensely early in their lives and to retire earlier. If jobs have larger human capital components over time, more workers will be observed retiring at relatively early ages.

Another possibility lies in the rapid increase in female participation in market work (Table 9.13). Because more women work, family income has expanded at a higher rate than overall productivity advances would suggest. Part of the higher family wealth accumulation may be reflected in earlier retirement by male spouses. In some sense, there is a lifetime reallocation of family leisure from earlier to later in the life cycle. If this is an important explanation for earlier retirement, the drift toward ever earlier retirement ages will not find equilibrium soon.

The mass withdrawal of older workers from the market economy over the past 40 years represents one of the most striking features of the U.S. labor market. Yet we do not have an adequate explanation of this phenomenon. This creates the potential for important and exciting work still to be done in this area of research, work that could have important implications for public policy toward retirement.

Notes

1. For further information on the NBS design, see U.S. Department of Health and Human Services (USDHHS; 1986).

2. Under the earnings test in 1987, $1 in benefits is withheld for every $2 in earnings above $6,000 for persons under age 65 or above $8,160 for those aged 65–69. At age 70 the earnings test no longer applies.

3. For more information on beneficiaries who work, see Iams (1986).

4. Pensions in this paper include government pensions, military pensions, private employer or union pensions, and railroad retirement benefits. These pensions are those received at the time of interview and are not necessarily pensions from the last job before retirement.

5. Some pension plans reduce benefits at age 65. Because more than half the NBS retired-worker beneficiaries were under age 65 when they were interviewed, it is probable that more than 5 percent will ultimately experience a benefit reduction.

6. Social Security and public transfer income may also include income from those programs received by the beneficiary's children, if there are children whose benefits are included in the beneficiary's check.

7. Imputation methodologies used on the NBS data are described in USDHHS (1986, chap. 10).

8. The estimate that 25 percent of new retired-worker beneficiaries left their last job because of health reasons applies only to the population of workers who received Social Security retired-worker benefits before receiving any other type of Social Security benefit. This population does not include those who first received disability insurance benefits or suvivor benefits. Neither does it include those who left their last job and died before receiving benefits or those who retired but did not apply for benefits. The percentage of all workers who retired primarily for health reasons might be higher than 25 percent if these other groups were included in the NBS population.

9. Marital status on the NBS was measured at the time of interview. It does not necessarily reflect the marital status at the time of retirement.

10. In principle, the earnings test is also applied during the ages 62–64. But the tax can be evaded simply by postponing receipt of Social Security benefits until age 65. Benefits are actuarially adjusted during ages 62–64; hence, there is no penalty to postponing receipt. If receipt is postponed after age 65, the earnings test is evaded but the worker absorbs a reduction in Social Security owing to unfair actuarial adjustments past age 65.

REFERENCES

Baily, Martin N. 1987. "Aging and the Ability to Work: Policy Issues and Recent Trends." In Gary Burtless, ed., *Work, Health, and Income Among the Elderly.* Washington, D.C.: Brookings Institution.

Barro, Robert. 1978. *The Impact of Social Security on Private Saving.* Washington, D.C.: American Enterprise Institute.

Blinder, Alan, Roger Gordon, and Donald Wise. 1980. "Reconsidering the Work Disincentives of Social Security." *National Tax Journal* 33:431–42.

Burkhauser, Richard, and John Turner. 1978. "A Time Series Analysis of Social Security and Its Effect on the Market Work of Men at Younger Ages." *Journal of Political Economy* 86:701–15.

————. 1981. "Can 25 Million Americans Be Wrong? A Response to Blinder, Gordon, and Wise." *National Tax Journal* 34:467–72.

Feldstein, Martin. 1974. "Social Security, Induced Retirement and Aggregate Capital Accumulation." *Journal of Political Economy* 82:905–26.

Fields, Gary, and Olivia Mitchell. 1984. *Retirement, Pensions and Social Security.* Cambridge, Mass.: MIT Press.

Gustman, Alan, and Thomas Steinmeier. 1986. "A Structural Model of Retirement." *Econometrica* 54:555–84.

Iams, Howard. 1986. "Transition to Retirement Jobs." Paper delivered at the annual meeting of the Gerontology Society of America, Chicago, Ill., November 22.

Ippolito, Richard A. 1986. *Pensions, Economics and Public Policy.* Homewood, Ill.: Dow Jones-Irwin.

Moffitt, Robert. 1977. "Trends in Social Security Wealth by Cohort." In Marilyn Moon, ed., *Economic Transfers in the United States.* Chicago: University of Chicago Press.

Reno, Virginia. 1976. "Why Men Stop Working Before Age 65." In U.S. Department of Health and Human Services, Social Security Administration, *Reaching Retirement Age.* Research Report no. 47. Washington, D.C.: GPO.

Reno, Virginia, and Daniel N. Price. 1985. "Relationship Between the Retirement, Disability and Unemployment Programs: The U.S. Experience." *Social Security Bulletin* 48:24–37.

Rones, Philip. 1985. "Using the CPS to Track Retirement Among Older Men." *Monthly Labor Review* 108:46–49.

Sherman, Sally R. 1985. "Reported Reasons Retired Workers Left Their Last Job: Findings from the New Beneficiary Survey." *Social Security Bulletin* 48:22–30.

U.S. Department of Health and Human Services, Social Security Administration, Office of Policy. 1986. *The 1982 New Beneficiary Survey: Users' Manual.* Washington, D.C.

————, Social Security Administration. 1988. *Social Security Bulletin Annual Statistical Supplement, 1987.* Washington, D.C.

U.S. General Accounting Office. 1986. *Retirement Before Age 65: Trends, Costs, and National Issues.* GAO/HRD-86-86. Washington, D.C.

10

THE RETIREMENT DECISION IN CROSS-NATIONAL PERSPECTIVE

Alex Inkeles and Chikako Usui

Retirement is one of the most pivotal events in a person's life. The decision to retire may be shaped by personal considerations, such as a preference for leisure, or by health or economic reasons. It may also be accounted for by mandatory legislation or any combination of these and other factors. Whatever the reasons, retirement usually brings about significant changes in lifestyle and standard of living. It also produces other subtle influences on the daily life of retirees, their spouses, the rest of their family members, and their friends. Aside from these personal aspects of retirement, rapid population aging, the growing number of retirees in the population, and the costs of maintaining them have significant impacts on the structure of the economy and on society as a whole.

Our approach is governed by two sets of assumptions. First, retirement is best conceptualized as a personal decision, in which objective and subjective forces are differently weighed and perceived by individual social actors. The implication is that retirement rates cannot be understood and predicted without taking into account cultural orientations, individual values, and personal preferences.

Since such orientations and preferences generally vary systematically in different world regions, and sometimes from country to country in the same cultural area, we are led to our second assumption—namely, that retirement can be most fully understood when viewed in a cross-national perspective. The reason for adopting such a perspective is perhaps obvious if one understands the main objective of social science to be the formulation of propositions having the greatest degree of generality. However, such a perspective also has relevance for those with more practical interests in setting public policy. Social experiments to test policy alternatives are costly and, in any event, require years to complete and assess. Variations in policy from nation to nation, therefore, provide a substitute for such experiments at low cost and with a quick response. Thus, cross-national comparisons permit us to judge numerous policy-relevant issues on the basis of experience in a larger number of nations. They can, for example, help us judge whether raising the legal age of retirement has any significant effect on the age at which people actually begin retirement.

With these considerations in mind, we present here a comparative analysis of social insurance systems and retirement patterns by potential and actual retirees in several sets of nations. Our paper is organized into two sections. The first part defines retirement and examines global trends in the development of the governmentally organized and funded benefit systems—better known in the United States as Social Security—in approximately 30 relatively advanced industrial countries. In this analysis we focus on the usual age at which individuals become entitled to receive benefits, special conditions that must be met to qualify for old-age benefits, provisions for early retirement, and the ratio by which old-age benefits replace wages.

In the second part of the paper we examine cross-national differences in actual retirement patterns. Although public programs targeted on the aged population now exist in all the industrial countries, there is not enough known about how retirement policies and practices impinge on actual retirement behavior in various systems. We will attempt, therefore, to explain cross-national variations in the rates of retirement by examining social insurance, public and private pension systems, and societal norms about retirement and old age in four leading industrial countries (the United States, the United Kingdom, France, and Japan).

In the first section of our paper we focus on benefits, following the criteria set by the U.S. Social Security Administration—that is, on payments from compulsory, national social insurance programs sponsored by a government. This focus is not by preference, but is a response to the availability of data. This criterion excludes corporate or private pensions that are established voluntarily, and it also excludes public employee pension systems such as civil service retirement and firemen and teachers' pensions. In the second section, however, we examine the actual patterns of retirement in relation to the availability of both old-age benefits and private pensions. As we shall see, in some countries such private pensions are received by as much as 50 percent of the elderly.

Throughout the paper, we restrict ourselves solely to the situation of men; we plan to give parallel treatment to the situation of women in a separate publication.

GLOBAL TRENDS IN THE DEVELOPMENT OF SOCIAL INSURANCE SYSTEMS

What Is Retirement?

Although there is no generally agreed upon definition of retirement, analysts of the issue usually describe it as a formal social role involving more or less permanent cessation of employment, close to some formal age limit, and accompanied by the receipt of income from a government old-age benefit and/or corporate and/or private retirement pension. In many individual cases and communities, however, retirement takes place prior to the formal entitlement age. Some people who have withdrawn from the labor force because of age may be without either a public old-age benefit or any form of pension. Moreover, in some social insurance systems, workers may continue to work even *after* reaching the entitlement age while receiving old-age benefits. Other systems require substantial or complete withdrawal from work on the part of those who claim benefits. Indeed, this is one of several areas of considerable change.

The topics we consider first—the usual age at which a person becomes entitled to old-age benefits, provisions for early retirement, and the replacement ratio of benefits to earnings—readily assert their claim to serious attention. It seems reasonable to assume that the official age set for receipt of old-age benefits should be more or less definitive in determining the age at which people actually retire. The readiness to retire, as against staying in the labor force past the entitlement age, should logically be influenced by the degree to which benefits can replace lost earnings. Any restrictions on additional earnings by retirees would be an obvious influence on their behavior. It is clearly tempting to sociologists to examine cross-national differences in the governmentally determined entitlement age and to explore whether that age reflects the special demographic, economic, and political conditions of individual nations.

Usual Entitlement Age

In 1889 Germany introduced a state old-age benefit program, fixing the retirement age at 70 (see Table 10.1). In 1911 this was changed to age 65. New Zealand was next in adopting a similar law before the turn of the

TABLE 10.1 _____

CHANGES OVER TIME IN THE ENTITLEMENT AGE
FOR OLD-AGE BENEFITS FOR MEN

Country	Original age*	1983 age
Germany (West)	70 (1889)	65
Germany (East)		65
New Zealand	65 (1898)	60
Austria	65 (1906)	65
Czechoslovakia	65 (1906)	60
Australia	65 (1908)	65
Ireland	70 (1908)	66
United Kingdom	70 (1908)	65
Iceland	67 (1909)	67
France	65 (1910)	60
Luxembourg	68 (1911)	65
Romania	65 (1912)	60
Netherlands	70 (1913)	65
Sweden	67 (1913)	65
Italy	65 (1919)	60
Spain	65 (1919)	65
Denmark	65 (1922)	67
Soviet Union	60 (1922)	60
Yugoslavia	70 (1922)	60
Belgium	65 (1924)	60
Bulgaria	60 (1924)	60
Poland	65 (1927)	65
Hungary	65 (1928)	60
Portugal	65 (1933)	65
Greece	65 (1934)	65
United States	65 (1935)	65
Norway	70 (1936)	67
Finland	65 (1937)	65
Japan	60 (1941)	60
Switzerland	65 (1946)	65
Canada	70 (1951)	65
mean (X)	65.9	63.5
S.D.	2.89	2.67
C.V.(%)	4.39	4.20
N	30	31

SOURCES: Pilcher, Ramirez, and Swihart (1968); U.S. Department of Health and Human Services (USDHHS) (1984).

*Refers to a normal entitlement age set by the first legislation in a given country.

century (1898), setting its entitlement age at 65. Gradually, other countries followed suit, although often covering only limited occupational groups and extending the coverage to others with the passage of time. In general, government social insurance systems were adopted earlier in more advanced countries as compared to the less developed. Curiously, however, within the set of advanced countries the level of development alone does little to explain the dates of adoption. The United States, for example, was a relative latecomer among industrial countries in adopting a social insurance system.

There has been a trend among nations to lower the age at which entitlement begins. Data in Table 10.1 show the age for each country as set in the original legislation compared to the current law (as of 1983) for 31 countries. The range of the male entitlement age set in the first laws was from 60 to 70 years, with a mean of 66 and a standard deviation of 2.89. In 1983, however, the male entitlement age varied from 60 to 67 years, and the mean and the standard deviation had decreased to 63.5 and 2.67, respectively. Moreover, the coefficient of variation, which summarizes the relative degree of dispersion among data points, was 4.39 percent for the original legislation and 4.2 percent in 1983. Thus, the 31 countries were neither clearly convergent nor divergent in their entitlement age over time. However, most of these countries moved from a higher to a lower formal entitlement age, at least up to the decade of the 1980s.

These same changes in the normal entitlement age (NEA) for men for the period 1950–1983 are presented in summarized form in Table 10.2. In this form the data more clearly show a decline. In 1950 age 65 was the most popular in 21 of the 30 countries (70 percent). Only one-tenth of the nations awarded any old-age benefit at age 60. By 1983, however, well over one-third (36 percent) of the countries set their entitlement age at 60 and another half (52 percent) at age 65. By 1983 no country required waiting until age 70 for a social insurance benefit. Only 13 percent of the countries retained age 66 or 67.

Although these changes are sufficient to be worthy of attention, they should not distract us from awareness of the relative stability of the entitlement age set by law. Over a span of 30 years, 13 of the 31 countries in Table 10.1 saw no change at all. Austria has made no change in the original age of 65 over an 80-year period. The United States went for almost 50 years without making a change. We assume that this is due to a combination of forces. First, the age selected represents a cultural norm that does not change readily. Second, expectations and complex programs, both for individuals and organizations, are built on the basis of the age set by law. Consequently, a change in that law becomes too destabilizing because of how it interacts with many other activities, and it will not be undertaken lightly. And third, the set age always reflects a political compromise painstakingly worked out

TABLE 10.2

CHANGES IN THE NORMAL ENTITLEMENT AGE
FOR MEN, 1950 AND 1983

	NUMBER OF COUNTRIES	
NEA	1950	1983
60	3 (10.0%)	11 (35.5%)
65	21 (70.0%)	16 (51.6%)
66	0	1 (3.2%)
67	3 (10.0%)	3 (9.7%)
70	3 (10.0%)	0
N	30* (100%)	31 (100%)
X	65.4	63.5

SOURCE: See Table 10.1.

*Nations having introduced changes in their original entitlement age before 1950 are: Germany (age 65, 1911); Luxembourg (age 65, 1925); the Netherlands (age 65, 1919); and Denmark (age 67, 1933). Canada did not introduce an old-age insurance program until after 1950. Thus, the number of countries for 1950 was 30.

to adjust to many competing interests. Once such a compromise is reached, therefore, the costs of changing the norm will always seem to be high in terms of the struggle required to find once again an acceptable balance between the relevant interests.

Nevertheless, pressures for change may become inexorable. The ever-rising costs due to a much larger elderly proportion of the population have forced countries to reverse the long-term trend of the postwar era and actually raise the age of retirement. For example, with the 1983 amendments to the Social Security law, the original entitlement age of 65 in the United States will be gradually increased to age 66 by the year 2009 and to 67 by 2027. Similarly, in 1986 Japan gradually began to raise its entitlement age for women under the Employee's Pension System from 55 to age 60 by 2005 (Ricketts 1986, 9). We may well expect other countries to follow suit.

*Qualifying Conditions for the Receipt
of Full Government Benefit*

There is considerable variation among countries in the conditions set to qualify for a full or maximum old-age benefit (see Table 10.3). We base this analysis on the evidence for the eighteen advanced nations, of the original total of thirty-one, for which detailed information is available. Sixty-five is the most commonly chosen age at which men become entitled. In many countries (eleven, or 61 percent of the eighteen countries), older individuals are permitted to receive benefits *and* continue to work. In seven (or 39 percent), however, workers must stop work in order to claim full benefits.

There are, of course, many variations on this theme. For example, in the United States a person may work while receiving old-age benefits, but earnings (if over a set amount) are offset by reductions in the benefit received. On the other hand, although the United States is generally listed as requiring

TABLE 10.3 _____

QUALIFYING CONDITIONS FOR THE RECEIPT
OF FULL (MAXIMUM) OLD-AGE BENEFITS

| | | | OTHER REQUIREMENTS | |
Country	NEA (for men)	Withdrawal from labor force	Years of contribution	Years of residency
Australia	65	Required		10[a]
Austria	65	Required	15	
Belgium	65	Required	45 (men)	
Canada	65	Not required	None[b]	10[a]
Denmark	67	Not required	3[b]	10–40[a]
France	60	Not required	37.5	
West Germany	65	Not required	15[e]	
Greece	65	Not required	11	
Ireland	66	Not required	3	
Italy	60	Required	15	
Japan	65	Required	25	
Luxembourg	65	Not required	5	
Netherlands	65	Not required	50	
New Zealand	60	Not required		10[a]
Sweden	65	Not required	3[b]	Residency[a]
Switzerland	65	Not required	Since 1948	
United Kingdom	65	Required	10	
United States[d]	65	Required	10 (40 qtrs)[c]	

SOURCE: USDHHS (1984).

a. Universal old-age benefit.

b. Employment-related old-age benefit; nonemployment-related benefit requires up to 40 years.

c. Applies to those born in 1926 or later.

d. Ages 65–69 may earn up to $8,160 (1987) annually without any reduction in benefit. After age 69 there is no penalty.

e. Alternatively, workers may retire at age 63 who have 35 years of contribution to insurance/taxes.

withdrawal from the labor force, the restrictions on earnings do not apply after age 70. Thus, the details of a system should be analyzed before reaching conclusions about any presumed proportion of nations that absolutely bar employment after a person has started to receive old-age benefits.

Turning next to the issue of how long a person must have contributed to the system before becoming eligible, we find in Table 10.3 that there are marked cross-national differences in the required years worked or years of residency for the receipt of full benefit. Only three years in the labor force is sufficient for a worker to qualify for the employment-related old-age benefits in Denmark, Ireland, and Sweden. In contrast, producing an almost bimodal distribution, more than 40 years of contribution is necessary in Belgium and the Netherlands, and almost as much in France. The United States, with a 10-year or 40-quarter requirement, falls near the middle of the range.

Provisions for Early Entitlement

Until the 1960s, full old-age benefits were generally awarded only to older individuals who had reached the age of 65 or beyond and who had 15–30 years of insurance contributions or taxes behind them. The main exception to these general rules was that those engaged in "arduous" work could, in some countries, retire up to five years earlier. During the 1970s, however, many systems began to introduce more general provisions for "early retirement" (as compared with "normal retirement") with little or no reduction in the amount of the benefit. By 1975, seven West European countries (Austria, Denmark, Finland, France, West Germany, Italy, and Luxembourg) had introduced "flexible" entitlement options for reasons of long service (usually 35 years or longer), poor health resulting in partial disability, or involuntary unemployment (Zeitzer 1983, 53). Of these only four provided full benefits at early retirement (ibid.). By 1983, however, nine out of seventeen countries had adopted policies permitting workers to take early retirement on full benefits (see Table 10.4). Information about Switzerland was not available. It seems worth noting that of the five countries *without* any early retirement provisions, three were former frontier offshoots of the British empire—namely, Australia, Canada, and New Zealand. The United States, although it had its own special set of rules, went along with the overwhelming majority of comparable countries in permitting a flexible approach to early retirement.

Old-Age Benefits as Replacements for Earnings

The literature on the replacement ratio of old-age benefits to earnings indicates that for many years the ideal replacement rate for the average man working in manufacturing was considered to be at least 40–50 percent of former earnings (Horlick 1970, 9; Haanes-Olsen 1978, 4). In 1952 the International Labor Conference urged that the old-age benefit for a couple should be at least 45 percent of the previous earnings of the worker (Convention no. 128). Current expectations, however, are closer to 60–65 percent. There is a trend to set a higher goal. For example, in 1968 the government of Belgium expressed its desire to attain an eventual replacement of 75 percent of lifetime earnings, and the 1968 Italian legislature set a goal of 80 percent to be attained by 1980. In 1967 the U.S. Committee on Ways and Means of the House of Representatives recommended 50 percent for a couple, but some in the United States propose 50 percent for a single worker and 66–70 percent for a couple (Horlick 1970, 9–12). These goals, though not always attained, have been approximated as actual replacement rates have grown steadily over time.

In many of the nations studied here, the replacement rate is 30–50 percent higher for a couple than for a single beneficiary. As can be seen from Table 10.5, in 1980 elderly couples in Canada, the Netherlands, the United Kingdom, the United States, and Switzerland received an additional 40–50 percent over what a single worker earned. In Sweden the benefit for a couple was 20 percent more than that for a single person, whereas the difference reached only 10 percent in France and Japan. Yet in countries such as Austria, West Germany, and Italy there are no such additional benefits for a dependent spouse. In some of these countries, however, the replacement ratio is set at a fairly high level. The mean replacement ratio among the nine countries with differential treatment of couples versus single workers was 61 percent in 1980. Among the three countries without special treatment for a dependent spouse, two are above and one below (at 49 percent) that level.

Returning to the issue of change over time, we find that there has been steady upward movement among the advanced nations in the wage-replacement ratio represented by old-age benefits. The average replacement level among thirteen industrially advanced nations, as shown in Table 10.5, went up from 37.6 percent of the earnings in manufacturing in 1965 to 49.4 percent in 1980 for a single worker, and from 49.2 percent in 1965 to 61.4 percent in 1980 for a couple. If we take the 50 percent level as an ideal level of replacement for a single worker and 60 percent for a couple, as was recommended by U.S. planners in 1970, then about half of the nations had achieved that goal by 1980. This can be seen more clearly in Table 10.6, in which the countries in Table 10.5 are rearranged according to the level of replacement in 1980, from highest to lowest. By 1980, seven out of the twelve nations had attained a 60 percent replacement level for a couple and five had attained the ideal 50 percent level for a single retiree. The benefit awarded to a single worker in the United States, at 44 percent, was slightly

TABLE 10.4
EARLY RETIREMENT OPTIONS

Country	NEA	Options[a]	
Australia	65	—	No early retirement provisions
Austria	65	1	Age 60 with 35 yrs of contribution or with a year of sickness or unemployment
Belgium	65	2	Reduced benefit (5% each year of early retirement) up to 5 yrs before normal age
		1	Age 64 with 45 yrs contribution
		1	Age 64 if worked in arduous jobs for 5 of the last 15 yrs
		3	Age 60 on condition if replaced by an unemployed worker under age 30
Canada	65	—	No early retirement provisions
Denmark	67	1	Age 55 with "adverse social- and employment-related reasons"
		3	Age 60 if the worker belongs to unemployment fund for 5 yrs during last 10 yrs
France	60	—	No early retirement provisions
West Germany	65	1	Age 63 with 35 yrs contribution
		1	Age 60 for a person unemployed for at least 1 yr in last 1.5 yrs
		1	Age 60 if disabled and with 35 yrs contribution
Greece	65	1	Age 62 depending on yrs of contribution
		1	Age 60 for workers in unhealthy occupations
		2	Reduced pension at age 60; 55 with 11 yrs contribution
Ireland	66	1	Age 65 with withdrawal from the labor force
Italy	60	1	Any age with 35 yrs contribution and withdrawal from labor force
		3	Pre-retirement benefit available at 55 for those unemployed due to economic crisis or industrial reorganization

Country			
Japan	65	2	Reduced benefit at age 60 with 20 yrs contribution and withdrawal from labor force
Luxembourg	65	1	Age 60 for manual workers with varying yrs contribution (maximum 40 yrs) and withdrawal from labor force
		1	Age 60 for nonmanual workers with 15 yrs contribution and withdrawal from labor force
Netherlands	65	—	No early retirement provisions
New Zealand	65	—	No early retirement provisions
Sweden	65	1	Up to 5 yrs before normal age if unemployed or disabled
		2	Reduced pension (.5% per month)
United Kingdom[b]	65	3	Job release schemes available at age 62 if replaced by young unemployed persons
		—	No early retirement provisions but numbers of yrs needed for full benefit reduced if caring for a child or elderly or disabled relative
United States	65	2	Age 62–64 on reduced benefit

SOURCE: USDHHS (1984).

a. The numbers refer to three types of early retirement provisions:
1—Early retirement on full benefit;
2—Early retirement on reduced benefit;
3—Early retirement on special benefits—that is, some schemes provide the payment of special interim benefits until old-age benefit becomes payable at the normal age.

b. Data derives from Industrial Relations Services (1979).

TABLE 10.5

REPLACEMENT OF AVERAGE WAGE IN MANUFACTURING BY OLD-AGE
BENEFITS FOR SINGLE WORKERS AND FOR COUPLES, 1965–1980
(PERCENTAGES)

	SINGLE WORKER				COUPLE			
Country	1965	1969	1975	1980	1965	1969	1975	1980
Austria	67	67	63	68	67	67	63	68
Canada	21	24	33	34	42	41	47	49
Denmark	35	31	29	29	51	45	44	52
France	49	41	60	66	65	56	74	75
West Germany	48	55	51	49	48	55	51	49
Italy	60	62	61	69	60	62	61	69
Japan	n.a.	26	37	54	n.a.	27	39	61
Netherlands	35	43	43	44	50	61	61	63
Norway	25	34	41	n.a.	38	49	55	n.a.
Sweden	31	42	57	68	44	56	73	83
Switzerland	28	28	40	37	45	45	60	55
United Kingdom	23	27	31	31	36	43	47	47
United States	29	30	38	44	44	44	45	66
Mean	37.6	39.2	44.9	49.4	49.2	50.1	56.4	61.4
Median	35.0	34.0	41.0	46.5	46.5	49.0	55.0	62.0
S.D.	15.0	14.2	12.0	15.0	10.1	10.8	10.6	11.4
C.V.(%)	39.9	36.2	26.7	30.4	20.5	21.6	18.8	18.6

SOURCES: Figures for 1965 were obtained from Haanes-Olsen (1978, 3–14); figures for 1969,
1975, and 1980 derive from Aldrich (1982, 3–11).

lower than the average, but the replacement rate for a couple, at 66 percent,
was higher.

Policymaking Options

Faced with the great burden of supporting an ever larger proportion of
the population who are elderly, policymakers will be tempted to increase the
age for entitlement. In addition, they may be motivated to increase, stabilize,
or even reduce the proportion of wages replaced by the pensions. These
changes can be made only at great political cost. Such costs can be justified
only if there is good evidence that manipulating these variables will substantially influence the decision of individuals as to whether to retire and when.

We do not believe that the legal norms governing old-age benefits are
without consequence. Yet, we think that the importance of these norms may

be exaggerated in the minds of some policymakers and of the economists who may advise them. In our view, cultural assumptions and individually held values also play important roles in shaping individuals' retirement decisions. Such factors interact with arbitrary, politically set rules and the economic facts of life. Indeed, they may operate independently of, and at times in seeming defiance of, the factors policymakers try to manipulate. This becomes especially apparent when one looks more closely at the *actual* age at which many people retire and at the proportion of individuals who continue to work past the entitlement age. Some facts about these patterns and the challenges they present are considered in the next part of our paper.

ACTUAL PATTERNS OF RETIREMENT

The act of retiring involves a personal decision, but like all such decisions it is inevitably made in a given socioeconomic environment and in a specific cultural milieu. Millions of such decisions are cumulated in the familiar population rates, such as the proportion of those over 60 who are classified as retired. If those rates show considerable similarity across national populations, there must have been common forces to produce that outcome. And if

TABLE 10.6

REPLACEMENT OF AVERAGE WAGE IN MANUFACTURING BY OLD-AGE BENEFITS FOR SINGLE WORKERS AND FOR COUPLES, 1980 (PERCENTAGES)

SINGLE WORKER		COUPLE	
Italy	69	Sweden	83
Austria	68	France	75
Sweden	68	Italy	69
France	66	Austria	68
Japan	54	United States	66
West Germany	49	Netherlands	63
Netherlands	44	Japan	61
United States	44	Switzerland	55
Switzerland	37	Denmark	52
Canada	34	Canada	49
United Kingdom	31	West Germany	49
Denmark	29	United Kingdom	47

SOURCE: See Table 10.5.

they vary considerably from country to country—as they do—we are challenged to explain that variation by reference to differences in the characteristics of nations and in the differential interaction of those attributes. Some of these qualities may be subject to influence and control, whereas others would be much more intractable, and this has obvious implications for policy. For example, if Americans put an exceptionally high value on leisure but the Japanese did not, there would not be much that their respective governments could do to change that situation. On the other hand, if we were to find that across a substantial set of countries each percent increase in the rate at which pensions replaced wages moved the average age of those taking early retirement down by three months, we would have uncovered something about which policymakers could take sensible action.

Being retired has a special status, but it is not one equally recognized everywhere. Indeed, it is a relatively young idea in modern parlance and in many places is not used as spontaneously and securely as in the United States. For example, in Japan people are much more likely to focus on being old aged rather than retired, and the latter concept has only come into widespread use in recent decades. Imprecision in the use of the term is not limited to cross-national communication. A person may be retired from a particular firm and job, but still be in the labor force. An individual over age 65 may or may not have a pension and may be out of a job but still looking for work. In other words, a person might be both pensioned and technically unemployed at the same time.

We think that it would be helpful to agree on a definition of retirees as individuals who have permanently withdrawn from the labor force for considerations of age.[1] We would thus exclude the elderly who are working and those who are actively seeking employment, even if they are receiving Social Security or private pensions. The sources of support for the retirees would also be a separate dimension, with the most important distinctions being those among social insurance (government-paid) benefits, private or corporate pensions, self-support, and support by relatives. Unfortunately, many of these distinctions are not regularly made, which complicates cross-national analysis just as it does research on a single country, although with even more disconcerting effects. At present, all we can do is try to stay as alert as possible to the potential for being misled by differences in the conventions about how retirement is defined and measured in different countries, and in different studies within the same country.

To understand the decision to retire, including its antecedents and consequences, we need at least four kinds of information about the forces that are likely to impinge on the individuals concerned. The first, in its collective manifestation, is demographic. All industrial societies have more aged people than do the less industrial or preindustrial, and for many decades the proportion of their population in the older age ranges has been steadily increasing. Older people suffer from limitations of health that may induce them to leave the labor force, and if they do not do so voluntarily, employers will nevertheless be less likely to hire or retain them for that reason. In addition, there has been a long-term trend for each generation to acquire more schooling than those that came before, and this too puts the older individuals, on average, at a disadvantage in labor markets in which the increasing technological level and the rising intrinsic complexity of work are interpreted, whether correctly or not, as undercutting the utility of less well educated labor.[2] Data on the age composition of national populations is plentiful, and moderately detailed information about the employment of the elderly in those populations has been collected over a span of some decades.

Second, on the side of political economy, we need details about legal regulations such as those setting retirement ages, defining rights to work while receiving a public or private pension, and determining the levels at which pensions replace earnings. This kind of information is available over a considerable span of time for some industrial nations. In the following sections, we give a large part of our attention to the presentation and analysis of that data. At the outset, we can state that those who assume almost everything of interest can be explained by the politicoeconomic factors are seriously misled. For example, we will see later that in most countries the formal age for retirement set by law is not a good indicator of the actual age at which people apply for that status and claim their benefits.[3]

The third type of information needed may be defined as cultural. We have in mind such matters as the formality and legitimacy—or what sociologists would call the degree of institutionalization—of the status of a retired person. Other cultural factors include: popular images of what it means to be old; the general values surrounding work and leisure; shared conceptions about what constitutes a good life; the closeness of familial ties and the dependence on them; and the availability of social services for the elderly. Unfortunately, only limited information for a motley array of countries is available on these topics, and little of that information provides coverage over time.

Even less cross-national data of a systematic nature is available on the fourth kind of information needed—namely, that of the individual. Whatever the law says about the appropriate age for retirement, individuals who are panicked by the thought that they may have to amuse or otherwise occupy themselves all day without a job to go to will fight hard to stay employed. Similarly, those with strong, unfulfilled aspirations for hobbies and other leisure-time activities will be more likely to search out ways to take early retirement, other things being reasonably equal. Insofar as we had such information, we could enter it into a more complex model of analysis in which we could observe the interaction of these individual-level variables with the politicoeconomic and the sociocultural forces that define the context of individual decisionmaking. In the few instances in which the literature reports this kind of individual orientation (for example, Shanas et al. 1968), it rarely shows the interactions we would like to see. Lacking the appropriate data, we have blended the reports of individual orientation with the materials we treat as cultural expectations, assumptions, standards, or norms.

These four sets of forces combine their influence in complex ways, so that by age 60 two-thirds or more of the men in most industrial countries have left the labor force. Moreover, the proportions withdrawing have increased at a seemingly inexorable rate in recent decades. These trends have been so massive and unmistakable that there can be no further debate about them as such. However, considerable energy has been concentrated in an effort to sort out the relative contributions that different forces have made to the observed rates of withdrawal from the labor force in different countries. In the more comprehensive of these researches (for example, Pampel and Weiss 1983), the authors have simultaneously considered two of the sets of explanatory variables identified above, that is, the demographic and the politicoeconomic variables. Unfortunately, few of the standard studies that loom large in the literature have simultaneously taken into account the cultural and sociopsychological factors we have identified as making up the third and fourth sets.[4] Since we consider this a serious gap, we made a concerted effort to locate sources that would permit us to assess the contribution of sociocultural and individual value factors in the context of information about the other two commonly analyzed sets of variables.

Data: The Role of Objective Forces

In our search for appropriate data sources to measure cultural factors, we found only one study that could meet our requirements. We recognize that this is a narrow base on which to rest our case, and we do not feel that it permits any kind of general proof. It can serve, however, to illustrate the line of reasoning we would hope to follow should data become available on a larger scale and with a fuller sample of industrial countries. As we hope we can demonstrate, even with this limited sample, a fairly convincing case can be made for the importance of cultural forces in shaping the standing of nations on measures of employment among the elderly.

The study in question was sponsored by the Prime Minister's Office of Japan in 1981, and it reached a national sample of people aged 60 and over in four important industrial countries: Japan, the United States, the United Kingdom, and France. The respondents were asked about their retirement

and employment status, their images of and feelings about aging, their interests and uses of time, and a number of other issues. The study describes both
cultural standards and individual values. The data, reported at the country
level, permit us to examine the relationship between some facts about retirement and employment among the elderly, on the one hand, and the cultural
and personal values and standards of the same sets of individuals, on the
other.[5] To avoid uncertainty as to the overall causal factors in the different
ocupational situation of men and women, we have decided to focus on the
men, leaving the analysis of the data on women to a later presentation.

In these four highly industrialized and technically advanced countries,
there were marked differences in the proportions of men over age 60 who
reported themselves as still having a paid job. Japan came first with 57
percent, and the United States was also on the high side with 32.6 percent, as
compared to only 13.2 and 7.8 percent in the United Kingdom and France,
respectively (Table 10.7).[6]

This is certainly a wide range of variation. We find that a simple explanation of this variation in terms of obvious demographic, economic, and
legal facts—such as life expectancy, the proportion of the elderly in the
population, per capita income, the occupational composition of the population, the entitlement age set by law, and the proportion of earnings replaced
by government benefits—prove inadequate to account for the pattern. By
contrast, differences in cultural and personal values held by these national
populations seem to go quite far in explaining the observed cross-national
variation in rates of employment among the elderly.

We begin by looking at what is almost universally used as the first step in
this type of comparative analysis: GNP per capita. As reflected in Table 10.7,
in 1980 the per capita income of the countries put the United States and
France closest together at $11,360 and $11,730, respectively, while for Japan
it was $9,890 and for the United Kingdom was $7,920. Clearly, differences in
per capita income cannot account for the observed ordering or the magnitudes in employment among those over age 60 in the four countries.

The next most obvious set of indicators falls in the demographic realm.
If the proportion of older people in a population is high, we might expect
pressure to keep them employed longer to ease the burden of sharing social
security taxes. But in this set of four countries it is Japan, with the highest
over-60 employment rate, that has the lowest proportion of the population
over age 60. In contrast, France, with very low labor force participation
after age 60, has a larger proportion of old people than the United States,
which keeps a higher percentage of the elderly at work after 60.

How accurately people perceive the years of life remaining to them is
problematic, but it might be argued that if people recognize they have longer
to live, they might be willing to work more of those remaining years. Consid-

TABLE 10.7

CONDITIONS AFFECTING MEN OVER AGE 60 IN FOUR COUNTRIES, 1980

	Japan	United States	United Kingdom	France
Number of respondents	593	432	409	399
Percentage in the labor force	57	33	13	8
Retirement level	Low	Moderate	High	High
GNP per capita (U.S. dollars)	9,890	11,360	7,920	11,730
Percentage of population age 60 and over	13.5	16.0	20.1	17.6
Life expectancy at age 60 (1979)	19.0	17.5	16.0	17.1
Percentage of total labor force in agriculture	10	4	3	9
Unemployment rate	2.0	7.0	6.8	6.3
Entitlement age (full benefit)	65	65	65	65
Early retirement age	60	62	62	60
Percentage of wage replacement by old-age benefits for a couple	61	66	45	75
Percentage receiving:				
Public benefits	64	78	83	73
Private pensions	10	29	46	54
Other income (savings, investments, help from children)	47	68	31	21

SOURCES: Japan Prime Minister's Office (1982); USDHHS (1982); World Bank (1981, 1982).

ering life expectancy for men at age 60, we do find Japan with a three-year edge over the United Kingdom and almost two years over France, and this might contribute some to the tendency of Japanese men to continue working in their old age (Table 10.7). The lack of a compelling pattern in the case of all four countries, however, makes a weak case for this line of argument.

Neither could the observed differences in employment be explained by variation in the occupational composition of the countries. That this is a critical issue may not be recognized unless one is aware that attitudes about retirement and the readiness to withdraw permanently from the labor force vary greatly by occupation. Professionals and managers, for example, are much less likely to seek or accept retirement than are manual workers.

Moreover, the idea of retirement is less widespread in rural communities, and farmers are less often covered by social security programs. Indeed, the size of the agricultural population is a key factor in explaining retirement patterns.[7]

All four countries, being advanced economically, showed the low rates of agricultural employment characteristic of such populations. However, even within that narrow range the ordering and magnitudes did not conform to those for employment among the elderly. Thus, in 1980 France employed 9 percent of its labor force in agriculture, which clustered with Japan at 10 percent. The United Kingdom, with 3 percent of the labor force in agriculture, was on this measure paired with a new partner, the United States, with just under 4 percent so employed.

An alternative explanation related to the condition of the labor force might be based on rates of unemployment. It is not obvious, however, what direction the influence, if any, should take. From one perspective it might be argued that living in an environment of high unemployment would create the sort of insecurity that would induce people to cling to jobs. From another perspective, however, it might be argued that high rates of unemployment would induce older workers to switch over to the greater security of the available social insurance system. Japan, as is well known, enjoyed very low rates of unemployment for a number of recent decades, and as of 1980 its rate was still only 2 percent. The plentiful number of jobs may, then, have contributed to keeping more older men in the labor force. In 1980, however, the unemployment rates of the other three countries were all in the same range, despite their quite different rates of labor force participation after age 60 (Table 10.7).[8]

In the context of this discussion, however, these economic factors might be ruled less critical than the retirement policies of the countries under examination. The usual age for entitlement to a government benefit is widely assumed to be an important factor influencing individual decisions about retirement. Obviously, if the usual legal age making one eligible to receive benefits were markedly different in our four cases, that might suffice to explain the variation in employment rates.

As of 1980 all four of the countries under examination set the age at which entitlements began at the 65th birthday.[9] It might be argued, however, that it is not so much the entitlement age as it is the loopholes that are critical. This suggests that we look at provisions for early retirement. But there is little here to solve our problem. Japan, with 57 percent of the elderly in the labor force, and France, with a mere 8 percent so engaged, both awarded benefits upon early retirement at age 60. Although the contrast in over-60 employment in the United States and United Kingdom was considerable, both paid benefits upon early retirement at age 62 (Table 10.7). Again we must conclude that we have not found a simple objective factor to account for the pattern of employment among those over age 60 in the four countries under examination.[10]

Knowing the age at which workers start collecting social security does not tell anything about how ample it is, and people would obviously feel pressure to stay in the labor force if the typical standard benefit received was inadequate for maintaining a given standard of living. This critical point has stimulated analysts to calculate the rate at which typical social insurance benefits replace typical earnings from work in various countries.

In Table 10.5 we indicated that the more advanced countries had a mean replacement rate of about 61 percent for an aged couple. The rate for Japan is exactly that figure, which would seem to rule out this factor as an explanation for the high level of over-60 employment in that country. The situation is similar in the United States, where, indeed, replacement rates are well above the average in other countries. By contrast, the United Kingdom—with a very low rate of over-60 employment—actually had by far the lowest replacement rate of the four countries. Indeed, the United Kingdom has one of the lowest rates among all the industrial nations. Of the four countries, only France had a replacement rate, at 75 percent, consistent with its low over-60 employment level. Once again, seemingly compelling and obvious objective factors fail to explain the pattern of over-60 retirement in our set of four countries.[11]

In the available international comparisons, only the benefits paid by government programs are assessed for their value in replacing earnings. It must be recognized, therefore, that where individuals regularly supplement government benefits with private pensions, the rate at which earnings are being replaced will be higher than is the case where such private pensions are not widely available. This might certainly influence the decision about whether or not to remain in the labor force. But if we add this consideration into the presumed matrix of decisionmaking, we should also consider the availability of other supplements to government benefits. It is the case that 54 percent of the elderly men in the French sample and 46 percent in the United Kingdom reported receiving private pensions, as compared to only 29 percent in the United States and a mere 10 percent in Japan. However, the differential availability of private pensions seems to have been offset by the variable ability of the elderly to draw on other sources of support, in particular income from savings and investments or help from children. These two sources combined were available to 47 percent of the Japanese men and to 68 percent in the United States but to only 31 percent in the United Kingdom and 21 percent in France (Table 10.7). Here, then, we find some evidence that might help to explain why a larger proportion of men over age 60 continue in the labor force in Japan.

The Role of Subjective Factors

On the whole, the objective economic and structural factors have not emerged as clear-cut or compelling explanations of the observed differences in labor force participation among the elderly. We think that the outcome can be fairly well explained by measures of popular values, preferred modes of behavior, and other responses that may be broadly conceived of as describing cultural orientations in our sample societies. We propose that in certain respects the values and aspirations of Americans and Japanese are more alike than one might think if they were viewed only in terms of the conventional distinction between countries of the East and West. Stated in an alternative way, we consider that the United States, France, and the United Kingdom, though sharing many features of Western culture, are nevertheless sharply differentiated in their relative emphasis on attitudes toward work, its intrinsic meaningfulness, and its relation to desired conditions such as autonomy and independence, as reflected in the data collected for the Japanese study.

Perhaps the sharpest and most revealing difference emerged in the answers to that survey question that most explicitly focused on the retirement decision. When asked, "What do you think is the best age at which to retire?", the elderly men in the United Kingdom and France concentrated their preferences at age 60, that standard being chosen by 55 and 54 percent, respectively. In sharp contrast, only 14 percent of the sampled men in Japan and 16 percent in the United States selected so early an age as the best at which to begin retirement (Table 10.8).

Of course, some researchers may be tempted to say that the facts just given are not so impressive, because these national groups may only be trying to be consistent by bringing their stated preference into line with what the employment data suggests they have already done in practice, thus manifesting what psychologists call the strain toward cognitive consistency. Since our samples were not studied prior to age 60, we cannot resolve any uncertainty as to whether the stated preferences determined the behavior or vice versa.[12] However, other differences in the values expressed in the Japanese study strongly suggest that values were determining the retirement behavior and not the reverse. We consider particularly revealing the question, "Where should an older person's income come from?" Two choices that were offered seem especially relevant to our inquiry. The first stated, "One should save while working and not have to rely on the state or one's family." The second alternative was, "One should be able to rely on social security." The ratio between the percentages selecting these alternatives is particularly revealing. In Japan and the United States, the proportion of men

TABLE 10.8 _____

PREFERRED AGE OF RETIREMENT
(PERCENTAGES)

Age	Japan	United States	United Kingdom	France
55	1	6	5	20
60	14	16	55	54
65	34	31	23	15
70 and over	42	22	2	3
Other	8	25	13	4
No answer	1	0	2	4

SOURCE: Japan Prime Minister's Office (1982).

favoring saving while working was at least twice that advising reliance on social security, the percentages being 60/24 and 64/25. By contrast, in France the situation was the opposite, with the great majority favoring social security in a reversed ratio of 29/67; in the United Kingdom there was also a reversal, although a less dramatic one, with the proportions being 42/50 (Table 10.9).

Again we should note that this striking difference cannot be explained away by reference to a new set of objective conditions brought in to bolster a theory alternative to ours. Such an approach might be called a "sour grapes" theory. The argument would be that the elderly Japanese and Americans advise not relying on public benefits for the obvious reason either that they can less often get them or that those they do get are inadequate. Such a theory would require showing that government benefits were either less available or were less adequate in Japan and the United States. We have already given national-level data (Table 10.7) to indicate that sort of explanation will not hold. The Japanese study provides additional information that has the virtue of coming from the same individuals who provided the value judgments. As the respondents in the study describe their own personal situation, much the same proportion was getting social security in the United States as in the sample from France and the United Kingdom; the range for men in those three countries was from 73 to 83 percent, with the United States in the middle at 78. Although it is lower, the proportion receiving social security in Japan, at 64 percent, was certainly not different enough to explain the variation in its over-60 employment rate (Table 10.7).

To sum up, we think we have made a persuasive case that the marked difference in the rate of employment among those over age 60 in Japan and the United States, as compared to the United Kingdom and France, rests mainly on attitudes and values about work and about reliance on oneself (and on relatives, in the case of Japan) rather than on the government and its social security apparatus. Of course those social security provisions influence most people to retire eventually. We are not challenging that idea. What we address are the residual, but notable, differences in the rate of working after age 60, and we find that these cannot be explained by differences in the availability or adequacy of social insurance benefits in the four countries. Instead, the differences seem to be explained by preferences, basic values, and conceptions about what is good and proper. These evidently induce considerably larger proportions of Japanese and, to a comparable if lesser extent, Americans to stay in the labor force after they reach age 60.

Although we consider our argument to be persuasive, we recognize that it is not airtight. A fuller account would have to consider other preferences and values with which we have not dealt. Moreover, we stress again that we mean the analysis presented to be mainly illustrative, designed to show the path to follow in studies in which the same kind of information, and more of it, would be gathered for a large sample of developed countries, thus permitting a systematic test of the hypothesis suggested but only partially tested here.

The potential power of individual-level analysis may be illustrated by additional information we have on the United States. Using data from a 1972 study of income dynamics, Prigerson (1986) found that an individual psychosocial characteristic—that is, the sense of control over one's life—was a much more powerful predictor of staying in the labor force than race or even education. Indeed, those variables only produced minor effects on retirement behavior. By contrast, men who felt that what happened to them

TABLE 10.9

"WHERE SHOULD OLD PEOPLE'S INCOME COME FROM?"
(MALE RESPONDENTS ONLY, PERCENTAGES)

	Japan	United States	United Kingdom	France
Save while working	60	64	42	29
Social Security	24	25	50	67
Family	12	1	0	1
Other	3	10	8	3

SOURCE: Japan Prime Minister's Office (1982).
NOTE: Due to rounding errors, not every column totals 100 percent.

was largely their own doing had a retirement rate 49 percent lower than the rate among men who felt they did not have enough control over their own lives, other things being equal.[13]

Striking as these results are, they are subject to doubt as to whether the retirement caused the sense of control or, as we believe, the sense of control determined the decision to stay in the labor force. This doubt remains because Prigerson's analysis was cross-sectional. Clearly it would be most useful to work with panel studies, following the same individuals over time. Then we might predict the probability that given individuals would still be in the labor force at age 60 or 65 on the basis of what we had found their attitudes and values to be when they were only ages 55–59. Thus, by determining the way in which attitudes, values, and expectations interact with other influences in shaping an individual's decision about when to retire, we would considerably enhance our ability to explain, predict, and shape the labor force participation of those in or approaching their last two or three decades of life.

A number of such longitudinal studies in the United States are actually available to test the idea that the attitudes and values that characterize individuals before they reach retirement age significantly influence the chance that they will continue in the labor force *beyond* the point where most others have retired. These studies have been reviewed, and new analyses performed, by Palmore et al. (1985). Their data show early retirement to be heavily influenced by subjective factors. Men who said, "I'd like to work even if I did not have to," and those who said they "prefer work to leisure," were much more likely to continue in the labor force after others had retired. Indeed, the attitude toward one's job was the single best predictor of the age of retirement when examined in a multiple regression including such objective facts as rural status, wages, occupation, health, and being subject to mandatory retirement.[14]

We think that the implication of these findings for our analysis is clear. Although objective factors are significant forces shaping the retirement decisions, individual values and attitudes can evidently exert influence of comparable magnitude. We believe that the data we presented from the study by the Japanese Prime Minister's Office (1982) fits this model. The objective forces likely to encourage continued labor force participation by those over age 60 have become broadly alike in Japan, the United States, France, and the United Kingdom. Nevertheless, those countries have continued to keep markedly different proportions of the older male population at work. These differences arise from the fact that attitudes toward work and retirement continue to be significantly different in these four nations.

DISCUSSION

Steven G. Allen

Economists model retirement in terms of a lifetime labor-leisure choice made by utility-maximizing individuals. The predictions of this model are not likely to shock the average person on the street—retirement comes earlier if someone is old or unhealthy, expects to get low wages, or receives generous pension benefits. Estimates of the impact of these variables on retirement behavior have been obtained in a number of empirical studies using cross-sectional and longitudinal data sets, mainly the Retirement History Survey (RHS) and the National Longitudinal Survey of Older Males. With relatively few exceptions, the studies tend to confirm the predictions of the theory, although the range of the estimates is quite large.

Alex Inkeles and Chikako Usui argue that the economist's approach is too narrow in terms of both theory and methodology. Theoretically, they claim that researchers must not limit themselves to the economist's framework; instead researchers should also focus on such variables as attitudes and values. This is an issue that has long divided economists and other social scientists. Most economists accept the notion that attitudes play an important role in making decisions. They also assume that the role of attitudes is independent from the role of other variables so that preferences wash out in the error term. Because of the availability of attitudinal variables in a large number of data sets, a few economists have been able to test these assumptions directly. The results indicate that attitudes help predict outcomes, but the coefficients of the economic variables change very little when the attitudinal variables are added to the equation.[15] In other words, data on attitudes help us understand why one person in the RHS retired at age 65 whereas another person with the same wage and pension benefits retired at age 62; however, such data are of no help at all in estimating how much both persons will delay retirement in response to any proposed cut in Social Security benefits.

I am much more enthusiastic about Inkeles and Usui's paper from a methodological standpoint. They argue that we can learn more about retirement from international and historical comparisons than we can learn from further mining of the RHS. Their methodological argument is most persuasive when applied to the impact of public pensions on retirement decisions. All of the studies based on U.S. micro data are confined to the late 1960s and the 1970s. In that time the key features of the system did not change (this is, reduced benefits at age 62, full benefits at age 65, no earnings test after age 69). The only potential sources of exogenous variation in key parameters were changes in real benefits and payroll taxes. Careful study of these data has yielded some insights about how modest changes in benefits affect retirement, but we must be skeptical about how much such studies can tell us about what would happen if reduced benefits were delayed until age 65 and full benefits were postponed to age 68. One possible way to get the additional information needed to study this type of question is to make international comparisons.

The international comparisons approach is also likely to be useful for understanding the factors that determine the existence and design of social insurance systems. In reading the paper and exploring the tables, a number of important questions immediately come to mind. For instance, why do some systems make women eligible for benefits before men, despite higher life expectancy? Why have many systems reduced the age of eligibility through most of this century and why are a few now beginning to raise it? When are countries most likely to increase benefits?

The first part of the Inkeles and Usui paper examines why the age of eligibility for full public pension benefits varies across countries, and the second compares retirement patterns in the United States, the United Kingdom, France, and Japan. In my comments below I will follow the order of their discussion and (1) discuss the problems involved with making inferences about the choice of public pension plan characteristics from international comparisons, and (2) show why I think economic variables are, contrary to the claims of Inkeles and Usui, useful in explaining international differences in retirement behavior.

Comparing Public Pension Systems

Inkeles and Usui focus on differences in the age at which persons become eligible for full public social insurance benefits (henceforth called the normal entitlement age or NEA) across countries. They find that the average NEA for men in 30 countries has dropped modestly from 65.2 in 1950 to 63.5 in 1983. Almost half of the countries in their sample made no change at all.

The NEA is but one key parameter in any social insurance system, a fact that future researchers should keep in mind. In explaining retirement behavior, the NEA cannot be viewed in isolation from tax rates and government benefit formulas. To see this, consider a Heckman-MaCurdy-style lifetime labor supply model where labor supply in each period depends on the wage in that period, the wage in other periods, and the marginal utility of initial wealth.

Government social insurance systems affect labor supply first by changing the wage in every period. Before workers reach the NEA in the United States, they must pay payroll taxes, the result of which is a lower wage. At ages 65–69, workers are potentially subject to the earnings test, which amounts to a 50 percent tax on earnings beyond a given threshold. The intertemporal substitution effects of these taxes on labor supply are difficult to sort out because of the nonlinearity of labor-leisure budget sets. Social Security offsets in private pension benefit formulas further complicate matters.

The other important channel through which public pension systems affect labor supply is through their impact on the lifetime budget constraint, which is sometimes called the net generosity effect. Conditional on wages and expected lifetime, the combined effects of the tax and benefit schedule will affect lifetime opportunities for consumption and bequests. Increases in benefits (taxes) will allow an individual to have more (less) of both.

Taking this broader view of the key parameters in a social insurance system, it is quite clear that focusing only on the NEA gives a misleading impression about how stable these parameters actually are. Both tax and benefit schedules are subject to frequent changes in most countries. A critical issue for positive analysis is to determine how societies choose these benefit parameters. The political power of older citizens would clearly be a key variable in such an analysis.

This immediately leads to the question of whether international differences in government social insurance systems are truly exogenous variables in studying retirement decisions. Inkeles and Usui claim in their introduction that one of the advantages of the international approach is that it is a low-cost substitute for social experiments. Yet if benefit parameters are themselves functions of economic, political, and demographic variables, then clearly retirement rates could have a big influence. This puts us back in the old conundrum of identifying whether x causes y, y causes x, or both. This problem does not arise when we study the RHS because social insurance parameters can fairly be treated as exogenous to individuals. Once we aggregate, this question cannot be ignored.

Comparing Retirement Rates

Inkeles and Usui argue that researchers must consider demographic, politico-economic, cultural, and sociopsychological variables to truly understand retirement patterns. Estimation of such a model is problematic; the international equivalent of the RHS has yet to be collected. So as a starting point the authors analyze a study of men aged 60 and over in Japan, the United Kingdom, France, and the United States conducted by the Prime Minister's Office of Japan in 1981. The survey showed that 57 percent of Japanese older men still had a job. In contrast, 33 percent were still working in the United States but only 13 percent in the United Kingdom and a mere 8 percent in France. Inkeles and Usui discuss the qualitative relationship between these summary statistics and a wide variety of variables. They find that economic variables such as per capita GNP, unemployment rates, and pension coverage have no relationship with retirement rates, whereas attitudes about work and self-reliance are strongly related with retirement patterns across these countries.

I do not think that such a conclusion actually follows from the data presented in the paper. Inkeles and Usui casually dismiss in a footnote (see Note 6) a glaring difference between the employment rate for Britain in the Japanese study and the rate the British government reports in its own surveys. According to the British figures published by the ILO, 29 percent of the men over 60 were employed in 1980. Inkeles and Usui provide no details on how the Japanese study was conducted, so we can only speculate as to why the two estimates are so different. Regardless of the reason, it seems odd indeed that the authors in effect assume that a one-time Japanese survey is a better indicator of British retirement rates than the standard sources.

Using the ILO data, the employment rate for older men in the United Kingdom is about the same as in the United States, and the rates in both countries are well above the rate in France and well below the rate in Japan. This does not really change any of the analysis of the demographic and economic variables in Table 10.7, but it upsets much of the analysis of the attitudinal variables in Tables 10.8 and 10.9. Even though older men in the United Kingdom and France have similar ideas about when they should retire and how they should finance their retirement, their actual retirement rates are quite different. Older men in the United Kingdom and United States have different ideas about when they should retire and how they should finance their retirement, but their actual retirement rates are about the same. Unless the attitudes of the older British men in the Japanese survey sample are just as unrepresentative as the retirement rates, it is hard to see how this evidence supports Inkeles and Usui's conclusion that attitudes are the key to understanding retirement.

I also have some reservations about their claim that economic variables do not provide a "compelling explanation" about retirement patterns. One variable in Table 10.7 is highly correlated with employment rates: the percentage receiving private pensions. Inkeles and Usui note this in their paper but claim it is offset by differences across the countries in other sources of income, such as savings and intrafamily transfer payments. Apparently they view retirement rates as a function of the availability of outside sources of income and fail to allow for the possibility that a dollar of pension benefits and a dollar of savings might have different effects on retirement decisions.

This possibility is quite likely. In the United States, most pension plans base benefits on years of service and final salary. At any point in time a worker is entitled to an annuity stream starting at a given age; the present value of this stream is called pension wealth. Every year a worker stays with a company, his pension wealth changes because he has more years of service and a different salary; this change in pension wealth is called pension compensation. Once a worker reaches the age of eligibility for early retirement benefits, he generally has negative pension compensation—because by failing to retire and accepting his pension, the loss in that year's pension turns out to be considerably larger than any possible increase in pension wealth associated with salary and years of service. This makes the economic return from working an extra year smaller and raises the odds that a person will retire. In contrast, income from investments and transfers from family members is unaffected by the retirement decision, so we should not expect it to offset the impact of pensions on retirement rates.

Another variable not included in Table 10.7—but one that may turn out to be quite important, especially for explaining the low employment rate for older men in France—is the availability of early retirement benefits through the unemployment insurance and disability insurance systems.[16] In the 1970s a number of countries—including France, Belgium, Austria, Sweden, and West Germany—made public benefits available to unemployed workers at age 60. The labor force participation rate for men aged 60–64 in these countries dropped by an average of 23 percentage points between 1970 and 1981. It would be worthwhile to find out whether these two events are correlated. During roughly the same period, the disability insurance programs in Sweden, West Germany, and the Netherlands started giving considerably more weight to labor market opportunities in defining those eligible for benefits, so this factor would also have to be considered.

Probably the most interesting puzzle posed by this part of Inkeles and Usui's paper is why employment rates for older men in Japan are so high. This finding is especially intriguing when we take into account that almost all firms in Japan have mandatory retirement between the ages of 55 and 60.[17] Clearly, one reason many people work after mandatory retirement is that they cannot receive full benefits until age 65. A compounding factor could be the tendency for private pension benefits to be paid in a single lump sum rather than an annuity. It is also possible that there are better labor market conditions for older men in Japan than elsewhere—the elderly represent a smaller share of the population and the national unemployment rate is much lower. Some data on the earnings of older men relative to women and younger men for different countries would be useful in examining this possibility.

Because it is so hard to prove or disprove anything with a data set containing four observations, I decided to re-examine with a larger sample the question of whether economic variables are useful for explaining international differences in retirement patterns. Labor force participation rates for men aged 55–59, 60–64, and 65–69 are reported in the ILO's *Yearbook of Labor Statistics*. These are regressed on GNP per capita, the age of eligibility for public old-age benefits, and the year in which the social insurance program was established. I expect GNP per capita to be inversely related to labor force participation rates (greater marginal utility of initial wealth) and the age of eligibility to be directly related (later eligibility, less wealth).

The last variable requires a more detailed explanation. A few economists might argue that a rational, forward-looking, utility-maximizing individual born in the last decades of the nineteenth century would have taken possible social insurance schemes into account as part of his lifetime budget constraint so that only unanticipated changes in that scheme (for example, pension available sooner or later than expected, pension more or less generous than expected) would have any effect on his choice of retirement age. Most economists would view such a model as extreme and allow for some inertia in human behavior. Once we allow for inertia, it becomes quite clear that the full effects of old-age benefits on retirement and saving cannot be estimated until generations after the pension plan was started. Enough time must pass for people to form expectations about the plan's key parameters and for a full life cycle of labor-supply behavior to be observed. If old-age benefits encourage (discourage) early retirement, then the labor force participation rate for older men should be lower (higher) in those countries where benefits have been around the longest, because a higher fraction of the older men in those countries have had time to take these benefits into account as part of their lifetime labor-leisure choice.

The results are summarized in Table 10.10. Data for labor force participation rates of men aged 65–69 are not available for 12 countries in my 36-country sample. The countries for which this information is not available tend to have lower per capita GNP than the rest of the sample, so I include two sets of results for the 55–59 and 60–64 groups to indicate the sensitivity of the results to possible selection bias.

TABLE 10.10

ECONOMIC ACTIVITY RATE REGRESSIONS FOR MEN, BY AGE GROUP

	36-COUNTRY SAMPLE			24-COUNTRY SAMPLE			
	Mean (S.D.)	55–59 (1)	60–64 (2)	Mean (S.D.)	55–59 (3)	60–64 (4)	65–69 (5)
Constant		−216.175	−823.660		−217.309	−1152.699	−1279.844
GNP per capita ÷ 1000	6.664 (4.969)	.024 (.368)	−.689 (.649)	8.417 (4.834)	−.092 (.401)	−.630 (.726)	−2.075 (.673)
NEA	62.6 (3.9)	.432 (.401)	−.793 (.707)	63.7 (2.8)	1.045 (.610)	2.701 (1.103)	2.056 (1.022)
Year old = age insurance program initiated	1933.6 (23.4)	.140 (.072)	.435 (.127)	1926.1 (21.2)	.121 (.088)	.543 (.160)	.622 (.148)
Standard error		8.254	14.534		8.169	14.776	13.687
R^2		.141	.419		.202	.520	.707
Mean (S.D.) of dependent variable		81.664 (8.396)	61.953 (17.981)		82.104 (8.347)	59.325 (19.477)	31.617 (23.085)

SOURCES: Economic activity rate from ILO (1985, 13–44, table 1); GNP per capita from World Bank (1983, 148–49, appendix table 1); NEA and year old-age insurance program initiated from U.S. Department of Health and Human Services (1982).

NOTE: The following countries are included in the sample in columns 3 through 5: Austria, Denmark, Spain, Finland, France, West Germany, Ireland, Italy, Norway, Switzerland, Sweden, United Kingdom, Argentina, Canada, Chile, Guatemala, Honduras, Mexico, Paraguay, United States, Japan, Singapore, Australia, and New Zealand. The larger sample in columns 1 and 2 also includes Greece, the Netherlands, Portugal, Yugoslavia, Peru, Venezuela, Hong Kong, Indonesia, Jordan, Malaysia, Pakistan, and Turkey.

In all three age groups, labor force participation rates are much higher in countries that have started their social insurance programs relatively recently than in those where such programs have been around a long time. To illustrate the magnitude of this effect, compare a country that started its program in 1930 to one that began in 1950. The labor force participation rate in the latter country would be 2–3 percentage points higher for men aged 55–59, 9–11 percentage points higher for men aged 60–64, and 12 percentage points higher for men aged 65–69.

For the 65–69 group, the age of eligibility for old-age benefits is positively correlated and per capita GNP is negatively correlated with labor force participation. Per capita GNP has no significant effect on labor force participation for the 55–59 and 60–64 age groups. Age of eligibility is positively correlated with labor force participation for the 60–64 age group in the smaller sample in column 4, but not in the larger sample in column 2. It is unassociated with labor force participation for those aged 55–59 in either sample, no doubt a reflection of the fact that in most countries the age of eligibility is 60 or over.

How well do these economic variables explain international differences in labor force participation among older men? In the age 65–69 sample, these three variables account for 71 percent of the variation in the dependent variable; in the age 60–64 sample, 42 or 52 percent. Only in the age 55–59 sample do the economic variables come up relatively short, which is not surprising given the smaller variation in the dependent variable.

Another way to test this simple model's ability to explain behavior is to compare actual and predicted values of labor force participation for France, the United Kingdom, the United States, and Japan. The predicted labor force participation rates for men aged 65–69 for these countries are 6, 22, 31, and 40 percent, respectively, whereas the actual rates are 9, 17, 24, and 56 percent. Even though it underpredicts the Japanese rate by a sizable margin, the model at least ranks the rates in these four countries accurately. With information on private pensions, unemployment insurance, disability insurance, and labor market conditions for older workers, the predictive capacity of this simple model would be even greater.

Based on these results and the inconclusive nature of Inkeles and Usui's empirical analysis, there can be little doubt that economic variables carry considerable weight when people make their retirement decisions. There can be equally little doubt that Inkeles and Usui's claim that "individual values and attitudes evidently can exert influence of comparable magnitude" is untenable.

Nonetheless, Inkeles and Usui deserve a considerable amount of credit for opening this line of research. It would no doubt be useful to design an international survey designed to collect information on demographic, economic, and attitudinal variables and see where this leads us. I also think that there would be a big payoff in exploring the data sets already available from a perspective that takes into account historical as well as international comparisons. In crude terms, this amounts to moving from cross-section to panel data. My main reason for advocating this approach is illustrated in Table 10.11, where I report economic activity rates for men aged 65 and over from the 1930s and the 1980s.

Labor force participation rates for older men declined in every country, but the rate of decline has been anything but uniform across different countries. In the 1930s roughly half of the older men in France and the Netherlands were in the labor force; today fewer than one out of twenty are in the labor force. Once again the Japanese experience provides a striking contrast. The labor force participation rate there has declined much more slowly than in any country in the sample except Peru.

We might immediately consider this to be further evidence that the

TABLE 10.11

COMPARISON OF ECONOMIC ACTIVITY RATES
FOR MEN AGED 65 AND OVER, 1930–1941 AND 1981–1986

Country	1930–1941	1981–1986	Absolute decrease	Percentage decrease
Peru	82.6	63.1	19.5	23.6
Japan	63.0	36.9	26.1	41.4
United States	41.5	15.2	26.3	63.4
Ireland	67.3	19.1	48.2	71.6
New Zealand	40.0	11.2	28.8	72.0
Australia	34.3	8.9	25.4	74.0
Canada	47.2	12.2	35.0	74.2
Portugal	86.4	19.9	66.5	77.0
United Kingdom	47.9	10.8	37.1	77.4
East Germany	29.7	5.7	24.0	80.8
Italy	61.7	8.4	53.3	86.4
Netherlands	42.6	3.9	38.7	90.8
France	59.4	4.3	55.1	92.8
Spain	86.7	5.9	80.8	93.2
Denmark	35.1	21.0[a]	14.1	40.2
Norway	55.4	27.1[a]	28.3	51.1
Sweden	49.8	11.2[a]	38.6	77.5

SOURCES: 1930–1941: Woytinsky and Woytinsky (1953, 353); 1981–1986: ILO (1986, table 1).

a. Economic activity rate for men aged 65–74.

Japanese culture is fundamentally different from that of major industrial nations. The experience in Norway and Sweden suggests that culture is not likely to be the only useful factor for explaining differential rates of decline of labor force participation. In 1930 about half of the men aged 65 and over in each country were in the labor force; today 27 percent of Norwegian men between ages 65 and 74 are in the labor force, in contrast to only 11 percent of Swedish men.

Viewed from an international perspective, the growth of retirement in the United States seems rather modest. In 1940, shortly after Social Security benefits started to become available, the labor force participation rate was 42 percent. Today, after considerable growth in Social Security benefits and in the private pension system, the labor force participation rate stands at 15 percent.

The patterns in Table 10.11 defy armchair analysis. Almost all of the countries had well-developed social security systems throughout the period. Most workers in these countries are covered by private pensions. Differences in pension generosity and marginal tax rates are possible explanations, but factors such as health and earnings opportunities would also have to be considered. The job will not be easy. There are no longitudinal micro-data files to which we can readily turn. Yet the payoff from studying retirement decisions in this way could very well be much greater than the gains from any further tortured econometric analysis of the RHS.

Notes

1. Palmore et al. (1985, 2–3) distinguish "subjective" from "objective" retirement." Furthermore, these authors use both continuous and dichotomous measures of objective retirement.

2. It is commonly argued that the development of an industrial economy and bureaucratic organizations undermines the value of older people as workers. In contrast to an agricultural economy, where the experience of old people is valued, industrial society demands a highly educated, geographically mobile young labor force (Cowgill 1974; Graebner 1980). Thus, more old people are expected to face employment discrimination and to retire from the labor force under conditions of industrial development.

3. We should acknowledge, however, that Poul Milhøj (in Shanas et al. 1968, 306) concluded that in comparison with Britain and the United States, "the higher Danish age limit for public pensions plays a large part in explaining the later retirement of blue collar workers" in that country. In addition, in the United States there is a big increase in retirement at age 62, the earliest age at which one can receive Social Security, and at age 65, the point at which one becomes eligible for full benefits.

4. Shanas et al. (1968) may be considered an important exception to this generalization. However, they used relatively few value and attitude questions in their approach to retirement. This may have played some role in leading them to conclude that the cross-national differences they observed between Denmark, the United Kingdom, and the United States were "the result of the institutional forms and the economic and social structure of the three countries rather than of differences in the citizens' attitudes" (p. 319).

5. The data from this survey were also used extensively by Palmore and Maeda (1985) in the revision of Palmore's *The Honorable Elders* (1975), to which they appended the word *Revisited*. Some readers may find it interesting to compare their analysis with ours.

6. The Japanese survey relied on personal reporting by individuals in a sample survey, and these results are therefore not strictly comparable with data from the standard International Labor Organization (ILO) reports on the economically active population by age, which are census, sample, or household survey data supplied by governments (see, for example, ILO 1984, 3, 11). Nevertheless, it is of interest to compare the relative magnitudes and standings yielded by both methods. According to the ILO data for 1980, the proportion of the male population over 60 employed in the four countries was: Japan, 56; United States, 32; United Kingdom, 29; and France, 13. It is apparent that for three of the countries the magnitudes given in the Japanese survey are broadly similar to those yielded by the ILO. However, for the United Kingdom there is a large discrepancy between the ILO figures and those given by respondents in the Japanese study. Since we base our analysis on the same set of

individuals who report both their employment and their attitudes, we held to the Japanese data.

7. Pampel and Weiss (1983) found the percentage employed in agriculture to be by far the most powerful factor in explaining the rate of employment among the elderly in eighteen industrial countries from 1950 to 1975. They obtained a standardized regression coefficient of 0.63, the strength of this association being also reflected in the fact that a 1 percent decline in the proportion of the population engaged in agriculture reduced participation of the elderly in the labor force by 0.68 percent.

8. We recognize that the proportion over age 60 still employed at any one point in time, such as 1980, includes individuals who made their retirement and labor force decisions at earlier points in time. This argues in favor of considering earlier levels of unemployment and *changes* in the unemployment rate, which calls for a complex analysis. It is worth noting that between 1975 and 1980 the unemployment rate in Japan was quite stable. The rate fell in that period in the United States, but it rose substantially in England, from 4 to 6.8 percent, and in France, from 4 to 6.3 percent. Consequently, it could be that in the five years prior to our study, more older workers in the United Kingdom and France were pressured to withdraw from the labor force because employment possibilities were so limited.

A different kind of economic pressure would be that created by a labor shortage, with unfilled jobs beckoning to older workers. This might help explain the high level of employment of those over 60 in Japan. The *World Development Report 1986* (World Bank 1986) shows that from 1973 to 1984 the GDP growth rate for Japan was 4.3, indicating considerable growth, which might be expected to produce a labor shortage. But France and the United States both grew at the *same* 2.3 percent rate while the United Kingdom experienced only 1 percent growth. When the growth-rate factor is combined with changes in the rate of unemployment over time, we can see that Japan faced a situation such that high demand for labor might have induced older men to continue in the labor force. However, the rates of economic growth and the levels of unemployment in the United States and France were similar even though their over-60 employment levels were quite different. As for the United Kingdom, its economy grew most slowly and its unemployment rate increased sharply. Thus, the labor demand in combination with changes in unemployment rates over time does appear to be consistently related to the high employment level of men over age 60 in Japan and to the low level of employment in the United Kingdom. However, the profile of the United States and France on these measures does not serve to explain their markedly different rates of over-60 employment.

9. In 1983 retirement with full benefits became available at age 60 in France, as shown in Table 10.1. In our analysis of actual retirement in the four countries, we used data that were collected in *1981*. For our comparisons to be meaningful, all the data should be the same year, 1980 or 1981. Therefore, the retirement age of 65, not 60, was used for France in the text.

10. In Japan, workers employed by large companies (that is, 500 or more employees) are usually subject to mandatory retirement at age 55 as a matter of company policy. However, they must then wait until age 60 for reduced benefits from the public pensions, and until age 65 for full benefits. Accordingly, we might argue that

uncertainty about the future and fear of the loss of jobs at age 55 would make the Japanese more savings-oriented and self-reliant. However, only a small proportion of Japanese workers work for large firms and are subject to mandatory retirement policies. In 1983, the number of workers employed by large companies constituted only 18 percent of the total work force, whereas self-employed persons, family workers, and employees of small firms (that is, less than 30 employees) made up 42.6 percent of the labor force (OECD 1985, 15). These small companies do not practice mandatory retirement policies.

Even among the large companies, the mandatory retirement age of 55 is no longer the norm. An increasing number of companies are raising their mandatory retirement age because of the aging of the work force. According to a survey conducted by the Japan Ministry of Labor (1980), 39.5 percent of companies with some kind of mandatory retirement policy placed the retirement age at 55, and 39.7 percent of them set it at age 60 or older. Although it is possible that setting the retirement age at 55 creates uncertainty for some workers, it is equally likely that, for many, the system of lifetime employment provides considerable security.

11. Since our analysis focuses on all men over age 60 by 1980, many of those in the samples would have faced the retirement decision at an earlier time, when the replacement rates of the different countries might have had a different relationship than they had in 1980. We therefore averaged the replacement rates for 1975 and 1980. These averages were below the 1980 levels but did not change the pattern reported above. Specifically, the United Kingdom still had the lowest average replacement rate at 47 percent. Japan, despite having more than four times as many older men working after 60 as the United Kingdom, had a similar replacement average rate of 50 percent. The United States was at 56 percent, and once again France had an average replacement of 75 percent.

12. Despite its obvious importance, longitudinal data is difficult to obtain. This gives special significance to Palmore et al. (1985), who were able to work with several different studies of men whose attitudes were ascertained before retirement yet whose retirement behavior could be examined at intervals five or more years later. The results are partially described below. Unfortunately for our purposes, however, all the samples were of men in the United States only.

13. Prigerson's analysis was based on a sample of 1,788 men aged 25 and over. The dependent variable was essentially a rate of survival, reflecting the proportion of a given group that remained employed after the passage of different amounts of time. Along with education and race, the explanatory variables that entered into the analysis included having grown up in a rural region, which reduced the rate of being retired by 38 percent. In addition, the number of children born to men before their 25th birthday increased their retirement rate by 10 percent for each additional child. Of course, putting other variables in the regression might have shown different effects. Even more critical, it would have been desirable to have the analysis run with a sample restricted to older men, say age 50 and over.

14. The beta for attitude toward a person's job was − 0.21 and for attitude toward retirement 0.14. The other betas were: rural, 0.12; wages, 0.16; occupation, 0.15; health limits, − 0.16; subject to mandatory retirement, − 0.18; and core

industry, − 0.11 (Palmore et al. 1985, 29). It should be noted, however, that the impact of attitudes as a predictor varied according to how the dependent variable of "retirement" was measured.

15. See Allen (1978) and Filer (1981) for examples of this type of study.

16. This discussion is adapted from Casey (1984).

17. According to the Japan Institute of Labour (1986), 87 percent of all firms with 30 or more employees have mandatory retirement.

REFERENCES

Aldrich, Jonathan. 1982. "The Earnings Replacement of Old-Age Benefits in 12 Countries, 1969–80." *Social Security Bulletin* 45:3–11, table 1.

Allen, Steven G. 1978. "Absenteeism and the Labor Market." Ph.D. dissertation, Harvard University.

Casey, Bernard. 1984. "Recent Trends in Retirement Policy and Practice in Europe and the USA." In Pauline K. Robinson, Judy Livingston, and James Birren, eds., *Aging and Technological Advances.* New York: Plenum Press.

Cowgill, Donald O. 1974. "Aging and Modernization: A Revision of the Theory." In Jaber F. Gubrium, ed., *Late Life, Communities and Environmental Policy.* Springfield, Ill.: Charles C. Thomas.

Filer, Randall K. 1981. "The Influence of Effective Human Capital on the Wage Equation." In Ronald G. Ehrenberg, ed., *Research in Labor Economics,* vol. 4. Greenwich, Conn.: JAI Press.

Graebner, William. 1980. *A History of Retirement: The Meaning and Function of an American Institution, 1885–1978.* New Haven, Conn.: Yale University Press.

Haanes-Olsen, Leif. 1978. "Earnings Replacement Rate of Old-Age Benefits, 1965–75, Selected Countries." *Social Security Bulletin* 41:3–14, table 1.

Horlick, Max. 1970. "The Earnings Replacement Rate of Old-Age Benefits: An International Comparison." *Social Security Bulletin* 33:3–16.

Industrial Relations Services. 1979. "Flexible Retirement and Pension Rights." *European Industrial Relations Review* 67:13–17.

International Labor Office. 1984. *Yearbook of Labor Statistics 1984.* Geneva: ILO.

———. 1985. *Yearbook of Labor Statistics 1985.* Geneva: ILO.

———. 1986. *Yearbook of Labor Statistics 1986.* Geneva: ILO.

Japan Institute of Labour. 1986. *Japanese Working Life Profile: Statistical Aspects.* Tokyo: Japan Institute of Labor.

Japan Ministry of Labor. 1980. *Survey of Employment Management.* Tokyo: Ministry of Labor.

Japan Prime Minister's Office. 1982. *International Comparative Survey of the Life and Perception of the Old.* Tokyo: Office of the Aged, Prime Minister's Office.

OECD. 1985. *OECD Economic Surveys: Japan.* Paris: Organization for Economic Cooperation and Development.

Palmore, Erdman B. 1975. *The Honorable Elders.* Durham, N.C.: Duke University Press.

Palmore, Erdman B., and Daisaku Maeda. 1985. *The Honorable Elders Revisited.* Durham, N.C.: Duke University Press.

Palmore, Erdman B., et al. 1985. *Retirement: Causes and Consequences.* New York: Springer.

Pampel, Fred C., and Jane A. Weiss. 1983. "Economic Development, Pension Policies, and the Labor Force Participation of Aged Males: A Cross-National, Longitudinal Approach." *American Journal of Sociology* 49:350–72.

Pilcher, Donald M., Charles J. Ramirez, and Judson J. Swihart. 1968. "Some Correlates of Normal Pensionable Age." *International Social Security Review* 21:387–411.

Prigerson, Holly. 1986. "The Significance of Retiree Characteristics in the Determinants of Retirement." Unpublished term paper, Department of Sociology, Stanford University.

Ricketts, Jean Marie. 1986. "Worldwide Trends and Developments in Social Security." *Social Security Bulletin* 49:5–11.

Shanas, Ethel, et al. 1968. *Old People in Three Industrial Societies.* New York: Atherton Press.

U.S. Department of Health and Human Services. 1982. *Social Security Programs Throughout the World 1981.* Washington, D.C.: GPO.

———. 1984. *Social Security Programs Throughout the World 1983.* Research Report no. 59. Washington, D.C.: GPO.

World Bank. 1981. *World Development Report 1981.* New York: Oxford University Press.

———. 1982. *World Development Report 1982.* New York: Oxford University Press.

———. 1983. *World Development Report 1983.* New York: Oxford University Press.

———. 1986. *World Development Report 1986.* New York: Oxford University Press.

Woytinsky, Emma S., and Wladimir S. Woytinsky. 1953. *World Population and Production Trends and Outlook.* New York: Twentieth Century Fund.

Zeitzer, Ilene R. 1983. "Social Security Trends and Development in Industrialized Countries." *Social Security Bulletin* 46:55–62.

II

SOCIAL SECURITY BENEFITS:
AN EMPIRICAL STUDY OF
EXPECTATIONS AND REALIZATIONS

B. Douglas Bernheim

Expectations play a key role in modern life-cycle theory. This is something of an embarrassment to applied economists, since perceptions are not, in general, directly observable. Little if any existing evidence sheds light on the plausibility of central life-cycle tenets, which hold that consumers think seriously and coherently about the relatively distant and uncertain future. The extent to which financial hardship among the elderly stems from myopia and inept financial planning therefore remains largely a matter of speculation. In addition, economists are frequently forced to invoke a variety of strong assumptions concerning the structure of expectations in order to identify behavioral models (for example, many studies are based on the supposition that consumers understand the Social Security benefit formulas and form their expectations "rationally"). Specific empirical results often depend heavily on the nature of these assumptions. An excellent example of this appears in the literature on Social Security and personal saving: when employing macroeconomic data, we can obtain virtually any desired result by altering assumptions concerning expectations (see Leimer and Lesnoy's

This research was funded by the Department of Health and Human Services (National Institute on Aging) through its grant, "The Economics of Aging," to the National Bureau of Economic Research. I would like to thank David Wise for valuable comments and Laurence Levin for research assistance. Any opinions expressed here are those of the author and should not be attributed to any other individual or organization.

[1982] criticism of Feldstein [1974]). The study of expectations is therefore absolutely central to a comprehensive understanding of life-cycle behavior.

Previous empirical work on household expectations has focused primarily on inflation (see Huizinga 1980; Curtin 1982; Gramlich 1983; and Papadia 1982. Aiginger [1979] considers a somewhat broader range of variables). To my knowledge, there has been no previous systematic analysis of expectations and realizations among the elderly. Since the concerns and characteristics of the elderly differ from those of the nonelderly, it would be unwise to generalize from existing evidence when considering problems associated with aging.

In this paper, I employ data drawn from the Social Security Administration's Retirement History Survey (RHS) to study the accuracy of preretirement expectations concerning Social Security benefits. This emphasis on Social Security is appropriate, since program benefits are typically the most important single financial resource of retired individuals, comprising on average more than half of net wealth (see Bernheim 1987a). In a separate piece (Bernheim 1987b), I examine the accuracy of expectations concerning the timing of retirement.

The major findings of this study are as follows. First, survey responses to questions about expected Social Security benefits are reasonably "noisy." It is extremely important to bear this in mind when interpreting the data. When the noise is filtered out appropriately, it appears that consumers do think seriously about future events and report expectations that may well reflect, albeit imperfectly, their true beliefs. Indeed, respondents' forecasts explain roughly 60 percent of the variance in realizations.

Second, consumers do not form expectations on the basis of all available information. The data strongly suggest that individuals ignore a great deal of information contained in concurrent Social Security statutes. Proper adjustment for this information could reduce the residual forecast error variance by roughly 15 percent. There is also somewhat weaker evidence that consumers at least partially ignore certain demographic factors that help to predict future events. However, the potential gains from more refined use of demographic information appear minimal; proper adjustment would reduce the residual forecast error variance by at most 5 percent.

Third, the evidence is broadly consistent with the view that individuals use the same information to form expectations concerning a variety of different variables (Social Security benefits, other income, and date of retirement). When forming expectations concerning Social Security, individuals do not appear to ignore information upon which they base other expectations at the same point in time. In addition, consumers have good memories, in that they do not ignore information upon which they based expectations at previous points in time.

Fourth, people seem to be reasonably competent at forming relatively accurate expectations conditional on the information that they do chose to use. In addition, it is somewhat comforting to note that few individuals exhibit the kind of extreme optimism that might be responsible for catastrophic errors in financial planning; indeed, there is a general bias toward conservatism. Surprisingly, there is little evidence to support the view that expectations were abnormally inaccurate during periods of significant statutory reform. Indeed, the data broadly suggest that consumers correctly anticipated the general effects of legislative action during the early 1970s, contrary to the supposition of most previous authors (see, for example, Hurd and Boskin 1981). Data on retirement expectations bear this conclusion out (see Bernheim 1987b).

Fifth, various population subgroups, widows and single women tend to form both the most conservative (that is, low relative to realizations) and most accurate (judged by correlations or mean squared errors) forecasts. The forecasts of married men are the least conservative and least accurate. There is no evidence that the poor or those with relatively little education have particular difficulties forming accurate expectations.

Sixth and finally, the properties of reported expectations conform more closely to theory as retirement grows imminent. This suggests that individuals may become more serious about forming expectations with the approach of retirement.

The paper is organized as follows. The next section describes a general conceptual framework for analyzing Social Security expectations. The third section contains a description of the data, and simple tabulations of the raw data appear in the fourth. The fifth section contains regression results that permit formal testing of certain aspects of the conceptual framework. Although the results are generally unfavorable, I attribute this to the noisiness of reported expectations. I take up the issue of measurement error in section six and present new results that motivate many of the conclusions described above. The last section summarizes my findings and discusses directions for subsequent research.

A Conceptual Framework

It is plainly unreasonable to expect that an elderly person could predict without error his financial resources several years hence. Uncertainty is simply a fact of life. For purposes of conducting behavioral analyses and designing public policy, the relevant issue is whether individuals have learned to deal with this uncertainty as well as their circumstances allow. Economists frequently employ the assumption that households form their expectations rationally—in the sense that they are not fooled systematically—and further-more that their forecasts are as precise as possible conditional on available information. Given data on expectations, we can test his hypothesis in a variety of ways. One approach is to determine whether or not forecast errors are systematically related to information that the individual possesses (or has access to) at the time his forecast is made. If they are, then we can actually identify the kind of information that individuals either ignore or use improp-erly. Another approach is to examine the accuracy of predictions and to see whether they become more accurate as knowledge improves. In this section, I develop these ideas formally.

Suppose that at each point in time, $t = 0, 1, \ldots, T - 1$, an individual forms an expectation, X_t^e, about the value of same variable X, which is realized at time T. During period t, he has access to certain information, which I denote as Ω_t. Throughout, I assume that the individual's memory is perfect, so that all information available at time t is also available in period τ $> t$.

In subsequent sections, I interpret X as Social Security benefits and T as date of retirement.[1] When an individual reports expected Social Security benefits, there is, of course, some ambiguity as to what this means. He may have in mind something like a mathematical expectation, but it is also possible that his report reflects his view of the most likely outcome (that is, the mode). So long as the distribution of X is approximately symmetric and single peaked, this ambiguity is probably of little consequence. Throughout this paper, therefore, I focus on the hypothesis that individuals report ex-pected values, that is:

$$X_t^e = E(X|\Omega_t). \tag{1}$$

From equation (1), we can derive a number of simple testable implica-tions, which I summarize below as Properties 1–4.

Property 1: Realizations should exhibit more variability than fore-casts.

Property 2: The variability of forecasts should increase as the date of realization approaches.

Property 3: The variance of the forecast error should decline as the date of realization approaches.

Property 4: The correlation between forecasts and realizations should rise as the date of realization approaches.

The intuition for these results is straightforward. Different individuals should make different forecasts only if their information differs. Thus, as individuals acquire more differentiated information, forecasts should become more heterogeneous. Since information improves over time, Property 2 follows naturally. Note also that the improvement of information immediately suggests Properties 3 and 4, which essentially state that forecasts become more accurate as the date of realization approaches. Finally, since a realization is equivalent to a forecast based upon perfect information, realizations should exhibit more heterogeneity than forecasts (Property 1). I refer the reader to Appendix A for formal demonstrations.

Tests of the four properties listed above can help to determine whether or not consumers efficiently process available information. If these tests should fail, further investigation would be warranted. In particular, we would want to identify the kinds of information that individuals tend to ignore or process incorrectly. It is possible to shed some light on this issue by adopting a somewhat different approach. Specifically, equation (1) suggests the following regression framework:

$$X_{it} = \alpha + \beta X_{it}^e + \omega_{it}\gamma + \epsilon_{it} \tag{2}$$

where the ω_{it} are variables that are observable at time t (that is, elements of Ω_{it}). Theory implies that $\alpha = 0$, $\beta = 1$, $\gamma = 0$, and ϵ_{it} is orthogonal to X_{it}^e and ω_{it}. Thus, least squares estimation of (2) generates an additional set of texts.[2] It also allows us to isolate particular types of information that consumers fail to process correctly and to determine the direction and magnitude of the resulting forecast bias. Note, in addition, that by omitting ω_{it} from the regression, one can test a weaker proposition—that individuals form unbiased (conditional on the information that they do use) although possibly inefficient expectations ($\alpha = 0$, $\beta = 1$).

DATA

The RHS, from which the data for this study are drawn, followed a sample of retirement-aged households (58–63 years old in 1969) for a period of ten years, beginning in 1969. Each household was surveyed once every two years. Although the initial wave included more than 11,000 households, there was substantial attrition over successive waves.

In 1969, 1971, and 1973, respondents reported the level of Social Security benefits they expected to receive on retirement. In subsequent sections of this paper, the variable Expected Social Security (ESS) equals the reported amount, adjusted to an annual basis. Unfortunately, data on expected benefits were extremely poor in 1969. Casual inspection revealed a low response rate (due in part to survey skip patterns), as well as a high frequency of nonsensical values. I have therefore confined attention to responses given in 1971 and 1973.

Unfortunately, interpretation of expected benefits is somewhat problematic in that the treatment of inflation is ambiguous. Certainly, the survey instrument does not specify whether the individual is to report a real or nominal figure. Throughout, I simply assume that respondents report expected benefits in current (that is, survey-year) dollars. This seems the most natural choice, since respondents would otherwise have had to forecast future inflation rates before formulating an answer to the question. To the extent my assumption is incorrect, the scale of expectations may be somewhat off.

The primary advantage of the RHS is that it allows the analyst to identify realizations by employing data from subsequent survey waves. In the case of Social Security benefits, this process is somewhat involved. Although respondents are asked to report Social Security income in each survey year, these data are of questionable reliability. For example, it is not uncommon to find households that first report the receipt of benefits in a particular year, only to report no Social Security income in one or more of the subsequent waves. Furthermore, reported benefits frequently vary by 50 percent or more between consecutive waves. Since most of this undoubtedly reflects noise, the use of such data would introduce spurious forecast error. I therefore opt to use calculated values instead. The calculation proceeds in several steps.

First, I identify the year in which each repondent began to receive Social Security benefits. Although it is safe to assume that individuals rarely report the receipt of benefits when they in fact receive none, failure to report positive benefits does not necessarily indicate that none have been received (see above). Accordingly, I use the minimum of the date at which each respondent first reported Social Security income and the respondent's reported date of retirement. Unfortunately, respondents are never asked to report their dates of retirement directly. Instead, they indicate whether or not they are retired at two-year intervals. I take the respondent's reported date of retirement to be the date at which he left his last job prior to first classifying himself as retired. When the respondent fails to report this date, I take it to be midway between successive survey years (that is, in the year prior to the survey year when he first reports himself as retired).

Second, I calculate yearly Social Security Income (SSI) for each individual by compiling his earnings history and applying the benefit formula in effect during the year when he first began receiving benefits. Fortunately, the Social Security Administration has provided matching administrative records on official earnings histories through 1975; the administration uses these same data to calculate benefits in practice. These records are, of course, incomplete for individuals who began to receive benefits after 1975. In these cases, I use survey data on reported earnings after 1975 to complete the records. Survey data are available only through 1979, but this turned out to be immaterial: according to the criterion described above, no individual who reports an expected benefit in either 1971 or 1973 actually began to receive Social Security benefits after 1979.

As described in the previous section, part of my objective here is to relate forecast errors to available information in order to identify the kinds of information that individuals either ignore or process incorrectly. I consider two dozen informational variables, which I group into three distinct categories.

The first category contains variables that measure other reported expectations. The inclusion of these variables allows me to determine whether or not individuals have internally consistent expectations in the sense that they base all expectations on the same set of information. By including lagged expectations, I can test the hypothesis that individuals have good memories in the sense that they never ignore information they employed at some prior point in time. Definitions of specific variables follow.

ERET: expected date of retirement.

EOI: expected retirement income, other than Social Security.

LESS: expected Social Security income, reported in the preceding survey wave.

LERET: expected date of retirement, reported in the preceding survey wave.

LEOI: expected income other than Social Security, reported in the preceding survey wave.

Data on expectations is, of course, incomplete—many individuals who report expected Social Security benefits do not, for example, report an expected date of retirement. Accordingly, I also use dummy variables, which equal one if the individual reports the associated expectation, and zero otherwise. I refer to the dummies corresponding to five of the expectational variables listed above as DRET, DOI, LDSS, LDRET, and LDOI, respectively.

The second category includes a single variable, which is the individual's current Social Security entitlement, CSS, defined as the level of benefits he would receive under current law if he retired immediately. CSS is, theoretically, part of each individual's information set, in that it depends only on his own past earnings history and on current law (which is public information). By including CSS, it is possible to determine the extent to which individuals ignore information related to existing statutes.

The third and final category includes various demographic variables and other household characteristics that might be useful in predicting future Social Security benefits. The list of variables includes:

MAR: a dummy variable, indicating whether or not the respondent is married (1 = married, 0 = other).

DIV: a dummy variable, indicating whether or not the respondent is divorced (1 = divorced, 0 = other).

WID: a dummy variable, indicating whether or not the respondent is a widow or widower (1 = widow or widower, 0 = other).

AGE: the respondent's age.

SAGE: the respondent's spouse's age.

ED: the respondent's level of educational attainment (measured in number of years).

SED: the respondent's spouse's level of educational attainment.

W: the household's net wealth (including financial assets, businesses, and real property).

GH: a dummy variable, indicating whether or not the respondent reports his health as being better than average for his age (1 = better, 0 = other)

PH: a dummy variable, indicating whether or not the respondent reports his health as being worse than average for his age (1 = worse, 0 = other).

KIDS: number of children.

COMPRET: a dummy variable, indicating whether or not the respondent's employer maintains a compulsory retirement age (1 = compulsory retirement, 0 = no compulsory retirement).

MOVE: a dummy variable, indicating whether or not the respondent has moved within the past two years.

Before moving on to analysis of the data, it is important to discuss two potential problems. The first concerns sample selection biases. For the regression results later in this paper, I drop observations from the analysis for four reasons: the respondent fails to report expected Social Security benefits; reported expectations are obviously nonsensical; data on net wealth are inadequate; or the household disappeared from the RHS prior to receiving Social Security benefits. Note that the first three items all reflect household characteristics that are known when the respondent makes his forecast. According to theory, these factors should therefore be uncorrelated with the forecast error; dropping these observations should not bias the regression results. The fourth item (subsequent attrition) does reflect events occurring after the forecast was made, and therefore it may well be correlated with the forecast error. Nevertheless, this seems relatively unlikely. Attrition occurs primarily because of death or because the respondent has moved. Death is, of course, highly correlated with realized Social Security benefits in the trivial sense that an individual who dies prior to retirement receives nothing. However, I strongly suspect that individuals report a conditional (on survival) expectation (that is, the respondent thinks, if I live until retirement, what will I get?). If so, no sample selection bias arises. When attrition occurs for other reasons, the same argument cannot be made. However, the RHS did successfully locate many respondents after they had moved. Consequently, the variable MOVE should give some indication as to whether the resulting sample selection bias is significant. As we shall see, the evidence suggests that it is not.

The second problem concerns the nonindependence of realizations. In a short panel such as the RHS, forecast errors are probably correlated across observations due to "macro" events. Suppose, for example, that subsequent to the date at which forecasts are recorded, Congress unexpectedly raises Social Security benefits by 20 percent. Then we would presumably discover that, on average, forecast errors are significantly positive. We should not construe this as contradictory to theory, since forecasts may indeed be unbiased given the *ex ante* distribution of macro events.

Because the 1970s witnessed several large and potentially unexpected real increases in Social Security benefits, this problem is potentially severe. I am particularly concerned about the 20 percent increase in benefits enacted in September 1972 and the double indexing for inflation that caused real benefit levels to rise substantially between 1975 and 1977. However, these were for the most part across-the-board increases in benefit levels. As a result, they probably affected little more than scale. To put it another way, it would not be surprising to find $\beta > 1$ in estimates of equation (2), and this should not be construed as contrary to theory. Indeed, through estimates of β we can hope to discern the extent to which these legislative changes were actually anticipated. However, we would still expect to find $\alpha = \gamma = 0$ under the hypothesis that the theory is accurate.

This last remark is somewhat debatable. Legislative changes during the 1970s did alter individuals' budget constraints (see Hurd and Boskin [1981] for an example). Presumably, this had behavioral consequences. To the extent that different types of individuals had systematically different behavioral responses to changes in their budget constraints, then the corresponding characteristics would, *ex post,* be correlated with forecast errors, even if the theory were valid. In the absence of more extensive longitudinal data, little can be done about this problem. The reader should bear this qualification in mind when evaluating the evidence.

A Comparison of Forecasts and Realizations

It is possible to learn a great deal about the raw data by tabulating simple summary statistics. I devote the current section to this task; the next two sections contain regression results.

In Tables 11.1 and 11.2 I provide a general picture of expectations and realizations, broken down by several different respondent categories, including married men, widows, widowers, single men, single women, wealthy married men, and highly educated married men.[3] I report the total number of observations not yet receiving Social Security, the fraction of these observations reporting expected Social Security benefits, the average expectation along with its standard error, the average realization for those reporting an expectation along with its standard error, the relative mean forecast error ($= (\overline{SSI} - \overline{ESS})/\overline{ESS}$, where bars denote means), the correlation between expectations and realizations, and the mean square forecast error (MSE).

Consider first the response rates to questions about expected benefits. Since respondents may fail to report expectations for a variety of reasons, we should not attach too much importance to any particular rate. However, since the quality of an individual's information almost certainly affects the likelihood that he will report an expectation, relative response rates may be informative. The overall rate was 44 percent in 1971 and 42 percent in 1973. Since the average individual is closer to his date of realization in 1973 than in 1971, this is somewhat surprising—we would expect information to improve, and hence reporting to rise, as individuals approach retirement.

A comparison of response rates across population subgroups reveals that in 1971, single women and widows were least likely to report expected benefits. Yet in 1973, these subgroups were the most likely to respond. We might conclude that the evidence on response rates does not establish a consistent pattern of intergroup differences, but it is also possible that women become substantially more serious about planning for retirement as it approaches. Single men and widowers have relatively high response rates, and these rates change very little between 1971 and 1973 (a slight decrease for single men and no change for widowers). In contrast, response rates for married men decline substantially over the two-year interval. This phenomenon—which is confined to married men (the aggregate response rate declines simply because married men dominate the sample)—is rather puzzling. Note also that highly

TABLE 11.1
SOCIAL SECURITY FORECASTS AND REALIZATIONS, 1971: SELECTED SUBGROUPS

Population subgroup	Total number of observations	Fraction reporting an expectation	Mean expectation (standard error)	Mean realization (standard error)	Relative mean forecast error	Correlation coefficient	MSE/10^6
Married men	3573	0.45	2316 (947)	2534 (1031)	0.094	0.42	1.20
Widows	682	0.42	1425 (487)	1649 (732)	0.158	0.56	0.42
Widowers	155	0.46	1732 (484)	1989 (692)	0.148	0.33	0.56
Single women	197	0.35	1630 (611)	1875 (663)	0.151	0.75	0.27
Single men	132	0.48	1494 (516)	1713 (576)	0.147	0.57	0.31
Wealthy married men	2268	0.47	2407 (987)	2661 (1039)	0.106	0.39	1.32
Highly educated married men	1671	0.47	2458 (1002)	2707 (1051)	0.101	0.35	1.43
Total	4739	0.44	2127 (931)	2349 (1023)	0.104	0.50	1.01

TABLE 11.2

SOCIAL SECURITY FORECASTS AND REALIZATIONS, 1973: SELECTED SUBGROUPS

Population subgroup	Total number of observations	Fraction reporting an expectation	Mean expectation (standard error)	Mean realization (standard error)	Relative mean forecast error	Correlation coefficient	$MSE/10^6$
Married men	1989	0.39	2363 (1227)	2519 (1029)	0.071	0.37	1.67
Widows	414	0.52	1653 (764)	1738 (674)	0.051	0.31	0.73
Widowers	96	0.46	1865 (823)	2158 (673)	0.157	0.19	1.01
Single women	110	0.50	1916 (745)	2045 (600)	0.068	0.49	0.49
Single men	73	0.45	1712 (757)	1772 (795)	0.035	0.31	0.83
Wealthy married men	1274	0.39	2484 (1237)	2619 (1056)	0.055	0.38	1.68
Highly educated married men	965	0.41	2392 (1230)	2651 (1052)	0.108	0.36	1.75
Total	2682	0.42	2159 (1144)	2310 (989)	0.070	0.41	1.38

educated married men are slightly more likely to report expectation than those who are less well educated. Although wealth is also positively related to the response rate in 1971, this difference disappears by 1973.

I turn next to the relative mean forecast errors. The data indicate that in 1971, the average forecast was about 10 percent lower than the average realization. In 1973, it was about 7 percent lower. At this level, the data are consistent with the view that at least some of the statutory benefit increases during this period were unanticipated. Note, however, that the mean error was less than the real increase in benefit levels, so these changes were apparently not fully unanticipated (Boskin [1987] reports that the real benefit increase in 1972 was 14.1 percent). Furthermore, we shall see that further disaggregation casts doubt on the view that the mean forecast error is attributable to unexpected statutory changes.

A further point about the overall average forecast error deserves mention. In conducting regression analysis, I also calculated averages for several other variables, including current Social Security entitlement (CSS). Astonishingly, in 1973 the mean value of expected Social Security benefits differed from the mean value of current Social Security entitlement by only 40 cents. Although this may be largely coincidence, it also raises the possibility that, once individuals have reached retirement age (recall that respondents were between 62 and 67 years old in 1973), they form expectations by observing the experiences of similarly situated acquaintances who, unlike the respondent, choose to retire and receive their current entitlements.

Differences between subgroups are apparent. In 1971, married men had the smallest relative mean forecast error. Widows and single women were, on average, furthest off; their expectations tended to be very conservative. In 1973, widowers appeared to be the most conservative, followed by married men (more on this later in the section). The average forecast for single men was quite close to the average realization. Once again, there appears to be no clear relationship with either education or wealth; if anything, the data indicate that the forecasts of educated individuals tend to be further off than those of uneducated individuals.

In the second-to-last columns of Tables 11.1 and 11.2, I report the correlation coefficient between expectations and realizations. Note that in 1971 this correlation is by far the highest for single women; widows and single men tie for second by this criterion, and widowers bring up the rear. A similar pattern is evident in 1973, although married men improved their performance relative to other groups. (Note that the correlations were generally lower in 1973—more on this below.) Mean squared errors (the final columns of Tables 11.1 and 11.2) also suggest that, despite their conservatism, women tend to make the most accurate forecasts and that married men tend to make the least accurate forecasts.

I can only speculate as to the causes of this pattern. Unmarried women (especially widows) may depend more heavily on Social Security benefits than other groups, and they may therefore have more of a stake in acquiring accurate information. In contrast, couples may have greater access to other resources and may therefore spend less time thinking about Social Security benefits. This explanation seems plausible, but it is apparently contradicted by the fact that the expectations of relatively poor married men are not systematically better than those of the relatively wealthy, despite the fact that the poor undoubtedly depend on Social Security to a greater extent. Conceivably, income could be correlated with ability and ability with accuracy; this might offset any correlation arising from a diminished stake in Social Security.

The data in Tables 11.1 and 11.2 also allow us to draw some tentative conclusions concerning Properties 1–4. I will take them in order. The data for 1971 are superficially consistent with Property 1 (for each subgroup, the variance of expectations is smaller than the variance of realizations). However, there are two reasons to question this evidence. First, as mentioned above, the average realization exceeds the average expectation by 10 percent. Assuming that this is attributable to some macro event that increased benefits proportionally across the board, we should adjust for scale by inflating the standard deviation of expectations by 10 percent, in which case the data appear inconsistent with Property 1. Second, the rather small differences between the standard errors of expectations and realizations suggest that relatively little new information became available between 1971 and retirement. The opposite conclusion is suggested by the rather low correlations between expectations and realizations. Note finally that the data for 1973 directly contradict Property 1.

Although the evidence seems contradictory to theory, strong inferences may be premature. In view of the fact that actual income is reported with a high level of noise (see data section above), it seems likely that expectations are also measured with error. In particular, respondents may report "ballpark figures" in surveys but use a more precise forecast for planning purposes. Measurement error could easily account for the apparent failure of Property 1. I will return to this issue later.

Next, note that the standard deviations of reported expectations are substantially higher in 1973 than in 1971. This is strongly consistent with Property 2 and supports the view that individuals remember information they used to form expectations at previous points in time.[4] If the theory is valid, we would expect to find this pattern even in the presence of measurement error.

Properties 3 and 4 indicate that the mean squared forecast error should fall and that the correlation between forecasts and realizations should rise as individuals approach retirement. A comparison of the data from 1971 and 1973 reveals precisely the opposite pattern. The mean squared errors rise for every subgroup and the correlation coefficient falls for six of seven groups. This suggests either that individuals process information incorrectly or, contrary to my assertion in the preceding paragraph, that they ignore information they have employed at previous points in time.

In Tables 11.3 and 11.4 I provide a more disaggregated tabulation of the data for married men (other subgroups simply did not contain enough observations to permit similar calculations). In particular, I report the same set of items broken down by the date of expected retirement. Since retirement is for the most part equivalent to realization of Social Security benefits, this disaggregation facilitates a more explicit analysis of Properties 2–4. I use expected date of retirement rather than the actual date because the actual date is presumably correlated with information that became available subsequent to the survey year and that therefore may well be correlated with forecast error.

Note first that, in 1971, the fraction of individuals reporting an expectation declines monotonically with the expected date of retirement. The same pattern holds in 1973, expect for one aberration (that is, those expecting to retire in 1974 had an unusually low response rate). This finding contrasts with the longitudinal result noted above, that response rates were lower in 1973.

The relative mean forecast errors in Tables 11.3 and 11.4 merit particularly close scrutiny. Consider first the results for 1971. Recall that legislative action raised benefit levels by about 20 percent in September 1972 and that most analysts have thought of this as an unanticipated change. I have already suggested that the overall mean forecast error is at least partially consistent with this view. However, the disaggregated results are not. Note that respondents who expected to retire in 1971, prior to the benefit increase, had the largest mean forecast error, in most cases by a wide margin. Those expecting to retire in 1972, 1973, and 1974, after the benefit increase, had much smaller mean forecast errors, and the magnitudes of these errors fell well short of the real benefit increase. Forecast errors were somewhat larger for those intending to retire after 1974, but smallest of all for those who planned to continue working indefinitely.

A somewhat different pattern holds for 1973. Those expecting to retire in the current year had the smallest mean forecast error, and the magnitude of this error moved around quite a bit with the date of expected retirement thereafter. Since benefits were double indexed from 1975 to 1977, it is particularly interesting to note that the relative mean forecast error was extremely large (0.19) for those expecting to retire after 1975. Although this

TABLE 11.3

SOCIAL SECURITY FORECASTS AND REALIZATIONS, 1971: MARRIED MEN

Year expect to retire	Total number of observations	Fraction reporting an expectation	Mean expectation (standard error)	Mean realization (standard error)	Relative mean forecast error	Correlation coefficient	MSE/10⁶
1971	236	0.58	2225 (805)	2651 (1068)	0.19	0.54	1.03
1972	323	0.51	2425 (910)	2620 (1051)	0.08	0.49	1.04
1973	261	0.48	2447 (987)	2662 (971)	0.09	0.46	1.07
1974	209	0.47	2385 (892)	2611 (905)	0.09	0.35	1.10
1975	230	0.45	2381 (814)	2750 (950)	0.16	0.36	1.14
After 1975	145	0.42	2358 (806)	2746 (1074)	0.16	0.46	1.15
Never retire	1176	0.37	2388 (1097)	2507 (1049)	0.05	0.28	1.67
No date reported	993	0.50	2176 (873)	2379 (1023)	0.09	0.50	0.95
Total	3573	0.45	2316 (947)	2534 (1031)	0.09	0.42	1.20

Table 11.4

Social Security Forecasts and Realizations, 1973: Married Men

Year expect to retire	*Total number of observations*	*Fraction reporting an expectation*	*Mean expectation (standard error)*	*Mean realization (standard error)*	*Relative mean forecast error*	*Correlation coefficient*	*MSE/10^6*
1973	158	0.45	2435 (1194)	2507 (922)	0.03	0.57	1.02
1974	182	0.37	2537 (1130)	2822 (942)	0.11	0.36	1.47
1975	212	0.42	2458 (1281)	2645 (1046)	0.07	0.30	1.98
After 1975	141	0.41	2528 (1224)	3015 (1021)	0.19	0.38	1.82
Never retire	524	0.27	2364 (1226)	2478 (1067)	0.05	0.30	1.87
No date reported	772	0.45	2241 (1227)	2368 (1004)	0.06	0.35	1.65
Total	1989	0.39	2353 (1227)	2519 (1029)	0.07	0.37	1.67

suggests that the windfall was unanticipated, the real gains from double indexing were insufficient to account for the magnitude of the forecast error. In addition, this inference is contradicted by the fact that those planning never to retire had relatively accurate expectations.

We might object that expected dates of retirement may differ substantially from actual realizations. If, for example, those expecting to retire in 1971 actually worked on average for several more years, we would not necessarily expect this group to exhibit a systematically lower mean forecast error, even if the 1972 legislation was unanticipated. In practice, the correspondence between expected and actual dates of retirement is quite close. Analysis of the data reveals that the expected date of retirement was always the modal realization. More specifically, in 1971 approximately 40 percent of those who expected to retire in the current year actually did so, whereas only 10 percent of those expecting to retire in 1972 actually retired in 1971 (see Bernheim [1987b] for more details). Accordingly, under the view that the 1972 legislation was indeed unanticipated, we would be hard pressed to account for the apparent differences between subgroups.

Taken together, the evidence contradicts the hypothesis that the overall mean forecast errors in 1971 and 1973 were attributable to unanticipated reforms. Individuals do not appear to form systematically less accurate forecasts during periods of legislative change.

Consider next the pattern of standard deviations on reported expectations. Property 2 suggests that these should rise as individuals age. The evidence from Tables 11.3 and 11.4 is mixed; the standard deviation does not move monotonically with expected date of retirement. This contrasts with the rather strong evidence in favor of Property 2 arising from a pure longitudinal comparison (see above).

Turn finally to correlations and mean squared errors. Note that in 1971 the correlation between forecasts and realizations declined almost monotonically with expected date of retirement (there is a significant departure from monotonicity for the group intending to retire after 1975), while the mean squared error rose monotonically. These results are supportive of Properties 3 and 4. The general pattern is basically the same, although perhaps somewhat weaker in 1973.

Tables 11.3 and 11.4 also jointly facilitate more refined longitudinal comparisons. For those who expected to retire in any given year (for example, 1974): the standard error of forecasts rises between 1971 and 1973; with only one exception, the mean squared forecast error rises; and the correlation between forecasts and realizations rises for some groups and falls for others. The first observation is consistent with Property 2; the second is inconsistent with Property 3; and the third is weakly inconsistent with Property 4. Thus, disaggregation does not alter the apparent implications of longitudinal comparisons.

One final observation of interest is that the relationship between expected and realized Social Security benefits for those who fail to report an expected date of retirement seems quite similar to the relationship for those who do report such a date. I find this result somewhat surprising, in that an accurate forecast of a person's retirement date seems essential when he or she is formulating an expectation about future Social Security benefits.

I close this section by addressing a somewhat different issue. Part of the motivation for studying expectations is to determine whether faulty expectations could be accountable for financial hardship. In the case of Social Security benefits, hardship could arise if individuals tended to be overly optimistic—those anticipating large benefits may make inadequate private provisions. In Table 11.5 I compute the fraction of each subsample for which expected benefits exceeded actual benefits by more than 5, 10, 25, 50, and 100 percent. According to these data, approximately one in five individuals believes that benefits will exceed their actual levels by more than 25 percent; approximately one in eight individuals expects over 50 percent more than they receive; and one in fourteen individuals receive less than half of what they expected. Single women are the most conservative by this criterion. Except at the extreme tail of the distribution, married men are the least conservative, regardless of wealth or educational attainment.

In interpreting these numbers, we should bear in mind the possibility raised earlier, that individuals may report expectations with substantial noise. If so, Table 11.5 may substantially exaggerate the extent of excessive optimism.

Because this section has touched on a large number of detailed points, it is useful to summarize the major findings. Women's forecasts tend to be relatively conservative, but also the most accurate of any subgroup. Married men tend to form the least conservative and least accurate expectations. Education and wealth appear to have very little to do with the quality of forecasts. Surprisingly, expectations are not systematically less accurate during periods of significant legislative changes. And although many individuals are overly optimistic, this does not appear to be an especially pernicious problem for the vast majority of households.

Evidence on the theory of expectations is mixed. Property 1 is generally contradicted by the data, but this is consistent with the presence of measurement error. Property 2 is weakly contradicted by cross-sectional evidence but supported by longitudinal evidence. The reverse is true of Properties 3 and 4. Overall, the evidence suggests some incomplete degree of coherence with the theory.

TABLE 11.5

OVERLY OPTIMISTIC HOUSEHOLDS: SELECTED SUBGROUPS

Population subgroup	Survey year	FRACTION OF SAMPLE IN WHICH FORECAST EXCEEDED REALIZATION BY MORE THAN				
		5%	10%	25%	50%	100%
Married men	1971	0.30	0.27	0.20	0.12	0.06
	1973	0.43	0.36	0.22	0.14	0.07
Widows	1971	0.23	0.20	0.15	0.10	0.08
	1973	0.33	0.27	0.19	0.10	0.07
Widowers	1971	0.22	0.21	0.15	0.08	0.04
	1973	0.34	0.23	0.07	0.05	0.02
Single women	1971	0.12	0.12	0.09	0.07	0.01
	1973	0.36	0.26	0.09	0.05	0.02
Single men	1971	0.19	0.19	0.11	0.08	0.05
	1973	0.36	0.27	0.21	0.15	0.09
Wealthy married men	1971	0.28	0.25	0.19	0.12	0.06
	1973	0.44	0.36	0.21	0.14	0.07
Highly educated married men	1971	0.29	0.26	0.18	0.11	0.06
	1973	0.40	0.36	0.21	0.13	0.06
Total	1971	0.28	0.25	0.18	0.11	0.06
	1973	0.40	0.33	0.20	0.13	0.07

REGRESSION ANALYSIS

In this section I present estimates of equation (2) based upon the data and variables described above. I provide separate results for 1971 and 1973. The 1971 sample contained 1,949 observations and the 1973 sample included 942 observations.

I will begin with tests of the comparatively weak hypothesis that individuals form unbiased (conditional on whatever information they do use) though possibly inefficient expectations. That is, I estimate equation (2) omitting all informational variables, ω_i. For 1971, I obtain:

$$\text{SSI}_i = 1212 + 0.560\ \text{ESS}_i + \epsilon_i$$
$$\quad\ (44.8)\quad (0.020)$$

$$\sigma_\epsilon^2 = 7.05 \times 10^5$$

Analysis of data for 1973 yields:

$$SSI_i = 1369 + 0.426 \ ESS_i + \epsilon_i$$
$$(56.6) \quad (0.024)$$

$$\sigma_\epsilon^2 = 7.20 \times 10^5$$

In both cases, the intercept is large and estimated precisely, whereas the slope coefficient is significantly less than unity. The point estimates imply that, if an individual responds to information by raising his expected benefits one dollar, his realization will, on average, rise by roughly 50 cents. This qualitative pattern persists when other informational variables are added.

Table 11.6 contains estimates of equation (2) where ω_i includes the full complement of informational variables described in the section on data, above. In 1971 a large number of informational variables have statistically significant coefficients. These include the respondent's expectation of other income (EOI), current Social Security entitlement (CSS), age (AGE and SAGE), education (ED and SED), poor health (PH), number of children (KIDS), and compulsory retirement (COMPRET). Marital status (MAR, DIV, WID) does not appear to matter, nor does mobility (MOVE). Wealth (W) is marginally significant.

In 1973, fewer informational variables have statistically significant coefficients. As before, CSS plays an important explanatory role. Note that the 1973 regressions also include lagged expectations (this was not possible in 1971 due to data quality). LESS, the lagged value of Social Security benefits, appears with a very significant coefficient, which suggests that individuals may have poor memories. Aside from CSS and LESS, only ED enters significantly.

These results strongly contradict the theory of expectations outlined at the beginning of this paper. Unfortunately, interpretation of the coefficients is problematic. Since the coefficient of ESS is in general rather small, other variables are probably explaining the magnitude of actual benefits, rather than the forecast error.

It would, however, be premature to reject the theory on the basis of this evidence alone. As previously mentioned, there is some indication that reported expectations are rather noisy. Measurement error could account for the positive intercept and small slope coefficient. Other informational variables (especially CSS and LESS) might then help to filter out the noise, in which case they would appear with spuriously significant coefficients. These observations motivate the following analysis.

TABLE 11.6

REGRESSIONS OF REALIZATIONS ON FORECASTS

Variable	1971	1973	Variable	1971	1973
Intercept	8708	1374	DIV	5.26	41.7
	(767)	(684)		(89.3)	(86.5)
ESS	0.286	0.040	WID	22.6	50.2
	(0.019)	(0.018)		(74.1)	(71.3)
ERET	13.5	62.8	AGE	−133	−19.7
	(11.1)	(14.2)		(12.7)	(11.2)
DRET	−930	−4670	SAGE	11.9	0.476
	(817)	(1067)		(1.99)	(2.17)
EOI/100	1.25	0.763	ED	6.54	5.15
	(0.46)	(0.613)		(2.14)	(2.24)
DOI	−11.4	21.1	SED	−4.57	2.29
	(50.4)	(63.4)		(2.52)	(3.07)
LESS		0.129	W/10^4	4.03	1.12
		(0.029)		(2.17)	(2.84)
LDSS		−331	GH	8.05	−10.2
		(68.3)		(33.2)	(36.3)
LERET		18.2	PH	−199	2.46
		(14.3)		(49.8)	(59.1)
LDRET		−1310	KIDS	−18.6	−7.71
		(1055)		(7.78)	(7.93)
LEOI/100		0.571	COMPRET	203	71.1
		(0.614)		(56.5)	(41.6)
LDOI		37.2	MOVE	−40.4	−47.4
		(50.4)		(49.0)	(53.4)
CSS	0.495	0.774	$\sigma^2/10^5$	4.50	2.60
	(0.021)	(0.025)			
MAR	−148	242			
	(131)	(135)			

A TREATMENT OF MEASUREMENT ERROR

In this section, I devote serious attention to the possibility that expected benefits are measured with error. I adopt two separate estimation strategies. The first is to regress forecast errors on information; the second is to re-estimate the regressions of the preceding section, instrumenting for expected benefits. I devote a separate subsection to each of these approaches. The section closes with an analysis of "true" forecast errors.

Forecast Error Regressions

For motivation, I return to the analysis of the second section. Note that we can rewrite equation (1) as

$$X - X_t^e = \epsilon_t \qquad (3)$$

where ϵ_t is uncorrelated with X_t^e. Suppose we observe X_t^e with error. In particular, survey responses measure $\tilde{X}_t^e$, where

$$\tilde{X}_t^e = X_t^e + \mu_t \qquad (4)$$

and where X_t^e and μ_t are uncorrelated. Substituting (4) into (3), we obtain

$$X - \tilde{X}_t^e = \epsilon_t - \mu_t. \qquad (5)$$

By hypothesis ϵ_t is uncorrelated with available information. It is also plausible to assume that μ_t is unrelated to other contemporaneous variables, including the measurement error on these variables. Accordingly, equation (5) suggests the following regression framework:

$$X_i - \tilde{X}_{it}^e = \alpha + \omega_{it}\gamma + (\epsilon_{it} - \mu_{it}). \qquad (6)$$

Theory predicts that $\alpha = \gamma = 0$. Estimates of (6) are not only robust with respect to measurement error but also easily interpretable: from the coefficients γ, we can infer the manner in which individuals misuse information when constructing forecasts.

Estimates of equation (6) are presented in Table 11.7. I begin with the results for 1971. Note first that the intercept is usually statistically significant, which, strictly speaking, is contrary to theory. However, neither expected date of retirement nor expected other income appears with a significant coefficient. This supports the hypothesis that individuals employ an internally consistent set of information when formulating expectations.

CSS continues to play an important explanatory role, which strongly suggests that individuals ignore much of the information embodied in current statutes. The coefficient of CSS is, however, substantially smaller than in the previous regression analysis, which is consistent with the view that CSS was, in part, filtering the noise in ESS.

Married individuals tend to make high forecasts relative to realizations—this conclusion is consistent with the simple tabulations in the data section. The other marital status dummies are insignificant.

AGE and SAGE both appear significantly. The negative coefficient on

TABLE 11.7 _____

FORECAST ERROR REGRESSIONS

Variable	1971	1973	Variable	1971	1973
Intercept	3313	−622	WID	16.2	−2.71
	(1004)	(1412)		(98.6)	(147)
ERET	3.68	58.0	AGE	−55.7	4.93
	(14.8)	(29.4)		(16.6)	(23.2)
DRET	−240	−4226	SAGE	10.3	−1.54
	(1087)	(2205)		(2.65)	(4.49)
EOI/100	−1.05	−1.40	ED	4.41	3.03
	(0.612)	(1.26)		(2.85)	(4.63)
DOI	−46.1	53.7	SED	−9.34	−7.03
	(67.0)	(131)		(3.34)	(6.32)
LESS		0.008	W/10^4	9.75	10.7
		(0.061)		(3.18)	(5.86)
LDSS		−238	GH	−14.6	−63.7
		(141)		(44.2)	(74.9)
LERET		−4.35	PH	−118	184
		(29.4)		(66.2)	(122)
LDRET		193	KIDS	−9.82	−22.0
		(2179)		(10.3)	(16.4)
LEOI/100		−0.509	COMPRET	113	81.2
		(1.27)		(75.1)	(86.0)
LDOI		120	MOVE	−39.5	27.2
		(104)		(65.1)	(110)
CSS	0.287	0.262	$\sigma^2/10^5$	7.96	11.01
	(0.027)	(0.047)			
MAR	−434	188			
	(174)	(280)			
DIV	22.5	−24.0			
	(119)	(179)			

AGE implies that older individuals tend to make high forecasts relative to realizations. Since the overall mean of expected benefits is lower than the mean realization, this implies that individuals tend to make more accurate forecasts as they approach retirement. Although this accords with intuition, note that SAGE has the opposite effect.

SED comes in significantly negative. This implies that men with highly educated spouses tend to make less conservative and more accurate forecasts of benefits. In contrast, the coefficient of ED is statistically insignificant.

Wealth enters with a significantly positive coefficient, which implies that wealthier individuals tend to be more pessimistic relative to realizations—in this sample, they are on average further off the mark. This result is consistent with the view that poorer individuals have a greater stake in finding out about their Social Security benefits. Finally, GH, PH, COMPRET, and MOVE do not enter with a significant coefficient.

Turn next to the results for 1973. Surprisingly, ERET appears with a significant coefficient, which suggests that individuals may not form expectations on the basis of an internally consistent set of information. However, note also that the coefficient of LESS falls to zero. This is consistent with the view that the coefficient of LESS was significant in the regression analysis only because ESS was measured with error. Furthermore, it supports the hypothesis that individuals do not ignore information they have used in the past.

As in 1971, the coefficient of CSS is still quite significant, though once again its magnitude has declined. Note also that none of the other demographic variables or other individual characteristics enter significantly. Only the coefficient of wealth appears to be even marginally significant.

In summary, these results suggest that although individuals ignore information embodied in current statutes, they do recall the bulk of information used in the past and, for the most part, base all their expectations on the same set of information. There is mixed evidence concerning the roles of marital status, age, and education. The partial correlation between wealth and forecast errors is marginally significant. Individual characteristics seem less important in 1973 than in 1971, which is consistent with the view that individuals get serious about planning for retirement as the date of retirement becomes more imminent (the apparent role of age confirms this view). Overall, these results suggest at least a partial degree of coherence with the theoretical framework.

Instrumented Regressions

The classic remedy for measurement error is, of course, the use of instrumental variables (IV). An instrument is required that is uncorrelated with both ϵ_t and μ_t but correlated with X_t^e. Accordingly, valid instruments must be related to information that the individual actually uses to construct X_t^e. Thus, the basic expectations hypothesis must necessarily be tested jointly with the assumption that individuals use certain information (that is, information contained in the instruments) efficiently.

This approach confers two important advantages. First, it allows us to estimate β. This facilitates a more powerful test of the theory. In addition, we can also allow for the possibility that, due to the macro-events problem discussed earlier, the scales of expectations and realizations differ slightly.

Second, it allows us to separate true forecast error from measurement error. I pursue this second point later in this section.

The choice of instruments is completely arbitrary: we can employ any informational variable and perform the associated joint test. I present results based upon the plausible assumption that individuals' expectations are internally consistent (that is, all expectations are based upon the same information). Accordingly, I instrument with the concurrent expectational variables.

Again, I begin with tests of the comparatively weak hypothesis that individuals form unbiased (conditional on information contained in other forecasts and whatever other information they use) though possibly inefficient expectations. That is, I estimate equation (2) omitting all informational variables, ω_t, and instrumenting with expectational variables. For 1971, I obtain:

$$SSI_i = 122 + 1.09\ ESS_i + \epsilon_i$$
$$\quad\quad (175)\quad (0.085)$$

$$\sigma_\epsilon^2 = 9.65 \times 10^5$$

Analysis of data for 1973 yields:

$$SSI_i = -57.1 + 1.12\ ESS_i + \epsilon_i$$
$$\quad\quad (245)\quad\ (0.118)$$

$$\sigma_\epsilon^2 = 13.58 \times 10^5$$

These results are quite striking. In both cases, the intercept becomes insignificant, as predicted by theory. The slope coefficient for 1971 is 1.09, which is consistent with the observation that forecasts are, on average, about nine percent lower than realizations. The slope coefficient for 1973 is slightly larger. In both cases, the standard errors are not terribly large. These estimates strongly support the view that, after a small scale adjustment, reported expectations are unbiased estimates of realizations, conditional on the information contained in other forecasts and whatever other information individuals actually use. Results to the contrary are apparently attributable to measurement error.

It is also possible to test jointly for the correct usage of other information. Accordingly, in Table 11.8 I present regressions of realized benefits on expected benefits (instrumented), current Social Security entitlement, and various individual characteristics for 1971 and 1973. In both equations, CSS still enters significantly (in fact, ESS and CSS roughly divide up the original coefficient on ESS), although, as expected, the coefficient of CSS is lower

TABLE 11.8

INSTRUMENTED REGRESSIONS

Variable	1971	1973	Variable	1971	1973
Intercept	5938	1470	COMPRET	184	66.1
	(1305)	(974)		(62.5)	(53.2)
ESS	0.676	0.489	MOVE	−41.5	−0.06
	(0.126)	(0.193)		(54.2)	(71.0)
CSS	0.383	0.548	$\sigma^2/10^5$	5.53	4.51
	(0.043)	(0.116)			
MAR	−304	180			
	(155)	(182)			
DIV	13.6	−0.662			
	(98.9)	(115)			
WID	18.6	13.6			
	(82.1)	(95.8)			
AGE	−94.0	−25.7			
	(19.9)	(15.4)			
SAGE	11.1	−0.003			
	(2.22)	(2.85)			
ED	5.58	4.84			
	(2.45)	(3.06)			
SED	−7.27	−0.900			
	(2.95)	(4.58)			
$W/10^4$	6.81	4.75			
	(2.16)	(2.55)			
GH	−5.65	−20.6			
	(37.4)	(48.2)			
PH	−158	84.9			
	(57.3)	(87.5)			
KIDS	−13.7	−11.2			
	(8.81)	(10.7)			

than in the regression analysis. This result confirms the view that individuals ignore information embodied in current statutes. In 1971, AGE, SAGE, ED, SED, W, and PH all enter significantly, but MAR is marginal. The direction of each effect is essentially the same as in Table 11.7. In 1973, *nothing* besides ESS and CSS is statistically significant (AGE and W come closest). Once again, it appears as though individuals used information better in 1973, when they were closer to retirement, than in 1971.

As mentioned at the outset of this subsection, there are a variety of candidates for instrumental variables. The alternative employed above is not only intuitively appealing, but it also yields results that are highly consistent with the basic theory. However, I have also estimated equation (2) with other instruments. One set of estimates tested the basic expectations hypothesis jointly with the assumption that respondents make proper use of available data on demographic characteristics when formulating expectations (that is, I used variables in the third category as instruments). Once again, the results supported the view that, after a small scale adjustment, reported expectations are unbiased estimates of realizations, conditional on demographic variables and whatever other information individuals actually use. The pattern of coefficients on the informational variables corroborated the findings presented in Table 11.7. I omit a complete tabulation of the results in order to conserve space.

Equation (2) could also be estimated by using CSS as an instrument, thereby testing the basic expectations hypothesis jointly with the assumption that individuals efficiently use all of the information contained in CSS. Since the preceding evidence uniformly contradicts this assumption, it is hardly surprising that the associated results (omitted) are nonsensical.

To summarize, estimates with instrumental variables support the joint hypotheses that individuals form all of their expectations on the basis of the same information and that expectations about Social Security benefits are unbiased (conditional on whatever information is used to construct them) up to a small scale adjustment. Individuals do not, however, make efficient use of all available information. Most important, they tend to ignore information embodied in statutory entitlements. In addition, there is some evidence that forecast errors are correlated with age, education, wealth, and health.

Recovering True Forecast Errors

One of the central objectives of this study is to assess the accuracy of individuals' expectations. If expectational variables are contaminated by measurement error, then inferences based upon simple indexes of accuracy can be highly misleading. Specifically, the variance of the observed forecast error reflects both the variance of the true forecast error and the variance of the measurement error (see equation [5]).

Fortunately, it is possible to recover the variance of the true forecast errors through IV estimates, such as those presented the preceding paragraphs. I provide a detailed description of the procedure in Appendix B. In essence, the variance of the measurement error can be recovered by comparing ordinary least squares (OLS) estimates from a regression of SSI on ESS with IV estimates. The variance of the true forecast error is then computed as a residual from the variance of the IV regression error. This procedure can also be used to assess the net reduction in true forecast error that would result from incorporating new information into the forecast.

To emphasize the importance of correcting for measurement error, I begin by presenting the unadjusted variances of regression errors (Table 11.9). The first row of Table 11.9 simply provides, as a basis for comparison, the population variance of realized Social Security income for 1971 and 1973. The second row contains the variances of error terms from IV estimates (using expectational variables as instruments) of the regressions reported in the text of the subsection above (that is, SSI on an intercept and ESS). The next three rows contain the variances of error terms from IV estimates of regressions that also incorporate other informational variables. The regressions corresponding to the entries in the final row appear in Table 11.8; I omit a complete tabulation of the other regression results in order to conserve space.

If we ignore the fact that regression errors are contaminated with measurement error, then the following picture emerges. In 1971, private forecasts explained almost none of the population variance in realized benefits. In 1973, these forecasts were actually worse than simply naming the population mean—a finding that is clearly at odds with the hypothesis that individuals use information rationally. Although a significant improvement results from augmenting the information contained in ESS with CSS (current entitlements), the proper use of demographic information seems, on the whole, more important.

When we adjust the numbers in Table 11.9 for the presence of measurement error in order to obtain the variance of true forecast error, a dramatically different picture emerges (see Table 11.10). Private forecasts for 1971 now explain 56 percent of the variance in realized benefits; 1973 forecasts explain 65 percent of the variance. Note in particular that, as predicted by theory, the explanatory power of these forecasts is clearly better in 1973 than in 1971. This finding contrasts sharply with the results of simple data tabulations, which in general produce longitudinal patterns that are unfavorable to the expectations hypothesis. We now see that these negative findings are largely attributable to measurement error.

Table 11.10 also suggests that individuals make excellent though incomplete use of available information. Augmentation of forecasts with demographic information would achieve a minimal gain (less than a 5 percent reduction in residual forecast error variance) in 1971 and no gain at all in 1973. On the other hand, augmentation with information about statutory entitlements (CSS) could achieve a reduction in residual forecast error variance of between 14 and 17 percent. Thus, CSS emerges as the most important piece of information that individuals fail to incorporate fully into their forecasts.

TABLE 11.9 _____

VARIANCE OF REGRESSION ERRORS

	VARIANCE OF REGRESSION ERROR/10^5	
Independent variables	*1971*	*1973*
Intercept only	9.91	9.59
ESS	9.65	13.58
ESS and CSS	8.36	8.89
ESS and demographics	6.93	8.99
ESS, CSS, and demographics	5.53	4.51

TABLE 11.10 _____

VARIANCE OF FORECAST ERRORS

	VARIANCE OF FORECAST ERROR/10^5	
Variables used for forecast	*1971*	*1973*
Intercept only	9.91	9.59
ESS	4.34	3.34
ESS and CSS	3.70	2.77
ESS and demographics	4.14	3.49
ESS, CSS, and demographics	3.50	2.56

I close this section with one final remark. Although the existence of measurement error is fully consistent with the results of this section, there is another interpretation of the model described in equations (3) through (6). Specifically, individuals may not know the true empirical model and may form expectations, $\tilde{X}^e_t$, that are related as in equation (5) to the objective expectation, X^e_t, by some randomly distributed term, μ_t, reflecting idiosyncrasies of the individual's calculations. Under this view, a reading of my results must be adjusted slightly. Specifically, the IV estimates indicate that individuals on average form unbiased expectations. Furthermore, the calculations of this subsection apply to the variance of the forecast error for a particular individual (that is, after adjusting the mean for the idiosyncratic component), rather than to the population variance.

Concluding Remarks

The evidence in this paper indicates partial coherence with the theory of expectations outlined at the beginning. In addition, inspection of the data reveals several interesting patterns. I have already summarized these patterns in the introduction.

One pattern does, however, deserve further comment in that it has an obvious policy implication. Specifically, the bulk of the evidence indicates that individuals are simply not completely familiar with their current statutory entitlements. Presumably, the government could improve individuals' forecasts, and hence financial planning, by providing this information. Indeed, there is a precedent in the private sector. TIAA-CREF provides participants with an annual statement, which specifies the level of annuity benefits available upon immediate retirement, and with projections of benefits based upon assumptions about continued employment. Presumably, the Social Security Administration could provide each participant with similar information. If necessary, the program could be restricted to individuals over a certain age. According to my findings, most individuals would find this quite useful.

This paper leaves many important questions unanswered. In subsequent work, I plan to focus on the evolution of expectations, testing the hypothesis that expectations follow a random walk and examining the manner in which individuals revise forecasts when confronted with new information. In addition, I plan to explore the link between expectations and behavior.

Appendix A

Equation (1) can be rewritten as

$$X = X_t^e + \epsilon_t, \tag{A.1}$$

where

$$E(\epsilon_t|\Omega_t) = 0. \tag{A.2}$$

From (A.1) and (A.2), it is evident that

$$var(X) = var(X_t^e) + var(\epsilon_t). \tag{A.3}$$

Accordingly, we obtain

$$var(X) < var(X_t^e), \tag{A.4}$$

which is Property 1.

Next, note that

$$E(X_{t+1}^e|\Omega_t) = E(E(X|\Omega_{t+1})/\Omega_t)$$
$$= E(X|\Omega_t) = X_t^e, \tag{A.5}$$

from which it follows that

$$X_{t+1}^e = X_t^e + \eta_t \tag{A.6}$$

where

$$E(\eta_t|\Omega_t) = 0. \tag{A.7}$$

From (A.6) and (A.7), it is clear that

$$var(X_{t+1}^e) = var(X_t^e) + var(\eta_t), \tag{A.8}$$

which gives us

$$var(X_{t+1}^e) > var(X_t^e), \tag{A.9}$$

which is Property 2.

Further properties follow from combining equations (A.1) and (A.6). In particular, recursive substitution yields

$$\epsilon_t = \epsilon_{T-1} + \sum_{\tau=t}^{T-2} \eta_\tau. \tag{A.10}$$

Since η_t is an element of the information set Ω_{t+1}, (A.2) and (A.7) then imply that

$$var(\epsilon_t) = var(\epsilon_{T-1}) + \sum_{\tau=t}^{T-2} var(\eta_\tau). \tag{A.11}$$

Accordingly, we see that $var(X - X_t^e)$ is declining in t (Property 3).

The final property of interest concerns the correlation between forecasts and realizations, $\rho(X, X_t^e)$. Note that

$$\rho(X, X_t^e) = cov(X, X_t^e)[var(X)var(X_t^e)]^{-1/2}$$
$$= var(X_t^e)[var(X)var(X_t^e)]^{-1/2} \tag{A.12}$$
$$= [var(X_t^e)/(var(X)]^{1/2},$$

where the second equality follows from (A.1) and (A.2). Combining (A.12) with (A.9), we see that $\rho(X,X_t^e)$ is increasing in t (Property 4).

Note that equation (A.6) suggests a regression much like equation (2) and could be used as the basis for additional tests. Although I do not exploit this relationship here, I do plan to examine the evolution of expectations in future work.

APPENDIX B

Consider the forecasting equation

$$Y_i = \alpha + \beta X_i^* + \epsilon_i. \tag{B.1}$$

Let

$$X_i = X_i^* + \eta_i, \tag{B.2}$$

and suppose that $E(\epsilon_i\eta_i) = E(X_i^*\eta_i) = E(X_i^*\epsilon_i) = E(\epsilon_i) = E(\eta_i) = 0$. Suppose further that we observe X_i, rather than X_i^*. Substitution of (B.2) into (B.1) yields

$$Y_i = \alpha + \beta X_i + (\epsilon_i - \beta\eta_i). \tag{B.3}$$

Let $\xi \equiv \epsilon - \beta\eta$, so that

$$\sigma_\xi^2 = \sigma_\epsilon^2 + \beta^2 \sigma_\eta^2. \tag{B.4}$$

Now let $\hat{\beta}_{\text{OLS}}$ be the OLS estimate of β. As is well known,

$$\beta_{\text{OLS}} \equiv plim\ \hat{\beta}_{\text{OLS}} = \beta\left(\frac{\sigma_x^2 - \sigma_\eta^2}{\sigma_x^2}\right). \tag{B.5}$$

From this it follows that

$$\sigma_\eta^2 = \sigma_x^2(1 - \beta_{\text{OLS}}/\beta) \tag{B.6}$$

One obtains a consistent estimate, $\hat{\sigma}_x^2$, of σ_x^2 simply by computing the population variance of X. $\hat{\beta}_{OLS}$ is a consistent estimate of β_{OLS}. Finally, the IV estimator, $\hat{\beta}_{\text{IV}}$, is a consistent estimate of β. Thus,

$$\hat{\sigma}_\eta^2 \equiv \hat{\sigma}_x^2(1 - \hat{\beta}_{\text{OLS}}/\hat{\beta}) \tag{B.7}$$

is a consistent estimator for σ_η^2. One obtains a consistent estimate, $\hat{\sigma}_\xi^2$, of σ_ξ^2 from the IV regression. From (B.4), it is then clear that

$$\hat{\sigma}_\epsilon^2 = \hat{\sigma}_\xi^2 - \hat{\beta}_{IV}^2 \sigma_\eta^2 \qquad\qquad (B.8)$$

is a consistent estimator for the true forecast error, σ_ϵ^2.

Next suppose that we augment the original forecast with some vector of informational variables, Z_i, so that

$$Y_i = a + bX_i^* + Z_i c + e_i \qquad\qquad (B.9)$$

and

$$Y_i = a + bX_i + Z_i c + (e - b\eta_i). \qquad\qquad (B.10)$$

Let $s_i \equiv e_i - b\eta_i$, so that

$$\sigma_s^2 = \sigma_e^2 + b^2\sigma_\eta^2 \qquad\qquad (B.11)$$

IV estimation of (B.10) yields consistent estimates, $\hat{\sigma}_s^2$ and $\hat{b}_{IV}$, of σ_s^2 and b. We have already derived a consistent estimator, $\hat{\sigma}_\eta^2$, of σ_η^2. Thus,

$$\hat{\sigma}_e^2 \equiv \hat{\sigma}_s^2 - \hat{b}_{IV}^2 \hat{\sigma}_\eta^2 \qquad\qquad (B.12)$$

is a consistent estimator for the variance of the error term from the augmented forecast.

DISCUSSION

David A. Wise

In his paper, Douglas Bernheim evaluates the extent to which individual forecasts of future Social Security benefits are accurate. He emphasizes the importance of rational expectations in traditional life-cycle theory analysis and points out that this assumption is almost never tested. Indeed, to my knowledge, this is the first serious investigation of this basic assumption. The implicit assumption that individuals know the future is in fact implicit in a great deal of empirical analysis, not only in life-cycle theory. Models of retirement, for example, are often based on the presumption of a "lifetime" budget constraint, based on knowledge not only of future Social Security benefits but of future wage rates and firm pension benefits as well. The provisions of private pension plans typically imply large discontinuous increases or decreases in the accrual of pension wealth at particular ages—for example, at the age of early retirement (see Kotlikoff and Wise 1985, 1987; Bulow 1979; Lazear 1981, 1983). There is often a large reward for working until the age of early retirement and a large penalty for working past the age of normal retirement, typically at age 65. Because Social Security benefits are not actuarially increased after age 65, there is typically a loss in Social Security wealth for working past that age. It is unclear whether individuals understand the Social Security provision. The private pension provisions that create retirement incentives are often complex, and the extent to which they are understood by employees is not apparent. It is likely that many individuals are unaware of the effect of an additional year's work on Social Security and private pension benefits. Yet the assumption of complete internalization of the provisions of the plans is a key assumption of the estimation procedure. Uncertainty about the future is rarely incorporated in the analysis of retirement decisions.[5] The analysis by Bernheim is an important beginning of systematic investigation of the relationship between expectations about the future and actual realizations.

Bernheim structures the analysis in a way that can be interpreted as testing two hypotheses: (1) that individual predictions are unbiased, and (2) that as individuals age their knowledge of future Social Security benefits increases so that their predictions explain more of the actual variance in benefits, the forecast variance increases, and the residual variance declines. In particular, he finds that expectations are roughly "unbiased" and, to the extent that they are inaccurate, tend to be conservative. The formal tests of the hypotheses, however, are possibly not the most interesting of his findings.

An important finding is that better information on current Social Security benefits could substantially improve individuals' forecasts of their future benefits. This suggests that periodic statements from the Social Security Administration presenting current accrued benefits, for example, could significantly aid in the evaluation of likely future benefits.

An apparent puzzle in the results is that predictions about future benefits seem to be relatively unbiased, even when predictions were made before substantial increases in Social Security benefits in the early 1970s. It might be argued that these increases should have been completely unexpected.[6]

Widows are among the groups that make the most accurate and conservative predictions about future benefits. They also make up a large proportion of the poor elderly. Indeed, the prior couples of poor widows apparently saved much less, given earnings, than the prior couples of nonpoor widows (see Hurd and Wise, forthcoming). It would be interesting to know whether poor widows are more likely to come from prior couples that overestimated Social Security benefits. Did they not save because they overestimated the future value of Social Security benefits?

More generally, it will be important to know more about the implications of forecast errors. Could it be shown, for example, that those who overpredict Social Security benefits save less in other forms? In other words, can it be shown that incorrect forecasts are associated with unforeseen and low levels of wealth among the elderly?

On the more technical side, this is a case where some experimentation with functional form may be informative. The assumption in this analysis is that the relationship between expectations and realizations is linear. It might be, however, that the extent to which predictions are too high or too low depends on the level of expected benefits. The nonlinearities in the Social Security benefit formula might motivate exploration of this possibility.

Finally, Bernheim's exploration of the effect of noise in the forecasts is sensible and shows that taking account of noise has important implications for interpretation of the results. It seems to me, however, that the proper interpretation of noise in predictions of this sort remains ambiguous. The assumption must be, for example, that individuals could make better predictions if they tried harder, or that they are not telling all that they know, or that they do not take the time when responding to the survey questions to make estimates to the nearest dollar instead of to the nearest thousand dollars. What should the analyst consider to be the true prediction? What should be filtered out? The IV estimates are intended to address this issue, but it is not clear to me that they automatically remove the noise that should be removed. That remains a matter of interpretation.

In short, this is a careful analysis of an important issue. An important result is that better information from the Social Security Administration could significantly improve individual forecasts of Social Security benefits. I know that this is only one of a series of papers on realizations versus expectations that Bernheim has planned for the future. I trust that his work will encourage others to undertake such analyses as well.

NOTES

1. I abstract from the possibility that T is itself uncertain. I take this issue up in Bernheim (1987b).

2. Since the variance of ϵ_{it} should, according to theory, depend on t, heteroscedasticity is a potential problem. I have ignored this issue throughout. Calculated standard errors may therefore be somewhat inaccurate.

3. The RHS does not include married women as a separate respondent category. When surveying couples, the RHS always classifies the husband as "respondent" and the wife as his spouse. In this study, data on Social Security benefits for married men include their spouse's benefits. For purposes of categorization, I take the dividing lines for high wealth and high education to be $20,000 and tenth grade, respectively; these figures correspond roughly to medians.

4. Of course, the 1973 sample is not identical to the 1971 sample, so caution is warranted. However, the average respondent in 1973 is 1.6 years older than the average respondent in 1971 and is accordingly more advanced in the life cycle. It is therefore appropriate to evaluate Properties 2–4 by comparing data from 1971 and 1973.

5. Recent work by Rust (forthcoming) is an exception.

6. A key aspect of the analysis by Burtless (1986) of the effect of Social Security benefits on retirement, for example, is that these increases were unforeseen.

REFERENCES

Aiginger, Karl. 1979. "Empirische Information zur Bildung von Erwartungen." *Ifo-Studien* 25:83–135.

Bernheim, B. D. 1987a. "Dissaving After Retirement: Testing the Pure Life Cycle Hypothesis." In Z. Bodie, J. Shoven, and D. Wise, eds., *Pensions and Retirement in the United States*. National Bureau of Economic Research Conference Volume. Chicago: University of Chicago Press.

———. 1987b. "The Timing of Retirement: An Empirical Study of Expectations and Realizations." Mimeo, Stanford University.

Boskin, Michael. 1987. *Too Many Promises: The Uncertain Future of Social Security*. Homewood, Ill.: Dow Jones-Irwin.

Bulow, Jeremy. 1979. "Analysis of Pension Funding Under ERISA." Working Paper no. 402, National Bureau of Economic Research, Cambridge, Mass.

Burtless, Gary. 1986. "Social Security, Unanticipated Benefit Increases, and the Timing of Retirement." *Review of Economic Studies* 53:781–805.

Curtin, Richard T. 1982. "Determinants of Price Expectations: Evidence from a

Panel Study." In M. Laumer and M. Ziegler, eds., *International Research on Business Cycle Surveys*. Aldershot, England: Gower.

Feldstein, Martin S. 1974. "Social Security, Induced Retirement, and Aggregate Capital Accumulation." *Journal of Political Economy* 82:905–26.

Gramlich, Edward M. 1983. "Models of Inflation Expectation Formation: A Comparison of Household and Economist Forecasts." *Journal of Money, Credit, and Banking* 11:155–73.

Huizinga, John. 1980. "Real Wages, Employment, and Expectations." Ph.D. diss., MIT.

Hurd, Michael, and Michael Boskin. 1981. "The Effect of Social Security on Retirement in the Early 1970s." Working Paper no. 659, National Bureau of Economic Research, Cambridge, Mass.

Hurd, Michael, and David A. Wise. Forthcoming. "The Wealth and Poverty of Widows: Assets Before and After the Husband's Death." In David Wise, ed., *Economics of Aging*. Chicago: University of Chicago Press.

Kotlikoff, Laurence J., and David A. Wise. 1985. "Labor Compensation and the Structure of Private Pension Plans: Evidence for Contractual Versus Spot Labor Markets." In David Wise, ed., *Pensions, Labor, and Individual Choice*. Chicago: University of Chicago Press, pp. 55–87.

———. 1987. "The Incentive Effects of Private Pension Plans." In Zvi Bodie, John Shoven, and David Wise, eds., *Issues in Pension Economics*. Chicago: University of Chicago Press, pp. 283–336.

Lazear, Edward P. 1981. "Severance Pay, Pensions, Mobility, and the Efficiency of Work Incentives." Mimeo, University of Chicago.

———. 1983. "Pensions as Severance Pay." In Zvi Bodie and John Shoven, eds., *Financial Aspects of the United States Pension System*. Chicago: University of Chicago Press, pp. 57–85.

Leimer, Dean R., and Selig D. Lesnoy. 1982. "Social Security and Private Saving: New Time Series Evidence." *Journal of Political Economy* 90:606–29.

Papadia, Francesco. 1982. "Rationality of Inflationary Expectations in the European Communities' Countries." Working Paper, European Economic Community, Brussels.

Rust, John. Forthcoming. "A Dynamic Programming Model of Retirement Behavior." In David Wise, ed., *Economics of Aging*. Chicago: University of Chicago Press.

PART III

POLICY IMPLICATIONS

12

POPULATION AGING AND THE TIMING OF OLD-AGE BENEFITS

Peter Uhlenberg

It is commonplace to begin discussions of the future of aging with comments on the aging of the population. The recently published report from the Carnegie Corporation–funded study of the aging society, for example, begins: "Few Americans realize that this country is in the midst of a demographic revolution that, sooner or later, will affect every individual and every institution in the society. This revolution is the inexorable aging of our population" (Pifer and Bronte 1986, 1). It may or may not be true that most Americans are still unaware of the graying of the population, but certainly no gerontologist questions the "inexorable aging" of the population. Demographers have provided precise population projections, broken down by age and sex, which clearly show the future growth in the relative and absolute size of the age category 65 and over. With so much uncertainty about the future, it is reassuring that demographers, at least, can provide precise numbers regarding the future size of the older population. Before uncritically accepting this contribution of demographers to the study of aging, however, we might remember the heading of an article that appeared in the *Wall Street Journal* a few years back: "Demographers Are Wrong Almost as Often as Economists."

This paper does not question the scientific and political significance of exploring the future of aging. Nor does it question the importance of giving demographic trends a central role in developing scenarios of future patterns of aging. Indeed, no discussion of future society can afford to ignore the unprecedented aging of the population that is anticipated in the next 50 years. However, in making and interpreting demographic projections, it is important to consider carefully the assumptions that are being made. Too often, initial assumptions are treated as if they were fixed parameters—that is, as if they were "natural" or "biologically determined." When assumptions are treated in this way, population aging is taken as inevitable and all attention is directed toward how other parts of the system might adapt to the potential problems this creates. In this paper, I focus on how variable the future course of population aging is and on how the size of the older population is politically determined.

The Problem of an Aging Population

The aging of a population from year to year, or even from decade to decade, is seldom impressive. But if we extend the time perspective to the lifetime of an individual, the change can be dramatic. The proportion of the American population over age 65 tripled between 1900 and 1987 (from 4 to 12 percent), and it is projected to nearly double again between now and 2050 (from 12 to 22 percent). Obviously, substantial chronological aging of the population has already occurred during the twentieth century, and continued aging for the next 60 years or so is almost guaranteed.

It is interesting that the doubling of the proportion of the population over age 65 during the past 50 years has not been accompanied by any deterioration in the relative social and economic well-being of older persons. Just the opposite has occurred. Cohorts entering old age in recent years have experienced remarkable improvements in well-being relative to those preceding them. The expected number of years of life remaining for those who reach age 65 increased from 12.7 in 1940 to 16.7 in 1983. The proportion of older persons with incomes below the official poverty line declined from 35.2 percent in 1960 (the first year in which this measure was calculated) to 12.4 percent in 1984. The elderly are the only age group in American society covered by national health insurance (Medicare) and with a guaranteed minimum income (Supplemental Security Income). Legislation has been enacted to protect the old against discrimination in the labor force and to abolish mandatory retirement. The Older American's Act supports an array of social services specifically for old persons. And, in general, opportunities for older persons to enjoy leisure activities have proliferated as fewer are working full-time and more have incomes above a subsistence level.

Given the positive correlation between population aging and the well-being of older persons in the recent past, why is there growing concern over the future position of the elderly? The primary reason is that all projections of current trends point to a financing crisis in old-age support programs before the middle of the twenty-first century (that is, within the expected lifetime of today's young adults). Projections show that continuing current programs would require that 50–60 percent of the federal budget be directed toward supporting older persons by the time the baby boom has entered old age (Morrison 1986; Torrey 1982a). It is not only the future growth of the older population, however, that produces this presumably untenable outcome. Rather, the potential crisis results from a combination of assumptions regarding (1) future population aging, (2) retirement age of the elderly from economically productive roles, (3) continued entitlement of the elderly to a variety of cash and noncash benefits, and (4) total size of the federal budget.

Although three factors (population aging, age of retirement, and levels of benefits) contribute to the projected cost of supporting the older population, discussions of options for the future usually focus only on the issue of economic transfer policies. Implicitly it is assumed that population aging and retirement rates are determined for the future. Thus, some possible options are: Will more responsibility for support be moved back to individuals and families? Will the cost of transfer programs be limited by imposing means tests? Will the tax burden on the working population be increased to meet the growing costs of these programs? Perhaps an alternative option, dealing with the aging of the population, merits more careful consideration. Should the proportion of elderly in the population be reduced by changing the age of old age? This possibility is explored later in this paper. First, however, let us look more carefully at those population projections that provide information on future age distributions.

Population Projections: The Uncertainty Factor

Discussions of the future of aging routinely include a statement such as "by the year 2030, 21 percent of the population will be over age 65." Sometimes it is mentioned that this number comes from a projection that is based on certain assumptions, but seldom is the uncertainty of this figure as a likely outcome emphasized. It is tedious and it disrupts the flow of an argument to consistently remind the reader that the future age distribution of the population is really unknown. A look at some recent population projections, however, indicates why caution should be exercised in using projections as forecasts.

Consider the series of population projections for the year 1980 made by the U.S. Bureau of the Census (USBC) between 1960 and 1975 (data are presented in Table 12.1). In making each projection, it was necessary to make assumptions about the future course of mortality, migration, and

TABLE 12.1.
PROJECTIONS OF THE ABSOLUTE AND RELATIVE SIZE
OF THE POPULATION AGED 65 AND OVER

Year projection made	PROJECTIONS FOR 1980 POP. 65+		PROJECTIONS FOR 2020 POP. 65+		PROJECTIONS FOR 2030 POP. 65+	
	Thousands	Percentages (low/med/high)	Thousands	Percentages*	Thousands	Percentages*
1960	24,526	9.0/9.7/10.6				
1964	23,086	9.2/9.6/9.9				
1966	23,063	9.2/9.7/10.2				
1967	23,063	9.2/9.6/10.1				
1971	23,703	10.0/10.2/10.4	40,261	10.8		
1972	24,051	10.4/10.6/10.8				
1975	24,523	10.9/11.0/11.3	42,791	14.6	55,024	18.3
1983			51,472	17.3	64,581	21.2
Actual: 1980	25,709	11.3				

SOURCES: USBC (1960, 1964, 1966, 1967, 1971, 1972, 1975, 1984b).
*Middle-range projections.

fertility. Prior to 1983, the USBC used only one assumption regarding future levels of mortality and migration each time it calculated a new projection, whereas several alternative scenarios of fertility behavior were included. Since future fertility could not affect the size of the older population over the time span of these projections, only one projected size of the older population was presented in each report. A range in the size of the total population at future dates was given, however, reflecting alternative fertility assumptions. Consequently, there is always a range in the *proportion* of the population over age 65 projected for 1980.

Focusing on the absolute and relative size of the older population reported for 1980 in the projections made from 1960 to 1975, we can assess how close recent, short-term projections have been to the actual outcome. As seen in Table 12.1, every projection underestimated the future size of the older population. Even the projection made in 1975 was almost 5 percent less than the actual number living five years later. A look at the range of projected proportions of the population over age 65 shows not only that the middle-range projection was consistently too low, but also that the range of projection did not even include (until 1975) the actual percentage of the population aged 65 and over in 1980. In each case the projection was technically correct: it showed what the population age distribution would be under a given set of assumptions. But the projections did not accurately forecast what would really happen over the succeeding 5–20 years. In light of this, one might want to avoid presenting 21.2 percent as a fact about the proportion of the population that will be old in the year 2030.

In retrospect, it is obvious why population projections made in the 1960s and early 1970s missed the target. No one anticipated the precipitous decline in childbearing after 1961 (the total fertility rate plummeted from 3.7 around 1960 to 1.7 in 1976), nor did anyone forecast the sharp decline in death rates among the elderly that occurred after the late 1960s (an average annual decline of 1.7 percent between 1968 and 1980). Current conventional wisdom at the USBC—the basis for middle assumptions in the 1983 projections—holds that fertility will increase slightly (the total fertility rate increasing from 1.8 to 1.9), while mortality rates gradually decline. The future of the third variable, migration, is difficult to anticipate, given the current state of flux regarding migration policy and control of illegal immigration. Thus, the middle assumption regarding migration is that the pattern of recent years (which is not actually known because of illegal immigration) will persist.

In addition to a projection based on the middle assumptions, the 1983 population projections (USBC 1984b) include a range of alternative scenarios, each based on a different combination of assumptions regarding the future of mortality, migration, and fertility. Lifetime births for women are allowed to range from 1.6 to 2.3, with a central value of 1.9. Expectation of life at birth in the year 2050 varies from 77.4 to 85.9, with a central value of 81.0. Assumptions of yearly net immigration range from 250,000 to 750,000, with a central value of 450,000. As of early 1987, none of these alternative values appeared to be unreasonable, and some demographers would argue that it is plausible that values outside of these ranges could occur. How does the proportion over age 65 vary under different combinations of these assumptions?

Assuming the middle value for each demographic variable produces the widely quoted census projection that 21.2 percent of the population will be 65 or older in 2030. But if the lowest value on each variable should occur, 25.4 percent would be old. On the other hand, the highest value on each variable produces a population with 17.5 percent old. Three observations about the future of population aging emerge from noting this range of plausible outcomes. First, each projection indicates a substantial future increase over the 12 percent of the population now aged 65 and over. Second, the range of plausible outcomes is substantial, the high figure being about 50 percent greater than the low figure. The economic and social implications of 17.5 versus 25.4 percent old are surely quite different. Third, we cannot be confident that the actual proportion of the elderly will in fact fall within this wide range. This last observation needs further elaboration.

What happens if the "low" mortality assumption of the 1983 projections (Table 12.1) is replaced with an even lower level of future mortality? This type of calculation was made by Siegel and Taeuber (1986), when they assumed that age-specific death rates would decline at the same rate in the future as they did over the past decade and a half—not a wholly implausible situation. Should this occur, in conjunction with low fertility and low immigration, 36 percent of the population would be over age 65 in the year 2050. At the other extreme of barely plausible scenarios, the proportion of the elderly in 2030 could be as low as 13 percent, should there be a combination of slow mortality improvements, medium immigration, and an increase in fertility to the level existing in the mid-1960s (a total fertility rate of 2.7). Admittedly, the extremes of 13 percent and 36 percent are unlikely outcomes. But substantial uncertainty regarding what the age distribution will be in 2030 does exist. Given this uncertainty, there is an advantage to incorporating flexibility in any social policy that will affect the future older population. Unless a policy can adapt to whatever course the demographic variables may follow, it is likely to produce untenable consequences.

Beyond Numbers: The Issue of Composition

Projections of the absolute and relative size of the older population are useful pieces of information, but standing alone they shed little light on the future of aging. Beyond numbers, we need to know something about the characteristics of the future old and non-old populations. To assume that the elderly in the future will be similar to the elderly of the past or present is absurd. The composition of the older population is constantly changing as individuals crossing the boundary marking old age replace those leaving old age via death. Over a single decade there is approximately a 60 percent turnover in the individuals that compose the older population (Uhlenberg 1987a). Since the entrants to old age have different historical backgrounds and different aggregate characteristics than do the decedents, the composition of the older population is never static. Equally important for the elderly of the future, the non-old population is also changing.

Social and economic change occurring over most of the twentieth century has produced a situation in which each successive cohort entering old age has been better educated, more urban, and wealthier than any preceding cohort (Uhlenberg 1979a). This same process of growth and expansion has meant that at each date the older population had, on average, less education and lower incomes than the middle-aged adult population. The gap in socioeconomic status between cohorts is maximized during periods of rapid transition, such as the first half of the twentieth century. In contrast, during periods of stability, the gap between age groups diminishes. As a result of stability (or stagnation) after 1970, it appears that the old/non-old differences in education and earnings will decline substantially in coming decades.

With respect to education, both the proportion of eighteen-year-olds completing high school and the proportion of high school graduates going on to college increased steadily until about 1970. Since that date, however, successive cohorts entering young adulthood have not surpassed earlier ones in years of school completed. For example, comparing 25- to 29-year-olds in 1980 and 1984 shows virtually no difference in levels of educational attainment (USBC 1985). Looking ahead, I believe that those entering old age after 2020 will be as well educated as the younger adults in the population.

Future earning trajectories of various cohorts is unknown, but since 1973 there has been no improvement between successive cohorts reaching middle adulthood. According to calculations made by Levy and Michel (1985), the average earnings of a man aged 30 grew rapidly up to 1973, when it was $23,500 (in 1984 dollars). After 1973 it declined, so that by 1983 it was only $17,520. To be sure, the 1970s were not a prosperous time. But future increases in real income per capita of successive cohorts over preceding ones is no longer a safe assumption (ibid.).

The potential leveling of education and earnings across cohorts has two interesting implications for the elderly in the future. First, if the elderly no longer suffer an educational disadvantage, their ability to compete with younger workers for desirable occupational positions may be enhanced.

This would occur especially if there is an increase in lifelong education that could keep skills from declining as workers age. Second, the ability or willingness of the young to support the elderly at levels considered adequate by the latter may become problematic. Up to the present, the income expectations of the elderly (based on their past earnings) have been modest compared to the actual incomes of middle-aged individuals. This may not be true in the future, as the middle-aged population is no longer advantaged vis-á-vis the elderly. Will middle-aged workers be willing to support retired persons who, on average, have a higher standard of living than themselves?

Further doubt regarding the ability of the young to support the elderly at relatively high income levels arises when the experience of adolescents over recent years is examined. If the early years of life are a time of accumulating human capital that determines future productivity, there is reason for concern. The academic performance of successive cohorts of young people, as measured on standardized exams, has deteriorated. Furthermore, there have been increasing rates of adolescent criminal behavior, drug and alcohol use, and out-of-wedlock births (Uhlenberg and Eggebeen 1986). An increasing number of children are living in poverty and are being raised in single-parent families. These children and adolescents of the 1970s and 1980s will be the middle-aged adults of the 2020s, to whom—if current arrangements persist—the elderly must look for support. Perhaps renewed concern for the well-being of children will produce changes that will reverse these pernicious trends of recent decades. But the recent experiences of children at least adds another note of uncertainty regarding the future security of the elderly.

A final observation regarding the changing composition of the population concerns the rapid growth of minority groups. In 1970, Hispanics, blacks, and Asians composed about 17 percent of the total U.S. population. Between 1970 and 1980, however, these minorities accounted for 44 percent of the total population growth. It is expected that they will contribute over 56 percent of the total population growth between 1980 and 2000 (Davis, Haub, and Willette 1983; Gardner, Robey, and Smith 1985). As a result of this differential growth, almost 30 percent of the population projected for 2000 will be members of minorities. The rapid growth of the Hispanic, black, and Asian groups is a consequence of both immigration patterns and fertility differences between groups. In the early 1980s, 83 percent of all immigrants to the United States came from either Asia or Latin America (Bouvier and Gardner 1986). In 1982 the general fertility rate was 50 percent higher for Hispanics than non-Hispanic whites, and 34 percent higher for blacks than whites (National Center for Health Statistics 1984; Ventura 1985). Conversely, the average length of life for whites in 1985 was 75.3, compared to 71.2 for nonwhites (National Center for Health Statistics 1986).

The changing racial-ethnic composition of the population is shown in Table 12.2, where the data for 2030 are based on the middle-range projections by the USBC. Several authors (Hayes-Bautista, Shinek, and Chapa 1984; Torres-Gil 1986) have noted that racial-ethnic stratification along age lines could become problematic. The projections for 2030 indicate that 41 percent of the children but only 24 percent of the elderly will be members of minorities. Thus, various racial-ethnic groups in the population will differ in the stake they have in programs supporting different age groups. Might the growing number of middle-aged minorities, who are parents of a disproportionate number of the children, resist increasing federal expenditures for the elderly, who are predominately nonminority whites?

With the institutionalization of retirement, the older population in the United States has become increasingly dependent on the middle-aged population for economic support. The changing dependency ratio that accompanies population aging leads to forecasts of substantial increases in the cost of supporting the elderly in the future. But this brief consideration of changing characteristics of various age groups raises a further question about the feasibility of increasing government support of the elderly. Those who will be called on to support the future elderly, compared to the current middle-aged population, may be less interested in playing that role.

WHO IS OLD?

This paper began by observing that any discussion of future problems associated with population aging must be based upon certain assumptions and that commonly accepted assumptions need critical examination. First, assumptions regarding future demographic trends were questioned. Because the future course of fertility, morality, and migration are uncertain, the range of plausible age distributions of the population at any particular date in the future is wide. Second, attention was given to assumptions concerning the characteristics of the future older and younger populations. Aging is not an immutable process, so it is naive to assume that the elderly (or the young) in the future will resemble closely those who are currently old (or young). The continuous process of cohorts flowing through historical time means that the current occupants of each age category are being replaced by newcomers, who may be quite different. Assumptions about size and composition of age categories include an implicit assumption that old age begins around 65, but to discuss the future of old age this assumption also must be questioned.

Research on aging by anthropologists and historians provides a useful perspective for considering the contemporary and future definitions of old

TABLE 12.2

AGE DISTRIBUTION OF THE POPULATION BY RACE, 1985 AND 2030
(PERCENTAGES)

	Proportion of total population	AGE			
		0–17	18–44	45–64	65 and over
1985					
White, non-Hispanic	78.3	72.0	77.5	82.9	87.5
Hispanic	6.8	9.4	7.2	5.1	3.0
Black	12.2	15.4	12.4	9.7	8.1
Other races	2.7	3.2	2.9	2.3	1.4
2030					
White, non-Hispanic	66.4	59.3	62.9	68.9	76.4
Hispanic	12.9	16.7	14.6	11.3	8.2
Black	15.6	18.6	17.1	14.5	11.3
Other races	5.1	5.4	5.4	5.3	4.1

SOURCE: USBC (1986).

age. Three useful generalizations can be extracted from the cross-cultural and historical literature on aging (for example, see Fry and Keith 1982; Laslett 1985). First, old age is a socially recognized phase of the life course in virtually every society. That is, certain individuals are recognized as "old," and having that status has consequences for how individuals are treated and how they are expected to behave. Second, societies differ greatly in the criteria they use to distinguish their old from their non-old members, and rites of passage into old age range from clear rituals to ambiguous transitions. Third, the meaning of "old age" is highly variable across cultures and across time. Using these generalizations as guides to the future, we anticipate that "old" will continue to be a meaningful status but that when it begins and what it means may change.

No one denies the social reality of old age in contemporary America, though many protest the assertion that it begins at 65. The choice of age 65 to mark the beginning of old age seems too arbitrary. Given the biological, social, psychological, and economic heterogeneity of individuals at any particular age, how can one chronological age be used to classify persons as old? Furthermore, few persons aged 65 identify themselves as old. Age 65 has little intrinsic meaning, heterogeneity is an important issue, and subjective age identity has some meaning. Nevertheless, most individuals do cross a threshold into old age by the time they celebrate their 65th birthday.

The identification of old age with 65 should be seen in the context of what can be called the increasing chronologization of the entire life course. Kohli and Meyer (1986), for example, write: "Life stages have become more clearly defined and set apart, and the boundaries between them—or transitions, in terms of the life course as a process—more strictly organized by chronological age" (p. 146). Two distinct changes, both highly correlated with chronological age, best mark the transition into the last stage of life. One is retirement, which has become a normative life event (Atchley 1982). The other is receipt of old-age benefits, which is nearly universal among those aged 65 and over. Regardless of other characteristics or attitudes, it is meaningful to say that a person has entered old age when he or she both receives old-age entitlements and is no longer significantly engaged in the labor force. In other words, old age begins around age 65.

Why does the relationship to the organization of production and to the welfare state tend to change around age 65? This age has figured prominently in social legislation enacted over the past 50 years. As old age became recognized as a social problem, policymakers were challenged to design social policies to alleviate the problem. Designing programs to aid a subpopulation (the elderly) that cannot be precisely defined might appear to be difficult. This was not, however, a major obstacle to legislatures. They simply selected a chronological age as the standard criterion for defining who would be eligible for old-age benefits. Starting with old-age insurance in 1935, a wide gamut of special benefits have been created for those individuals who can prove that they have been alive for more than a fixed number of years. These benefits are essential for making retirement a viable option for most older persons.

Several different ages (55, 60, 62, and 65) are used in various federal (and other) programs designed to benefit the elderly. But the most significant age is clearly 65—that age at which full Social Security benefits, Medicare, and (until recently) special tax advantages are available. Reflecting the semiofficial status of age 65 as the marker of old age, official statistics reporting on the older population routinely use a category of 65 and over. Researchers, after noting the arbitrariness of any particular chronological age, follow suit by operationalizing old age as 65 and over. Thus, despite the diversity of opinions regarding who is truly old, chronological age has become the indicator. Many have achieved the status "old" by age 62 (they are substantially retired and receive old-age benefits), and most are in the category "old" by age 65.

In recent years, several experts on aging have urged that the trend toward increasing use of chronological age to structure the life course be reversed. Neugarten (1986), for example, sees chronological age as an irrelevant basis for defining groups in contemporary society, and she advocates removing "the irrelevant age constraints that now exist for the young as well as for the young-old in various areas of employment, housing, education, and community participation" (p. 46; see also Neugarten 1979, 1982). Best (1980), Morrison (1978), Riley (1978), and Wirtz (1975) all protest the increasing division of life into three boxes—education, work, and leisure—based on chronological age. They support a reorganization of the social structure in a way that will encourage interspersing each of these activities throughout the life course. The case for beginning to deinstitutionalize the life course is persuasive, given the heterogeneity of the population within each age category. It is not likely, however, that old age will be eliminated as a distinctive stage of life.

Aging is a multifaceted process, involving biological and psychological change as well as social change. Attempts to socially eliminate old age as a distinctive last phase of life, without breaking the association of biological decline with aging, are probably futile and counterproductive. The absence of a chronological age to mark the transition to old age would leave old age to be defined by negative biological changes—physical and/or mental deterioration. Under this condition, old age could be viewed only as an unmitigated disaster—that phase of life characterized by undesirable losses. Despite its arbitrariness, the use of chronological age to determine when old age begins has certain advantages.

Establishing an age for entitlement to old-age benefits enables individuals and governments to engage in long-range planning. Further, this approach to old age leaves open how the meaning of old age is to be defined. It simply says that, after a set age, the social expectation of being engaged in the labor force is lifted and the person qualifies for special benefits. Having a clear marker of old age does not limit the flexibility of what older persons do, nor does it necessarily encourage an unproductive old age. On the other hand, it does provide added protection during a stage of life when physical limitations are increasingly likely to restrict activities.

Determining an Old-Age Threshold

I am arguing that it is reasonable to establish an official chronological age to mark old age, but that this age should be variable over time. If age 65 was a reasonable choice in 1935, it is so no longer. With increasing life expectancy and aging of the population, the age of old age should be rising. Support for increasing the age of eligibility for Social Security benefits has been growing in recent years. Four successive commissions studying the future of the Social Security system have recommended increasing the age for full eligibility (Congressional Quarterly 1983). In 1983 Congress finally accepted this proposal and passed an amendment to the Social Security Act that includes the gradual increase in the age of full benefit eligibility to 67 by 2027. This change in age eligibility is a significant step toward removing age 65 as an untouchable symbol. Nevertheless, it does not deal with the issue of how the marker of old age can be shifted upward in the future as demographic conditions continue to change. Rather than replacing one fixed age with another, it is possible to think of "old" as a variable.

Any method for selecting a chronological age to mark the transition to old age will involve some arbitrariness. It is possible, however, to develop a formula that would provide a logical basis for periodically shifting the age of eligibility by a certain amount. Such a formula should include the following characteristics: simple to calculate and easy to explain to the general public; responsive to demographic changes; and capable of preventing the future population from becoming excessively old. Details regarding its implementation would need to be specified, perhaps along the following lines: every ten years, using current information, a revised marker of old age would be calculated; and the new marker of old age would be gradually phased in, beginning twenty years later (when, for example, old age could be advanced two months per year until the new level was obtained).

Four alternative formulas for establishing a variable marker of old age are described below. Many variations on these proposals could be suggested, as well as altogether different approaches. The essential point, however, is that a feasible formula could be established and implemented to guide planning for the future older population.

Proposal 1. Fixed limit to the span of old age. Rather than defining the beginning of old age by a fixed number of years after birth (such as 65), this approach suggests counting *back* a fixed number of years from expected age at death. (This definition of old age was first discussed by Ryder [1975] and developed briefly in a recent *Current Population Reports* [USBC 1984a].) Using a current life table, it is simple to calculate the age at which the average number of remaining years of life is fifteen (or whatever number is preferred). As life expectancy increases, the onset of old age also increases. Thus, any added years of life would expand the length of the middle years of life rather than old age. Nevertheless, with this definition most members of each cohort could anticipate a substantial period of life in the privileged status of old.

Proposal 2. Old age limited to one-fourth of the adult life. Torrey (1982b) suggests a formula for calculating a normal retirement age that is also determined by using life-table values. By selecting the age at which life expectancy is equal to 25 percent of the life expectancy at age twenty, individuals would spend an average of one-fourth of their adult lives as older persons. Compared with Proposal 1, this alternative allows the length of both old age and middle age to grow in response to increasing expectation of life.

Proposal 3. Fixed ratio of old to middle-age populations. Rather than starting with life tables, this approach keeps constant the ratio of older to middle-aged adults in the population. The age distribution of the population, as provided by the USBC, would be used to determine an age X such that the population over age X was equal to 17 percent of the population aged twenty to X. Thus, the old-age dependency ratio would not increase as the population aged chronologically.

Proposal 4. Fixed proportion of elderly in the population. A variation on the previous proposal would keep the proportion of elderly in the population constant at 10 percent. Again, this involves a simple calculation using the age distribution of the population. Under this proposal, there would be no future growth in the relative size of the older population, regardless of what demographic changes might occur.

Using any of the above proposals, the age of old age would become a variable determined by future demographic trends. The age of old age in 2030 under each proposal can be illustrated by calculating the age based upon the most recent middle-range projections for that year. The results of these calculations are shown in Table 12.3. For comparison, 1985 is used as a baseline, with age 67 as the starting age marker of old age in that year (reflecting the change in future age eligibility for full Social Security benefits). Proposal 1 (old age begins when average years of life remaining equals fifteen) and Proposal 2 (ratio of older years to middle years of life equals 0.25) produce the same result: the transition to old age would occur at age 72. By advancing old age five years (from 67 to 72) over the next 40 years, there would be about a 24 percent increase in the ratio of old to middle-aged adults. Proposal 3, which keeps this ratio of old to middle-aged years constant, would require advancing the beginning of old age to 74 years. Under this schema, average length of the last stage of life would decline to 13.7 years. Finally, Proposal 4, which keeps the proportion of elderly in the population constant at 10 percent, requires the biggest change: old age would begin at 75. This alternative, which still provides an average of 13 years of life remaining for those who reach old age, would reduce the proportion of all adults who were old.

Each proposal has a certain internal logic, and none of them results in changes that are unimaginable. In contrast, should age 62 be selected for the beginning of old age, the results, under conditions projected for 2030, would be quite remarkable. The ratio of old to middle-aged adults would

TABLE 12.3

IMPLICATIONS OF ALTERNATIVE DEFINITIONS OF OLD AGE

	Old-age threshold	Average length of old age (years)	Proportion of adult life as old	Proportion of elderly in adult population	Proportion of elderly in total population
1985 (baseline)	67	15.4	.275	.17	.10
2030 (projection)					
Proposal 1[a]	72	15.0	.250	.21	.13
Proposal 2[b]	72	15.0	.250	.21	.13
Proposal 3[c]	74	13.7	.229	.17	.11
Proposal 4[d]	75	13.0	.219	.15	.10

SOURCES: Population data are from USBC (1984a); life-table values are from Faber and Wade (1983).

a. Old age begins at X, $\overset{\circ}{e}_x = 15$ years.

b. Old age begins at X, such that $\overset{\circ}{e}_x / \overset{\circ}{e}_{20} = .25$.

c. Old age begins at X, such that Pop $(X+)$/Pop $(20-X) = .17$.

d. Old age begins at X, such that Pop $(X+)$/Pop (total) $= .10$.

rise to 0.48, and the ratio of years lived in old age to years lived in middle age would increase to .36. Once the implications of maintaining the status quo are understood, the idea of changing the age of old age may not appear preposterous. Indeed, raising the age for entrance into old age to 72 or 74 becomes a modest proposal.

Implications of the Proposed Change

Any proposal to enact legislation to make the future age for entitlement to old age benefits a variable will generate a number of important questions. A thorough discussion of issues underlying these potential questions is necessary, but cannot be included in this brief paper. Nevertheless, initial responses to three questions that surely will arise are suggested in this section.

Question 1.   Is there evidence that older people desire this type of change? Absolutely not. All evidence indicates a preference for early retirement and early eligibility for old-age benefits. Other things being equal, people would prefer to receive higher benefits and to receive them earlier in life. But this first question is irrelevant to the proposal to change the age of old age for three reasons. First, no change is proposed that would affect those who will be approaching age 65 over the next twenty years. Cohorts who will be entering old age in the future have different backgrounds and different characteristics than those currently entering old age, and we cannot assume that attitudes will remain constant. Second, the issue for future cohorts must be framed in terms of alternatives. The alternatives to increasing the age for eligibility are likely to be even less attractive to future cohorts than to the current one. Third, decisions regarding transfer payments cannot be decided by considering only the interests of those receiving the benefits. The interests of the working-age population (who must pay the benefits) and of children also must be weighed in arriving at an equitable policy. An open discussion now of how to support the future elderly can prepare the population for necessary changes and can begin to change attitudes.

Question 2.   Given the differences in life expectancy by sex (in 1984, life expectancy was 7.0 years greater for women than men) and by race (in 1984, life expectancy was 5.6 years greater for whites than blacks), would this proposal create inequalities? No. Changing the age for benefit-eligibility continues the current policy, which uses one age criterion for the total population rather than treating various subgroups differentially. Different ages to mark the old-age-threshold could be calculated (for example, see McMillen 1984), but to design a policy that treats subgroups differentially surely would be unworkable. The number of characteristics related to life expectation is quite large. Should those who smoke, are obese, or have low education be provided with benefits earlier because, on average, their life expectancy is below the average of the population? The current approach of refusing to discriminate on the basis of individual characteristics appears to be the only reasonable way to avoid splintering the population into numerous competing factions. (For a more complete discussion of changes that could make the Social Security system more equitable, see Ricardo-Campbell [1984]).

Question 3. Given the existing social structure, would the proposed change not seriously harm the welfare of the near-old population? Yes. If advancing the age for entitlement is accepted, other changes must also be made to protect the well-being of individuals in later life. These changes are not simple, and each one will need careful consideration. Four types of changes needed to complement advancing the age of old age are rather obvious.

First, changes must be made in the organization of work. The increased frequency of early retirement has occurred because it makes economic sense within the existing structure of work. Morrison (1986) provides useful observations on the types of changes that would promote reform in the social institution of retirement. These changes are relevant both for those in later middle age and for those in old age. Rather than accepting the norm of upward mobility and increasing rewards over an entire worklife, he argues for "horizontal job mobility without increasing pay, reduced responsibility and income, and gradual diminution of responsibility and reward" (p. 287). Further, he lists a variety of work options (such as part-time, flexible hours, and contract work), which, if expanded, would permit an individual to choose an option that meets his or her particular work needs and abilities.

Second, changes are needed in the organization of education. If older workers are to have skills needed to be productive or to make job changes, opportunities for education and learning throughout adulthood must be expanded. Moody (1986) offers a number of provocative ideas regarding the emergence of "nontraditional higher education" that are relevant to this concern. Lifelong education not only increases possibilities for extending the worklife but also promises greater opportunities for continuing productivity in noneconomic areas of life.

Third, extending the middle years of life into the seventies requires that more attention be given to problems of disability before old age. Despite some contrary views (for example, Fries 1983), most studies of morbidity trends in recent years suggest that declining mortality has not been accompanied by improved health status (Chapman, LaPlante, and Wilensky 1986; Verbrugge, 1984). If disability in later adulthood does not decline (or if it increases), then advancing the normal retirement age would increase the number of persons unable to work because of physical disabilities. Increased efforts to prevent disability should be encouraged, but ways to provide more adequately for those with disabilities must also be developed.

Finally, attention to delaying entrance into old age does not address the equally important question of what happens during old age. Shortening the duration of old age and reducing the proportion of the population who are old may facilitate efforts to improve the quality of the last years of life. But how to make old age a productive and meaningful stage of life also needs direct attention.

Conclusion

In contemporary society, old age is best defined as that stage of life during which an individual both receives old age benefits and plays a minor (or no) role in economic production. With this definition, the state largely controls access to old age by establishing a chronological age at which individuals become entitled to major old-age benefits. Despite some arbitrariness involved in selecting any particular age for the beginning of entitlements, there are advantages to using age criteria in some social policies. It allows for long-term planning, recognizes the reality of increasing risks in later life, and avoids old age being defined as physical disability at the end of life. If chronological age is a relevant component of an aging policy, however, it is crucial that increased attention be given to the process of selecting the marker of old age. Ways to make the age of old age a variable that changes in response to other social and demographic variables are suggested above.

Allowing the age of old age to continue drifting downward, as it has in recent years, makes little sense. Indeed, recent social and demographic changes point to the need to substantially increase the age for entitlement to old-age benefits. Among many valid reasons for increasing the age of old age, four points seem particularly salient.

First, the aging of the population, combined with expanding old-age benefits, is creating economic problems. Currently about 30 percent of the federal budget supports benefits for the population aged 65 and over. A continuation of present expenditure patterns is projected to increase the proportion of the budget going to support older persons to 60 percent by 2030 (Morrison 1986). Given the growing concern over the size of the federal budget deficit, substantial increases in expenditures on older persons is sure to receive increasing attention. Reducing the size of the future older population by increasing the age for entering old age is an attractive alternative to the choices of reducing the level of per capita benefits or increasing taxes.

Second, the challenge of creating meaningful social roles for older persons is exacerbated by the expanding average length of time spent in old age. But the added years of life after age 60 resulting from declining mortality do not need to extend the old-age stage of life. Rather, these added years can extend the middle-aged adult phase of the life course, when individuals are expected to be economically productive. At the same time, a distinctive and, it is hoped, a more positive last phase of the life course can be developed.

Third, the potential productive contributions by cohorts after reaching age 60 or 65 has been increasing while actual productivity has declined. There is a growing gulf between what older persons could contribute to societal welfare and what they actually contribute in the areas of work, leadership in organizations, and family (Uhlenberg 1987a). The members of cohorts reaching age 65 now and in the future, as compared to those in earlier cohorts, are better educated and more skilled in participating in a complex bureaucratic society (Uhlenberg 1979a, 1979b). As argued earlier, the gap in education and background between the elderly and the middle-aged population is declining as the societal transformations from low education and rural residence to high education and urban residence are nearing completion. Advancing the age of old age will encourage continued independence and productivity among individuals who are capable of making significant contributions to the larger society.

Fourth and finally, the widely discussed issues of conflict between age groups (Daniels 1985; Longman 1985; Preston 1984) is closely related to the changing age distribution. Concern that increasing government expenditures for older persons causes underinvesting in children cannot be ignored. Increasing the economically productive years of adulthood and decreasing the size of the older population by increasing the age threshold of old age offers a partial solution to this problem. The level of resources allocated to dependent children involves separate political decisions, but having more resources available certainly increases the feasibility of allocating more to children.

The general proposal to make the age of old age a variable requires further debate. The idea has not yet received much attention, and potential mechanisms to accomplish such a goal are still sketchy and tentative. Nevertheless, the number of options for dealing with the potential problems of future population aging is not very large, and there are risks involved in postponing a decision about which one will be selected. To avoid serious social disruption, substantial lead time is needed to implement any significant change in supporting older persons. In addition, the unknowns about future conditions suggest the need for a policy that is sufficiently flexible to adapt to a range of possibilities. A schema for periodically adjusting the age of old age for cohorts who will be entering old age twenty years later is a reasonable and not terribly painful way to meet these requirements.

DISCUSSION

Sherwin Rosen

This paper by Peter Uhlenberg is an interesting and thoughtful one, and it makes a strong case for the idea of relative lifetime stages, particularly that portion labeled as old age for institutional purposes and for entitlements to age-related social insurance. The main point is that adopting a chronological age benchmark, such as 65, changes the proportion of a lifetime that a person is classified as "old" when the expected length of life changes. In a society where the average person lives until 55 years of age, age 50 is old, yet in one where the expected lifetime is 80 years, age 50 is still only middle-age status.

Two compelling factors make the point in the past three decades. One is the remarkable increase in longevity of the average person, particularly of the elderly. There has been an enormous increase in life expectancy conditional on reaching age 65 for the U.S. population. This is one of the most dramatic social changes we have experienced in the past 25 years or so, and these conditional expectations are derived from cross-section life tables, which are biased downward due to cohort effects. The other is the better-known "graying" of the population—that is, the rising proportion of elderly in the total population. Although Uhlenberg recognizes the uncertainty of demographic projections, there is little question that the elderly will account for an increasing proportion of total population in the next three or four decades. Both of these factors contribute to an increasing share of total resources claimed by the elderly, whereas production is increasingly concentrated on a declining share of nonelderly persons in the total population. Changing the definition of elderly certainly restores balance in these proportions.

Uhlenberg concentrates on the ratio of the elderly to the nonelderly, yet for the problem that motivates the discussion, the more interesting ratio is the dependency ratio: the ratio of working to nonworking population. The first point to be made is that the nonworking population includes both the elderly and the young. It is not sufficiently emphasized that the ratio of the young to the total population will be decreasing at the same time as the ratio of the elderly to the nonelderly is increasing, so the dependency ratio is not going to increase as fast as he indicates. The accounting case for changing the definition of old age rests on the increasing fraction of claims on total production going to the elderly. Yet this will be accompanied by a decreasing fraction going to the young. Certainly resources are highly mobile in the time units of generations implicit in the paper. Over one or two generations it is not unthinkable to transform elementary school teachers to geriatric social workers.

The second point that must be noted is prospects for productivity growth, because the social burden of changes in the dependency ratio is inversely proportional to the rate of income growth. Admittedly, there is great uncertainty in productivity growth projections (though no more than in population projections), and the U.S. economy has not grown much lately. But the point remains that high productivity growth relaxes many constraints on the dependency ratio.

The third and final qualification relates to the remarkable increase in labor force participation of women. This is just the other side of the coin of falling birth rates and a declining proportion of young people in the population. Not only has the time of women been largely released from the care of the young and household production, but the substitution of time toward market-goods production also decreases the social burden of market-based transfers to the elderly.

Surely this paper will stimulate more thinking on the definition of old age. The next tasks are to identify precisely the social problem to be solved by changing the age of old age and to make that definition consistent with people's behavior. By increasing this age we reduce the institutional claims on resources by the elderly, but casting the discussion in the terms of the paper tends to conceal the fact that changing the age of old age takes benefits away from the elderly. Why not be precise on this point? Furthermore, we know that people adapt their private behavior to social policy, and these things have to be considered in choosing the entitlement age. For example, in the case of Social Security, the possible offset of private transfers through Ricardian Equivalence means that the Social Security retirement age may have less effect on resource claims by the elderly than meets the eye. Whether the federal government taxes or borrows to finance the Social Security benefits could, under some circumstances, have the same effect. And how are medicare entitlements to be treated? It is hard to conceive of a political decision to increase that age of entitlement, and it is well known that the bulk of medical resources are spent on the elderly.

There are also the behavioral determinants of retirement itself to be concerned about. For example, it is stated in the paper that increased longevity extends the period of productive life. True enough, but I am not so sure that the implicit definition of productivity used here has universal appeal. Most people do not like to work, and the most compelling evidence we have on the point is the fact that they have to get paid to do it. There is little doubt that the Social Security Act has hastened the age of retirement, but so too has the general growth of wealth and of private pensions. The age of retirement is declining and is likely to continue, however we define old age. Families in which both spouses work and there are few children to care for will naturally accumulate greater money wealth to sustain themselves in old age and can afford to retire earlier than those in previous generations. For those who are in less fortunate circumstances, there is the old saying that disability insurance is the old-age annuity of the poor. Surely there is much truth in this, and advancing the age of retirement must be examined in conjunction with what will be done to the disability system. Who is it that will determine who the productive elderly are? All of these points are not so much criticisms of Uhlenberg's work as additional thoughts that are inspired by it. Changing the age of old age is a rather more complicated business than it appears on the surface.

REFERENCES

Atchley, Robert C. 1982. "Retirement as a Social Institution." *Annual Review of Sociology* 8:263–87.

Best, Fred. 1980. *Flexible Life Scheduling*. New York: Praeger.

Bouvier, Leon F., and Robert W. Gardner. 1986. "Immigration to the U.S.: The Unfinished Story." *Population Bulletin* 41:4.

Chapman, Stephen H., Mitchell P. LaPlante, and Gail Wilensky. 1986. "Life Expectancy and Health Status of the Aged." *Social Security Bulletin* 49:24–48.

Congressional Quarterly. 1983. *Social Security and Retirement: Private Goals and Public Policy*. Washington, D.C.: Congressional Quarterly.

Daniels, Norman. 1985. "Justice Between Age Groups: Am I My Parents' Keeper?" *Milbank Memorial Fund Quarterly* 61:489–522.

Davis, Cary, Carl Haub, and Jo Anne Willette. 1983. "U.S. Hispanics: Changing the Face of America." *Population Bulletin* 38:3.

Faber, J. E., and A. H. Wade. 1983. *Life Tables for the United States: 1900–2050*. Actuarial Study no. 89. Washington, D.C.: Social Security Administration.

Fries, James F. 1983. "The Compression of Morbidity." *Milbank Memorial Fund Quarterly* 61:397–419.

Fry, Christine L., and Jennie Keith. 1982. "The Life Course as a Cultural Unit." In M. W. Riley, R. P. Abeler, and M. S. Teitelbaum, eds., *Aging from Birth to Death*, vol. 2. Boulder, Colo.: Westview.

Gardner, Robert W., Bryant Robey, and Peter C. Smith. 1985. "Asian Americans: Growth, Change, and Diversity." *Population Bulletin* 40:4.

Hayes-Bautista, David E., Werner O. Shinek, and Jorge Chapa. 1984. "Young Latinos in an Aging American Society." *Social Policy* 15:49–52.

Kohli, Martin, and John W. Meyer. 1986. "Social Structure and Social Construction of Life Stages." *Human Development* 29:145–49.

Laslett, Peter. 1985. "Societal Development and Aging." In Robert H. Binstock and Ethel Shanas, eds., *Handbook of Aging and the Social Sciences*. New York: Van Nostrand Reinhold.

Levy, Frank S., and Richard C. Michel. 1985. "The Economic Future of the Baby Boom." Report from the Urban Institute, Washington, D.C.

Longman, Phillip. 1985. "Justice between Generations." *The Atlantic Monthly* 255:73–81.

McMillen, Marilyn M. 1984. "Sex-Specific Equivalent Retirement Ages: 1940–2050." *Social Security Bulletin* 47:3–10.

Moody, Harry R. 1986. "Education in an Aging Society." *Daedalus* 115:191–210.

Morrison, Malcolm H. 1978. "Flexible Distribution of Work, Leisure and Education: Potentials for the Aging." In B. Herzod, ed., *Aging and Income*. New York: Human Sciences Press.

————. 1986. "Work and Retirement in an Aging Society." *Daedalus* 115:269–93.

National Center for Health Statistics. 1984. "Advance Report of Final Natality Statistics, 1982." *Monthly Vital Statistics Report* 33.

————. 1986. "Annual Summary of Births, Marriages, Divorces, and Deaths: United States, 1985." *Monthly Vital Statistics Report* 34.

Neugarten, Bernice L. 1979. "Policy for the 1980s: Age or Need Entitlement." In *Aging: Agenda for the Eighties*. Washington, D.C.: National Journal Issues Book.

————. 1986. "Age in the Aging Society." *Daedalus* 115:31–49.

————, ed. 1982. *Age or Need? Public Policies for Older People*. Beverly Hills, Calif.: Sage Publications.

Pifer, Alan, and D. Lydia Bronte. 1986. "Introduction: Squaring the Pyramid." *Daedalus* 115:1–11.

Preston, Samuel H. 1984. "Children and the Elderly in the U.S." *Scientific American* 251:44–49.

Ricardo-Campbell, Rita. 1984. "Social Security Reform: A Mature System in an Aging Society." In J. H. Moore, ed., *To Promote Prosperity: U.S. Domestic Policy in the Mid-1980s*. Stanford: Hoover Institution Press.

Riley, Matilda White. 1978. "Aging, Social Change, and the Power of Ideas." *Daedalus* 107:39–52.

Ryder, Norman B. 1975. "Notes on Stationary Populations." *Population Index* 41:3–28.

Siegel, Jacob S., and Cynthia M. Taeuber. 1986. "Demographic Perspectives on the Long-Lived Society." *Daedalus* 115:77–117.

Torres-Gil, Fernando. 1986. "The Latinization of a Multigenerational Population: Hispanics in an Aging Society." *Daedalus* 115:325–48.

Torrey, Barbara Boyle. 1982a. "Guns vs. Canes: The Fiscal Implications of an Aging Population." *American Economic Review* 72:309–13.

————. 1982b. "The Lengthening of Retirement." In M. W. Riley, R. P. Abeles, and M. S. Teitelbaum, eds., *Aging from Birth to Death*, vol. 2. Boulder, Colo.: Westview.

Uhlenberg, Peter. 1979a. "Demographic Change and Problems of the Aged." In Matilda White Riley, ed., *Aging from Birth to Death*. Boulder, Colo.: Westview.

————. 1979b. "Older Women: The Growing Challenge to Design Constructive Roles." *Gerontologist* 19:236–41.

————. 1987a. "A Demographic Perspective on Aging." In Philip Silverman, ed., *Elderly People, Modern Pioneers: Interdisciplinary Research on Aging*. Bloomington: Indiana University Press.

————. 1987b. "Aging and the Societal Significance of Cohorts." In James E. Birren and Vern L. Bengtson, eds., *Theories of Aging: Psychological and Social Perspectives*. New York: Springer.

Uhlenberg, Peter, and David Eggebeen. 1986, "The Declining Well-Being of American Adolescents." *Public Interest* 82:25–38.

U.S. Bureau of the Census. 1960. *Current Population Reports.* Series P-25, no. 187. Washington, D.C.: GPO.

———. 1964. *Current Population Reports.* Series P-25, no. 286. Washington, D.C.: GPO.

———. 1966. *Current Population Reports.* Series P-25, no. 345. Washington, D.C.: GPO.

———. 1967. *Current Population Reports.* Series P-25, no. 381. Washington, D.C.: GPO.

———. 1971. *Current Population Reports.* Series P-25, no. 470. Washington, D.C.: GPO.

———. 1972. *Current Population Reports.* Series P-25, no. 493. Washington, D.C.: GPO.

———. 1975. *Current Population Reports.* Series P-25, no. 601. Washington, D.C.: GPO.

———. 1984a. *Current Population Reports.* Series P-23, no. 138. Washington, D.C.: GPO.

———. 1984b. *Current Population Reports.* Series P-25, no. 952. Washington, D.C.: GPO.

———. 1985. *Statistical Abstract of the United States: 1986.* Washington, D.C.: GPO.

———. 1986. *Current Population Reports.* Series P-25, no. 995. Washington, D.C.: GPO.

Ventura, Stephanie J. 1985. "Births of Hispanic Parentage, 1982." *Monthly Vital Statistics Report* 34.

Verbrugge, Lois M. 1984. "Longer Life but Worsening Health? Trends in Health and Mortality of Middle-Aged and Older Persons." *Milbank Memorial Fund Quarterly* 62:475–519.

Wirtz, Willard. 1975. *The Boundless Resource.* Washington, D.C.: New Republic.

— 13 —

CHANGES IN THE LEGAL MANDATORY RETIREMENT AGE: LABOR FORCE PARTICIPATION IMPLICATIONS

Malcolm H. Morrison

Recent congressional action has eliminated the mandatory retirement age and has required continuing pension accruals for persons working beyond the normal retirement age in qualified pension plans (USDOL 1981). This legislation was enacted after extensive studies, conducted by the U.S. Department of Labor (USDOL), indicated that eliminating mandatory retirement and requiring continued pension accruals would not result in a significant increase in labor force participation by older workers (ibid.).

The studies were developed primarily to evaluate the labor force consequences of raising or eliminating the mandatory retirement age. At their inception, many analysts believed that the existence of mandatory retire-

This chapter represents an excerpted and edited version (with some additional material) of the U.S. Department of Labor's Interim Report to Congress on Age Discrimination in Employment Act Amendments submitted in 1981. At that time, Morrison was Director of the National Studies of Mandatory Retirement and the Effects of the Age Discrimination in Employment Act for the Department of Labor; he contributed substantially to, and was responsible for, the production of this report. In carrying out the research on this issue, the Labor Department procured a study from the Urban Institute, which in turn secured the services of Joseph Quinn of Boston College and Richard Burkhauser of Vanderbilt University, to formulate specific simulation models for the purpose of assisting Labor Department analysts in their assessment.

ment rules significantly reduced labor force participation by older workers and that, if these rules were liberalized or eliminated, labor force participation would increase significantly (Harris 1979; Givens 1978; McConnell and Corson 1956; Slavik 1966; USDOL 1965a, 1965b, 1977). As is often the case in studying policy issues, research both confirmed and denied these assumptions. Mandatory retirement policies were shown to have certain independent though modest effects on reducing labor supply. However, these effects are significantly mitigated, because mandatory retirement rules are usually accompanied by available public and private pensions and it is difficult to separate the effects of these factors when analyzing labor force participation (USDOL 1981). When public and private pension incentives are taken into account, it becomes clear that eliminating the mandatory retirement age will have only limited effects on labor force participation by older workers. For this reason, if increased labor force participation by the aging becomes a policy goal, then modification of retirement eligibility ages and payment options in public and private pension plans will be necessary to encourage a significant increase of older workers in the labor force (Burkhauser 1976, 1979, 1980; Meier 1975; Meier and Dittmar 1980; Mitchell and Fields 1985; Morrison 1982a; Reno 1971; USDOL 1981).

Mandatory retirement rules are only one method of ensuring that a worker leaves a job at a given age. The lifting of such rules, though protecting the worker's right to continue at the same job at an older age, will not ensure that he or she will actually do so. This is because, in addition to forced retirement rules, pension plans have been widely used to induce job exit (Barfield and Morgan 1969; Blinder, Gordon, and Wise 1978a; Boskin 1975; Bowen and Finegan 1969; Burkhauser 1979; Hall and Johnson 1980; Lazear 1979; Parnes and Nestel 1979; Quinn 1977, 1978; Rones 1978; Schulz 1974).

Pension plans can and do exert economic pressure on individuals to leave a job or even leave the labor force. Of course, the very existence of a pension that can be taken at a given age will provide workers with the option of leaving their jobs and accepting payments at that age. Thus, generous pension plans will eliminate to some degree the need for mandatory retirement rules. But pension plans have been designed to induce retirement with even greater certainty. If those who continue working were rewarded with increased yearly benefits that fully compensated them for not immediately taking a pension, only individual preferences would enter into such a choice. This type of pension system would be neutral with respect to the timing of payments. It would encourage or discourage the acceptance of these payments and subsequent job separation at any particular age only to the extent that any kind of asset affects such a decision. A pension system is not neutral when the lifetime value of payments changes with the timing of payment acceptance. It is this aspect of pensions that greatly facilitates their use as alternative mechanisms for encouraging specific patterns of retirement (Blinder 1973; Blinder, Gordon, and Wise 1978b; Burkhauser and Turner 1978; Hammermesh and Grant 1979; Quinn 1977).

Most pensions decrease in lifetime value when postponed and therefore put economic pressure on workers to leave their jobs and accept a pension. Employers can affect the age of retirement by ensuring that the optimal time for acceptance of pensions occurs at the age they desire employees to leave the firm. Nonneutral pension plans can therefore strongly influence retirement-age decisions. Rather than forcing retirement at a given age, they reduce the advantage of continued employment by effectively reducing the future pension provided for continued work (Anderson 1978; Burkhauser 1976; Meier and Dittmar 1980; Morrison 1982b; Schulz 1974; Walker and Lazer 1978).

In order to examine the effects of mandatory retirement rules on labor supply and estimate potential changes in labor force participation without mandatory retirement, two labor supply models were used: a retirement transition model (Burkhauser and Quinn 1980), and a retirement simulation model. Both models were tested using existing survey data, and labor force participation estimates were derived based on the results of the models.

RETIREMENT TRANSITION MODEL

Estimates of retirement behavior were derived from data in the Social Security Administration Retirement History Survey (RHS), a ten-year longitudinal study by the Social Security Administration of a national sample of older workers approaching retirement age (Quinn 1978; U.S. Department of Health, Education and Welfare [USDHEW] 1976a). The research was undertaken to develop, from survey responses, reliable estimates of Social Security and pension benefit amounts and the wealth such benefits represent and to combine these data with information on mandatory retirement effects in order to predict retirement behavior.

The basic approach was to estimate, over two-year intervals, the probabilities that employed workers would remain in the same job, move to a new job, or leave the work force altogether. Separate estimates were made by sex, by employed versus self-employed status (for men only), and by age group (58–61, 62–64, and 65–67). Analysis was performed on a series of variables for those respondents who were not subject to mandatory retirement during the two-year intervals. By then applying the resulting predictions to respondents who were subject to mandatory retirement, and by comparing predicted with actual labor force transitions for these people, upper limits were derived for the marginal impact that mandatory retirement *alone* may have had on these transitions.

The explanatory variables used in the job transition equations included the following: indexes of eligibility for a full pension or a reduced pension during the transition periods; wealth measures for lifetime pension and Social Security benefits; estimates of the net costs in terms of foregone benefits of a one-year delay in acceptance of a pension and of Social Security; indexes for the presence of a mandatory retirement constraint occurring after the two-year transition interval; marital status; indexes for health limitations and evidence of deteriorating health; and market wage rates.

Groups Subject to Analysis

With four waves of RHS data, the labor market transitions of employed respondents were studied over two periods, 1969–1971 and 1973–1975. The methodology consisted of two stages. First, those employed individuals who did not face a mandatory retirement constraint during the two-year transition period were isolated, and the factors explaining their observed transitions (same job, new job, no job) were analyzed. These results were then used to predict transitions for respondents facing mandatory retirement, and their predicted and observed behaviors were compared.

The age disaggregations isolated three different groups with regard to mandatory retirement. Those people aged 58–61 are not yet eligible for Social Security retirement benefits and are rarely subject to mandatory retirement. For this reason, there was little to be learned from this subsample about the impact of immediate mandatory retirement.

Those aged 65–67 are eligible for full Social Security benefits, and nearly all are beyond the former age of mandatory retirement (65). Those still employed after 65 are rare and unrepresentative.

The remaining group, those aged 62–64 during the base year (1973), are the most important. These workers, who were ages 64–66 by 1975, were nearly all eligible for Social Security benefits during that two-year peroid. In addition, many were or became eligible for reduced or full pension payments, and this is the group with the largest percentage of workers encountering a mandatory retirement restriction.

Results

The principal findings of the analysis are summarized below. The determinants of labor force transitions for persons not subject to mandatory retirement during the transition period differed by sex and age. For men in the youngest cohort (58–61 in the base year), health and retirement income eligibility were the most important factors. Both initial health limitations and a deterioration in health over the two years induced men out of the labor force, as did full pension eligibility or the combination of Social Security and either a full or a reduced pension (Anderson, Burkhauser, and Quinn 1986; Parnes and Nestel 1979; Reno 1971; Schwab 1974). For women aged 58–61, the wage rate was significant; those women with higher wages were more likely to continue working.

In the analysis of men and women aged 62–64 in 1973—the groups of primary interest—the financial variables were most important. The terms, which described the losses in Social Security and pension payments that would occur during an additional year of work, were highly significant. Men and women were less likely to continue work the larger the pensions and Social Security benefits they would have to forego. These more sophisticated variables, which reflected the size of the payments, were better predictors of behavior than simple dummy variables denoting pension and Social Security eligibility.

In addition, the wage rates were important for men (the higher the wage, the more likely they were to continue to work) as were marital and self-employment statuses for women. Married women were more likely to retire, and self-employed women were less so. Health and changes in health were important for both. The behavior of the oldest cohorts—those aged 65–67 and still employed in the base year—was the most difficult to predict. This difficulty was not surprising, since these respondents had largely ignored any retirement incentives that existed at ages 62 and 65. Only a few variables were significant predictors of retirement: the wage rate and full pension eligibility for men, and full pension eligibility and the pension amount change for women. Health was generally insignificant as a predictor of work behavior for this age group (Ehrenberg 1979; Mitchell and Fields 1985; USDHEW 1976b).

At the risk of oversimplification, it could be concluded that health and retirement income eligibility status are the most important predictors of retirement behavior for the youngest group, that the details of the financial incentives dominate for the "normal retirement" (62–65) group, and that the behavior of the late retirees, with the exception of those waiting for full pension eligibility after 65, is the hardest to predict.

The above labor force transition results are based on the behavior of respondents who were *not* subject to mandatory retirement during the transition period; the following discussion focuses on those aged 62–64 who were. In Table 13.1 we show the actual transition behavior of the entire sample between 1973 and 1975. Of those subject to mandatory retirement, 80 percent were out of the labor force by 1975. Of those remaining, 11 percent were still on their 1973 job and 9 percent had switched jobs. This

TABLE 13.1

ACTUAL TRANSITION BEHAVIOR, 1973–1975,
FOR MEN AND WOMEN AGED 62–64 AND EMPLOYED IN 1973
(NUMBER AND PERCENTAGE OF RESPONDENTS)

	Same job[a]	New job[b]	No job[c]	N
Subject to mandatory retirement by 1975				
Men	16 (11.4%)	10 (7.2%)	114 (81.4%)	140
Women	3 (8.8)	5 (14.7)	26 (76.5)	34
Total	19 (10.9)	15 (8.6)	140 (80.5)	174
Not subject to mandatory retirement by 1975				
Men	581 (50.8)	107 (9.3)	456 (39.9)	1,144
Women	232 (59.8)	25 (6.4)	131 (33.8)	388
Total	813 (53.1)	132 (8.6)	587 (38.3)	1,532
Difference in percentages				
Men	−39.4	−2.2	+41.5	
Women	−51.0	+8.3	+42.7	
Total	−42.2	0.0	+42.1	

SOURCE: USDOL (1981).

NOTE: Sample of employed men does not include those who were self-employed.
a. During the subsequent two years, the worker has remained on his/her same job.
b. During the subsequent two years, the worker has taken a new job.
c. During the subsequent two years, the worker has completely moved out of employment.

behavior contrasts strongly with that of workers who were not subject to mandatory retirement by 1975. Of these, only 38 percent moved out of the labor force, 53 percent stayed on the 1973 job, and 9 percent changed jobs. The differences in these numbers represent a potentially large mandatory retirement effect (Clark, Barker, and Cantrell 1979; Copperman, Montgomery, and Keast 1979; Halpern 1978; Reno 1972; Sheppard 1978; U.S. Congress 1977).

In Table 13.2 we present predictions on how those people subject to mandatory retirement would have behaved had this constraint not existed but all their other characteristics remained the same. These predictions were derived by applying results from persons not subject to mandatory retirement to the mandatory retirement populations. The larger the gap in predicted versus actual behavior, the greater the unexplained differential and the larger the potential effect of mandatory retirement.

TABLE 13.2

TRANSITION BEHAVIOR, ACTUAL AND PREDICTED,
FOR MEN AND WOMEN AGED 62–64 AND EMPLOYED IN 1973
(PERCENTAGES)

	Same job	New job	No job	N
Men				
Not subject to mandatory retirement (MR)	50.8	9.3	39.9	1,144
Subject to MR, predicted	40.7	5.9	53.4	140
Subject to MR, actual	11.4	7.2	81.4	140
Women				
Not subject to MR	59.8	6.4	33.8	388
Subject to MR, predicted	43.3	8.7	48.0	34
Subject to MR, actual	8.8	14.7	76.5	34
Total				
Not subject to MR	53.1	8.6	38.3	1,532
Subject to MR, predicted	41.2	6.4	52.4	174
Subject to MR, actual	10.9	8.6	80.5	174

SOURCE: USDOL (1981).

As is seen in Table 13.2, differences in other variables explain some, but certainly not all, of the differences between those who were and were not subject to mandatory retirement. For men, half of those who were not subject remained on the same jobs. Of those who were subject, it was predicted that 40.7 percent would remain, but only 11.4 percent did. Taking another view of the same transition, only 39.9 percent of those not facing mandatory retirement left employment by 1975. It was predicted that 53.4 percent of those who did face it would leave, but 81.4 percent actually left. Of the 41.5-point differential in actual behavior (81.4 minus 39.9), 14 points (53.4 minus 39.9) or a third of the total difference are explained, whereas 28 points (81.4 minus 53.4) are not.

In summary, there are large differences in labor force behavior when those people who were and were not subject to mandatory retirement are compared. For example, those who did face mandatory retirement were over twice as likely to leave the labor force as those who were not forced to leave. About a third of this difference, however, can be attributed to other factors, such as the different pension incentives that influenced the retirement decision. The remainder, about 28 percentage points for both men and women, cannot be so explained and might be attributed to mandatory retirement.

These effects, however, probably represent upper bounds for the impact of mandatory retirement and quite likely overstate its importance for two basic reasons. First, the distribution of workers among jobs with and without mandatory retirement is probably not random; instead, it is likely to be correlated with unmeasured retirement age preferences. For individuals who prefer to remain working after age 65, a compulsory retirement rule is a serious drawback. Such individuals might tend to stay away from jobs with this constraint, either by avoiding them completely or by moving out long before the compulsory date arrives.

Second, since the methodology concentrates on transitions over time, it starts with a sample of employed workers. Those respondents who were especially sensitive to the Social Security and pension effects have been eliminated, since they have already withdrawn from the labor force by age 62. Compulsory retirement for these individuals is irrelevant. The remaining sample is more likely than average to have ignored these incentives, and therefore it is more likely than average to encounter and be influenced by mandatory retirement.

Little evidence was found of job switching in response to mandatory retirement. Neither was much evidence found of an anticipatory mandatory retirement effect among men and women aged 62–64.

Estimation of Labor Supply Effects

The following analysis examines the effects of changing the mandatory retirement age on the labor force participation rate of men aged 62–64 over a two-year transition period. In Table 13.3 we compare the actual labor force participation of this cohort in 1975 with the predicted labor force participation if the law had been changed to permit mandatory retirement at age 70 during the transition period.

Only 14.5 percent of the men in this age cohort who were working in 1973 were subject to mandatory retirement during the next two years. Using Social Security population data, this group was estimated to include 238,000 men. Of this group, only 17 percent (40,000) remained in the labor force in 1975. If the labor force withdrawal not explained by the predictive equations is the result of mandatory retirement, its removal would have increased the labor supply of those who faced mandatory retirement in the transition period by 28 percentage points. Thus, their overall labor force participation rate would rise to 45 percent (107,000 workers). This change in the law would have resulted in an estimated additional 67,000 men remaining at work who otherwise would have exited from the labor force.

Of the 1,641,000 men aged 62–64 and working in 1973, 843,000 (51 percent) continued to work in 1975. If the mandatory retirement law had

TABLE 13.3

INITIAL EFFECT OF CHANGING MINIMUM MANDATORY RETIREMENT (MR) FROM AGE 65 TO 70
ON THE 1975 LABOR SUPPLY OF MEN AGED 62–64 IN 1973
(SIMULATED FOR THE TRANSITION PERIOD 1973–1975)

Subject to MR rules	(1) MR status of working population (percentages)[f]	(2) Number of workers subject to MR (thousands)[g]	(3) Actual labor force participation rate in 1975 (percentages)[h]	(4) Number of workers in labor force in 1975 (thousands)	(5) Labor force participation rate in 1975 given a minimum MR Age of 70 (percentages)	(6) Number of workers in labor force in 1975 given a minimum MR Age of 70 (thousands)	(7) Change in number of workers in labor force (thousands)
Now[a]	14.5	238	16.8	40[k]	44.8[n]	107[p]	67
Later[b]	22.2	364	54.9	200[k]	57.0[n]	207[p]	7
Never[c]	63.3	1,039	58.1	603[k]	58.1	603[p]	0
In labor force in 1973[d]	—	1,641	51.4	843[k]	55.9	917[p]	74
Out of labor force in 1973[e]	—	735	0.0	0	0.0	—	—
Total population	—	2,376	37.7	2,236[m]	41.0	—	—

SOURCE: USDOL (1981).

a. Subject to a mandatory retirement age on current job during 1973–1975.

b. Subject to a mandatory retirement age on current job at some time but not during 1973–1975.

c. Not subject to mandatory retirement age on current job.

d. Working at a job in 1973.

e. Not working at a job in 1973.

f. Based on data from RHS.

g. In 1973, 2.328 million men aged 62–64 were eligible to receive Old Age and Survivors Insurance benefits (USDHEW 1976a, table 51), and 98 percent of the total male population were so eligible (USDHEW 1976b, table 49). The labor force participation rate for men aged 60–64 in 1973 was 69.1 percent.

h. Based on data from RHS.

k. Column 2 multiplied by Column 3.

m. Survivor rate based on life table for men.

n. Based on regression results from USDOL (1981).

p. Column 2 multiplied by Column 5.

been changed in 1973, the estimated additional 74,000 workers would have raised the total working to 917,000 men (8 percent). Overall, that would have increased the 1975 labor force participation rate for men aged 64–66 from 38 to 41 percent.

Overall, as indicated in Table 13.4, the estimated initial effect of increasing the minimum mandatory retirement age from 65 to 70 for those aged 58–67 in 1973 would have been an increase in the labor force participation of this group in 1975 by 114,000 men and 86,000 women. That is, 200,000 workers would have continued in the labor force who otherwise left their jobs because of mandatory retirement.

These estimates should not cause great concern regarding the potential effect of increasing the mandatory retirement age on job displacement or career retardation of younger workers. The estimate of 200,000 additional workers due to the change in law would have resulted in increases of 0.16 percentage points in the male labor force participation rate and 0.11 percent in the female rate. Such changes would be smaller in magnitude than those caused by the seasonal movement of students into and out of the labor force. They would be totally swamped by business cycle changes.

The original 1978 change in the law raising the mandatory retirement age to 70 was expected to increase the labor force participation rates of older workers directly by allowing workers to remain on jobs they otherwise would have been forced to leave and by reducing the number of workers who left in anticipation of a mandatory retirement age. The initial estimated effect was that at most 5 percent (200,000 workers) continued working who otherwise would have left the labor force. Although the change in the law was expected to have some measurable effect, in the context of the entire economy the overall impact was expected to be small, on the basis of this research.

Interaction of Effects on Labor Supply from Mandatory Retirement and Pension Provisions

It is apparent that the incidence of mandatory retirement rules during the transition period was most important for workers aged 62–64 in 1973. The fact that only 20 percent of such workers remained in the work force suggests that mandatory retirement rules are important. But as indicated in Table 13.5, such rules were only one aspect of the retirement system that had a major impact during this transition period.

As can be seen from Table 13.5, of the 217 RHS respondents aged 62–64 in 1973 who would be subject to a mandatory retirement rule by 1975, nearly three out of four were also eligible to collect a pension during those two years, and most were eligible for full payments. (For pension plans that

TABLE 13.4

INITIAL EFFECT OF CHANGING MINIMUM MANDATORY RETIREMENT (MMR) FROM AGE 65 TO 70 ON THE LABOR SUPPLY OF OLDER WORKERS IN 1975 (SIMULATED FOR THE TRANSITION PERIOD 1973–1975)

Age in 1975	MEN		WOMEN		Net change in workers who would remain in labor force in 1975 (thousands)
	Labor force participation rates in 1975 (percentages)	Number in labor force in 1975 (thousands)	Labor force participation rates in 1975 (percentages)	Number in labor force in 1975 (thousands)	
60–63					
MMR = 65	71.3	2,403	36.5	1,489	
MMR = 70	72.1	2,432	37.6	1,534	
Net effect	0.8	29	1.1	45	+74
64–66					
MMR = 65	37.7	843	20.4	542	
MMR = 70	41.0	917	21.6	573	
Net effect	3.3	74	1.2	31	+105
67–69					
MMR = 65	22.5	402	10.4	240	
MMR = 70	23.1	413	10.8	250	
Net effect,	0.6	11	0.4	10	+21
Total population age 16 and over					
MMR = 65	80.40	58,984	46.62	37,207	
MMR = 70	80.56	59,098	46.73	37,293	
Net effect	0.16	114	0.11	86	+200

SOURCE: USDOL (1981).

TABLE 13.5

RELATIONSHIP BETWEEN MR PROVISIONS
AND ELIGIBILITY FOR PENSION BENEFITS
FOR MEN AND WOMEN AGED 62–64 AND EMPLOYED IN 1973
(NUMBER AND PERCENTAGE OF RESPONDENTS)

Subject to MR rules	ELIGIBLE TO COLLECT PRIVATE PENSION BENEFITS				
	Eligible for reduced benefits by 1975	Eligible for full benefits by 1975	Eligible later than 1975	Never eligible	N
1973–1975					
Men	15 (9)	117 (68)	30 (17)	11 (6)	173
Women	3 (7)	27 (61)	5 (11)	9 (21)	44
Total	18 (8%)	144 (67%)	35 (16%)	20 (9%)	217
Later					
Men	67 (25)	76 (29)	92 (35)	29 (11)	264
Women	15 (28)	15 (28)	16 (31)	7 (13)	53
Total	82 (26)	91 (29)	108 (34)	36 (11)	317
Never					
Men	59 (8)	107 (14)	190 (25)	398 (53)	754
Women	3 (1)	17 (7)	35 (14)	198 (78)	253
Total	62 (6)	124 (12)	225 (23)	596 (59)	1,007
Total population					
Men	141 (12)	300 (25)	312 (26)	438 (37)	1,191
Women	21 (6)	59 (17)	56 (16)	214 (61)	350
Total	162 (11)	359 (23)	368 (24)	652 (42)	1,541

SOURCE: Retirement History Survey (1969 through 1975).

are "integrated" with Social Security, these payments include amounts to make up the difference in Social Security benefits for retirees who would have elected [or in some cases who do elect] to accept reduced Social Security benefits between ages 62 and 64. Once the recipient reaches age 65, the pension payment is reduced by a percentage of the Social Security benefit. Thus, in many cases, persons electing to retire between ages 62 and 64 will suffer no economic loss in pension payments.) Only 9 percent would never be eligible for any pension payments. Of those subject to mandatory retirement at a later age, nine in ten were also eligible for pensions, either during the transition period (55 percent) or later. Of all the workers subject to mandatory retirement rules either during the transition or at a later time, only 10 percent were not eligible for pension payments.

These pension eligibility rates are in sharp contrast to those for workers not subject to mandatory retirement rules. Although 40 percent of the latter group were eligible to receive private pensions, 60 percent had no private pension coverage. There was clearly a strong correlation between mandatory retirement rules and pension plans, not only with respect to coverage but also with respect to the age at which they both became effective. The vast majority of workers, both male and female, who were subject to a mandatory retirement age were also eligible to receive pension payments at that age. Thus, the impact of either retirement rules or pensions should not be considered without explicitly taking into account the importance of the other.

The impact of both of these potential inducements to change jobs or leave the labor force can be seen quite clearly in Table 13.6. Two out of every three workers remained in the labor force over the transition period if they were neither eligible to collect a pension nor subject to a mandatory retirement provision on their current jobs. This result is in sharp contrast to the one worker in ten who remained in the labor force among those both eligible to collect a full pension and subject to a mandatory retirement age during the transition period. The combined impact of pensions and mandatory retirement almost completely reduced labor force participation.

Another insight from Table 13.6 is that pension plans may have pre-empted the impact of mandatory rules for workers. The highest labor force participation rate (73 percent) was registered for those subject to mandatory retirement later but not yet eligible to collect a pension. The rate was only 33 percent for those eventually subject to mandatory retirement but currently eligible for full pension benefits.

Conclusions of Labor Supply Research

This study indicated that the prior existence of age-65 mandatory retirement rules had a significant impact on the likelihood that workers reaching that age would withdraw from the labor force. For example, the probability that men aged 62–64 who were wage or salary workers in 1973 would continue to work at any job over the next two years diminished by about 28 percentage points due to the age-65 mandatory retirement rule.

Had the 1978 Age Discrimination in Employment Act (ADEA) Amendments become effective during 1973–1975, the result of raising the mandatory retirement age from 65 to 70 would have been that at most 200,000 older workers would have been working in 1975 instead of retired. The level of the permitted mandatory retirement age was, of course, of great significance to individual workers approaching age 65 who wanted to continue working and were unlikely to have much opportunity at that age to move to

TABLE 13.6

LABOR FORCE PARTICIPATION RATES IN 1975 FOR EMPLOYED
MEN AND WOMEN AGED 62–64
BY MR PROVISIONS AND PENSION ARRANGEMENTS
(PERCENTAGES)

| Subject to MR rules | ELIGIBLE TO COLLECT PRIVATE PENSION BENEFITS | | | | |
	Eligible for reduced benefits by 1975	Eligible for full benefits by 1975	Eligible later than 1975	Never eligible	Total
1975–1977					
Men	a	8.5	33.3[b]	a	16.8
Women	a	14.8[b]	a	a	18.2[b]
Total	a	9.7	31.4[b]	55.0[b]	17.1
Later					
Men	50.7	34.2	71.7	65.5[b]	54.9
Women	a	a	a	a	58.5
Total	51.2	33.0	73.1	69.4[b]	55.5
Never					
Men	44.1	29.0	64.2	65.1	58.1
Women	a	a	54.3[b]	69.2	64.8
Total	45.2	29.8	62.7	66.4	59.8
Total population					
Men	43.5	22.3	63.5	65.3	
Women	47.6[b]	23.7	58.9	68.2	
Total	48.5	22.5	62.8	66.3	

SOURCE: Retirement History Survey (1969 through 1975).
NOTE: Labor force participation is 100 percent in 1973.
a. Based on fewer than 20 observations.
b. Based on 20–50 observations.

other jobs, but it was less important in the degree of impact it had in the measurable increment to the *total* number of such workers. For example, the maximum figure (200,000) implied a 3 percent labor force increase for men aged 64–66 in 1975. However, viewed in the context of the national economy, this change in labor supply would have been a minuscule increase in the total workforce (less than two-tenths of one percent).

This study also estimated the relative importance of Social Security benefit and pension entitlements to the retirement decision, both in terms of the current year tradeoff (loss of a year's wages versus loss of retirement benefits) and the wealth effect (the present asset value of a lifetime of future benefits). The current tradeoff of benefits versus wages was found to be especially important, reflecting the fact that Social Security and the bulk of pension plans are designed to facilitate retirement.

Since mandatory retirement provisions are closely tied to private pensions, this research indicates that the incentives inherent in pension plans are important determinants of behavior—people do respond to these incentives. Therefore, the eventual impact of changes in mandatory retirement age legislation depends critically on how pension characteristics change. If employers cannot dismiss employees at age 65 on the basis of age but are permitted to structure fringe benefits to make it expensive for workers to forego retirement benefits beyond that point, changes in mandatory retirement rules will have only a modest aggregate impact (Burkhauser and Talley 1978; Ross 1978; Rosenfeld and Brown 1979).

RETIREMENT SIMULATION MODEL

This section describes research on the long-term labor supply effects of alternative mandatory retirement policies. Estimates of changes in the labor force participation of older workers were projected to the year 2000 for three policy options: the old law (age-65 mandatory retirement); the 1978 ADEA Amendments (age-70 mandatory retirement); and a policy that prohibits employers' use of mandatory retirement (the 1986 ADEA Amendments). In addition, the sensitivity of these estimates was tested to a possible change in retirement benefits—larger benefits under employer-provided pensions when retirement is delayed past the normal retirement age.

Estimated effects of changes in labor force participation rates are based upon the retirement transition model. This model was applied to data for a sample of 60,000 persons from the 1973 Current Population Survey (CPS) and matched Social Security Earnings Records (SER). The projections to the year 2000 involved use of dynamic simulation techniques that take into account expected changes in demographic and economic characteristics of individuals as they age and compute entitlement to Social Security and employer pensions. The retirement transition model—which takes into account individuals' Social Security benefits and pension payments and mandatory retirement constraints as well as age, wage rate, health status, and other variables—was applied to estimate the labor force participation of persons between ages 60 and 70 for three points in time (1985, 1990, and 2000).

Methodology

The basic data base used as input was the March 1973 CPS-SER Exact Match File. Included in the Social Security data on the file are each person's covered wages for each year since 1951 and each year's quarters of coverage since 1937. The amount of the Social Security benefit is an important determinant of the timing of the retirement decision, since workers reaching retirement age in 2000 will have Social Security benefits based upon earnings back to the mid-1950s.

For this project, a subsample of half the March 1973 CPS-SER was used. This sample was aged year by year from 1973 to the year 2000 using the Family Earnings History (FEH) model. This model updates a sample by projecting, for each year and for each person in the sample, whether the person's basic demographic status will change and what his or her labor force activity and earnings will be. Basic demographic characteristics that are updated are age, marital status, educational attainment, disability status, number of children for women, and whether the person will die during that period. Labor force characteristics projected are participation in the labor force, wage rate, hours worked, and hours unemployed. For this analysis, simulated earnings for each year after 1972 were saved on each person's record to be able to calculate Social Security benefits in the year 2000 or any earlier year.

The output file from the FEH model with each person's characteristics for the year 2000 and earlier years was used as input into a second simulation model, the JOBS model. This model added to each person's records simulated job histories to match the labor force histories. These histories included number of jobs held, the years the jobs were held, the industry of the job, and whether the worker was covered by a private pension plan on the job. These data were needed to compute employer pension payments—another major determinant of the timing of the retirement decision.

Using the data from the 1973 CPS-SER file augmented by data from the FEH and JOBS models, it was possible to put together all of the data required to simulate retirement using the retirement transition model. Application of the retirement transition model was the last step in estimating the long-term impact of alternative mandatory retirement policies. The model estimates the age at which persons in the labor force at age 58 will retire. Included in the determinants of retirement is whether the worker is subject to mandatory retirement and at what age. The steps in the development of the data base are summarized in the Appendix.[1]

Policy Simulations

The data bases and the retirement transition model were used to estimate older workers' labor force participation rates under three alternative mandatory retirement policies.

The first policy was a continuation of the law in effect prior to passage of the 1978 ADEA Amendments. Under this law, workers could be required to leave their jobs at age 65 at the earliest (Edelman and Siegler 1978–79; MacDonald 1978; Morrison 1982b). Prior to the 1978 ADEA Amendments, 56 percent of private-sector workers over age 40 were subject to mandatory retirement. Of these workers, 90 percent were subject to mandatory retirement at age 65, an additional 6 percent were subject to mandatory retirement at ages 66–69, and 4 percent were subject to mandatory retirement at age 70. The simulations assume this distribution would not change greatly between 1980 and the year 2000 without a change in the law.

The second mandatory retirement policy simulated is the 1978 ADEA law. This law specified 70 as the earliest mandatory retirement age but for a few exceptions (Morrison 1982b; Ross 1978). Of private sector workers age 40 or older in early 1980, 47 percent were subject to mandatory retirement. With rare exceptions, the mandatory retirement age for these workers was 70. The simulations assumed there would be no change in the percentage of workers subject to mandatory retirement or in the age requirements between 1980 and the year 2000 without legislation to raise the legal minimum mandatory retirement age.

The third mandatory retirement policy simulated assumed the elimination of mandatory retirement, effective January 1980.

A fourth set of simulations was also performed as part of this research. These simulations attempted to estimate the impact on older workers' labor force participation not only of raising or eliminating the mandatory retirement age but also of requiring employers to offer fair increases in retirement pension benefits to employees who continue to work after fulfilling the age and service requirements for normal retirement. This anticipated the provision in the 1986 ADEA Amendments requiring continued pension accruals for persons working beyond the normal retirement age in qualified pension plans.

The fourth simulation assumed that all provisions that restrict benefit accruals after normal retirement eligibility would be prohibited by law. Furthermore, the simulation assumed employers would be required to give near actuarially fair increases in benefits to workers who were eligible for normal retirement benefits but continued to work. "Near actuarially fair" was defined as a 10 percent increase in the benefit for each year retirement was postponed between ages 65 and 70. (For workers who were eligible for

normal retirement before age 65, the simulation assumed a 5 percent increase in benefits for each year retirement was postponed.)[2]

Research Findings

Labor supply effects of mandatory retirement policy options. The retirement behavior of these samples was estimated under each of the mandatory retirement standards described above, and the results for each of the
simulation years were tabulated. Labor force participants and nonparticipants were tabulated separately for men and women in the age groups 60–
61, 62–64, 65–67, and 68–70. The resulting labor force participation rates
for men are shown in Table 13.7 for the years 1985, 1990, and 2000 for
each age group and under each alternative mandatory retirement policy.

Raising the mandatory retirement age increases the labor force participation rates in all age groups between 60 and 70. This is true both in the near
future and in the longer run—say, in the year 2000. Among workers aged
60–64, raising the mandatory retirement age to 70 increases the labor force
participation only slightly, however. As expected, the increase in participation rates is largest for workers between 65 and 67. Hence, raising the
mandatory retirement age from 65 to 70 increases the labor force participation rate by nearly 7 percentage points in the year 2000, which represents an
increase of 20 percent in the number of male workers aged 65–67. Increases
in the labor force participation rate of workers under age 65 and over 67 are
very much smaller.

For workers between ages 68 and 70, the effect of raising the mandatory
retirement age from 65 to 70 was also very small, although more than twice
as large in percentage terms than the impact on workers under 65. For this
group, the higher age represents almost a 5 percent increase in labor force
participation. This increase is in part the result of more workers having
remained in the work force to age 68 because they were no longer subject to
mandatory retirement at age 65 or were no longer subject to mandatory
retirement at all.

As shown in Table 13.7, eliminating mandatory retirement altogether
results in still further increases in labor force participation rates among older
men. In moving from mandatory retirement at age 70 to no mandatory
retirement, the greatest increase in labor force participation is among men
aged 67—70. In the year 2000, the increase from 19.8 to 23.9 percent
participation is a 21 percent increase in the number of men in this age group
who would be working. The primary reason for this increase is a difference
in the behavior of men over age 65 when they leave their current jobs.
According to the retirement transition results, whether or not a worker takes

TABLE 13.7

LABOR FORCE PARTICIPATION RATES FOR MEN
UNDER ALTERNATIVE MR POLICIES, 1985, 1990, AND 2000
(PERCENTAGES)

Year and age group	MINIMUM MR AGE		
	65	70	None allowed
1985[a]			
60–61	84.6	85.3	86.5
62–64	69.5	69.7	69.9
65–67	33.1	41.0	41.1
68–70	17.6	22.0	27.8
1990			
60–61[b]	84.9	85.2	86.0
62–64	68.2	69.5	71.8
65–67	32.9	40.4	42.2
68–70[b]	18.6	19.4	23.9
2000[c]			
60–61	87.9	88.6	89.3
62–64	67.9	69.3	70.6
65–67	33.4	40.1	42.9
68–70	18.9	19.8	23.9

SOURCE: USDOL (1981).
a. Two outlying estimates were eliminated. Based on five replications.
b. Age group 60–61 estimates based on four selected runs. Age 65 rate for age group 68–70 based on first seven simulations.
c. Based on seven replications; no judgmental selections.

a new job when he leaves his current employer is strongly dependent on whether the worker is subject to mandatory retirement. Older men of all ages are less likely to seek other jobs if they were covered by mandatory retirement on the jobs they just left. According to the results, the elimination of mandatory retirement would result in a 15 percent increase in the probability that workers who leave their jobs would continue to work in other jobs for at least one more year.

The increases in labor force participation rates for workers aged 60–67 are smaller than those for workers between 68 and 70. However, the increase in the absolute number of men aged 65–67 in the labor force would actually be larger—roughly 200,000 as compared to 100,000 for men aged 68–70.

TABLE 13.8

INCREASES IN MALE LABOR FORCE PARTICIPATION RATES
IN THE YEAR 2000 RESULTING FROM ALTERNATIVE MR POLICIES
(PERCENTAGES)

| | MR AGE CHANGED | |
Age group	From 65 to 70	From 70 to no MR
60–61	0.8	0.8
62–64	2.0	1.9
65–67	20.0	7.0
68–70	4.8	20.7

SOURCE: USDOL (1981).

In Table 13.8 we summarize older male workers' labor force responses in the year 2000 due to changing the mandatory retirement age from 65 to 70 and from 70 to elimination of mandatory retirement. The responses are percentage increases in the labor force participation rates of the age groups.

Because of the 1978 change in the mandatory retirement age from 65 to 70, the simulations predict increased labor force participation among all ages of male workers between 60 and 70. The largest predicted increase will be among workers aged 65–67; their labor force participation will increase 20 percent.

Moving from the age-70 mandatory retirement policy to elimination of mandatory retirement would further increase labor force participation rates. As shown in Table 13.8, the additional response of workers aged 60–64 would be as large as their response to the change of mandatory retirement from age 65 to 70. The response of those aged 65–67 to elimination of mandatory retirement would not be as great as their response to changing the mandatory retirement age from 65 to 70; however, it would still be substantial (7 percent increase).

The largest long-term labor force response to eliminating mandatory retirement would be among workers aged 68–70. In the absence of changes due to other factors, the labor force participation rate of this group would increase by about 21 percent.

Clearly, in the absence of other offsetting changes, the changes in law enacted in 1978 and 1986 will increase the labor force participation of older workers significantly. In particular, the elimination of mandatory retirement would result in increases of a lesser but still significant magnitude. The next section estimates the actual number of older workers under alternative mandatory retirement policies.

Projected increases in numbers of older workers. Labor force participation rates and the projected number of male workers in each age group are shown in Table 13.9 under an age-65 mandatory retirement policy assumption; the table also shows the number of additional older men who are predicted to continue working in the year 2000 because of the change in the mandatory retirement age to 70. In all, 217,000 more men between ages 60 and 70 can be expected to be in the work force as a result of the 1978 ADEA Amendments. This represents a total increase in labor force participation of this group of a little over 5 percent. Well over half of the increase is among those aged 65–67, who would have been most directly affected by age-65 mandatory retirement.

According to the predictions of the retirement transition model, a substantial additional increase of 195,000 male workers would result if mandatory retirement were eliminated entirely as the 1986 ADEA Amendments require. These workers would represent a 4.5 percent increase in the male work force aged 60–70 above the level expected with mandatory retirement at age 70.

The largest single impact of eliminating mandatory retirement altogether would be among those aged 68–70; an estimated additional 90,000 of these workers would then remain in the labor force. With elimination of

TABLE 13.9

OLDER MEN IN THE LABOR FORCE IN THE YEAR 2000
UNDER ALTERNATIVE MR POLICIES

| | AGE = 65 MR | | INCREASE IN WORK FORCE FOR MR AGE CHANGE | |
| | *Adjusted participation rate* | *Total male work force* | *From 65 to 70* | *From 70 to no MR* |
Age group	*(percentages)*	*(thousands)*	*(thousands)*	*(thousands)*
60–61	70.3	1,491	12.4	12.2
62–64	54.3	1,458	30.0	27.9
65–67	30.7	772	155.5	64.7
68–70	17.4	417	19.3	90.3
Total	—	4,138	217.2	195.1

SOURCE: USDOL (1981).

mandatory retirement, these workers are far more likely when they leave their preretirement jobs to seek new employment, possibly with more flexible hours and/or a less demanding work load. The overall results indicate that mandatory retirement ages affect employee behavior through a complex process that results in earlier departure from employment and lack of re-employment after leaving the current job (Becker 1964; Bixby 1976; Kasschau 1976).

Effects of adjusting pension benefit accruals after normal retirement eligibility. There is currently a lack of analysis of how employer pension plans treat the accrual of benefits after a worker fulfills all requirements for normal (unreduced) retirement benefits. In the prior simulations, it was assumed that benefits of all workers were frozen at the point of normal retirement eligibility (Hewitt Associates 1980).

At the time the simulations were run, it was known that not all workers' benefits were frozen at the age of normal retirement eligibility. In particular, defined contribution plans, which apply to roughly 20 percent of covered workers, must permit increases in benefits if they continue to collect contributions.

In Table 13.10 we show the distribution of workers covered by various types of late retirement provisions. Almost 27 percent of covered workers were in plans that offer no increases in benefits after normal retirement eligibility. An additional 22 percent were covered by plans that have age and/or service limits on the accrual of benefits. Thirty-six percent of workers were clearly covered by plans where benefits continue to accrue without limit after normal retirement eligibility. In a minority of these cases, the accrual is on some actuarial basis. In short, it is certain that about 36 percent of covered workers continue to accrue benefits without limit and that as many as 22 percent more may receive benefit increases if they do not exceed age or service limits.

In Table 13.11 we present results from a simulation that gave all covered workers new actuarial benefit increases for postponing retirement. These increases were 5 percent of the normal benefit for each year of postponement if normal retirement eligibility occurred before age 65 and 10 percent per year of postponement for normal retirement at or after age 65. Currently, using an assumed 6 percent interest rate, an actuarially fair increase in benefits for postponing retirement one year would be 16–17 percent for men between ages 65 and 70. For women, the fair increase would be about 12 percent for each year retirement was postponed between ages 65 and 70. The lower unisex rate of 10 percent was selected because of expected increases in longevity over the next twenty years and because pension plans tend to be conservative in their actuarial assumptions.

TABLE 13.10

TREATMENT OF BENEFIT ACCRUALS TO WORKERS
WHO POSTPONE RETIREMENT PAST NORMAL ELIGIBILITY

Plan's late retirement provision	Covered workers (percentages)
No provision in plan for late retirement	15.6
No benefit accruals after normal retirement eligibility	26.8
Continued benefit accruals subject to age and/or service limitations	21.6
Benefits actuarially increased based on data at start of retirement	4.8
Benefits continue to accrue with no age or service limits	31.2
Total	100.0
Number of employers	2,602

SOURCE: USDOL (1981).

Under the age-70 mandatory retirement policy, male labor force participation rates at the turn of the century would not be much affected by increases in employer pension benefits for delayed retirement of the magnitude simulated. In all, only 50,000 more men aged 60–70 would be working, which is only a 1 percent increase in labor force participation for this group. The primary reason for this low response is that for workers below age 65, a 5 percent increase in the normal pension payment is an inducement to retire.

For workers aged 65 and older, the net effect of the 10 percent yearly increase in the normal retirement benefit is to increase labor force participation by about 15 percent. Under the age-70 mandatory retirement policy, this is the only age group with a strong response to the 10 percent increases in delayed normal retirement benefits.

With mandatory retirement eliminated, the increase in labor force participation (because of increases in employer pension benefits after normal retirement) would be somewhat stronger than under mandatory retirement at age 70. Without mandatory retirement, it is estimated that about 68,000 additional men aged 60–70 would be in the work force in the year 2000.

Table 13.11

Effect of Requiring Upward Adjustments in Employer Pension
Benefits After the Normal Retirement Age on
Male Labor Force Participation in the Year 2000

	LABOR FORCE PARTICIPATION WITH[a]		
Age group	No adjustment in benefit (percentages)	Near actuarial adjustments (percentages)[b]	Change in size of work force (thousands)
MR at age 70			
60–61	70.9	69.7	−25.4
62–64	55.4	55.4	0.0
65–67	36.9	37.3	9.8
68–70	18.2	20.9	64.7
No MR			
60–61	71.4	70.6	−18.3
62–64	56.5	58.5	55.4
65–67	39.5	40.1	15.5
68–70	22.0	22.6	15.1

Source: USDOL (1981).

a. Labor force participation rates adjusted to reflect projected trends.

b. Workers eligible for normal benefits before age 65 had their benefits increased 5 percent for each year retirement was delayed. Workers eligible for normal benefits at age 65 or later had their benefits increased 10 percent for each year retirement was delayed.

This is a 1.5 percent increase in the work force, as opposed to the 1 percent predicted under the policy allowing for mandatory retirement at age 70.

Conclusions of Retirement Simulations

This section has described research on the long-term labor supply effects of alternative mandatory retirement policies. Estimates of changes in the labor force participation of older workers were projected to the year 2000 for three policy options: the old law (age-65 mandatory retirement); the 1978 ADEA Amendments (age-70 mandatory retirement); and a policy that prohibits employers' use of mandatory retirement (the 1986 ADEA Amendments). In addition, the sensitivity of the estimates was tested to a possible change in retirement benefits: larger benefits under employer-provided pensions when retirement is delayed past the normal retirement age.

Estimated effects of changes in labor force participation rates were based on a retirement transition model developed for use in estimating the effects of mandatory retirement age on employment. This model was applied to data for a sample of 60,000 persons from the 1973 CPS-SER. The projections to the year 2000 involved use of dynamic simulation techniques that take into account expected changes in demographic and economic characteristics of individuals as they age and that compute entitlements to Social Security and employer pension benefits, assuming moderate inflation, economic growth, and a continuation of current retirement policies and trends. The retirement decision model—which takes into account individuals' Social Security and pension wealth and mandatory retirement constraints as well as age, wage, rate, health status, and other variables—was applied to estimate the labor force participation of persons between ages 60 and 70 for three points in time (1985, 1990, and 2000).

The estimates indicated that labor force participation of older men should rise as a result of the 1978 ADEA Amendments prohibiting mandatory retirement before age 70. Slight increases in the participation rate were forecast for older men under age 65. The most significant impacts on older workers remaining in the labor force were found for those aged 65 and over. In all three years (1985, 1990, and 2000), men aged 65–67 were estimated to experience a participation rate increase from about 33 to about 40 percent. For men aged 68–70, a significant increase was also found, although the pattern was not as uniform. In 1985 the participation rate was estimated to rise from 17.6 to 22.0 percent. In 2000, however, the rate should increase only about 5 percent of the base rate at that time. This difference over time results from the interaction of mandatory retirement policies with trends in Social Security and pension income for this age group, with the retirement benefit effects becoming stronger than mandatory retirement for workers aged 68–70.

Other factors being equal, the change in mandatory retirement from age 65 to 70 will result in approximately 217,000 more older men being in the labor force in 2000, or approximately 5 percent of all male workers aged 60–70 estimated for that year. The bulk of this increase is in the age 65 to 67 range.

As in the policy changes described above, moving from the current age-70 mandatory retirement policy to a situation in which mandatory retirement is prohibited affects, but only modestly, older men who are not yet at the mandatory age. However, for the age bracket that includes age 70, the participation rate rises sharply, from 22.0 to 27.8 percent in 1985 (a 26 percent increase in participation) and from 19.8 to 23.9 percent in 2000 (a 21 percent increase in participation).

Compared to the age-70 policy, elimination of mandatory retirement would result in 195,000 additional older men being in the labor force in

2000. Almost half (90,300) would be in the 68–70 age group. If this figure is added to the estimated rise in the labor force size caused by the increase in the mandatory retirement age from 65 to 70, eliminating any mandatory retirement age would induce 412,000 men to remain in the labor force in 2000. This number constitutes about 10 percent of all male workers aged 60–70 estimated for that year.

The adjustment to employer pension benefits for delayed retirement that was analyzed assumed that all plans provided a 10 percent increase in accrued benefits for each year worked after the normal retirement age (or 5 percent for plans with normal retirement ages younger than 65). This adjustment is more generous than that assumed to exist currently in the majority of plans.

The more generous pension accrual adjustment simulation results indicated an increase in labor force participation both under the age-70 mandatory retirement policy and under a prohibition of mandatory retirement. It was estimated that, if pension plans were revised to encourage later retirement, the number of men aged 60–70 in the labor force in the year 2000 would increase by an additional 49,000 in the age-70 mandatory retirement case and by an additional 68,000 with no mandatory retirement.

Several important conclusions may be drawn from these projections of the labor supply effects of alternative mandatory retirement policies. First, the rate of increase of the downward trend in the labor force participation of older men that has prevailed for two decades could be reversed, at least temporarily, by the 1978 and 1986 ADEA Amendments unless other more powerful economic forces offset the effects attributable to the new policy eliminating mandatory retirement. However, the long-term decline in older men's labor force participation can be expected to resume, so long as other significant policy changes or economic trends that depart sharply from previous experience are absent. Elimination of mandatory retirement constitutes such a policy change, and in this case the projections found that older men's labor force participation would rise not only immediately after enactment of such a policy but would also continue to rise slightly over the longer term.

Second, the order of magnitude of the increase in the work force that should result from the age-70 policy (a 5 percent increase in labor force participation by older workers) found in other studies was confirmed here and found to apply even when viewed over a long period of time.

Third, the total elimination of mandatory retirement would have a similar impact (an additional 5 percent increase in labor force participation) on the male work force when compared to the labor force participation expected under the age-70 policy. Altogether, assuming a continuation of current retirement policies and the 1986 ADEA Amendments eliminating mandatory retirement, an additional 412,000 men aged 60–70 would be added to the labor force by the year 2000. Thus, elimination of mandatory retirement, though helpful to employment aspirations in thousands of individual cases, would be expected to have a marginal impact on the overall labor force—that is, no greater an impact than when the mandatory retirement age was changed from 65 to 70.

Finally, targeted pension adjustments such as an increase in the rate of benefit accruals for delayed retirement could be expected to slightly increase older workers' labor force participation.

APPENDIX

Steps in the Development of Data Base for Year 2000 Application of the Retirement Decision Model

1. Base year data file: matched 1973 CPS-SER with Social Security histories through 1972.
2. Application of family and earnings history model: added demographic and labor force characteristics for each year, 1973–2000.
3. Application of JOBS model: added data on jobs held, years each job held, industry of each job, and private pension coverage.
4. Application of Social Security model: added data on Social Security retired workers' benefits from ages 58 to 71.
5. Employer pension assignment: added data on nomral retirement age, early retirement age, and immediately payable pension benefit for each age from 58 to 70.
6. Mandatory retirement provision assignments: added data on whether or not worker was subject to mandatory retirement and on mandatory retirement statutes.
7. Retirement decision model: computed Social Security and employer pension wealth and year and age at retirement.

SOURCE: USDOL (1981).

DISCUSSION

Robert Hutchens

It is a pleasure to discuss Malcolm Morrison's paper. Morrison is one of a handful of authors who have written about the employer side of the older worker labor market. I have followed his writings with much interest.

The present paper focuses on the supply side of the older worker labor market. It examines the effect of mandatory retirement rules on the labor supply behavior of older workers. Of course, a literature does exist on this issue (see summaries in Rones 1978; Burkhauser and Quinn 1983). The consensus in that literature would seem to be that, prior to the 1978 restrictions on mandatory retirement rules, (a) these rules significantly decreased labor force participation of men who were subject to them, and (b) since only a small fraction of older men were actually subject to mandatory retirement, the overall labor force participation effects of the 1978 restrictions were rather small. Although Morrison's paper comes to essentially the same conclusion, it makes some interesting contributions along the way.

The paper is divided into two parts. The first part addresses the question of whether the retirement behavior of workers who were subject to mandatory retirement provisions differs significantly from that of workers who were not. The attack on this question is reminiscent of Burkhauser and Quinn (1983), but this piece is different in that it extends the analysis to women and to a broader range of ages. The analysis begins by estimating a model of retirement behavior in a sample of people who were not subject to mandatory retirement. This model is then used to predict the behavior of people who were subject to mandatory retirement. Of course, there is a difference between the predicted and actual behavior of people subject to mandatory retirement. For example, the predicted labor force participation rate of men aged 64–66 who were subject to mandatory retirement in 1975 was 45 percent; their actual labor force participation rate was 17 percent.

This gap between actual and predicted behavior is then attributed to mandatory retirement rules.

I have no argument with this line of research so long as it is recognized that the resulting estimates are upper-bound estimates. After all, the gap between actual and predicted behavior may be attributable to several factors other than mandatory retirement rules. For example, the measure of pensions in this work is rather rough. People subject to mandatory retirement may have unobserved pension characteristics that make retirement more likely and that would contribute to the gap. Alternatively, there may be unobserved taste differences between people who were subject to mandatory retirement and people who were not. People who want to work until age 70 would probably select themselves out of jobs with mandatory retirement at age 65. Such factors will tend to widen the gap between actual and predicted behavior, implying that the gap in this paper probably overestimates the effect of mandatory retirement. Since the paper is quite clear about these results representing upper-bound estimates, I have no argument with the first part of the paper.

The question addressed by the second part of the paper is, what effect do various policy changes have on the retirement behavior of older workers? In essence, the paper projects the characteristics of the older population in the years 1985, 1990, and 2000, and it simulates how changes in government policy with respect to mandatory retirement and pensions affect labor force participation rates in those years.

My only complaint about this part of the paper is that the simulations assume no behavioral response by employers. Employers are extremely passive in this model; the government changes a firm's pension or mandatory retirement provisions and increases its costs, and the firm does nothing in response. I think that is a rather strong assumption. Consider, for example, the 1978 prohibition against mandatory retirement before age 70. As argued in Lazear (1979), mandatory retirement provisions may be one component of a compensation plan that is used to elicit worker effort. In that case it is likely that employers will respond to such legislation by finding ways around it. After all, potential substitutes do exist for a mandatory retirement clause. In response to a prohibition against mandatory retirement, employers might increase the actuarial unfairness of their pensions. Alternatively, they might alter working conditions in a way that induces more retirements. The point is that if employers want to encourage retirement at age 65, there are alternative ways of doing so besides a mandatory retirement provision. If the government places restrictions on mandatory retirement, employers are likely to consider those alternatives.

In fact, something similar may have occurred after the 1978 legislation prohibiting mandatory retirement before age 70. Lazear (1983) and Mitchell and Luzadis (1986) examine changes in pension characteristics around the time of the 1978 legislation. Both find evidence (albeit not conclusive evidence) indicating that pensions put greater emphasis on encouraging early retirement. Moreover, in another paper by Morrison (1985), he presents data on a 1983 survey of employers. The survey inquired whether there had been any change in employer policies toward early retirement between 1978 and 1983. Fourteen percent of the employers said that they were providing more encouragement for early retirement, 4 percent said they were providing less encouragement, and the remaining 82 percent said no change. The fact that 14 percent were providing more encouragement for early retirement is interesting. It is conceivable that this was due to the 1978 legislation.

In these simulations, employers do not react to changes in government policy. The government restricts the employer's options with regard to mandatory retirement, yet employers do not change other components of the compensation package (like wages and pensions). Only workers react. Under these assumptions, the simulations indicate that workers retire later. For example, by the year 2000 elimination of mandatory retirement results in a 4.5 percent increase in the number of male workers between ages 60 and 70.

But this is an upper-bound estimate for two reasons. First, if employers respond to the policy change by introducing substitutes for a mandatory retirement clause, then there would be less of a change in worker behavior. Second, the simulations are based on the models in the first part of the paper, and, as noted above, those models yield upper-bound estimates. For both reasons the true effects are probably much smaller than those in the paper.

Finally, let me make a pitch for more research on the employer side of this labor market. I think we have pretty well nailed down the issues addressed by this paper. Elimination of mandatory retirement clauses probably has small positive effects on older worker labor force participation. What we are missing is information on how employers respond to such policies. What happens to compensation packages, pensions, and wages? To my knowledge we know very little about such issues.

Notes

1. The specific components and assumptions of each of the models and details on the development of the data base are documented in USDOL (1981).

2. The 10 percent figure is a crude approximation of what plans could reasonably be expected to do. For men at age 65, a truly fair increase based on mortality rates slightly lower than the current rates would be about 16–17 percent per year between ages 65 and 70. For women, the fair increase between ages 65 and 70 would be roughly 12–13 percent a year.

References

Anderson, Joseph. 1978. "Substitution Among Age Groups in the United States Labor Force." Research Paper no. 18, Economics Department, Williams College.

Anderson, Kathryn H., Richard V. Burkhauser, and Joseph F. Quinn. 1986. "Do Retirement Dreams Come True? The Effect of Unanticipated Events on Retirement Plans." *Industrial and Labor Relations Review* 39.

Barfield, Richard, and James Morgan. 1969. *Early Retirement: The Decision and the Experience*. Ann Arbor: University of Michigan Press.

Becker, Gary S. 1964. *Human Capital*. New York: Columbia University Press.

Bixby, Lenore E. 1976. "Retirement Patterns in the United States: Research and Policy Interaction." *Social Security Bulletin* 39: 3–19.

Blinder, Alan S. 1973. "Wage Discrimination: Reduced Form and Structural Estimates." *Journal of Human Resources* 7: 436–55.

Blinder, Alan S., Roger H. Gordon, and Donald E. Wise. 1978a. "An Empirical Study of the Effects of Pensions and the Saving and Labor Supply Decisions of Older Men."

———. 1978b. "Market Wages, Reservation Wages, and Retirement Decision." Paper prepared for the National Bureau of Economic Research Workshop on Social Security, Stanford University.

Boskin, Michael. 1975. "Social Security and Retirement Decisions." Working Paper no. 107, National Bureau of Economic Research, Stanford University.

Bowen, William, and Thomas Finegan. 1969. *The Economics of Labor Force Participation*. Princeton, N.J.: Princeton University Press.

Burkhauser, Richard V. 1976. "The Early Pension Decision and Its Effect on Exit from the Labor Market." Unpublished Ph.D. dissertation, University of Chicago.

———. 1979. "The Pension Acceptance Decision of Older Workers." *Journal of Human Resources* 14: 63–75.

———. 1980. "The Early Acceptance of Social Security—An Asset Maximization Approach." *Industrial Labor Relations Review* 33: 484–92.

Burkhauser, Richard V., and Joseph Quinn. 1980. "Mandatory Retirement Study (Part I): Task Completion Report on the Relationship Between Mandatory Retirement Age Limits and Pension Rules in the Retirement Decision." Washington, D.C.: The Urban Institute.

———. 1983. "Is Mandatory Retirement Overrated? Evidence from the 1970s." *Journal of Human Resources* 18:337–58.

Burkhauser, Richard, and George Talley. 1978. "Older Americans and Market Work." *Gerontologist* 18: 449–53.

Burkhauser, Richard, and John Turner. 1978. "A Time Series Analysis on Social Security and Its Effects on the Market Work of Men at Younger Ages." *Journal of Political Economy* 86: 701–15.

Clark, Robert L., David T. Barker, and R. Steven Cantrell. 1979. *Outlawing Age Discrimination: Economic and Institutional Responses of the Elimination of Mandatory Retirement.* Report to the Administration on Aging (Grant no. 90-A-1938), Washington, D.C.

Copperman, Lois F., Douglas G. Montgomery, and Fred Keast. 1979. *The Impact of the Age Discrimination in Employment Amendments of 1978 on the Private Business Community.* Oregon: Institute on Aging, Portland State University.

Edelman, Charles, and Ilene Siegler. 1978–79. *Federal Age Discrimination in Employment Law.* Charlottesville, Virginia: The Michie Company.

Ehrenberg, Ronald. 1979. "Retirement Policies, Employment and Unemployment." *American Economic Review* 69: 131–36.

Givens, Harrison, Jr. 1978. "An Evaluation of Mandatory Retirement." *Annals of the American Academy of Political and Social Science* 438: 50–57.

Hall, Arden, and Terry Johnson. 1980. "The Determinants of Planned Retirement Age." *Industrial and Labor Relations Review* 33: 241–55.

Halpern, Janice. 1978. "Raising the Mandatory Retirement Age: Its Effect on the Employment of Older Workers." *New England Economic Review* 3:23–35.

Hammermesh, Daniel S., and James Grant. 1979. "Econometric Studies of Labor–Labor Substitution and Their Implications for Policy." *Journal of Human Resources* 14:518–42.

Harris, Louis, and Associates, Inc. 1979. *1979 Study of American Attitudes Toward Pensions and Retirement.* New York: Johnson and Higgins.

Hewitt Associates. 1980. "Hot Topics in Employee Benefits." *Compensation Exchange* (pamphlet).

Kasschau, Patricia L. 1976. "Retirement and the Social System." *Industrial Gerontology* 3: 11–24.

Lazear, Edward. 1979. "Why Is There Mandatory Retirement?" *Journal of Political Economy* 87: 1261–84.

———. 1983. "Pensions as Severance Pay." In Z. Bodles and J. Shoven, eds., *Financial Aspects of the U.S. Pension System*. Chicago: University of Chicago Press.

MacDonald, R. M. 1978. *Mandatory Retirement and the Law*. Washington, D.C.: American Enterprise Institute.

McConnell, John, and John J. Corson. 1956. *The Economic Needs of Older People*. Baltimore, Md.: Lord Baltimore Press.

Meier, Elizabeth. 1975. "Over 65: Expectations and Realities of Work and Retirement." *Industrial Gerontology* 2: 95–109.

Meier, Elizabeth, and Cynthia Dittmar. 1980. *Varieties of Retirement Ages*. Staff Working Paper, President's Commission on Pension Policy, Washington, D.C.

Mitchell, Olivia, and Gary S. Fields. 1985. "Rewards for Continued Work: The Economic Incentives for Postponing Retirement." In Martin David and Timothy Smeeding, eds., *Horizontal Equity, Uncertainty and Economic Well Being*. Chicago: University of Chicago Press.

Mitchell, Olivia, and Rebecca Luzadis. 1986. "Pension Rewards for Delayed Retirement: Changes in Incentives Through Time." Mimeo. Department of Economics, Cornell University.

Morrison, Malcolm H. 1982a. *Economics of Aging: The Future of Retirement*. New York: Van Nostrand.

———. 1982b. "The Future of the ADEA: An Analysis of the Impact of the 1978 Amendments to the Act." In Monte B. Lake, ed., *Age Discrimination in Employment Act, A Compliance and Litigation Manual for Lawyers and Personnel Practitioners*. Washington, D.C.: Equal Employment Advisory Council.

———. 1985. "The Transition to Retirement: The Employer's Perspective." Washington, D.C.: Bureau of Social Science Research.

Parnes, Herbert, and Gilbert Nestel. 1979. "The Retirement Experience." In U.S. Department of Labor, *The Pre-Retirement Years*. Washington, D.C.: GPO.

Quinn, Joseph F. 1977. "Microeconomic Determinants of Early Retirement: A Cross-Sectional View of White Married Men." *Journal of Human Resources* 12: 329–46.

———. 1978. *The Early Retirement Decision: Evidence from the 1967 Retirement History Study*. Staff Paper no. 29, Social Security Administration, HEW Publication no. (SSA) 78-11855.

Reno, Virginia. 1971. "Why Men Stop Working at or Before Age 65." *Survey of New Beneficiaries Report*. Working Paper no. 3, U.S. Dept. of Health, Education and Welfare. Washington, D.C.: GPO.

———. 1972. "Compulsory Retirement Among Newly Entitled Workers." *Social Security Bulletin* 35:3–15.

Rones, Philip L. 1978. "Older Men: The Choice Between Work and Retirement." *Monthly Labor Review* 10: 3–10.

Rosenfeld, Carl, and Scott Campbell Brown. 1979. "The Labor Force Status of Older Workers." *Monthly Labor Review* 102: 12–18.

Ross, Irwin. 1978. "Retirement at Seventy: A New Trauma for Management." *Fortune,* May 8, pp. 106–12.

Schulz, James. 1974. "The Economics of Mandatory Retirement." *Industrial Gerontology* 1:1–10.

Schwab, Karen. 1974. "Early Labor Force Withdrawal: Participants and Nonparticipants Aged 58–63." *Social Security Bulletin* 37: 24–38.

Sheppard, Harold. 1978. "The Issue of Mandatory Retirement." *Annals of the American Academy of Political and Social Science* 438: 40–49.

Slavik, Fred. 1966. *Compulsory and Flexible Retirement in the American Economy.* Ithaca, N.Y.: Cornell University Press.

U.S. Congress, House Select Committee on Aging. 1977. *Mandatory Retirement: The Social and Human Cost of Enforced Idleness.* Washington, D.C.: GPO.

U.S. Department of Health, Education and Welfare, Social Security Administration. 1976a. *Almost 65: Baseline Data from the Retirement History Survey.* Washington, D.C.: GPO.

———. 1976b. *Reaching Retirement Age: Findings from the SNEB 1968–1970.* Washington, D.C.: GPO.

U.S. Department of Labor. 1965a. *The Older American Worker.* Washington, D.C.: DOL.

———. 1965b. *The Older American Worker: Research Materials.* Washington, D.C.: DOL.

———. 1977. "Questions and Issues Relating to the Age Discrimination in Employment Act of 1967." Report to the Subcommittee on Labor, U.S. Senate Committee on Human Resources.

———. 1981. *Interim Report to Congress on Age Discrimination in Employment Act Amendments.* Washington, D.C.

Walker, James W., and Harriet L. Lazer. 1978. *The End of Mandatory Retirement: Implications for Management.* New York: John Wiley and Sons.

INDEX